D1453494

PR 756 .U86 H65 1987
Holstun, James.
 A rational millennium : Puritan
utopias of seventeenth-century
England and America

A
Rational
Millennium

Title page of Sir Francis Bacon, Instauratio Magna *(London, 1620). The legend is from the prophecy of the end time in the Book of Daniel: "Many shall run to and fro, and knowledge shall be increased" (12:4).*

A
Rational
Millennium

Puritan Utopias of Seventeenth-Century England and America

James Holstun

New York   Oxford

OXFORD UNIVERSITY PRESS

1987

PR
756
.U86
H65
1987

Oxford University Press

Oxford   New York   Toronto
Delhi   Bombay   Calcutta   Madras   Karachi
Petaling Jaya   Singapore   Hong Kong   Tokyo
Nairobi   Dar es Salaam   Cape Town
Melbourne   Auckland

and associated companies in
Beirut   Berlin   Ibadan   Nicosia

Copyright © 1987 by Oxford University Press, Inc.

Published by Oxford University Press, Inc.,
200 Madison Avenue, New York, New York 10016

Oxford is a registered trademark of Oxford University Press.

All rights reserved. No part of this publication may be reproduced,
stored in a retrieval system, or transmitted, in any form or by any means,
electronic, mechanical, photocopying, recording, or otherwise,
without the prior permission of Oxford University Press.

Library of Congress Cataloging-in-Publication Data
Holstun, James.
A rational millennium.
Bibliography: p.
Includes index.
1. English prose literature—17th century—History and criticism.
2. Utopias.   3. English prose literature—Puritan authors—History and
criticism.   4. American prose literature—Colonial period, ca. 1600–1775—
History and criticism.   5. American prose literature—Puritan
authors—History and criticism.   6. Puritans.   7. Millennialism
in literature.   8. Rationalism in literature.   I. Title.
PR756.U86   1987   828'.408'09372   86-8450
ISBN 0-19-504141-0

1 3 5 7 9 8 6 4 2

Printed in the United States of America
on acid-free paper

For Joanna

Acknowledgments

My parents, Janet Marcia Donnet Holstun and John Tucker Holstun, Jr., helped me write this in more ways than they lived to know and more ways than I know yet. I'm grateful to the Department of English and Comparative Literature of the University of California at Irvine for giving its students both a quickening course of instruction and the freedom to follow their own odd bents; UCI screws up my distinction between arcadia and utopia by being a pleasant spot for the advancement of learning. Five friends and teachers were indispensable. Harold Toliver, Robert L. Montgomery, and John Carlos Rowe guided me through the prototype version and beyond. Molly Rothenberg (now at Beloit College) and Alan Bewell (now at Yale University) gave me constant encouragement and suggested important revisions that are now part of the book. My students at UCI and UCLA helped me learn how to read. In my discussion of Utopian warfare, I draw on papers by Sean Brunwin, Christopher Carter, Shelly Furry, and Christopher Gulli, all students in one of my English 4 classes at UCLA. I benefited from the congenial and efficient editorial work of William Sisler, Henry Krawitz, and Linda Robbins at Oxford, and from the expert copy editing of Janet W. Falcone. Leonard Tennenhouse reviewed the manuscript with critical sympathy, gently pointing out that I'd neglected to write an introduction. I've also profited from readings by Richard Halpern and Mitchell Breitwieser. An earlier version of the third chapter appeared in *Rep-

resentations 4 (Fall 1983) as "John Eliot's Empirical Millenarianism" (© 1983 by the Regents of the University of California, 128–53). Suggestions by the editorial board and by J. G. A. Pocock strengthened that article, and I'm grateful for permission to rework and republish it. I read yet an earlier version at the 1982 meeting of the Philological Association of the Pacific Coast. I've reproduced the frontispiece of Bacon's *Instauratio Magna* by permission of the Huntington Library, San Marino, California. My greatest debt is to Joanna Tinker, my wife. She helped me get on with the work, sometimes by making me put it down.

With the exception of titles, I've modernized spelling, punctuation, and typographic conventions. When willing and able, I've modified the standard translations I quote.

Burlington, Vermont   J.H.
July 1986

Contents

A
Rational
Millennium

Why do Englishmen so eagerly kill all snakes?

Algonquian to Puritan missionary, 1649

1

Introduction

Vasco de Quiroga Misreads *Utopia*

Puritan utopia is a literary form, political rhetoric, and social practice that envisions the displaced populations of early modern Europe and North America as the raw materials for an act of millennial poiesis. It promises to subject these populations to a revolutionary program of civil and ecclesiastical discipline, replace customary secular monarchy with a rational, nonhierarchical theocracy, and inaugurate the millennium. Later in this introduction I will discuss certain aspects of my approach implicit in this definition: why I make a point of describing Puritan utopia as a combination of form, rhetoric, and practice; what I mean by *discipline* and *rational;* and the critical framework I see myself working inside. Chapter 2 examines Puritan utopia in the contexts of the utopian tradition, Puritanism, and early modern culture. Chapters 3 and 4 study the projects of two utopists active during the middle of the seventeenth century: John Eliot of Massachusetts and James Harrington of England. The fifth and final chapter considers the fate of Puritan utopia at the Restoration and its mode of presence to us today. Along the way I examine the writings of certain utopian and nonutopian predecessors, contemporaries, and successors to the Puritan utopists, including several corporate projects of the seventeenth century that meet my definition of utopia: the Congregationalist church, the Massachusetts Bay Colony, and the New Model Army.

But first, all these matters may well seem less problematic than does the cohesiveness of my title. "Puritan utopia" sticks in the craw. It is easier to link Thomas More with the Enlightenment than with Puritanism, easier to see the rational ideal animating his imaginary state as a humanist anticipation of Enlightenment secularism than as a phenomenon contemporary with the Reformation.[1] *Puritan utopia* links these secular and sacred aspects of early modern culture, muddling the terms of several conceptual binaries that continue to organize an enormous body of literary, political, and religious history: binaries between the traditional and the modern, the Age of Faith and the Age of Reason, the Renaissance and the Reformation. From the point of view of the history of ideas, *Puritan utopia* is something of an oxymoron, one that spontaneously generates such cognate absurdities as "theocratic rationalism" and "secular millennialism." If we do allow ourselves to see utopianism in Puritanism, it should be no more than an embryonic tendency: the semiconscious stirrings to life of a movement from a sacred to a secular idea of progress.

For literary criticism there are problems of a different sort, since there seems to be such a generic distance between More's ironic and self-negating apologue and the Puritan utopists' nonfictional programs for reform, which insist stridently on their own feasibility and their imminent realization in a determinate geographical site. The relevant oxymorons here might be "whimsical jeremiad" or "Calvinist romance." So far as they read More (which is infrequently), the Puritan utopists seem to misread him, ignoring the literary textures that put More's political programs into context. Stephen Greenblatt's chapter on More in *Renaissance Self-Fashioning* is the best recent warning to those who would ignore the tensions inhabiting More's work. He reads *Utopia* as an unresolved autobiographical debate between Raphael Hythloday (More as the proponent of an ascetic state instituted by direct political action) and the character More, or "Morus" (More as the detached, ironic, and self-dramatizing creator of fictions). Those ignoring the part played in the dialogue by Morus have typically appeared most foolish, sometimes going so far as to imagine that Utopia was or is a real place. In a letter to Peter Giles, More mentions his first such gull: the unnamed (and possibly fictitious) "devout man" and "professor of theology" who wants the pope to make him the missionary bishop to the Utopians (More 111–12). And in *Nowhere Was Somewhere,* Arthur E. Morgan argues that *Utopia* is a more or less factual account of the Inca empire that More based on the report of some unidentifiable traveler. Few of More's readers have been so literal-minded, but most readers, from the Renaissance to the present, have been guilty at times of simply identifying More the author with Raphael, often despite themselves. In their self-confident advocacy of a program of civic perfection, the Puritan utopists (or critics designating these Puritan writers as utopists) would seem to join this foolish Raphaelite Brotherhood, leaving themselves exposed to a literary critique anchored in More's ironic vision.

To deal with the problems suggested by my crossbred title and subject matter, I will approach them obliquely, through the person of Vasco de Quiroga, a sixteenth-century Spanish lawyer and Erasmian with impeccable Humanist credentials, whose Raphaelite reading of More nonetheless brings him rather close to the Puritan utopists. In a sense, Quiroga also wished to become the missionary bishop to the Utopians, but unlike More's gull he realized that he would have to create his Utopians before doing so—that he would have to assume the role of King Utopus shaping the conquered populace of barbarian Abraxa into ideal citizens before he could minister to their spiritual needs.

Quiroga has largely been ignored by English and American literary scholars and historians of utopian writing. But Silvio Zavala has shown that Quiroga used More's fictional work as a pattern for the civil settlement of the newly conquered Indian populations of New Spain. Quiroga was sent to New Spain in 1531 as one of the judges of the second *audiencia,* or high court of justice. In his writings he reveals that he sees the Indians as the innocent inhabitants of "what is to them a golden world," while the European world is "already one of iron and steel and worse." But Quiroga feels the classic Western ambivalence toward the noble savage, for he also condemns what he sees as the "lawlessness and the savage and tyrannical way of life of these natives" (Zavala 106). The Spanish conquest has only aggravated this condition. Because of it, the Indians are in a state of disarray, desperately in need of civil organization and order.

This state of disarray, however, is a utopian opportunity as well as an administrative problem. Because the Indians are, in Quiroga's eyes, a soft wax awaiting rational molding, they hold out the possibility of a pure reformed Catholic church in the New World and are therefore an implicit reproach to degenerate Europe. Quiroga says that "it seems certain to me that I see . . . in the new primitive and reborn Church of this New World, a reflection and an outline of the Primitive Church in our known world in the Age of the Apostles" (Phelan 44). Like More's Utopians, these Indians seem to hold out the possibility of a reformation of church discipline within Catholicism—a reformation curiously like that being proposed by Quiroga's Protestant contemporaries.

Soon after his arrival, Quiroga and his fellow judges sent Spain their appraisals of the state of colonial affairs and their recommendations for the civil settlement of the conquered Indians. In his *Información en Derecho,* a legal brief of 1535 referring to his part of this report, Quiroga reveals that he turned to *Utopia* for an organizational "pattern," calling More "an illustrious and ingenious man, more than human." His first step in establishing a New World utopia would be to gather the displaced and scattered Indians in one spot, for "one alone may be but ill secure, and the man who has neither a craft nor a trade may be very bad for himself, if not for others" (Zavala 111). Even after these Indians are gathered together, however, the "disorderly pieces and patches of laws and ordinances" governing colonial Spain will be of little help, making it necessary to "remake the thing anew"using *Utopia* (Warren 33).

Quiroga's proposal was not sympathetically received in Spain. To his distress, the royal decree of February 20, 1534, permitted the enslavement of the Indians. But by scaling down his plans and using considerable sums of his own money, he established on his own authority two "hospital pueblos," one near Mexico City and the other in Michoacán. Sometime between 1554 and 1565 he drew up the *Ordinances* by which the pueblos had been and continued to be governed. These reveal that although the pueblos never attained anything like the national scale of More's ideal state, they incorporated a remarkable number of his Utopian principles, as we can see in Fintan Warren's summary comparison (34–42). Both utopias propose the communal ownership of property. As the fundamental social unit of Utopia is the *familia* composed of from ten to twenty adults and ruled over by male elders, so that of the pueblos is the *familia* composed of from twenty to twenty-four adults ruled over by a *padre de familia.* Both guard against the accumulation of power by any individual familia, for any household exceeding the maximum size must split up and regroup. In both states the inhabitants wear simple and unadorned clothing, work communally for six hours daily, and avoid ridiculing anyone because of poverty or physical deformity. In both, all men and women practice agriculture and some secondary trade. Both prescribe a regular rotation of persons between city and farm. Hythloday describes a complex form of republican government in Utopia, with a ruling hierarchy of phylarchs elected by the households, and head phylarchs and a prince elected by the phylarchs. Though ultimately subordinate to Spanish colonial rule, Quiroga's pueblos have a similar self-rule, with a governing body of *principals, regidores,* and *jurados* elected by the padres. In both states political matters are decided some days after they are debated to allow for a period of reasoned deliberation.

Quiroga's hospital pueblos remained small, and despite his continuing advocacy, they inspired no imitation. But they did, in fact, survive him and, according to a traveler's report, maintained a recognizably Utopian form well into the seventeenth century. Like so many utopists before and after him, Quiroga became the object of an interpretive struggle, for both Mexico's religious right and its socialist left attempted to add him to their heroic genealogies.

In Quiroga's New Spanish sixteenth-century utopia, we can see a number of themes that we will encounter again and again in the utopias of the English and the New English seventeenth century:

1. *Utopia has a bifocal vision.* Because Quiroga focuses alternately on the texts he reads and the displaced populations he uses them to shape, we cannot classify his project as either essentially literary or essentially nonliterary.

2. *Utopia is born ex libris, not ab nihilo.* Quiroga's utopia arises not just from some concept or historical spirit but from a reading of an earlier utopia (*Utopia*) and of an earlier work (the Book of Acts) *as* a utopia.

3. *Utopia is the site of a textual/practical dialectic.* Quiroga's texts become practices (*Utopia* becomes the communal life of a hospital pueblo), and these practices in turn become texts (that life is formalized in a written code of utopian behavior).

4. *Utopian social practice is inseparable from the practice of warfare.* The Spanish Conquest produces the anomic population comprising Quiroga's utopian raw material, and his utopias prevent further Indian resistance.

5. *Utopia is something done to others.* Quiroga's utopia goes beyond an act of individual or collective self-fashioning to an act of fashioning selves for others, whether they like it or not. In the model of a republican government imposed from outside, the pueblos combine liberty and domination.

6. *Utopia is a factory for the disciplinary production of subjectivities.* Quiroga's utopia aims to produce new models of regenerate individual

conscience and new corporate "subjects"—all distinct from those produced by hierarchical organic monarchy, whether Aztec or Spanish.

7. *Utopia is the marginal defense of reason against centralized custom.* Quiroga casts himself as the individual advocate of a revolutionary
program in rational domination on the borders of the empire, in conflict
with (and yet dependent on) a traditional legal order of customary domination centered in Spain.

8. *Utopia's isolation is not withdrawal, but insular preparation for
rational expansion.* In an era of world unification through European conquest, Quiroga sees his hospital pueblos as the sites for a repeatable
experiment in organizational technology.

9. *Utopia's theory of history is not regressive and nostalgic, but progressive and prophetic.* Quiroga adopts the model of apostolic communism not because he longs for mythical return but because he wishes to
institute a (potentially millennial) program of radical renovation. This
program promises not a pastoral golden age but a rational reorganization
of urban and rural space.

10. *Utopia exceeds the intention of the utopist.* Quiroga's utopian
project outlived him in a local, nonuniversal form, and it entered into
interpretive disputes he did not foresee.

Later in this chapter I group these ten utopian themes under Max
Weber's concept of *rationalization,* arguing that a desire for universal
rationalization animates early modern utopia and Puritan utopia in
particular.

Before we move on too quickly to Puritan utopia, we should consider Quiroga's project more carefully, since his distinctly eccentric
and marginal position in the utopian tradition might seem to compromise my attempt to use him to mediate between More's political
romance and the Puritans' earnest political projects. Was Quiroga's
curiously literal reading of More's work a misreading? Should his hospital pueblos be excluded from the history of utopia proper? In the
absence of any explicit consideration, we may reasonably assume that
many scholars who have recently attempted to define utopia would
answer yes to both questions. Edward Surtz argues that More's fantasies of the utopian reorganization of society are necessarily divorced
from any real proposal for social practice, since they depend on a total
Christian regeneration producing ideal men and women that we are
unlikely to see this side of the New Jerusalem (*Pleasure* 189). Frank
Manuel and Fritzie Manuel have a more secular version of the same
reluctance. They see utopian projects like Quiroga's as appropriate
subjects for what they call the infant science of "applied utopistics,"

but they are happy to leave this science to others, fearing a move from a purely imaginative realm to some realm of social practice "too dangerously close to reality." Indeed, "utopian practice" may even be a "contradiction in terms" (8–9). In *The Quest for Utopia* Glenn Negley and J. Max Patrick define utopia as a fictional work describing a particular state or community with the political structure of that community as its theme (3). In his construction of a particular community with a fictional work as its theme, Quiroga seems to have gotten things backward. Negley adds that a great advantage of his and Patrick's definition is that it distinguishes utopias from "political tracts and dissertations" (Negley xii). Darko Suvin is generally leery of the taxonomic reflex of "literary or non-literary?" Still, he finds it necessary to differentiate utopia from "general beliefs, programs, and unlocalized projects" and from "blueprints" (59). Michael Holquist sets utopia off from "other fiction on the one hand" and from "political programs on the other." Literal-minded persons like Quiroga have forgotten that utopia is a game and, by "transgressing the limits of what marks it off as play, have wrought great harm to themselves and others" (112, 121). Northrop Frye makes clearest the post-Kantian imperative to distinguish between aesthetic vision and nonaesthetic functionalism: "The utopia is a *speculative* myth; it is designed to contain or provide a vision for one's social ideas, not to be a theory connecting social facts together. There have been one or two attempts to take utopian constructions literally by trying to set them up as actual communities, but the histories of these communities make melancholy reading" ("Varieties" 25–26).

The problem with these essays at generic definition is not simply the utopian figure they trace but also the nonutopian ground on which the figure emerges. They make only a token effort to describe that area outside the confines of the definition, which remains the murky but seemingly self-evident world of the applied utopia, the theory connecting social facts together, the political tract, dissertation, program, or blueprint. This world of political discourse and social practice is an agglomeration of brute facts, unshaped by the utopian imagination. Utopia assumes its properly literary identity in distinction from, and opposition to, this world of political life and the referential, instrumental language that serves it.

The danger of such an attempt to define utopia is not just that it depoliticizes literature but also that it de-formalizes political writing and social practice. As Stanley Fish has argued in a series of essays on literary stylistics and language theory, most attempts to establish a

rigid division between literature and nonliterature on the basis of formal properties of "literary" and "ordinary" language begin by defining
the latter as a purely representational, value-free language and conclude by defining literary language as a deviation from this norm,
impoverishing our experience of both the norm and the deviation in
the process (*Text* 97). The utopian version of this separation (which
divides literary from nonliterary utopia, imaginative from applied utopia, or utopia from merely instrumental writing) typically presents
itself with the bland self-assurance of an innocent heuristic. But no
heuristic in the history of utopian criticism has had such a pernicious
effect, for it erodes works on both sides of the divide, hiding both the
social and political affiliations of literary utopia and the fictive and
imaginative qualities of nonliterary utopia. This study will adopt a different heuristic: it will look for the ways in which the formal traits of
utopian writing (literary and nonliterary) and its exercise of power
imply each other. For instance, beginning in the next chapter we will
see that utopia frequently depicts itself as an act of rational writing on
the human tabula rasa of a displaced population. Even in literary utopia, this metaphor implies a relation of power in which someone writes
and someone is written on. Even in nonliterary or applied utopia, it
implies an imaginative ability to envision a population as a utopian
blank page. An a priori separation of literary from nonliterary utopia
would tend to hide the complexities of the metaphor.[2]

Certainly, not all critics have said that utopia's fictionality cuts it off
from political life. Karl Kautsky, in his much-attacked reading of *Utopia,* sees More as a political prophet of European communism and a
critic of the nascent capitalism of his own day. Karl Mannheim's influential distinction between ideology and utopia depends on a similar
temporal separation between the utopian signifier and signified. Both
ideology and utopia describe situations counter to the prevailing world
order, but while ideology simply provides unrealizable fantasies as an
escapist pleasure compensating for present oppression, utopias
actually transcend reality and "tend to shatter, either partially or
wholly, the order of things prevailing at the time" (192). More's *Utopia*
may be considered utopian, but only so far as it participates in a larger
utopian history of ideas and social practice. Utopias find their true definition and acknowledgment in the future: "If we look into the past, it
seems possible to find a fairly adequate criterion of what is to be
regarded as ideological and what as utopia. This criterion is their realization. Ideas which later turned out to have been only distorted representations of a past or potential social order were ideological, while

those which were adequately realized in the succeeding social order were relative utopias" (204). Here, too, utopia takes its definition from its opposition to a self-evident Other: those instrumental, local, and ephemeral political ideas and practices that simply serve a dominant social order. From our later viewpoint we may designate these ideas and practices as self-evidently ideological, for we can see that they have not realized themselves in a later stage of development as utopia has. Ideology signifies its present by distorting and concealing it, while utopia signifies its future by prophesying and giving birth to it.

We can see a more sophisticated version of the Mannheim distinction at work in Fredric Jameson's "The Dialectic of Utopia and Ideology," a chapter of his *Political Unconscious*. Jameson writes, "If the Mannheimian overtones of this dual perspective—ideology and Utopia—remain active enough to offer communicational noise and conceptual interference, then alternative formulations may be proposed, in which an *instrumental* analysis is coordinated with a *collective-associational* or *communal* reading of culture, or in which a *functional* method for describing cultural texts is articulated with an *anticipatory* one" (296). The problem with these reformulations is that they are already implicit in Mannheim. And as in Mannheim, they tend to slight the present-directed quality of utopia—its refusal simply to anticipate. Throughout this study I will be arguing that utopia attempts to envision an oppositional collectivity utterly distinct from that of the dominant order (and so non-"ideological"), yet utterly permeated by a program of domination.

These two approaches to defining utopia tend to be antagonistic, and they tend to form alternative canons of utopia.[3] The first, which sees utopia more as a literary genre, favors the more satiric, playful, and conservative romance or "dystopia," or at least the more self-consciously and self-questioning fictional sort of utopia. The second, which sees utopia more as a historical idea or spirit, favors revolutionary utopian politics or social practice. However, they would seem to agree in their exclusion of Quiroga's writing and social practice from their canons: the first because Quiroga misread More's fiction as a workable social blueprint, the second because his hospital pueblos failed to transcend the present in any world-historical form by providing a model for a new social order. Both definitions trace the utopian figure on the ground of an attenuated and self-evident political present: the first argues that utopia takes a humane and reflective distance from this present, while the second argues that utopia prophesies the future that the ideological present tries to hide. Different though they may be in many ways, these definitions share a belief that definition is logically prior to relationship, that the fundamentally oppositional nature of utopia must be stated before we can discuss its particular relation to those social forms contemporary with it.

As a way around this effacement of utopia's concern with and complex relation to its own present, this study will argue two related theses. First, utopia, like any genre, assumes its generic identity not by its congruence with some preexistent definition but from the concrete relationship it forms with other works of other genres. Going far beyond mere logical opposition, these are relations of filiation, supersession, predecession, complementarity, antagonism, parallelism, and even complete independence. And individual utopias form a relation of "tradition" with earlier and later utopias. This irreducible complexity, which I will call a materialist or "conjunctural" conception of genre, means that one never has criteria for classification in advance. We should not pose the question of Quiroga's New World utopianism in strictly yes-or-no terms. Rather, we should see his project as a conjuncture of its relations to other genres and other utopias: to More's text (a relation of filial tradition, since he reads *Utopia* as social theory demanding realization), to noble savagism (a complementary relation, since he sees the Indians as ideal experimental subjects for utopian discipline because they are uncontaminated by European civility), to warfare (a relation of supersession, since Quiroga's utopia aims to take up the project of colonial domination where warfare leaves off), and to slavery (an antagonistic relation, since Quiroga's fellow judges propose domination through the unmediated force of slavery, Quiroga through the utopian creation of Indian self-government). There are no doubt a great many more such relations, and one might go on to establish hierarchies of and relations among them. But there is no "utopia" logically or temporally prior to some conjuncture of generic relations. Definition becomes a matter of charting relations of generic forces, and the meaning of *utopia* becomes not the cause of its relations to other genres but the effect of those relations.

This is not to say that Puritan utopists of the Interregnum do not participate in the continuous history that literary historians usually refer to as a genre, only that this is one relationship among others, with no necessary priority over them. Indeed, we will see that John Eliot and James Harrington construct utopias with remarkable formal and thematic similarities to More's great work, even though Harrington alludes to More infrequently and Eliot seems never to have read him.

But they also engage in generic disputes and alliances in which he never thought to engage.

J. C. Davis also constructs a conjunctural definition of utopia in his *Utopia and the Ideal Society,* for he defines utopia by distinguishing it from the literatures dealing with arcadia, the Land of Cockaigne, the perfect moral commonwealth, and the millennium (12–40). Here, too, however, definition precedes relationship, for in Davis's eyes utopia maintains the same oppositional relation to these alternative genres throughout its history. He repeatedly faults other interpretations of utopia for straying unwittingly into a discussion of one of his other four ideal types, as if the distinctions were absolute and eternal. But to insist that utopia maintains the same oppositional relation to other genres throughout its history is, in a sense, to deny it a history altogether. Such a procedure relies, more or less explicitly, on a political psychology that locates some such constants as "the millenarian mentality" and "the utopian mentality" at determinate sites in an invariant and ahistorical collective unconscious. But the history of utopia, like the history of any genre, consists not of its patrolling its generic frontiers and expelling transgeneric interlopers and half-breeds, but of the very changes in its relations with other genres. I will argue, for instance, that it is impossible to understand Puritan utopia without seeing its changing relation to millennialism. Whereas utopia is largely independent of millennialism in England under the two Charleses (and completely so in, say, Plato's *Republic* and Le Guin's *The Dispossessed*), Interregnum writers see utopia as the organizational means to the millennium. This conjunctural and dynamic approach to the history of a genre is particularly important for utopia. Since (as we will see) a central utopian imperative is its impulse to subject what it sees as a disorganized raw material to a rational ordering, and since this impulse extends to other genres as well as to displaced populations, we will frequently find utopia colonizing nonutopia, or nonutopia present in rationalized form inside utopia.

This conjunctural approach to the definition of a genre makes possible a generic history that is not simply the history of an identity. Theodor Adorno's discussion of the utopian truth content of modernist literature is equally relevant to utopia itself: "Unconsciously, every work asks itself whether, and if so how, it can exist as a Utopia. And the answer invariably is: through the constellation of its elements. Thus the art work transcends the immutable not merely because of its sheer abstract difference, but also because it appropriates the immutable, dismantling it and putting it together again in an act of aesthetic creation, as they say. One criterion of the truth content of art works is their ability to compose the other out of elements of the immutable" (*Theory* 431). Quiroga's relation to More, then, becomes a relation of dismantling and aesthetic re-creation: More's literary text, which circulated (at first, anyway) among a relatively small coterie of Humanist friends, becomes a political program circulated across the Atlantic from a radical colonist to a monarch and used to initiate a social practice. The gap between Quiroga's project and More's (a gap not altogether unlike that between More and his immutable sources in Plato, Lucian, and Plutarch) does not disqualify Quiroga from consideration as a utopist. We will see similar acts of dismantling and re-creation in the projects of the Puritan utopists.

My second thesis about utopia's relation to its present (the need for which may be apparent in my idiosyncratic reference to war, slavery, and noble savagism as genres) is that Puritan utopia may be understood as simultaneously a literary form, a political rhetoric, and a social practice—a triune concept I will frequently refer to as a genre. I do not advance this thesis with the idea that Puritan utopia is the unique intersection of these three categories. It seems almost self-evident, in fact, that writing in any literary mode, engaging in any political rhetoric, is a social practice; that all literature and all social practice are at some level political (whether they actively criticize existing distributions of power, tacitly accept them, withdraw from them, or all three); and that all political rhetoric and social practice have a formal structure open to analysis. It may even be proper to say that these three categories name three modes of analysis rather than three kinds of object—that we, for instance, call a certain work literary only as a form of shorthand when we find it difficult or unprofitable to establish its mediations to politics and social practice.

Still, a remarkable number of studies of utopia begin with a claim that the literary identity of a written utopia precedes its political or social identity, or with the implicit assumption that the verbal and formal quality of utopian political writing or social practice is self-evident and so unworthy of explicit consideration. This approach is particularly damaging for Puritan utopia, which is itself a criticism insisting on the radical interconnectedness of these modes. Never in England before or since the Interregnum have the barriers between literary form, political rhetoric, and social practice seemed so permeable. The political fictions of individual utopists are printed and rapidly enter into the national debate over a political settlement. Utopian political rhetoric like Harrington's has a will to practical truth, producing not accurate descriptions of preexistent states or political abstractions but models for future states. Local social experiments like John Eliot's praying towns and Gerrard Winstanley's Digger commune at George's Hill, not content to remain mute practices, translate themselves into print and force a way into the national political debate. So it is vital for a study of Puritan utopia to take as its object a complex three-dimensional space of transformations among utopian form, rhetoric, and practice, not a two-dimensional field in which one term becomes foreground, the others background.

We might characterize this focus on form, rhetoric, and practice negatively by saying that it is specifically not a focus on utopian thought; throughout this study I will deny myself access to "the utopian mind" as a means of historical explanation. In this regard I find very suggestive J. G. A. Pocock's "State of the Art," the theoretical introduction to his *Virtue, Commerce, and History.*[4] Here Pocock describes a recent shift in political history away from "the history of political thought" (an approach modeled on philosophical analysis, which takes political writing as the expression of the writer's controlling consciousness) to "the history of political discourse" (an approach modeled on rhetoric, which takes political language itself as a complex, historically embedded object of analysis, not merely the instrument of a unified controlling consciousness). Political writing is not just the neutral reflection of political thought but has its own substance. It is "formed over time, in response to many external and internal pressures," so we should not suppose that this language "simply denotes, reflects, or is an effect of the experience of the moment" (28). Because of the historical materiality of political language, the political writer finds that he must work as much on it as with it, that "languages are the objects as well as the instruments of consciousness" (15).

Adapting Thomas S. Kuhn's *Structure of Scientific Revolutions* to the history of political discourse, Pocock argues that political thought can exist only inside a system of enabling and constraining conventions that he calls "discursive paradigms." Such a paradigm, Pocock says, "will present information selectively as relevant to the conduct and character of politics, and it will encourage the definition of political problems and values in certain ways and not in others" (8). It provides the political writer with a certain vocabulary of terms, with rules of usage and combination for them, and even with the power to change the paradigm itself under certain circumstances—to make the individual *parole* modify the paradigmatic *langue.*

In adapting Kuhn's theory of scientific paradigms, Pocock modifies it in two important ways. First, he argues that whereas a single scientific paradigm may authorize a vast array of scientific practices, a single political speech act may operate in several different paradigms at once: the political speech act is "by its nature polyvalent" (9). For instance, he has argued that James Harrington's claim in *Oceana* to have shown the way to an eternal commonwealth operates both inside the secular Machiavellian paradigm of classical republicanism and inside the sacred English paradigm of the millennial elect nation. Much of Pocock's work has been a paradigmatic archaeology recovering the languages and the dialects of Western political discourse, particularly republicanism. This polyvalent or multiparadigmatic quality of the political speech act seems to me analogous to my conjunctural conception of utopia as a genre, and it has helped me to open up the complex materiality of utopian discourse so easily hidden by static taxonomies.

Pocock also modifies Kuhn's conception of the relationship between language and practice. Whereas Kuhn's scientific paradigms require no absolute distinction between scientific languages and the practice of "normal science" (in fact, they are mutually constitutive), Pocock insists that his paradigms are strictly discursive. Though he concedes that a history of political practice is possible, Pocock says that "we are in search . . . less of the text's 'practical' than of its discursive performance" (13–14). Turning to *The Prince* and *Leviathan* as examples (of all political writing, we assume), he says, "This is to say, of course, that we are historians of discourse, not of behavior, but it is also to read Machiavelli and Hobbes as they were read by everyone whose response to them we possess in written form; these responses are, without exception, concerned not with their practical consequences, but with the challenges they present to the normal structures of discourse" (14).

I will return to this remarkable claim when I examine Harrington's impassioned attention to the practical consequences of Machiavelli's writing (and Hobbes's). For the moment, we should note the paradigmatic qualities of Pocock's own argument. His absolute distinction between the linguistic focus of discursive history and the practical focus of social history (as if discourse were not a practice, and as if social history were somehow a version of the history of ideas, with no possible methodological grounding in language) functions primarily as part of an anti-Marxist polemic in contemporary historiography. Indeed, Pocock says frankly that he is advocating a "Whig history" of politics in opposition to a "modernist history of consciousness organized around such poles as repression and liberation, solitude and community, false consciousness and species being" (34). Consistently enough, this Whig history works from a model of politics as a deliberative, even parliamentary, activity—a politics existing inside "communities of debate" as "a history of utterance and response by relatively autonomous agents" (13, 34).

Now there is, in fact, a sense in which utopia upholds the humanist ideal of reasoned conversation, with its vision of a *vivere civile* of reciprocal discourse in which "agents perform upon other agents, who perform acts in response to theirs" (17; see also Pocock, *Moment* 64–67). Indeed, I will argue in the second section of chapter 2 that a particular humanist conversation—that between the traveler and the philosopher—is a recurrent motif in early modern utopia. But there is also a sense in which utopia is an instrumental discourse aimed at *producing* "relatively autonomous agents" and a social practice in which agents act upon patients whose task it is to comply, not to reply—patients who can become agents only by following the agenda set by another agent. True, we will see John Eliot engaged with fellow Puritans of the Bay Colony and of England in a community of debate; but we will also see his language and his social practice aimed at shaping a (to him) fundamentally mute group: the conquered Algonquian nation. True, James Harrington does enter into civil conversation with Machiavelli, Hobbes, Matthew Wren, and a number of other political writers; but he also enters into an essentially one-sided conversation with the "formless" English people, whom he hopes his utopian orders will form into a utopian commonwealth. This study will not attempt to give voice to these voiceless persons (though, at times, we will see that their mute resistances become vocal and break into utopian discourse). But it will try to show how they are articulated in the texts of Puritan utopia *as* voiceless, as the passive patients subject to utopian agents. It will argue that utopian social practice is an appropriate domain for textual analysis: neither as the real ground to which discursivity must be made to refer, nor as the authorizing substance visible to us beneath merely phenomenal writing, but as a complex entity visible to us almost exclusively in writing and subject to the same interpretive transformations and strategies as are political polemics and philosophy.[5]

However, these two theses about Puritan utopia—that we should define it conjuncturally and that we should see it as a combination of literary form, political rhetoric, and social practice—remain somewhat abstract, not much more relevant to Puritan utopia then to other genres of other periods. To begin moving toward a more concrete understanding of the particular place of Puritan utopia in early modern culture, I will now discuss three related concepts that illuminate the will to power governing Puritan utopia's particular external relation to other genres and its internal metamorphoses among form, rhetoric, and practice. These are Max Weber's concept of rationalization, Max Horkheimer and Theodor W. Adorno's concept of enlightenment, and Michel Foucault's concept of discipline.

Rationalization, Enlightenment, and Discipline

The ten utopian themes I earlier derived from Vasco de Quiroga's New World utopianism might be conveniently grouped under the heading *rationalization,* which H. H. Gerth and C. Wright Mills call "the most general element in Weber's philosophy of history" (Weber, *From Max Weber* 51).[6] By rationalization Weber means something quite different from what philosophy means by the history of reason. Rationalizaton cannot be characterized as a simple progress on the level of mind: it leads not to the Enlightenment or to Absolute Spirit's contemplation of itself, but to the "iron cage" of modern bureaucratic domination (*Ethic* 181–82). It is fundamentally a transformative activity: that process by which an array of preexistent particulars is ordered, sorted into manageable groups, submitted to a procedure, and above all made *calculable.* In a favorite phrase (taken from Schiller) Weber calls rationalization *die Entzauberung der Welt,* "the disenchantment of the world": the substitution of a single form of abstract and quantifying bureaucractic domination for all merely customary, magical, or ad hoc human actions.

In its most general sense, rationalization is the name of a nearly universal activity, "an historical concept which covers a whole world of different things" (78), and Weber takes pains to avoid any absolute distinction between the rational and the irrational. In *The Protestant Ethic and the Spirit of Capitalism,* he notes, "A thing is never irrational in itself, but only from a particular rational point of view. . . . If this essay makes any contribution at all, may it be to bring out the complexity of the only superficially simple concept of the rational" (194). Rationalization may aim to direct social action to some new, more calculable end. It may only attempt to modify the means adopted to achieve a given "irrational" end, so that we can accurately speak of the rationalization of magical practices or the rationalization of mysticism in the Ignatian exercises. It may even refer to the collapsing of means and ends, so that rational means become their own ends (*Max Weber: The Interpretation* 57–58). Weber's wide-ranging and complex study of world religions, economic formations, and politics testifies to the fact that rationalization cannot itself be rationalized and brought under the rule of a neo-Hegelian universal history. Weber is careful to note that one cannot locate rationalization neatly in time and space: "The history of rationalism shows a development which by no means follows parallel lines in the various departments of life." Rome, for instance, rationalized its legal system in late antiquity, whereas law in England (the birthplace of rational industrial capitalism) remains unrationalized to the present day (*Ethic* 77)—a matter of perennial concern to English utopists, as we will see.

But in another sense, rationalization is for Weber geographically locatable and historically specific: it is that modern transformation of the West that has enabled it to submit all mankind to its own vision of rationality by disenchanting first itself, then the world as a whole. In the opening pages of *The Protestant Ethic*, Weber argues that we can specify a "path of rationalization which is peculiar to the Occident" (25). In this work Weber develops his much-contested thesis that an important constituent of modern world-historical rationalism (in the form of capitalism) was a spirit of self-disciplinary "worldly asceticism" centered in Protestant northern Europe and North America. The progressive elimination of nonrational or "magical" means to salvation, which was already under way among the ancient Hebrew monotheists, reached its culmination in the predestinarian sects of early modern Protestantism (*Ethic* 105, *Sociology* 203, *Economy* 630). Unable any longer to think of themselves as placating or manipulating the deity through local magical technics, sacrifice, or sacraments, such Protestants turned to the rational and this-worldly discipline of an ascetic "system of life" (*Ethic* 116–17). By submitting himself (and others) to a program of constant and methodical labor in a vocation or calling *(Beruf)*, the Puritan individual searches for, or attempts to create, worldly economic signs of spiritual election. The ascetic Puritan is constantly drawing up a spiritual balance sheet, rationalizing his own use of time, his spiritual state, and worldly testimony to that state. According to Weber, Protestantism profoundly modified Christian asceticism. Whereas asceticism at first fled from the daily life of the world into the monastery, now "it strode into the market-place of life, slammed the door of the monastery behind it, and undertook to penetrate just that daily routine of life with its methodicalness, to fashion it into a life in the world, but neither of nor for this world" (154). (We will see a related version of such extroverted monasticism in More's Utopia and Campanella's City of the Sun.)

The idea of labor in a calling, Weber argues, was a rational concept at the service of an irrational end: "The life of the saint was directed solely toward a transcendental end, salvation. But precisely for that reason it was thoroughly rationalized in this world and dominated entirely by the aim to add to the glory of God on earth" (118). But when this idea of systematic labor in a worldly calling combines with an ascetic limitation on consumption, it leads inevitably to an accumulation of capital (172). The Puritan disciplines of self-inspection and self-calculation give rise to a different *ratio*—the regular calculation in a double-entry account book of the relation between credit and debit: "Everything is done in terms of balances: at the beginning of the enterprise, an initial balance, before every individual decision, a calculation to ascertain its probable profitableness, and at the end a final balance to ascertain how much profit has been made. . . . It is one of the fundamental characteristics of an individualistic capitalistic economy that it is rationalized on the basis of a rigorous calculation" (18, 76). Puritanism, then, helped to form three prerequisites for capitalism: a fund of capital, a system of rational calculation amenable to capital accounting, and a disciplined labor force of persons who find themselves (often despite themselves) methodically at work in a calling (180–81).

Weber's non-Marxist critics have frequently faulted him as an economic determinist who ignores the specifically religious aspects of Puritanism (*Ethic* 8–12; Walzer, "Puritanism"). This is in part the product of their willingness to overlook Weber's scrupulous signposting. His anti-idealist scheme of history (which is closer to Nietzschean genealogy than to Marxist dialectics) insists on the possibility of a radical discontinuity between the origin of some social phenomenon and the uses that may later be made of it: "We shall thus have to admit that the cultural consequences of the Reformation were to a great extent, perhaps in the particular aspects with which we are dealing predominantly, unforeseen and even unwished-for results of the labors of the reformers" (*Ethic* 90). For Weber the Protestant ethic was not by any means a ruse of history: it was not an unconscious anticipation of capitalism, and capitalism is not the threat implicitly veiled in it. He denies the imputation of a scheme of simple causality: "We have no intention whatever of maintaining such a foolish or doctrinaire thesis as that the spirit of capitalism ... could only have arisen as the result of certain effects of the Reformation, or even that capitalism as an economic system is a creation of the Reformation" (91). Rather, the accumulative asceticism of Puritanism was an important but historically contingent constituent of rational capitalism, which was itself the product of a contingent conjunction of forces that happened to come together in the West, not the necessary result of a historical dialectic. From the point of view of Puritan worldly asceticism, capitalism was an irrational (because uncalculated) by-product.

I do not want to rehearse the Weberian controversy in any detail, only to argue the importance of the concept of rationalization for understanding early modern utopia, Puritanism, and (a fortiori) Puritan utopia. Early modern utopia presents itself as the genre of universal (but Europocentric) rationalization. It advocates not the local transformation of discrete technics and social practices that will leave the surrounding customary state untouched, but the universal rationalization of all the world and every aspect of life. We can see this impulse to universal rationalization in the very form of utopian writing, for its chapter-by-chapter movement from one clearly labeled topic to another (religion, warfare, agriculture, education) suggests the dream of a rationally compartmentalized and administered universe. More important, we can see this impulse in the concrete transformative project proposed by early modern utopia: by submitting the dangerously displaced human populations of the Old World and the New World to a program of rational discipline, it promises to produce a unified state that will provide the model for, or a martial means to, the unification of the world. In a sense, Puritan utopia is a prophecy of the increasingly rationalized, bureaucratized, and threatening world that Weber sees around himself with dread (*From Max Weber* 139, 155)— a totalizing conception of rationality that has drawn criticism from (among others) the Frankfurt School and Michel Foucault, as we will see. But regardless of the truth of Weber's claim, we can at least locate in early modern utopia a dream of such universal rationalization.

Similarly, with some reservations, Weber's concept is important for understanding the specifically Puritan aspects of Puritan utopia. This study implicitly participates in the critique of Weber for having overemphasized the specifically economic components of Puritanism, for it will focus on political rather than economic rationalization. It also participates in the critique of Weber for having located early modern rationalization too exclusively in Protestant northern Europe and North America; for while it focuses on a group of Puritan (or at least antiprelatical) utopists, it argues that they frequently have more in common with their Roman Catholic and Anglican predecessors (Quiroga, Machiavelli, Bacon, Campanella, and, above all, More) than with their anti-utopian compatriots and coreligionists. But there is a sense in which early modern rationalization had a special affinity with radical Protestantism, for both readily define themselves as the negation of *custom*—the omnipresent and almost demonic Other of Puritan utopia. Weber argues in *Economy and Society* that "one of the most important aspects of the process of 'rationalization' of action is the substitution for the unthinking acceptance of ancient custom, of deliberate adaptation to situations in terms of self-interest" (30). In the polemical religious wars of early modern Europe, Protestantism was better able than Catholicism to employ a rhetoric of anticustomary rationalization. It could denounce the irrational "magic" of Roman Catholic priests, sacraments, and icons as a customary corporate ideology, whereas Catholics could only stigmatize Protestantism as a newly erupted individual heresy, or at worst as the return of some chronic heresy—not as the voice of an entrenched and irrational custom. As Keith Thomas has shown in eloquent detail in *Religion and the Decline of Magic,* English Puritans transposed this Protestant theme into a higher key when they took it upon themselves to disenchant the English countryside and root out the vestigial "magic" in the Anglican church.

Early modern utopia works well as a test case for Weber's distinction between Protestant and non-Protestant Europe. We can certainly see a rational critique of custom in the writings of the Roman Catholic utopists (*Utopia, The Discourses, The City of the Sun*); much of chapter 2 of this study will consider this critique. But compared with the utopias of radical Protestantism (the reforming Swiss cantons, the Protestant armies, Puritan New England, the various utopian projects of Interregnum England), these writings remained largely unrealized, suggesting that, as Weber argues, the impulse to rationalize encountered greater customary resistance in non-Protestant nations. Roman Catholic utopists were unable to attach themselves successfully to extra-utopian political rhetorics and social practices of revolutionary rationalization such as flourished in the Protestant nations. Catholic utopian projects like Quiroga's, the Jesuit *reducciones* in Paraguay, and the eighteenth-century California missions of Junípero Serra are exceptions that prove the rule, since they spring up in the New World, on the margins of imperial and papal power.

Weber's distinction between the relatively rational means adopted by some social activity and the relatively irrational ends it may serve can help us avoid a certain idealist periodization that typically controls the history of utopian literature—a scheme that centers on a definition of utopia in relation to a seismic shift at the Enlightenment. Like most schemes of periodization, this one not only sets historical borders for its object of study but, in the very act of setting those borders, determines the nature of those objects. In "The Political Theory of Utopia," Judith Shklar sees a fundamental division between "classical"utopias (which are basically Platonic, focused on contemplation of a paradigmatic and timeless ideal) and "action-minded" utopias of the Enlightenment and later (which are basically historical, focused on achieving future reforms in actual social processes). The Puritan utopias of Harrington, Samuel Hartlib, and Winstanley, which would seem to be activist utopias inhabiting the era of classical utopias, are, in fact, no more than local, quirky, and "pathetic" exceptions to "the general course of utopian thought," which reaches the point of radical rupture between the classical and the activist utopia only at the French Revolution (107). Drawing in part on Shklar, Elisabeth Hansot has kinder words for Puritan utopia in *Perfection and Progress: Two Modes of Utopian Thought;* but she formulates a history of much the same sort. She organizes her study around a historical contrast between the classical utopia (which is static, organized according to a logical schema implying a supersensible and transcendent reality, and aimed at reforming the individual) and the modern utopia (which is dynamic, organized according to a spatial and temporal schema implying a historical and this-worldly reality, and aimed at reforming society as a whole) (8–16). Even a study such as Ernest Tuveson's *Millennium and Utopia: A Study in the Background of the Idea of Progress,* which recognizes the importance of premodern models of history, subscribes to this periodization in its argument for a critical moment of transition in the seventeenth century: "With the arrival of chiliasm and the emergence of the new science, the Western Christian world took the first step away from the ideal of world-transcendence and toward that of world reform" (112). The history of the idea of progress is itself linear and progressive: as Tuveson's title indicates, there is a single idea of progress ("utopia") that is born at some certain point after a lengthy sacred gestation ("millennium"). Though these periodizations may locate the seismic shift at different moments, they all rely on some version of the prefabricated and fundamentally metaphysical opposition between the paradigmatic stasis of the pre-Enlightenment idea and the programmatic activity of Enlightenment reform.

This study, on the other hand, will examine the connections constantly charted in early modern utopia between paradigm and program, between transcendence and reform. Weber's "rationalization" (as the nominalized verbalized adjective suggests) also bridges the opposition and questions the periodization it gives rise to. We cannot move immediately from naming the professed end of some modern writing, rhetoric, or practice to characterizing its social actuality. Just as Weber's Puritans promote an ascetic system of life in order to produce signs of election but also produce the seeds of rational capital, so the Puritan utopists promote political rationalization in order to institute the New Jerusalem but also produce secular models of social discipline. Weber's model of rationalization allows us to see the rationalities at work inside what may be to us a prerational frame of ideas without writing them off as eccentric and unimportant, or as embryonic anticipations of "the modern." My calling Puritan utopia a rational millennialism, like Weber calling Puritanism a worldly asceticism, may be presenting an oxymoron in place of a proper definition, from the point of view of the history of ideas. But this particular oxymoron marks out the specifically early modern moment of Puritan utopia.

The Frankfurt School's analysis of the history of rationality, in part a development of Weber's, illuminates the relation between reason and domination in Puritan utopia. A prerequisite for Frankfurt's analysis was its redefinition in the 1940s of *Enlightenment:* whereas the term had previously designated a period in intellectual history tied to the eighteenth-century rise of the bourgeoisie, it now became a synonym for the course of Western thought as a whole—the name of a will to power analogous, in a sense, to Weber's *rationalization.* Along with this redefinition came a modification of Frankfurt's Marxist analysis of history—as Martin Jay characterizes it, its "replacement of class conflict, that foundation stone of any truly Marxist theory, with a new motor of history. The focus was now on the larger conflict between man and nature both without and within, a conflict whose origins went back to before capitalism and whose continuation, indeed intensification, appeared likely after capitalism would end" (256). *Enlightenment* becomes not a discretely periodized ideology that can be examined objectively from without, but a horizon of rationality that can be examined only with difficulty from within.

Max Horkheimer and Theodor W. Adorno's *Dialectic of Enlightenment,* written in America during their wartime exile and published in 1947, is in part a philosophical meditation on the contemporary state of reason—a latter-day version of Kant's *Was Ist Aufklärung?* But it is also a study of the disastrous effects of enlightenment's attempts to actualize itself—in Weber's terms, a study of accelerating rationalization. They call their study "an attempt to focus understanding more clearly upon the nexus of rationality and social actuality, and upon what is inseparable therefrom—that of nature and the mastery of nature" (xv–xvi). Their central claim is that it is impossible simply to oppose *Vernunft* and *Herrschaft,* "reason" and "domination," since enlightenment reason contains within itself a will to mastery. Drawing on Nietzsche, they argue that enlightenment has always combined an antipathy to superstition and priestly domination with a willingness to manipulate masses of men (44). It may be tempting, in the aftermath of the Holocaust and with the arrival of a moment for reflection on the triumph of barbarism in the twentieth century, to denounce such barbarism as a betrayal of rationality and to call for a return to an enlightened way of thinking; nevertheless, "the notion of this very way of thinking, no less than the actual historical forms—the social institutions—with which it is interwoven, already contains the seed of the reversal universally apparent today" (xiii).

The promise that enlightenment holds out is the realization of the Baconian equation of knowledge and power: "The human mind, which overcomes superstition, is to hold sway over a disenchanted nature" (4). Like Weber's Puritan ascetic, Horkheimer and Adorno's enlightened bourgeois is a calculating animal whose very existence is dependent on "the requirement of sobriety and common sense—a proficient estimate of the ratio of forces" (57), and he submits himself, others, and nature itself to a program of rationalization and disenchantment. But the result of this ascetic calculation is that the knowing subject subjects both itself and the object known to a single system of abstract, quantifying reason, in which "the multiplicity of forms is reduced to position and arrangement, history to fact, things to matter" (7). All things are ruled by a principal of self-denying equivalence:

> World domination over nature turns against the thinking subject himself; nothing is left of him but that eternally same *I think* that must accompany all my ideas. Subject and object are both rendered ineffectual. The abstract self, which justifies record-making and systematization, has nothing set over against it but the abstract material which possesses no other quality than to be a substrate of such possession. The

equation of spirit and world arises eventually, but only with a mutual
restriction of both sides. (26)

This model of self-denying power, which marks utopia off clearly from
absolutist models of sovereignty, is one we will encounter frequently.
The utopist's will-to-blankness longs to see human populations as an
inert raw material awaiting the infusion of rational form, but he himself is no more than the conduit of this form, and he is unable to envision any utopian place for himself save as part of the blank populace.

It is possible to see Horkheimer and Adorno's expansion of the term
enlightenment to the extent that it fills the entirety of Western culture
as a radically antihistoricist move. In the first excursus to their study,
"Odysseus or Myth and Enlightenment" (43–80), they argue that we
can find the Western program of rational domination in place at the
dawn of recorded Western history, for Odysseus appears as the archetypal enlightenment man. Using his skills of linguistic and technological calculation to defeat the Cyclops, listening to (and so disenchanting) the song of the Sirens while he is bound to the mast of his ship
and while his men pull at the oars with their ears plugged, he becomes
a figure for enlightenment domination over nature, other men, and the
self. In their second excursus, "Juliette or Enlightenment and Morality" (81–119), they tie Homer to the Enlightenment by comparing
Odysseus's ascetic rationality with the instrumental reason implicit in
the projects of both Kant and Sade—a reason "neutral in regard to
ends," assimilated to the condition of mere planning (88).

But their study is also a project in critical history, one that is constantly aware that it is insufficient simply to confront barbarism with
enlightenment (since enlightenment is already a kind of barbarism),
impossible simply to speak the truth to power (since power is already
loquacious, extending its dominion by speaking its truth effects into
existence). Critical reason must now be able to think of history as
simultaneously continuous and discontinuous. In an era of near-universal catastrophe, the Hegelian model of universal history, with its
steady progress to Absolute Spirit, is no longer conscionable. Still,
there is a "unity that cements the discontinuous, chaotically splintered
moments and phases of history—the unity of the control of nature,
progressing to rule over men, and finally to that over men's inner
nature. No universal history leads from savagery to humanitarianism,
but there is one leading from the slingshot to the megaton bomb"
(Adorno, *Negative Dialectics* 320). Like Weber's rationalization,
Horkheimer and Adorno's enlightenment is a means of conceptualiz-

ing a discontinuous totality. A critique of enlightenment's totalizing metaphysics and of utopia's claims to universal rationalization should not overlook the accelerating, universalizing, and irreversible power of their technics.

The proper activity for the critic of enlightenment, say Horkheimer and Adorno, is to construct not an extrinsic critique reproaching it for having failed to live up to its rational promise (it has, with a vengeance), but an immanent critique questioning it for the relations it reveals between reason and domination, critical reason and instrumental reason, truth and power—pairings that are always intimately connected, never precisely identical. This nonidentity, this capacity for a rational critique of rational domination that does not simply contribute to the global process of rationalization, is the most important difference between Horkheimer and Adorno's analysis of the history of rationality and Weber's relatively pessimistic analysis (Dreyfus and Rabinow 165–66). In the rest of this study I will use the term *enlightenment* (lowercase, with no article) for two purposes: first, to indicate that such a critical project is under way, and second, to indicate an implicit ongoing critique of schemes of historical periodization that cannot recognize pre-Enlightenment rationalities. I am not claiming that the Enlightenment is present in germinal form in the rational prophesies of these early modern writers (as Horkheimer and Adorno sometimes seem to be claiming it is in Homer), only that they are engaged in confronting a certain irrationality, custom, and magic with a certain rational oppositional practice. Any attempt to distinguish between early modern and Enlightenment utopia (I will make no such attempt in this study) cannot begin simply with a claim about the eighteenth-century birth of rationality, but must instead compare the particular rationalities at work in early modern and Enlightenment utopian forms, political rhetorics, and social practices.

This immanent critique of enlightenment is particularly important for utopia, since utopian criticism too frequently presents itself as the liberal proponent of the utopian ideal of critical reason ("utopia as satire") and opponent to the dystopian nightmare of instrumental domination ("utopia as blueprint") without seeing the connections between the two. But early modern utopia reveals the intertwining of critical and instrumental reason, of a rational and liberating critique of monarchy and custom with an instrumental impulse to transform, disenchant, and dominate. In its critical aspect utopian reason enables the early modern intellectual to think an oppositional cultural totality. In its instrumental aspect it enables him to envision new technics for disciplining human populations and gridding a natural landscape conceived of as objects without qualities. John Eliot's theocratic rationalism is simultaneously a critique of customary English monarchy and an attempt to disenchant the Massachusetts landscape by bringing this critique to bear on the Algonquian "monarchy." James Harrington's utopian writing is simultaneously a critique of English monarchy, dynastic patriarchalism, and Hobbesian schemes of absolute sovereignty, and a proposal to mold a rational imperialist state out of malleable English bodies and minds. The critical and instrumental aspects of utopian reason are not separable. But their articulation is intelligible, and so is the way their articulation articulates us. One of the peculiarities of the denunciation of the "totalitarian" implications of utopia by liberal dystopists (Eugene Zamiatin, Aldous Huxley, and George Orwell), literary critics, and cold war intellectuals is that they are themselves the more or less unwitting products (beneficiaries or victims) of the disciplinary rigors they denounce. We are all, in a more or less mediated sense, the products of enlightenment, of utopian reason and domination.

Still, for all Horkheimer and Adorno's insistence on the possibility of resistance by critical reason to domination by instrumental reason, they spend little time specifying the material forms such resistance can take. History seems to be on the side of enlightenment, which consequently becomes a unified force threatening to extinguish the embattled reflective consciousness of the critical individual. Michel Foucault's concept of the disciplinary formation of subjectivity will help us bridge the binary opposition between the rationalized and rationalizing collective and the individual subject in a way that helps explain the relation between collectivity and individuality in utopia.

But first, it is important to note the similarities (more striking than the differences) between Foucault's history of rational forms and those of Weber and Horkheimer and Adorno. In a surprisingly Weberian critique of "Weberians," Foucault says that we should speak not of rationality itself as an absolute but only of various rationalities, and then only in "an instrumental and relative sense." No practice is rational or irrational in itself (indeed, it is impossible to conceive of any practice outside some scheme of rationality), but only from the point of view of some other practice. Our object of study should not be rationality considered as a unified philosophical abstraction, but the ways in which "forms of rationalities inscribe themselves in practices or in systems of practices, and the roles they play there" (Perrot 47). Foucault compares the independent lines of development of the historical analysis of rational forms in Germany (from Weber to Frankfurt) and France (from Georges Canguilhem to, among others, himself), calling his relation to Frankfurt "a strange case of non-penetration between two very similar types of thing which is explained, perhaps, by that very similarity. . . . Now obviously, if I had been familiar with the Frankfurt School, if I had been aware of it at the time, I would not have said a number of stupid things that I did say and I would have avoided many of the detours which I made while trying to pursue my own humble path" (Foucault, "Structuralism" 200).

Much of Foucault's work has centered on the languages and practices of the eighteenth and nineteenth centuries, but he is no closer than are Weber and Horkheimer and Adorno to a traditional periodization of the Enlightenment. To begin with, he resists the periodizing temptation to see the birth of the Enlightenment as an isolatable event on the level of mind conceived of either as the liberation of reason from unreflective mind or as the oppressive alienation of subject and object: "I would not speak about *one* bifurcation of reason, but about an endless, multiple bifurcation—a kind of abundant ramification. I do not address the point at which reason became instrumental" (201). Second, like Horkheimer and Adorno, Foucault resists what he calls the critical "blackmail" of the Enlightenment, by which we are presented with an "authoritarian alternative: you either accept the Enlightenment and remain with the tradition of rationalism . . . or else you criticize the Enlightenment and then try to escape from its principles of rationality. . . . We must try to proceed with the analysis of ourselves as beings who are historically determined, to a certain extent, by the Enlightenment" (*Reader* 42, 43). Theories of history that propose a return to some pre-Enlightenment, prealienated unity, or define themselves as the voice of a radical present freed from the Enlightenment by some fundamental and universal rupture, are to be profoundly mistrusted ("Structuralism" 200).

Foucault has directed his most important critique of Weber and Horkheimer and Adorno to a certain premature or false totalization: "It may be wise not to take as a whole the rationalization of society or of culture, but to analyze such a process in several fields, each with a reference to a fundamental experience: madness, illess, death, crime, sexuality, and so forth. I think that the word *rationalization* is dangerous. What we have to do is analyze specific rationalities rather than always invoking the progress of rationalization in general" (Dreyfus and Rabinow 210). This emphasis on local rationalities has led Foucault into studies of what he calls "the disciplines": those relatively independent but still interconnected systems of rationalization comprising material structures and sites, an array of practices, a local power or authority, and a human subject matter assigned to (or created by) its practices. Defining discipline as "a political anatomy of detail," Foucault argues that "there is a whole history to be written . . . of the utilitarian rationalization of detail in more accountability and political control" (*Discipline* 139). In *Discipline and Punish,* his study of the rationalization of modern penal practices, he argues that while the jurists and philosophes of the Enlightenment were elaborating their critiques of monarchical sovereignty, their theories of social contract and right, and their systems of global reason, the "technicians of discipline were elaborating procedures for the individual and collective coercion of bodies" (169). He examines the techniques of disciplinary detail at work in the modern prison: techniques for enclosing and partitioning spaces, for classifying criminals and distributing them in spaces, and for transforming them into citizens or more docile and manageable prisoners through corrective training, constant surveillance, and carefully calculated punishments and rewards. Penal discipline becomes the foundation for a new science of criminal pathology, which preserves the bodies and consciences of prisoners as objects of knowledge and power. This power tends to disseminate itself, creating (on the analogy of the prison) new spaces and procedures for the discipline of workers, schoolchildren, soldiers, and the sick: "Is it surprising that prisons resemble factories, schools, barracks, hospitals, which all resemble prisons?" (228).

Though Foucault's study of the disciplines focuses on the French eighteenth and nineteenth centuries, it has some suggestive implications for a study of seventeenth-century Puritan utopia. In the first place, French demands for liberal prison reform arise at an eighteenth-century juncture reminiscent of the Puritan Interregnum: a moment defined by the intersection of a struggle against an absolutist model of sovereignty (with its retributive systems of penal torture) and of an emerging struggle against an unmanaged populace (displaced, potentially turbulent, and clinging to their customary "tolerated illegalities") (87).

Second, and more important, we will see at work in Puritan utopia a version of the postmonarchical power Foucault sees at work in the disciplines of the Enlightenment and later. One of Foucault's primary aims in his later work has been to formulate a new theory of power, moving away from a view of power as a negative instrument of repression toward a view of it as a positive instrument of production: "It seems to me now that the notion of repression is quite inadequate for capturing what is precisely the productive aspect of power. In defining the effects of power as repression, one adopts a purely juridical conception of such power; one identifies power with a law that says no; power is taken above all as carrying the force of a prohibition" (*Reader* 60–61). An analysis of the disciplines reveals power to be a complex force disseminated through a wide array of disciplinary authorities, aimed at achieving a rational and calculable economy of disciplinary effects and at producing a body of experimental truth that becomes, in turn, a vehicle for the further exercise of power. So long as we continue to see the exercise of power in modern society under the heading of juridical denial and repression, we are using a monarchical model of power to examine a postmonarchical society: "What we need ... is a political philosophy that isn't erected around the problem of sovereignty, nor therefore around the problems of law and prohibition. We need to cut off the king's head: in political theory, that still has to be done" (63). We will see the regicide Puritan political theorists busily at work fabricating a new corporate body animated by a postmonarchical model of power to replace the body politic they have decapitated.

Though it is explicitly critical of totalizing conceptions like rationalization and enlightenment, Foucault's concept of power tends toward a premature totalization of its own, for it sometimes claims that an analysis of power on the level of the disciplines automatically brings with it a knowledge of power on the level of class relations and national or global conflict.[7] But he does not altogether ignore the relation between the micropowers of the disciplines and the macropowers of the state, as we can see in his discussion of the modern state's development of a "pastoral of power." While the church's detailed pastoral care of souls, with its minute attention to the individual, may have lost most of its force in the eighteenth century, it reappears in a secular form in the social institutions and disciplines that take over its individualizing function. Whereas pastoral power had been confined to the church, in early modern Europe it suddenly expands into a number of disciplinary institutions aimed at policing health, penality, family life, education, the workplace, and so on. Therefore, we should not see the rise of the modern state simply as the rise of a vast impersonal rationalizing apparatus indifferent to the persons it dominates (there are elements of this critique in Weber and in Horkheimer and Adorno), but as "a modern matrix of individualization, or a new form of pastoral power" (Dreyfus and Rabinow 213–15).

Puritan utopia exists in a political universe anterior to the "disciplinary archipelago" that Foucault describes: it is some distance from the discrete and quasi-scientific disciplines of the Enlightenment to the Congregationalist church discipline at the center of Eliot's utopia and the military discipline at the center of Harrington's. Yet, on a more general level, they have the same objective: the production of calculable subjectivities. Foucault describes his work as essentially "a history of the different modes by which, in our culture, human beings are made subjects" (Dreyfus and Rabinow 208). Speaking explicitly of penal discipline but implicitly of discipline in general, Foucault says that its aim is simultaneously to produce and analyze certain forms of subjectivity: "This is the historical reality of this soul, which, unlike the soul represented by Christian theology, is not born in sin and subject to punishment, but is born rather out of methods of punishment, supervision, and constraint. . . . The soul is the effect of a political anatomy; the soul is the prison of the body" (*Discipline* 29, 30). The history of utopia all too often proceeds on the basis of a sterile antinomy between the individual and the repressive totalitarian state set over against the individual. We will see that the aim of early modern utopia is, in Foucault's terms, to conduct a pastoral of power by creating and regulating certain models of subjectivity. *Discipline* in the following pages is the means by which utopia attempts to regulate the production of certain models of individual subjectivity; it is also the means by which utopia proposes to reconstruct the state from below by using previously subpolitical pastoral technics (Congregationalist church discipline, military discipline, pedagogy) as technics of revolution that will ultimately restructure the entire state.

Chapter 2, Paradise New-Modeled, examines the course of rationalization, enlightenment, and discipline in early modern utopias, Puritan and non-Puritan alike. The first section, Millennial Demographics, argues that we can best see early modern utopia as an attempt to rationalize the displaced populations of the Old World and the New World; Puritan utopia conceives of this act of secular shaping as part of the sacred history of the latter days. The next section, Enlightenment and Utopia, argues that utopian rationality contains within itself a program of domination and imperial expansion. The third section, Cain and Agrarian Utopia, suggests that we should see utopia not as the urban negation of the rural but as a disenchantment of arcadian nature that aims to produce a readjustment of the relation between urban and rural space; this section also attempts to distinguish between utopia and arcadia and to draw an analogy between utopia and georgic. The fourth section, Lamech and Martial Utopia, examines a key disciplinary model for, and component of, utopia: its rational armies. The expansive armies depicted by early modern utopia (along with the Puritan New Model Army, which is itself a kind of utopia) are a key corrective to the view of the pre-Enlightenment utopia as a static ethical paradigm. The last section, The Body Politic and the *Rex Absconditus,* discusses the postmonarchical vision of political power implicit in a recurrent figure of early modern utopia: the abdicating legislator who assumes all power, disseminates that power into a rational nonmonarchical state, and then abdicates. After examining these utopian themes and technics at work in the concrete utopian projects of John Eliot (chapter 3) and James Harrington (chapter 4), we return in the final chapter to the question of discipline by examining the relation between utopia and social contract theory in the seventeenth century and later.

We begin, however, more modestly, for utopia begins not with a prelinguistic yearning for rational universality but with an act of reading—frequently with a reading of some earlier utopia. Quiroga's project is a convenient example, but by no means unique. No genre is more self-allusive than is utopia; even Plato's archetypal utopia invokes and preserves earlier models of an ideal state. But the early modern utopist, after consulting his predecessors, reading his textual authorities, and constructing his paradigms or models, looks up from his text and begins to search for groups of real persons to embody those models.

2

Paradise New-Modeled

Millennial Demographics

The rebirth of utopian writing in the Renaissance is the product neither of some radically new literary imagination nor of some unprecedented social practice. It is the product of a new encounter between a body of texts and a subject matter: the displaced population. If we concentrate on the newness of either party to this encounter at the expense of the encounter itself, then we quickly run into problems. True, certain textual authorities for early modern utopia seem to be absolutely original: Bacon's program for scientific revolution in *Novum Organum* and *Advancement of Learning* authorizes his own *New Atlantis* and the utopian writings of John Amos Comenius and the circle of Samuel Hartlib. But other authorities were discovered, not invented: the newly read and translated political philosophy of Plato, Aristotle, Plutarch, and Polybius authorized such works as More's *Utopia,* Machiavelli's *Discourses* and *The Prince,* and James Harrington's *Oceana.* Still other authorities were rediscovered: the Bible, perhaps the most important text for Puritan utopists, acquired its utopian authority only through a reinterpretation that gave it a previously unimagined relevance to social reorganization in such utopian communities and writings as Gerrard Winstanley's community of Diggers at George's Hill and his *Law of Freedom* and John Eliot's Massachusetts Indian praying towns and his *Christian Commonwealth.* These texts seem to offer themselves as patterns for social organization that can be applied immediately, with little or no concern for the inertial authority of preexisting social and political forms.

Likewise, these texts encounter displaced populations that are variously created, discovered, and rediscovered. The economic development of the sixteenth century, with its by-products of enclosure and eviction, created those roaming hordes that haunt both the colloquists of More's Book 1 and Gerrard Winstanley, just as the new mobile collective of the Puritan New Model Army inspired Harrington's meditation on the relation among land tenure, military discipline, and political power in *Oceana.* The discovery of New World cultures revealed a body of peoples ripe for utopian molding, whether their displaced and anomic condition was the fictional product of European unwillingness to see non-European political organization or the actual product of European conquest and disease. And early modern millennial utopianism rediscovered Europe's archetypal displaced population, the Hebrew nation, seeing its conversion and utopian fixing as a pressing political project for the latter days. The displaced population, once an amorphous and threatening mob, the "beast with many heads," is now the raw material for constructing an eternal commonwealth.[1]

I characterize this meeting of texts and populations as an "encounter" to avoid reducing one party to a simple cause and the other to a simple effect, while at the same time preserving the possibility of various causalities. This is to say, the displaced population may cause the utopist to turn to or write an organizing text, or his text may bring him to look for a population on which to try it out. Typically, we see a complex dialectic of text and population: the encounter of classical political theory and the wandering populations of sixteenth-century England produces *Utopia;* the encounter of *Utopia* and the conquered Indians of New Spain produces Quiroga's hospital pueblos. Early modern utopia presents this radically new encounter between text and population and promises the transformation of each: the revelation of the political nature of texts and the restructuring of human nature itself according to a textual plan.

Of course, utopia envisioned the reorganization of populations according to some textual scheme long before the Renaissance. In

Book 6 of *The Republic,* Socrates suggests that a carefully applied program of educational discipline will allow the philosophers to reform individuals and then the entire state. But they must first have the proper utopian raw materials. In his description of the formation of these materials, Socrates reveals the fundamentally aesthetic attitude of utopian discourse toward these human populations and introduces us to a utopian image we will frequently encounter: "They will take the city and the characters of men, as if they were a tablet, and wipe them clean—no easy task. But at any rate you know that this would be their first point of difference from ordinary reformers, that they would refuse to take in hand either individual or state or to legislate before they have received a clean slate or themselves made it clean" (2.71–73). The utopian philosophers will then proceed with their creation, constantly rubbing out and correcting their image of the ideal character and state according to their divine pattern; the image of the tabula rasa has at least as long a history in political philosophy as in epistemology. Still, Socrates leaves the precise manner of this "wiping" somewhat vague; he does have a plan for the forced rustication of all inhabitants of the city over the age of ten in order to have complete control over the children, but he seems to have no great faith in its feasibility (2.233). His problem remains the excess of pedagogical and civil alternatives to his utopia, and to the extent that he is unable to suggest some practical method for erasing previous ideological contamination from the minds of his pupils, his plan for reform is doomed. In *The Republic* the true art of reducing the study of the populace to a science is sophistry, not philosophy. Only the sophist is sordid enough to study the monstrously heterogeneous crowd and reduce it to a system.

The advantage of early modern utopia is that it can so readily identify (or claim to identify) blank, nonpolitical, displaced populations. The interest of Raphael's audience in his description of an orderly state in More's Book 2 is more than idle curiosity, for most of Book 1 has been a discussion of the need for some new organizational technique to discipline the thieving vagabonds of England. These populations are by no means qualitatively new. But the large-scale European wars of More's time have created both massive armies during wartime and massive peacetime armies of unemployed soldiers, just as the European market economy's demand for English wool has created a host of unemployed peasants driven out of agriculture by the enclosure of commons lands.

The sixteenth-century voyagers to the New World find a similar raw material awaiting rational inscription. In *The Decades of the Newe Worlde, or Weste India,* Peter Martyr (Pietro Martire d'Anghiera) draws a simile from writing: "For like as rased or unpainted tables are apt to receive what forms soever are first drawn thereon by the hand of the painter, even so these naked and simple people do soon receive the customs of our religion, and by conversation with our men, shake off their fierce and native barbarousness" (52). Both Vasco de Quiroga and the later Franciscan missionary Gerónimo de Mendieta describe the Indians of New Spain as "soft wax" capable of being molded into any new form (Phelan 58, 132n). Like More's Raphael, Quiroga and Mendieta dream of a return to the Christian communism of the Book of Acts. When confronted with the displaced populations of both the Old World and the New World, these Roman Catholics are possessed by a quasi-Protestant fantasy of reliving the history of the church by erasing the centuries of intervening corruption separating them from the era of apostolic simplicity. The utopian subject matter accompanies the utopian intention and almost calls it into existence: More and these other utopists and explorers are presented with a clean slate and need not find some way to wipe it clean themselves.

The social and political tumult of the Puritan seventeenth century simply accelerates this simultaneous disorder and utopian potential. For the Puritans of England and New England, utopian thought has not only an imaginative orientation but a subject matter: the "unformed" raw material of displaced and disorganized populations who are to be gathered together and submitted to a new organization of social space, time, and procedure. Confronted with the seventeenth-century populations displaced by continuing enclosure, the breakdown of rural housekeeping, and a sheer increase in numbers, the Puritans did not mourn the loss of traditional social cohesion but took the chaotic situation as an opportunity to form a radically new social covenant. Christopher Hill argues that Puritanism instinctively turned to the wandering rural poor and the urban unemployed as objects of disciplinary organization in the local congregations and the workplace (*Society* 219–58). Michael Walzer writes that the "Puritans confronted a disorder and confusion whose particular, material causes they hardly needed to know: they expected nothing else; organic harmony was never their presupposition. Calvinist theology already mirrored the new social reality and suggested a general explanation: nothing but disorder could possibly follow from the activity of fallen men, restless, lustful, and disobedient" (*Revolution* 203–04).

Indeed, we should see Puritanism not simply as a reaction to these populations but also as one cause of their displacement. It encouraged the individual's removal from the customary social matrix of rural household, parish, and secular monarchy and reintegration in the new corporate bodies of the Puritan family, the congregation, and the theocratic state or regenerate community in continental or colonial exile. Puritanism is itself an itinerant ideal: William Haller has shown Puritanism's interest in the metaphor of the true "wayfaring Christian" walking the strait path to God (*Rise* 147–72). We can see fictional and literal types of this wandering in the narratives of the Marian exiles and the Pilgrim and Puritan emigrants, in John Bunyan's picture of Christian and Christiana in *Pilgrim's Progress* and of himself in *Grace Abounding to the Chief of Sinners,* in the careers of the wandering mechanic preachers of the seventeenth century, in Mary Rowlandson's captivity narrative, and in the compulsive voyaging of Defoe's Crusoe. When the Puritan encounters the displaced person, he sees a prerationalized type of himself; the wayfaring Christian walking the strait path is a rationalized and regenerate version of the displaced and degenerate person wandering aimlessly.

During the Interregnum, Puritan church discipline overflowed into social discipline of other kinds. Everywhere the saints turned, they discovered new displaced populations or new opportunities for organizing old ones; the years of the Commonwealth saw a series of acts creating orphanages, workhouses, and joint stock companies for the propagation of the gospel and Puritan civility in Ireland, Wales, the north of England, and Massachusetts. Valerie Pearl examines the writings preceding and relating to the establishment of the Corporation for the Poor. William Steele, later recorder of the radical government of London, first president of the Society for Propagation of the Gospel in New England, and lord chief justice of Ireland, proposed legislation for "the maintenance of the impotent and aged poor, and for employing and punishing the beggars and vagabonds." Workhouses and houses of correction were to be established in every county, and movements of displaced populations were to be limited by setting apprehended vagrants to work in the nearest workhouse rather than returning them to the parishes of their birth (Pearl 216). Samuel Hartlib, associate of Comenius and John Dury, wrote three pamphlets proposing new ways to settle the poor. In *The Parliament's Reformation* he proposes a nationwide system similar to Steele's: in each county, workhouses will "provide" work and preaching for young and old alike and education for the young. Houses of correction will exercise sterner discipline on those who shrug off the lessons of the workhouse, returning them to the workhouses when they become more tractable (1646; rpt. Webster, *Hartlib* 111–19).

Pearl remarks that Hartlib's plans "are essentially empirical, marked by hard-headed notions of social discipline far removed from the utopianism with which he is sometimes charged" (219). But hardheaded empiricism and utopianism are by no means incompatible. In fact, both of the major utopian projects we will examine practice a peculiar sort of empiricism that takes human bodies as the building blocks of the regenerate city. Defending John Eliot's painfully slow process of utopian conversion, Richard Mather writes, "And therefore no marvel if the building of a spiritual temple, an holy church to Christ, and a church out of such rubbish as amongst Indians, be not begun and ended on a sudden; it is rather to be wondered at, that in so short time, the thing is in so much forwardness as it is" (*Tracts* 221). James Harrington defends the English people from those who rail against their seeming inclination to revert to monarchy during the closing days of the Protectorate, arguing that they remain an uncorrupted raw material ready for utopian shaping: "But men that go upon picking up arguments against a house out of the rubbish, and distinguish not between the people under the ruins of the old government and what they must needs be when raised into the proper structure of a new frame, will say that the people have a general aversion from being built into any new form at all. So hath the rubbish, and yet it may have good stones and beams in it" (750). One reason Puritan utopia has largely escaped the attention of historians of utopia attuned to the spatial and architectural imagination is that its building blocks are also its citizens.

But here we run into an antecedent problem of definition: What is a Puritan? For early modern Englishmen as for contemporary critics, the term is distressingly versatile, with everyone from the most radical sectary to Charles I and the party of Queen Henrietta Maria smarting under its hostile application (Hill, *Society* 13–29). So eclectic is its usage that it seems more pronominal than nominal, allowing any speaker to deride anyone lower in social class, further from Rome in religion, or less inclined to support absolute monarchy than himself. But whether *Puritan* refers to class, religion, politics, or to some combination of the three, it would seem difficult to indicate a vantage point outside Rome from which my two primary utopists, John Eliot and James Harrington, might be seen as Puritans. Eliot was by birth a son of the Hertfordshire yeomanry, by religion a Congregationalist minister and New England theocrat, and by political affiliation a democratic supporter of regicide. Harrington was by birth the eldest son of an ancient noble family of Lincolnshire and Rutlandshire, by religion a tolerationist Erastian, and by political affiliation in turns a gentleman of the bedchamber to Charles I, a republican opponent of Cromwell, and a political prisoner of Charles II. It is difficult, in fact, to refer to Harrington as a Puritan of any sort; only J. W. Gough has tried ("Harrington"). The most important sense in which he might be seen as a Puritan writer (I will argue that it is, in fact, quite an important sense) is that his writings emerged and took their shape in the context of the "Puritan" religious and political languages of the Protectorate. If we turn to the other radical Protestant utopists of the Interregnum— Gabriel Plattes, Pieter Cornelisz Plockhoy, John Amos Comenius, Gerrard Winstanley, and the organizers of the New Model Army—we discover an even more confusing mixture of class, religious, political, and even national backgrounds.

For the purposes of this study, *Puritanism* is to some extent, like *utopia,* a label of convenience that will have to justify itself retroactively. I will not begin by championing any previous definition of Puritanism or by adding one of my own, but will content myself, first, by employing it in a rather conventional sense to indicate a number of writers and practices previously convened under the heading of Puritan, then by trying to show some of the tensions inhabiting this convention. However we separate Puritanism from early modern culture as a whole by immuring it through definition, we will find more of interest in the gates breaching the wall, the tunnels undermining it, and the factions inside it than in the wall itself; this study will argue that we can see some surprising continuities between Puritan and non-Puritan utopists and some surprising differences among utopian and anti-utopian Puritans.

In an older tradition of the history of ideas, Puritanism appears as an internally coherent world view clearly demarcated from Roman Catholicism and Anglicanism on the one hand, from radical sectarianism on the other. William Haller sees the proliferation of warring sects as a token of the energetic unity of the great Puritan middle (*Rise* 17–18). Perry Miller sees the New England Way of Non-separating Independency as a relatively moderate unity that rejects the antinomian "enthusiasm" of the left and the Arminian "rationalism" of the right (*Seventeenth Century* 286, 367–71). Even Michael Walzer's more recent *Revolution of the Saints* begins with an act of definitional main force, excluding the English sects from the Calvinist "mainstream" of

English Puritanism, and he has little or nothing to say about the Levellers, Diggers, radical spiritists, and millenarians (viii).

In more recent histories Puritanism has become less the name of a unified logical structure or "mind," more the name of a complex field of social, theological, and political controversy with no clear center. Whereas Perry Miller claimed that the dispute between John Cotton and Roger Williams in the Bay Colony of the 1630s was a dispute between Cotton's orthodox Puritan Ramism and Williams's heretical, non-Puritan typologizing, Sacvan Bercovitch shows that it was rather a thoroughly Puritan dispute between Cotton's "historical" and Eusebian view of typology and the millennium, and Williams's "allegorical" and Augustinian (but no less Puritan) view (Bercovitch, "Typology"). Recent studies of Puritan political thought such as Christopher Hill's *World Turned Upside Down* and Philip F. Gura's *Glimpse of Sion's Glory* have shown the internal contradictions inhabiting or constituting the conservative Puritan world view—contradictions that led Puritanism to generate its own radical sectarian opposition. In this study, particularly in the final chapter, I will be arguing that while the Puritan utopists are certainly not at the center of Puritan orthodoxy (wherever that center might be), their obsession with techniques for disciplinary rationalization of the world can show us something of interest about Puritan theories of contract and covenant, even those of overtly anti-utopian Puritans.

I will suggest here that one crucial trait of Puritanism—by no means a definition of it—is the central importance it lends to the printed world. In *Foxe's Book of Martyrs and the Elect Nation*, William Haller argues that the religious experience of sixteenth-century England was decisively shaped by the simultaneous processes of the Marian executions and exiles, the translation of the Bible, and the composition of Foxe's *Book of Martyrs,* which crystallized the myth of England as an elect nation and a people of the Book: "The endeavour initiated by the martyrs and exiles of Mary's reign to convert the English people to a religion based upon the reading of the Word in print became an inseparable part of the great folk movement of their age and nation" (51). Initially this movement inhabited the Anglican church, and as Haller shows, Foxe did much to solidify Elizabeth's mythical reputation as a godly prince. But with the growth of Presbyterianism and Independency, the printed Scriptures became more and more an authority turned against the Anglican hierarchy and Laudian sacramentalism and toward a new religious culture. Speaking of the importance of the printed and preached Word for Old and New World Puritans, Larzer

Ziff says that "Puritanism, taking its rise in the days of the Armada, never relinquished its overwhelming insistence on the centrality of the word. . . . Once let loose, the word united men in revolt and divided them in victory" (5). The Puritan congregation, like early modern utopia more generally, is the site for a dialectic of text and practice. Congregational discipline bases itself on a reading and reinterpretation of the Bible and the church fathers, and this discipline is in turn the font of a stream of print: devotional manuals, catechisms, social polemics, theories of church polity, scriptural commentaries, and volumes of printed sermons. We will see a version of this dialectic when we turn to John Eliot's praying towns.

Perhaps the most instinctively satisfying way to unify any group of writers characterized as Puritan is through their theological roots. But the theory of political writing espoused by these Puritan utopists takes them some distance from the Continental Reformers who based their political theory on the concept of natural law. This concept allowed the Reformers (like the fathers and the Scholastics before them) to account for the presence of seemingly Christian virtues in pagan states and philosophers. The key text for the natural law theorists was Romans 2:14–15, where Paul argues that gentile conscience is premarked by God's hand: "For when the Gentiles, which have not the law, do by nature the things contained in the law, these, having not the law, are a law unto themselves: which shows the work of the law written in their hearts." When they moved from ethics to political theory, natural law theory provided the Reformers with a casuistic theory of saintly accommodation to contemporary political authority: no matter how secular that authority might seem to be, it has been shaped by God, so a Protestant may submit to it in good conscience. John T. McNeill shows that Luther, Melanchthon, and Calvin made much of this scriptural text. Luther claims that it shows that "'the law of nature has been naturally and indelibly stamped [*impressa*] upon the mind' of man" (McNeill 168). Melanchthon defines natural law as "the common judgment to which all men alike assent, which God has engraved upon the mind of each, [and which is] designed to fashion morals" (172).

In his *Institutes of the Christian Religion* Calvin condemns the typical utopian conception of Scripture as a magical compendium of political models. He partitions God's law, saying, "It is necessary to observe that common distinction which distributes all the laws of God promulgated by Moses into moral, ceremonial, and judicial; and these different kinds of laws are to be distinctly examined, that we may ascertain what belongs to us, and what does not" (Calvin 63). Only the moral law is universal, and its very universality (which connects it to natural law) makes it impossible to imagine a truly blank, displaced population: "Now . . . it is certain that the law of God, which we call the moral law, is no other than a declaration of natural law, and of that conscience which has been engraven by God on the minds of men" (65). On the other hand, Calvin says, the "ceremonial" and "judicial" laws of the Bible have no transcendent authority. Whereas both Harrington and Eliot see the model of government presented in Exodus 18 as a divinely sanctioned political model of universal validity, Calvin denounces as "dangerous and seditious" the opinion of those who "deny that a state is well constituted which neglects the polity of Moses and is governed by the common laws of nature" (63). The Scriptures hold no special authority, for Moses framed a polity for the Hebrews according to their "peculiar circumstances" of "time, place, and nation" (60).

The utopists' disinterest in natural law theory brings them closer to Zwingli than to any other Continental Reformer. McNeill suggests that Zwingli downplayed natural law because his "defence of the reformed community of Zurich necessitated the affirmation of a common divine authority for both church and civil government. For Zwingli these were closely integrated, and both became equally Christian" (178n). The Puritan utopists, too, are quite unconcerned with accommodating a new form of church government to a preexisting secular government, for the City of God and the City of Man are about to become one and the same, subject to the same theocratic principles. Rather than seeing God's shaping hand in the moral conscience of pagan human nature, the utopist sees all humankind, pagan and Christian alike, as a blank page on which God stands poised to write.

The similarity of the Puritan utopists lies less in the content of their theologies than in the relationship they see between the individual and the state. Here they side with Raphael Hythloday, who claims that there can be no permanent reform of individuals until there has been a fundamental reform of political institutions (More 31–32). James Harrington states the utopian attitude most succinctly: "'Give us good men and they will make us good laws' is the maxim of a demagogue, and (through the alteration which is commonly perceivable in men, when they have the power to work their own wills) exceedingly fallible. But 'give us good orders, and they will make us good men' is the maxim of a legislator and the most infallible in the politics" (205). The virtuous citizen is the product of the virtuous utopian state, not its precondition; the anomic and displaced population is not a portent of impending social chaos but a blank tablet awaiting the utopist's inscription.

This attitude unites the Puritan utopists in opposition to an equally diverse anti-utopian group: Hobbesian monarchists, who hold that the virtue of a king is a precondition for and a guarantor of the virtuous state; Presbyterian aristocrats; the Milton of *The Ready and Easy Way,* who holds that his aristocratic ideal commonwealth must be ruled by "the rightly-qualified"; most Fifth Monarchist millenarians (Eliot is a notable exception), who await the millennial rule of an aristocracy of visible saints; and even the Levellers, who hope for a new democratic state based in part on the rule of man's unconstrained native liberties. These anti-utopian theorists all agree with the premise of Hythloday's opponent, "More," who says, "It is impossible to make all institutions good unless you make all men good, and that I don't expect to see for a long time to come" (29). Here we may take the conservative Puritan Independent, Richard Baxter, opponent both of Harrington's utopian civil government in *Oceana* and of Eliot's utopian church government in *Communion of Churches,* as a more contemporary spokesman for the anti-utopian opposition. He is writing specifically in criticism of *Oceana:* "From hence the question may be resolved, whether it be better to be ruled by good laws and bad governors, or by good governors and bad laws? Answer: It is as if you should ask, is it better to be warmed by cold snow, or cooled by the fire? Laws are nothing but acts of government: effects and significations of the governor's will concerning what shall be the subject's duty. Laws antecedent to the sovereign's will are effects before the cause. Good rulers will make and continue good laws, and bad ones the contrary" (*Baxter* 95). The Fifth Monarchist John Rogers agrees, saying, "Nor can we trust that maxim of his [Harrington's], 'Give us good orders, and they will make us good men,' so much as give us good men and they will make us good orders, and government with God's blessing" (Barker 95). The clash between the nonutopist and the utopist is certainly related to matters of class, religion, and political affiliation, but it does not derive immediately and predictably from them. It would be more accurate to see it as a clash between an ethical politics, which envisions the virtuous state as the product of rule by an aristocracy of birth, property, or grace, and a disciplinary politics, which envisions the virtuous citizen as the product of virtuous state orders.

For the Puritan utopists of the Interregnum, this virtuous commonwealth always takes on a millennial glow. Doing an injustice to the complexities of millennialist writing and practice, I will here simply draw a distinction between the nonutopians practicing a "hermeneutical" millennialism and the utopians practicing a "catalytic" millennialism.[2] By the first group I mean those writers (certainly in the majority both before and after the Interregnum) who argue that if one interprets Biblical apocalyptic in a particular way, collating it properly with contemporary events, one may accurately predict the end of secular history and the beginning of the end time. This category includes those learned, "more responsible" scholars Tuveson examines in *Millennium and Utopia*: Joseph Mede, Henry More, Thomas Brightman, John Henry Alstead, and Thomas Burnet (89). It also includes Fifth Monarchist radicals like William Aspinwall, Independent conservatives like Richard Baxter, and perplexing radical conservatives like John Cotton. Their common bond lies not in any theological or ideological solidarity but in their attitude toward millennialist writing. They may speculate on the structure of daily life in the New Jerusalem, identify the four successive monarchies of Nebuchadnezzar's dream and prophesy the fifth, predict the dates of the pouring out of the seventh vial and the conquest of Antichrist, recalculate these dates when events prove them wrong, and argue with each other over all the above activities. But in no sense are the Last Things dependent on their writing. They are utterly self-contained events in the future reaching back into their own past, calling the writings of the hermeneutical millennialists into existence. There is an irreducible distance between these future final events, which are absolutely certain however obscure they now appear, and the writing that attempts to clarify, prophesy, and comprehend them.

By the catalytic millennialism of the utopists, I mean a millennial writing and practice that claims an authority exceeding prophecy and interpretation by claiming to show the way to the reign of Christ on earth, or even to constitute that reign. The utopists' precursors in this millennialism are the authors of the Jewish apocalyptic of the second century B.C. (Dan. 7–12, The Apocalypse of Animals, The Testament of Moses), who participated in the Maccabean political struggle by attempting "to move groups to adopt particular responses or courses of action in the face of the events of the moment" (McGinn 15). The catalytic millennialist does not simply comment on those prophesies recorded scribally by Daniel or John: he immediately takes on their role, breaking down the barrier between his writing and what he aims to describe. In the seventeenth-century utopias of Eliot, the early Winstanley, Comenius, and Harrington, we can see a writing that seems to call to its readers from somewhere inside the walls of jasper and gold.

Here again Richard Baxter (at least temporarily soured on the prospect of a millennial Godly Magistrate) provides us with a key contrast. In a letter of 1663 to Baxter, Eliot suggests a reformation of learning and of civil government in order "to advance the kingdom of Jesus Christ, which shall be extended over all the kingdoms and nations of the earth (Rev. 11:15), not by the personal presence of Christ, but by putting power and rule into the hands of the godly learned in all nations." Baxter demurs, saying, "As for the divine government of the saints which you mention, I dare not expect such great matters upon Earth, lest I encroach upon the privilege of heaven, and tempt my own affections downward, and forget that our kingdom is not of this world" (Baxter, *Reliquiae* 293–97). Human activity in the saeculum must not intrude upon the divine institution of the millennium.

In some ways the millennialism of the Puritan utopists is closest to that of the radical medieval sects Norman Cohn analyzes in *The Pursuit of the Millennium*. Both propose a millennium that will totally transform and perfect life on earth and that will be enjoyed by the faithful as a collective. But Cohn also says that these earlier millenarians believed that their millennium would be "miraculous, in the sense that it is to be accomplished by, or with the help of, supernatural agencies" (15). There is still an element of hermeneutical and predictive millennialism here. We need only look to the desperate reign of Jan Bockelson (John of Leyden) and the Anabaptists at Münster to see that like so many millenarian sects before and after them, they revolted in anticipation of supernatural or supernaturally inspired reinforcements that never arrived.

But the catalytic millennialism of the utopists is so reluctant to admit any need for special divine intervention, so eager to see God working through second causes, that we may reasonably call it a rationalist millennialism. God need not intervene in any miraculous way, for he is already immanent in the material conditions of the historical present: in the anomic populations he has created and in the textual models he has provided to shape them with. All the utopist need do is commence writing. Consequently, Puritan utopianism becomes millennial not (or not at first) on the level of its universal and totalizing claims but on the level of its minute organizational practices, and we find millennialism invading utopian works whose overt subject matter would seem too modest to warrant it.

We can see this juxtaposition of the quotidian and the apocalyptic in the educational theory of John Amos Comenius (1592–1670), Moravian Protestant exile, temporary guest of the Commonwealth, associate of John Dury and Samuel Hartlib, and advocate of a reformed "pansophy," or universal education. His proposals for educational reform are replete with scrupulously detailed systems of classroom discipline and so at first would seem more narrowly focused than overtly political Puritan utopia. But in Comenius these systems always promise to realize the Platonic ideal of a reformation of the state through a reformation of pedagogy: "The world is a school, since it is entirely made up of an order of teachers, learners, and disciplines." Just as "you might not improperly call the world the home of discipline," so the reformed schools might rightly be called "the workshops of humanity" (*Way* 1, 2; *Great Didactic* 71). Comenius sees in his reformed classroom what James Harrington sees in an orderly military muster, John Eliot in a well-disciplined congregation: a small-scale model for creating a regenerate millennial nation. His pansophic didactic is the means to a reformed state, a countermetaphysics or "art of arts" whose aim is universal reformation, not just universal description (*Great Didactic* 20, 6). He announces that the subject matter of his work is "the universal art of teaching all things to all men, and indeed of teaching them certainly, so that the result cannot fail to follow. . . . We wish to prove this a priori . . . so that we may establish the universal art of erecting schools" (5).

The principles of reformed education emerge at a moment when history shimmers just this side of complete millennial intelligibility: "The construction, the management of the world itself is very like a comedy" in that it gradually leads its spectators and actors further into the complexities of the plot "till at length all the actions converge more and more upon the denouement" (*Way* 32). God has foreshadowed his coming universal didactic reformation of man through the annunciatory chaos of the collapse of older methods of schooling, "for he who intends to raise a new structure always levels the site ahead of time, demolishing the decaying or inferior structures" (*Great Didactic* 8).

Comenius acknowledges the corruption of man's fallen state, but he sees this corruption as an opportunity, not a hindrance, for it produces the human raw materials for a utopian reformation of learning: "In our corrupt condition, it is all that much more necessary for us to learn by experience, since in truth our minds are bare, like a tabula rasa. . . . Out of every piece of humanity a man can be fashioned, if it is not utterly corrupt. Someone, I know, will object, 'But our inner power has been weakened by the Fall.' 'Weakened,' I reply, 'but not extinguished'" (85). Throughout his writing Comenius depicts this fashioning as the purely instrumental and aesthetic act of subject upon object: "Just as the writer can write or the painter paint whatever he wishes on a bare tablet, if he is not ignorant of his art, so anyone not ignorant of the art of teaching can just as easily write all things on the human mind" (44).

For Comenius as for Plato, the ideal materials for a universal transformation are the young: "You have seen that there is no better time than early youth to fight against the evils humans are prone to as a breed, no better way to plant a tree destined for eternity than to plant it and train it up while it is young, no better time to raise Zion on the site of Babylon than when the living buildingstones of God, the young, are easily hewn, shaped, polished, and fitted for the heavenly edifice" (18). Comenius's *Reformation of Schooles* (1642) concludes with a millenarian conceit comparing the construction of a "temple" of pansophy to that of the temple in Jerusalem, and so also to the promised construction of its latter-day type, the Book of Revelation's New Jerusalem (60–93). Like the political architecture of James Harrington and the Puritan missionaries, Comenius's pedagogical architecture promises to shape the heavenly city out of disciplined human bodies.

We will return to some of Comenius's proposals in chapter 5. For the moment, though, we should note the presence in his writing of a characteristically utopian zoom focus which moves in a moment from a microscopic organizational detail to the telescopic unification of the world and its history in the millennium. Utopian millennialism is a fetishism of the detail. It frequently makes its appearance in the juxtaposition of the most banal, seemingly everyday occurrence (the organization of a classroom, a proposal for the cultivation of commons grounds, the weeping of an Indian convert, a plan for assembling voters or a militia or an ecclesiastical synod) with a vista of the New Jerusalem. Puritan utopia is both the organizational means to the millennium and the means by which an apocalyptic fervor permeates everyday life. By bringing together his utopian textual authorities and his displaced populations according to certain readily specifiable procedures, the utopist promises to inaugurate the reign of Christ on earth. Puritan utopia is do-it-yourself millennialism.

Enlightenment and Utopia

The engraved title page of Bacon's *Instauratio Magna* (1620; see frontispiece of this book) seems a perfect emblem for a study of the seventeenth-century anticipation of secular Enlightenment science. Framing the title and Bacon's name are two Doric columns on pedestals representing the Pillars of Hercules, the traditional symbol for the ne plus ultra of premodern Europe. One ship is passing through the narrow strait between the two pillars (whether into or out of the Mediterranean we cannot tell), with another ship in the near distance. In 1517 Charles V adopted a similar device as the emblem for the Spanish royal family, with the legend *plus ultra* to indicate Spain's imperial destiny in the West. With the rise of British seapower and the defeat of the Armada, Britain frequently affixed the emblem to representations of Elizabeth and James as iconographic booty (Yates). In his dedication to James at the beginning of Book 2 of *Advancement of Learning,* Bacon connects this emblem with his own revolutionary program in antischolastic science: "There is not any more noble or more worthy [project for your patronage] than the further endowment of the world with sound and fruitful knowledge. For how long shall we let a few received authors stand up like Hercules' columns, beyond which there shall be no sailing or discovery in science, when we have so bright and benign a star as your Majesty to conduct and prosper us?" (4.283). As Bacon uses it, then, we may see this plate as an emblem for the "new spirit of inquiry" that was to produce the Royal Society, the Enlightenment, and ultimately the modern world (Medawar 438)—a spirit that would have to vanquish the vestiges of religious superstition before it could prevail (Corbett and Lightbown 186–87).

But the plate is more complexly emblematic than this, as we can see when we note that Bacon or his engraver has changed the legend from *plus ultra* to *Multi pertransibunt et augebitur scientia*—a quote from the Book of Daniel that later provided the title for Bacon's *De Dignitate et Augmentis Scientiarum* (1623). In *Novum Organum* Bacon quotes the passage again and comments:

> Nor should the prophecy of Daniel be forgotten, touching on the last ages of the world, "Many shall run to and fro, and knowledge shall be increased," clearly intimating that the thorough passage of the world (which by so many distant voyages seems to be accomplished, or in the course of accomplishment), and the advancement of sciences, are destined by fate, that is by Divine Providence, to meet in the same age. (4.92)

The millennial legend binds together the imperial/geographical and the scientific levels of the emblem. The prospect we see through the pillars is not just secular but millennial: a vision of the course of empire to be followed by an expansive elect nation led by a godly prince like Elizabeth or James, after the annunciatory defeat of the Armada of Antichrist. This imperial expansion is not just a simile for the advancement of learning but a historical sign of it, for the two are to occur simultaneously in the final days of the world. In *A Reformation of Schooles* Comenius comments, "Many have already passed to and fro, and have searched out (in this our age more than ever) both heaven, and earth, seas, and islands, even the whole kingdom of nature, as also the Holy Scriptures. . . . And what remains then, but that the other part of the prophecy should also take its turn to be fulfilled?" (29).

Charles Webster has shown that this verse from Daniel was a favorite of the millenarian Puritan heirs to Bacon, who were eager to advance the causes of Christ, knowledge, and empire (*Instauration* 1– 31). For the Puritan pre-Enlightenment of the earlier seventeenth century, millennialism and enlightenment are related to each other not as sacred precursor and secular successor but as coexistent signs of each other. Both promise the submission of all places, times, and ways of knowing to a single domination, historical plot, and reason. Puritan utopia is one of the key early modern intersections of millennialism and enlightenment: the *Multi pertransibunt* of Daniel points toward utopia's displaced populations wandering the Old World and the New World, the scriptural authorities it will use to shape them into a millennial state, and the advancement of learning that will result. Puritan utopia is equally comfortable with millennialism and enlightenment, the sacred and secular fantasies of geographical, historical, and epistemological totality. In this section we will examine the implications for early modern and Puritan utopia of this enlightenment advancement of learning dramatized by geographical expansion and backlit by millennialism.

In the last two aphorisms of the first book of *Novum Organum,* Bacon moves from his discussion of the nature of the new science he proposes to a consideration of the benefits it will bring to society and the honors it should receive in return. He offers as a lesson the praise the ancients awarded two kinds of innovators. First are the merely civil and political innovators "such as founders of cities and empires, legislators, saviours of their country from long endured evils, quellers of tyrannies, and the like." The ancients gave these persons honors no higher than heroic, for they bring "civil benefits only to particular places." These blessings are not only local but mixed, for "the reformation of a state in civil matters is seldom brought in without violence and confusion."

Second are the "authors of inventions," whom the ancients granted not merely heroic but divine honors. They bring benefits that are universal and that "may extend to the whole race of man." Furthermore, these discoveries carry "blessings with them, and confer benefits without causing harm or sorrow to any" (4.113). The author of an invention is the winner of a game of hide-and-seek with God, for, as Solomon says, "'The glory of God is to conceal a thing; the glory of a king to search it out.'"

But when Bacon elaborates on this distinction between these two kinds of innovators, problems arise: "Again, let a man only consider what a difference there is between the life of men in the most civilised province of Europe, and in the wildest and most barbarous districts of New India; he will feel it be great enough to justify the saying that 'man is a god to man,' not only in regard of aid and benefit, but also by a comparison of condition. And this difference comes not from soil, not from climate, not from race, but from the arts." Though Bacon does not say this difference will be permanent, his emphasis has shifted disconcertingly. Relative godhead is no longer a matter of the relation betwen a single inventor and the beneficiaries of his invention—those who will themselves become godlike by putting it to use. It is now a matter of the relation between one culture—one "particular place"—and another. Bacon shifts from a definition of man as the abstract universal "mankind" to one of man as the varied product of different cultures with different technologies. He shifts from seeing technology as a unifier of men to seeing it as a distinguisher among them.

Of course, Europe may simply be preparing to share its technology with the rest of the world. But Bacon's greater emphasis on the "comparison of condition" here (which would, of course, be wiped out by technological "aid and benefit") suggests otherwise. And the nature of the examples of invention Bacon brings forward makes the "aid and benefit" seem less and less beneficial:

> Again, it is well to observe the force and virtue and consequences of discoveries; and these are to be seen nowhere more conspicuously than in those three which were unknown to the ancients, and of which the origin, though recent, is obscure and inglorious; namely, printing, gunpowder, and the magnet. For these three have changed the whole face and state of things throughout the world; the first in literature, the second in warfare, the third in navigation; whence have followed innumerable

changes; insomuch that no empire, no sect, no star seems to have exerted greater power and influence in human affairs than these mechanical discoveries.

The ancients, only recently invoked as exemplars, have been utterly superseded, almost reduced to the level of New Indians in their lack of technology.

More important, it is difficult to think of these inventions as gifts of an inventor to all mankind. Their relation to the appearance of the "godlike" Europeans in the Indies makes their nature even more problematic. Print allows the dissemination of the language of the country inventing the printing, not (at least at first) that of the country without printing, which may not even have a written language. Gunpowder, of course, was instrumental in the westward course of European empire, but it was hardly one of the discoveries that carry "blessings with them, and confer benefits without causing harm or sorrow to any." And the very unidirectional quality of the compass symbolizes its one-sided and instrumental nature; it is the means by which Europe "discovers" the Indies, not that by which the Indies discover Europe. If this technology is to become a universal possession of mankind, it will do so only by enabling a particular culture to conquer the rest of the world. Bacon draws two antithetical pictures of enlightment technology: technology as universal and disinterested knowledge and technology as the instrument of European domination.[3]

He goes on to make a distinction among "the three kinds and as it were grades of ambition in mankind." The first of these is the ambition "of those who desire to extend their own power in their native country." This kind is "vulgar and degenerate," and we seem to be safely inside a traditional ethics condemning temporal ambition. The second kind of ambition, which resembles that of the civil innovators Bacon has previously discussed, is "of those who labour to extend the power of their country and its dominion among men." We might expect that because this kind simply enlarges the scope of the first, it would be so much the worse. Indeed, Bacon admits that it has "not less covetousness." But he also says (without telling us why) that it has "more dignity." The move to a more universal ambition is actually a progress, and it begins to appear that the first kind was "vulgar and degenerate" because of its scope, not its nature. Finally, the third: "But if a man endeavour to establish and extend the power and dominion of the human race itself over the universe, his ambition (if ambition it can be called) is without doubt both a more wholesome thing and a more noble than the other two" (4.114). At first this seems unobjectionable, for we have moved beyond one man's domination of another to man's domination of nature. Yet the distinction seems tenuous: Bacon tells us that this last ambition is for the "empire of man over things," but the progression established by the first two ambitions might lead us to suspect that it is rather (or also) the domination of all men by some men—that what we have here is a distinction among three "grades" of ambition, not among three "kinds," though Bacon begins by implying no difference between grades and kinds. We have previously seen that modern Europe's advance over the ancients and its domination of the Indians are, for Bacon, somehow the same as the conquest of nature. How can the domination of mankind appear in the form of the domination of nature? How can technology appear to be disinterestedly universal and at the same time act as an instrument of domination?

In *Dialectic of Enlightenment* Max Horkheimer and Theodor Adorno suggest an answer. Enlightenment philosophy and political practice see their central task as the "disenchantment of the world," or the destruction of preenlightenment man's attempt to anthropomorphize the world through animism. There is no assault upon nature that is not simultaneously an assault upon the men or cultures who would anthropomorphize it, so dominion over nature is always dominion over men as well. Enlightenment is both a positive program of research and a negation of anthropomorphic myth: "Enlightenment has always taken the basic principle of myth to be anthropomorphism, the projection onto nature of the subjective. In this view, the supernatural, spirits and demons, are mirror images of men who allow themselves to be frightened by natural phenomena. Consequently, the many mythic figures can all be brought to a common denominator, and reduced to the human subject. Oedipus's answer to the Sphinx's riddle: 'It is man!' is the Enlightenment stereotype repeatedly offered as information, irrespective of whether it is faced with a piece of objective intelligence, a bare schematization, fear of evil powers, or hope of redemption" (6–7). From Plato's proposal in *The Republic* to censor tales of the gods' anthropomorphic savagery; to Bacon's critique of the idols of the tribe, cave, marketplace, and theater in *Novum Organum;* to Vico's account of the origins of human culture and religion in primitive man's projection of human desires and fears upon his inanimate environment; to Marx's account of commodity fetishism and of the social function of religion—enlightenment attempts to search out and destroy hidden images of man.[4] Enlightenment's critique of myth, magic, and monarchy as anthropomorphic fictions is simultaneously true and a tool of domination, and Bacon's "empire of men over things" is always also an empire over men considered as things: "What men want to learn from nature is how to use it in order wholly to dominate it and other men" (Horkheimer and Adorno 4). The basic impulse of enlightenment is to establish dominion over men through the mastery of nature on the basis of unified, antianthropomorphic science.

Bacon's *New Atlantis* realizes this impulse in fictional form. The researchers of Salomon's House, its national research academy, are not interested so much in giving nature man's form as in molding it to his will, making "trees and flowers to come earlier or later than their seasons." They make animals "greater or taller than their kind is; and contrariwise dwarf them, and stay their growth; we make them more fruitful and bearing than their kind is; and contrariwise barren and not generative" (3.158–59). In contrast with Bacon's usual insistence on the subordination of knowledge to use, the researchers seem to see an inherent value in the technological domination of nature. And despite the fact that they live in an island kingdom unknown to the outside world, this domination soon takes on a familiarly martial cast: they also construct "ordnance and instruments of war, and engines of all kinds: and likewise new mixtures and compositions of gun-powder, wildfires burning in water, and unquenchable" (3.163). At the conclusion of Bacon's fragment, the Father of Salomon's House gives the narrator leave to "publish" all this information "for the good of other nations" (3.166). But as Bacon's trinity of inventions suggests, "publication" is indissolubly linked with geographical exploration and warfare. The researchers of Salomon's House are guided in their research by an enlightenment aesthetic, pursuing for now a program of pure, useless domination with the secret dream that, one day, they will integrate it with a program of useful domination.

Utopia, as the genre of universal political rationalization, suggests that Bacon's distinction between the political innovator and the author of inventions can disappear. Solamona, the king who established the civil perpetuity of Bacon's ideal state nineteen hundred years before his narrator comes ashore, also founded its institution of scientific research, Salomon's House, which helps to ensure that perpetuity. Political innovation is not opposed to scientific innovation but is built on it. Salomon's House contains a statuary pantheon honoring, among others, Christopher Columbus and the inventors of ships, gunpowder, ordnance, writing, and the printing press.

The utopist is the *inventor* of a new political system, not a jurist commenting on his state's laws, not a polemicist writing in defense of some certain existing state, not a philosopher of state authority, contract, and right. Puritan utopia is typically less concerned with scientific technology than are other early modern utopias. Still, it does constantly attempt to invent new political technologies. James Harrington compares his invention of a utopian platform with William Harvey's discovery of the circulation of the blood, calling his platform "as ancient in nature as herself, and yet as new in art as my writings" (411). The civil innovator and the author of inventions come together in the figure of the utopist as political scientist, who has discovered his subject matter, the object of his technic, in the displaced population. He describes the domination of man not just *through* the domination of nature but *as* the domination of nature.

Utopia's affinity for islands and isolated sites comes not from a desire to flee the world but from its need for a controlled experimental site in which to prepare for the conquest and reorganization of the world—for submitting the world to its own vision of reason. After conquering the "barbarians" inhabiting the peninsula of Abraxa, King Utopus's first act is to create such an experimental site. He puts his soldiers and the Abraxans to work cutting the neck of land connecting Abraxa to the mainland—a miracle of civil engineering that makes him the secular and rational opposite of Moses at the shores of the Red Sea. Raphael tells us that "the neighboring peoples, who at first had laughed at his folly, were struck with wonder and terror at his success" (More 35). Given Utopia's imperial destiny, this terror is prophetic. After Utopus transforms Abraxa into Utopia, these very neighbors, we can assume, become the victims and beneficiaries of Utopia's armies and colonies. Similarly, Campanella's City of the Sun is a type of island. Its outer wall is defensive, for it seals out the nonutopian world; but its inner surface reproduces that world in a rationalized form: "On the . . . wall there is a map of the entire world with charts for each country setting forth their rites, customs, and laws; and the alphabet of each is inscribed above the native one" (33). Utopia is an island experimental site that aims eventually to destroy all political, religious, and epistemological insularity.

As Campanella's wall indicates, utopia also aims to destroy linguistic insularity. Bacon's New Atlantis hides from the rest of the world, but it has managed to master all the European languages, along with Hebrew, ancient Greek, and Latin. More's Utopians show an astonishing curiosity about other languages and great skill in acquiring them.

After giving them a few lessons in Greek, Raphael finds that "they picked up the forms of the letters so quickly, pronounced the language so aptly, memorized it so quickly, and began to recite so accurately that it seemed like a miracle" (62). Acquiring a new language establishes the possibility of a linguistic universality; print establishes the reality. The two great European contributions to Utopian technology are paper and print, but the Utopians' use of them is surprising: they take the few Greek texts that Raphael brings them, and before long, they have printed thousands of copies. There seems never to have been any thought of printing Utopian books. European technology makes possible the replication of European culture, not the development of a Utopian literature. The "scholar" of Gabriel Plattes's utopian dialogue *Macaria* predicts that the art of printing will soon spread knowledge so wide that the common people will throw off oppression, and "little by little all kingdoms will be like to Macaria"—which is to say, like England (89). We will see that such a one-sided publication forms an important part of John Eliot's Utopian Indian communities.

Early modern utopia's ideal civic perpetuity is by no means the same as sheer civil stasis (that totalitarian petrification of the imagination so frequently attributed to utopias old and new), for it incorporates this internal generic tendency to replicate itself. In More's Utopia, the spur for this replication is the pressure of population. When internal organization can no longer restore order, Raphael says, the only solution is colonization:

> They enroll citizens out of every city and plant a colony under their own laws on the mainland near them, wherever the natives have plenty of unoccupied and uncultivated land. Those natives who want to live with the Utopian settlers are taken in. When such a merger occurs, the two peoples gradually and easily blend together, sharing the same way of life and customs, much to the advantage of both. For by their policies the Utopians make the land yield an abundance for all, which had previously seemed too barren and paltry even to support the natives. But if the natives will not join in living under their laws, the Utopians drive them out of the land they claim for themselves, and if they resist make war on them. The Utopians say it's perfectly justifiable to make war on people who leave their land idle and waste, yet forbid the use of it to others who, by the law of nature, ought to be supported by it. (44–45)

More's paragraph begins with the promise of enlightened Utopian civility, for the Utopians thoughtfully choose "uncultivated" lands and "take in" those few native inhabitants inclined to "blend" with

Utopian culture in a new civil hybrid. But one begins to suspect that in relation to agriculturally advanced Utopia, most other lands are uncultivated. Contrary to the initial promise of this paragraph, we do not see the peaceful blending of two different cultures, for we never see what these non-Utopian cultures have to contribute. The Utopians have an almost European ethnocentrism, and Raphael shows us only the cultivation of Utopian civility among waste peoples in a wasteland. Those natives who refrain from blending in are no longer precivil but anticivil and so are justly driven out or killed. Utopian civility invokes the "law of nature" (a version based in political economy, not ethics) to rationalize its destruction of those natural or "native" inhabitants who resist civility and so become subnatural or demonic. We will see this sequence of colonization, utopian replication, and conquest repeated literally in John Eliot's Massachusetts and prophesied for James Harrington's Oceana. The replication of utopia, which originates in its production of an excessive, unmanageable, and so displaced population, produces other displaced populations in turn, though they are never displaced in precisely the same fashion. Utopia is *ou topos,* "no place," not just because it has an imaginative quality that removes it from any determinate location, but also because it is a vagabond colonial paradigm, eager to replicate its social structures in any new waste ground and people it meets.

Passages similar to the paragraph quoted above abound in *Utopia.* We begin with the promise of a six-hour workday and conclude with almost every waking minute of the day accounted for in some rational organized activity, with idleness strictly forbidden (40–41). We begin with the promise of free travel and conclude with a host of overlapping restrictions that would seem to make travel almost impossible (48–49). Speaking of these two passages, Stephen Greenblatt says, "The pattern is repeated again and again in Hythlodaeus's account: freedoms are heralded, only to shrink in the course of the description" (*Self-Fashioning* 40–41). I would add only that we do not see so much the disappearance of a promised freedom as the gradual revelation of reason's unbreakable link to domination.[5]

We might call the formal unit in which such links emerge the Möbius paragraph. When we focus on an isolated section of a Möbius strip, it seems to be a topologically ordinary, two-sided piece of paper. But when we move along one side of it, in what seems to be a circle, we soon find ourselves at a spot on the opposite side of the paper from our starting point, forced to come to the counterintuitive conclusion that we have in our hands a one-sided piece of paper. So in More's

Möbius papagraphs, we begin with what seem to be two clear sides: the Utopian world of enlightened reason and reform and, diametrically opposite, the European world of customary unreason and domination. As we read along in Raphael's account of the Utopian side, however, we find that its inital *promesse de bonheur* begins to fade. The distinction between reason and domination blurs, and we soon find ourselves in a spot disturbingly like that originally opposite our starting point— here, inside an ideology of imperialist domination. It is not that Utopia and Europe are the same place, but that enlightenment reason, working against customary domination, produces not freedom but rational domination. This link is by no means unique to More's utopia. But whereas Bacon, Johann Andreae, and Campanella joyously proclaim the identity of reason and domination, More disturbs us again and again by first allowing us to distinguish between the two, then forcing us to admit that the distinction cannot hold. *Utopia* is a painful and repetitive course in the paradoxes of rationalization.

This linkage between reason and domination is ubiquitous in *Utopia* and is inwardly as well as outwardly directed. In the first half of that paragraph quoted above, we can see the remarkable facility with which Utopia rationalizes customary forms of domination in order to replicate itself:

> Each city, then, consists of households, the households consisting generally of blood relations. When the women grow up and are married, they move into their husbands' households. On the other hand, male children and grandchildren remain in the family, and are subject to the oldest parent. . . . To keep the city from becoming too large or too small, they have decreed that there shall be no more than six thousand households in it (exclusive of the surrounding countryside), each family containing between ten and sixteen adults. They do not, of course, try to regulate the number of minor children in a family. The limit on adults is easily observed by transferring individuals from a household with too many into a household with not enough. Likewise, if a city has too many people, the extra persons serve to make up the shortage of population in other cities. And if the population throughout the entire island exceeds the quota, then they enroll citizens out of every city. . . . (44–45)

We begin with a reassuring assertion of permanence, for the cities seem to be stable civil units composed of stable households. But the second sentence introduces us to the first of several categories of movable bodies: Utopian women of marriageable age, who are rationally distributed among Utopia's patriarchal households. Of course, this is hardly a Utopian innovation; what is new here is that this customary distribution of women becomes, in the implicit logic of More's paragraph, a model for other, more radical distributions. Males cannot retain the customary fixedness promised in the third sentence, for Utopia transfers adult individuals of both sexes from household to household, entire households from city to city, and a national surplus from Utopia to its colonies. And as we have seen, Utopia does not hesitate to transfer an entire "native" population in these neighboring lands to yet other lands.

Taking the ancient and customary model of women as a symbolic currency that must circulate among patriarchal households, Utopia uses it to shape all of its own population and those of surrounding lands into a rationally distributable commodity. Working the other way around, we could also say that Utopia turns its techniques for managing and distributing foreign populations upon its own populace; in a sense, it feminizes and colonizes itself. Raphael introduces the chapter that contains this paragraph by promising to describe "the way the citizens behave toward one another, and how they distribute their goods within the society." But this is a false distinction: their behavior toward one another consists of their distribution of one another *as* goods.

If tragedy rises and falls, epic encompasses, lyric moves inward, romance moves outward then inward, then utopia moves westward and stays there; it is the heliotropic narrative of occidental enlightenment. As far back as Plato's *Republic,* the sun stands as the symbol of utopia's universalizing reason, with all of enlightenment's antagonism to animism and diffuse theology. The sun is a symbol of epistemological universality, for it links the eye and the visible just as the good links reason and the objects of reason (2.101–13). In *Critias* Plato shows such a linking of reason and the objects of reason in an Atlantean state west of the Pillars of Hercules.

But in describing this state, Plato simply retells an ancient myth. In early modern utopia, on the other hand, the enlightenment fascination with the west begins to take on a complex material form, and utopia begins to promise the universality of world dominion in addition to the epistemological universality Plato argues for. With the aid of the three revolutionary inventions Bacon describes, utopia begins actually to move westward, and the west becomes not just a mythical theme but a source of news: news of anthropological discovery, conquest, colonies, even of political organization and experimentation. More's Hythloday is a voyager who has traveled westward with Vespucci.

Bacon's voyagers to the New Atlantis are on a westward voyage to China and Japan. Campanella's Genoese sailor discovers the City of the Sun is somewhere near India, but he arrives there only by following the course of the sun—on a westward voyage with Columbus. This is the east, but it is a new east. And we have seen that despite *Utopia*'s fictional and satiric elements—its classical punning, elaborate dialogic structure, and unreliable narrators—it became even before More's death the textual authority for Vasco de Quiroga's construction of a utopian community in the New World.

Though less enamored of the utopian device of the imaginary voyage than More, Bacon, and Campanella, Puritan utopists had a similar westward fixation. Samuel Hartlib hoped that the principles of Plattes's *Macaria* might be realized in the New World, perhaps in Bermuda, as an ideal state named Antilia (Webster, *Hartlib* 71). The Dutch Mennonite Pieter Cornelisz Plockhoy, after presenting an unsympathetic Parliament and Cromwell with two pamphlets advocating the utopian and communist reform of English church and civil government, established a communist colony based on his utopian principles in New Netherland (present-day Delaware). James Harrington saw the utopian distinction of his ideal republic Oceana arising from its organization as a "commonwealth for increase"—as an imperial power that would put all the world under its rational dominion—rather than as a "commonwealth for preservation" like static Venice. John Eliot attempted to organize the Algonquians of Massachusetts into millennial utopian communities on the basis of Congregationalist church discipline and a utopian model he "discovered" in Exodus. The Puritans even found "western" wastelands much closer to home in the ranks of the urban poor and in the Roman Catholic peoples inhabiting Ireland, Wales, and the relatively agricultural and underdeveloped north and west of England, sparking organized efforts at evangelism and the reform of civil and church government (Hill, *Change* 3–47). Miriam Eliav-Feldon says that "it is quite striking, in fact, how little influence the New World had on the content of utopias during the Renaissance; one has the impression that they could all have been written even if Columbus had never set sail" (12). It might be better to say that the era of exploration enabled European utopists to notice the "Indian" raw material of displaced populations all around them.

Utopia's westward fixation brings it a theory of historical irreversibility characteristic of enlightenment theories of history in general, uniting sacred and secular theories of progress that we customarily separate. John Eliot's theocratic Christian utopianism aims to inaugurate the millennium, while Harrington's less overtly millennial utopianism suggests a way out of the rise and fall of secular republics, but both reject models or civil stasis or cyclicity. Comenius's *Way of Light* prophesies the irreversible spread of utopian enlightenment in a lengthy and complex conceit tying together a pedagogical epistemology, a pre-Newtonian theory of optics, and a millennial scheme of history. He constructs a seven-stage history of enlightenment based on the invention of seven diverse technics that bring the millenial unity of all peoples and all times closer and closer. These are direct empirical observation or "autopsy," speech between persons, public assembly, writing, printing, navigation, and his own pansophy, which will clarify and methodize all these technics, and institute the millennium. Comenius comments, "And as these two inventions (the arts, namely, of printing and of navigation) are in their very nature such as to multiply the light, I do not see why we should doubt that they are also the forerunners of a still greater, namely, that Universal light" (107).

The compass is a fitting emblem for utopia's scheme of unidirectional and irreversible history. Raphael Hythloday proceeds on his exploratory voyage by showing his New World crew the use of the compass, which contains within it all the dangerous power of enlightenment: "The seamen . . . were most grateful to him, Raphael said, for showing them the use of the compass, of which they had been ignorant. For that reason, they had formerly sailed with great timidity, and only in summer. Now they have such trust in the compass that they no longer fear winter at all, and tend to be overconfident rather than secure. There is some danger that through their imprudence, this discovery, which they thought would be so advantageous to them, may become the cause of much mischief" (More 8). In *The Philosophy of History* Hegel says that the progress of reason is like the path of the sun, with a determinate east in Asia and a progress to full European self-consciousness. Utopia argues that this progress has an unlocalized but no less determinate west in the New World and the various waste grounds and disorganized peoples of the Old World who are to be submitted to a process of rational organization. The advancement of learning is an irreversible scientific, geographical, and historical advance.

Of course, utopia is not the only rationalizing genre. Romance, for instance, often incorporates a disenchanting voyage through some mythical west. But romance also typically leaves this outer world behind—looted, deflowered, and purged of magic. The voyage of Odysseus, as Horkheimer and Adorno remark, is a disenchantment of the mythical world. They argue that Odysseus's cunning breaks the power of the Sirens' song, converting its previously irresistible effect into "the merely neutral longing of the passer-by. The epic says nothing of what happened to the Sirens once the ship had disappeared" (59). Odysseus comes home and reestablishes his patriarchal monarchy, and the mythical world he has visited becomes a postmythical narrative told around the Ithakan hearth. In his quest Sir Gawain encounters the seemingly enchanted Green Knight and Green Chapel, but after he discovers the hoax underlying their appearance, he returns to Camelot, where he initiates the custom of wearing the green girdle as a token of the passage from innocence to experience. In *The Tempest* a wiser Prospero restores family order by overcoming and forgiving his rebellious brother and by marrying off his daughter. He then returns to his ducal responsibilities in Milan, leaving behind him his island of exile, an anomic Caliban, the magic with which he ruled both, and Gonzalo's Montaignesque fantasies of an ideal state in the New World. The *nostos* of romance returns the protagonist to his homeland, where he reestablishes family order and contemplates the mythical world he has disenchanted from a perspective of domestic calm.

But the westward voyager of early modern utopia has a different return, for he never truly leaves the western utopia behind him. It continues to exist outside him as a source of news, superior to and independent of him; he can never internalize his voyage as the chronicle of his education. If he returns to Europe at all, it is to spread the utopian gospel or to sign on for another westward voyage. If we hear about his family at all, we hear that like Raphael's, it has been adequately provided for and has no further claims to make on him, or that like the unregenerate family of the Puritan emigrant, it has been left behind in the City of Man. The utopian traveler is not a romantic/heroic raconteur but a transmitter of information gained on a research expedition—not so much a character in a fiction as a blank medium of communication, a mobile tool in the antischolastic new science.

Montaigne's "Of Cannibals," an account of his conversations with a traveler, shows us the fascination that unlettered returned sailors have for the utopian philosophers of Old Europe: "Men of intelligence notice more things and view them more carefully, but they comment on them; and to establish and substantiate their interpretation, they cannot refrain from altering the facts a little. . . . We need either a very truthful man, or one so ignorant that he has no material with which to construct false theories and make them credible: a man wedded to no idea. My man was like that. . . . Therefore I am satisfied with his information and do not inquire what the cosmographers say about it" (108). Montaigne trusts the sailor who tells him about the wonders of savage life in Brazil precisely because he is the blank bearer of accurate information. In this he is strangely like both the utopian writer and the displaced population he writes on. His divorce from previous ideas resembles both the supposed objectivity of the ideal, inductive new scientist, liberated from scholastic custom and prejudice and immersed in empirical particulars, and the natural state or anomie of the New World populations that makes them ideal subjects for observation (for Montaigne) or for utopian experiments (for Quiroga and Eliot).

In Montaigne's conversations with this sailor, we encounter a recurrent motif of early modern utopia: the dialogue between the traveler and the philosopher. The newly returned (or letter-writing) traveler enters into dialogue with the European philosopher, who pumps him for news of this previously unknown civilization. We can see this in the conversation of Raphael Hythloday with the learned "More" and Peter Giles, in the dialogue of the Genoese sailor and the Knight Hospitaler in *The City of the Sun,* and in the very subtitle of Gabriel Plattes's *Macaria . . . a Dialogue between a Schollar and a Traveller.* We can even see variants on this dialogue in nonfictional utopias. John Eliot sends reports on the language and customs of the Algonquians to Robert Boyle and to numerous English divines; more important, he sends to England the results of his Indian experiments in antimonarchical utopian government. James Harrington claims to have been a "traveller" to the republics of ancient Israel, Greece, and Rome and of modern Italy, both in his historical research and in his actual visit to the Continent. He opposes his method of writing to that of "philosophers" like Matthew Wren and Thomas Hobbes, who have an inadequate understanding of the empirical particulars of these republics: "No man can be a politician, except he be first an historian or a traveller" (310).

Utopian dialogue lies halfway between the empirical report and the dream vision. It is ruled not by a progressive self-questioning in search of a preexistent truth, but by the traveler's utter repression of his commenting consciousness as he moves about the utopian state, with his repetitions of "and then I saw . . . and then . . . and then. . . ." He must report on secular visions as striking as St. John's dream with the self-effacing accuracy of an inventory clerk. As Darko Suvin says, the utopian dialogue is not so much Socratic as deictic: "At the basis of all utopian debates, in its open or hidden dialogues, is a gesture of pointing, a wide-eyed glance from here to there, a 'travelling shot' moving from the author's everyday lookout to the wondrous panorama of a far-off land" (37). The traveler's obsessed pointing does not bore his colloquist but draws him in. The philosopher constantly prods him, forcing him to continue, for his previous faith in the adequacy of his preenlightenment scholastic discipline has been punctured by the traveler's tale of an unanticipated social organization, which must be built on an alternative system of reason. Campanella glories in the empirical refutation of Augustine and Lactantius, who had denied the existence of the antipodes through syllogisms: "A sailor has proved them liars because he had *seen*" (Garin 216). Even anti-utopian philosophers like "More" become obsessed with these tales: "Then let me implore you, my dear Raphael ... to describe that island to us. Do not try to be brief, but explain in order everything relating to their land, their rivers, towns, people, manners, institutions, laws—everything, in short, that you think we would like to know. And you can take it for granted that we want to know everything that we don't know yet" (More 33). With brusque, empiricist rudeness, Campanella's Knight Hospitaler even skips the conversational amenities of More's Book 1 and begins the dialogue by instructing the returned traveler, "Tell me, please, all that happened to you on this voyage" (27). Some early modern utopias even internalize and incorporate this dialogue: the New Atlantis, the City of the Sun, and Oceana all have institutionalized programs of travel and research into the political organization and technologies of other states.

This conversation between the traveler and the philosopher about two different places, Europe and the utopian west, is also a conversation Europe has with itself about its own future, present, and past. We have already seen that the utopian advance of learning is tied to a prophecy of the westward course of empire; these sailors voyaging outward from a newly expansive Europe discover expansive, imperial, quasi Europes in the west. In the following sections of this chapter we will see that utopia is a rationalization and an acceleration of the social displacement of Europe's own present. But early modern utopia is also Europe's dialogue with its own past. Eugenio Garin shows that the Italian humanists set themselves the task of replacing Scholastic logic with a new method founded on philology, grammar, and rhetoric, thus substituting a conversation based on the particularities of human language for the abstract mediation of Scholastic universals (50–56, 151–69). J. G. A. Pocock comments, "The philological consciousness is very much a consciousness of the mind as expressed, and the world as seen, in prose; the humanist rhetoricians were converting the intellectual life into a conversation between men in time" (*Moment* 61). The utopian traveler removes the difficulties of this philological conversation with the remote past by spatializing it. He embodies the fantasy of objective anthropology and perfect translation, for he allows the European philosopher to enter into an unmediated conversation with modern-day versions of the virtuous pagans of classical antiquity. The traveler's blankness allows the European philosopher to see the heights to which human reason alone can rise when unhampered by religious dogma and Scholasticism, thereby restoring to Europe its own alienated history. At the same time the traveler allows the philosopher to envision the conversion of these virtuous pagans, effecting that rational integration of secular wisdom and Christianity lost in the turbulent course of European history. It overcomes the melancholy estrangement of Dante from Vergil and the other virtuous pagans of *The Divine Comedy.*

This encounter is not exactly one between Utopian reason and European revelation, such as R. W. Chambers sees forming the underlying moral of *Utopia:* "With nothing save Reason to guide them, the Utopians do this; and yet we Christian Englishmen, we Christian Europeans . . . !" (127). As Shlomo Avineri points out, More's work itself seems largely unconscious of this opposition: the parting censure of Utopian institutions by the dystopist "More" is not that they are impious, but that they take away all hierarchical "majesty" (Avineri 286, More 91).

There are other problems: the orthodox Utopian religion is already a form of Roman Catholicism (monotheistic, priest-run, based on a belief in an afterlife of punishment and reward, inclined to persecute Mortalist heretics), as the Utopians themselves notice (More 79). And the diverse Utopian religions seem to be on the verge of a Trinitarian unification. Raphael tells us that "there are some who worship a man of past ages who was conspicuous either for virtue or glory; they consider him not only a god but the supreme god." An antagonistic group believes in "a single power, unknown, eternal, infinite, inexplicable, far beyond the grasp of the human mind, and diffused throughout the universe, not physically, but in influence. Him they call father, and to him alone they attribute the origin, increase, progress, change, and end of all visible things" (78). All that the Utopians require to realize the deceptive quality of this apparent opposition between the religions of the Son and of the Father is some special intercession of the Holy Ghost, and that is already well under way, as Raphael reveals. At the time he speaks, a good many Utopians have converted to Christianity, perhaps because of their attraction to the principles of apostolic communism, perhaps "through the mysterious inspiration of God" (79). At the time Raphael leaves for Europe, the converts are considering a proposal to solicit Europe for a missionary bishop. True, all Utopians do not wish to convert, but those who do are not in any way persecuted. Utopia does exile one overly zealous convert, but only because he strays from King Utopus's directive that all proselytizing be conducted "quietly, modestly, rationally, and without bitterness toward others" (80). The conversation of conversion must continue in a rational manner.

Similarly, Campanella's Genoese sailor predicts that when the Solarian wandering spies discover Christianity, the entire city will quickly convert: "When the people learn the living truths of Christianity, proved by miracles, they will submit to them, for they are very pliant people" (67). The rational discipline of the pagan religions is essential for Christianity, for it produces pliant potential converts. In the New Atlantis the virtuous pagan and the Christian convert have miraculously become one; the inhabitants of Bacon's utopia have existed outside the European chronicle of gentile history and so have developed their scientific and political wisdom free of the tyranny of custom, yet through special conversion they are already thoroughly Christian. Similarly, the Jewish inhabitants of Samuel Gott's utopian state in *Nova Solyma* have undergone a rational conversion to Christianity. We can even see this utopian ideal of rational conversion in the Puritan missionary literature. In a preface to one of John Eliot's missionary pamphlets, Edward Reynolds speaks of the importance of convincing Indians by their own "natural and implanted light" as well as by the force of Scripture (Eliot, *A Further Accompt,* "Preface," n. pag.). Utopia is the home of neither reason nor revelation alone, but of their rational integration.

So we may locate early modern utopia at the revolutionary intersection of millennialism and enlightenment. At the conclusion of Campanella's *City of the Sun,* his Knight Hospitaler concludes from the report of his Genoese sailor that "Christianity is the true law and that, once its abuses have been corrected, it will become mistress of the world" (121). He speculates that the Spanish greed for gold is just a ruse of providential history, God's indirect means of spreading the gospel westward. The sailor agrees, telling him of the Solarians' millenarian interest in the recent European advancement of learning, particularly "our stupendous inventions—the compass, the printing press, the harquebus—mighty signs of the imminent union of the world."

The two colloquists tie these terrestrial portents to recent astrological ones, concluding that "there will be a great new monarchy, reformation of the laws and of arts, new prophets, and a general renewal. . . . But first the world will be uprooted and cleansed, and then it will be replanted and rebuilt" (123).

Early modern utopia is just as concerned with the practical means to this secular and sacred totality as with the totality itself. To examine some of these means in more detail, the last three sections of this chapter will investigate the relation between utopia and two literary forms (pastoral and georgic), the dialectic of utopia and a particular social practice (warfare), and utopia's connection to two political rhetorics (absolutist body politic theory and republicanism).

Cain and Agrarian Utopia

Utopia and pastoral arcadia have a long and complex fraternal relation, at least as old as the story of Cain, the first builder of cities, and Abel, the first pastoralist we meet in the Bible. Both genres critique existent society through an idealized topography: *eu topos* is practically a translation of the arcadian *locus amoenus*. And some kinds of myth criticism collapse the two forms, seeing them as products of the same primordial human longing for paradise (Eliade). But utopia and arcadia are finally distinct; they promise different kinds of good in different kinds of places.

The distinction between the two has often been seen as analogous to that between culture and nature. Darko Suvin says that arcadia "is primarily a *unomia,* a land without formalized institutions, without organized superstructures of community life" (58). J. C. Davis says that it is a radical alternative to utopia because "it not only rejects . . . the institutions of an acquisitive society, but it rejects all institutions whatsoever and so highlights the institutional preoccupations of the utopian" (*Utopia* 24). Northrop Frye suggests that the archetype underlying all pastoral is an anthropomorphic identification of the vegetable world with the human body (*Anatomy* 144).

Frye's generalization is useful so long as we remember that the human body itself (like nature more generally) has been subject to various conceptualizations and is not necessarily egalitarian as Frye says it is ("Varieties" 41). When we become aware of these conflicting models of nature, we begin to see that arcadia is thoroughly institutional. True, the pastoral landscape may be a democratic body politic animated by natural sympathies that put peasants and courtiers on a level. But as Harold Toliver shows, pastoral often feels an opposite inclination toward a hierarchized nature. The topography of pastoral landscape may represent a monarchical body politic, with all of nature organized around the figure of a perfect prince who alone can provide the commanding head that will return the body of nature to the Golden Age (20–44). In *A Midsummer Night's Dream* Oberon's kingdom is a corrective sylvan translation of Theseus's civil monarchy in Athens—one that allows him to celebrate his restored patriarchal authority in the concluding masque. Louis Adrian Montrose says that we should see a "dialectic between Elizabethan *pastoral forms* and Elizabethan *social categories*," since pastoral "variously marked and obfuscated the hierarchical distinctions—the symbolic boundaries— upon which the Elizabethan social order was predicated" (417–18). Montrose says that Elizabethan pastoral, which is thoroughly hostile both to georgic poetry and to actual country life, allows the court poet to criticize court life indirectly and to make a place for himself within it by purging him of any lingering rusticity.

Pastoral may even present a struggle between alternative modes of presenting a sympathetic, anthropomorphic nature. Sidney's *Countess of Pembroke's Arcadia* shows a pitched battle between rebellious peasants and tradesmen (nature as untamed passion) and courtly aristocrats (nature as controlled rational violence) (376–81). Milton's *Comus* takes a different point of view on a similar conflict between natures: one in sympathy with princely dominion and profligacy (Comus himself) and the other in sympathy with a relative egalitarianism and chastened appetite (the Lady and Sabrina). Far from being a realm outside institutional culture, arcadia is the institutional site for a more or less explicit battle between rival definitions of "natural" culture. So the distinction between arcadia and utopia cannot be usefully aligned with an opposition between nature and culture. No more can it be aligned with the conflict between religious and political radicalism and conservatism. Both genres are open to all factions.

All the same, they do form different models of the natural landscape and make different uses of these models. Arcadia is the site for a sympathetic meshing of nature and culture (however defined)—for a demonstration of the natural basis of an ideal cultural order, whether that order is customary and hierarchical or revolutionary and egalitarian. The site of arcadia is properly three-dimensional, with a topographically *given* quality that grounds human culture in something outside itself, just as the natural cycles of the days and seasons determine the human time of arcadian life. Utopia is the experimental site for the formation of a new cultural order—for a demonstration of the transformable quality of human and physical nature, whether that transformation leads to greater human liberty, greater social integration, or a social philosophy that questions the distinction between the two. The site of utopia is properly two-dimensional, with a topographically *blank* quality suggesting the future enclosure and gridding of new civil spaces—a human organization of space that will follow from human reason, just as the ritual times of utopian life will follow a rational rather than a natural necessity.

The rationalizing analogy between population and site is common in early modern utopia. (We saw it in the colonial policy of More's Utopians.) Andreae builds his utopia on it: just as there is in Christianopolis "not a foot of soil to be seen which was not under cultivation or in some way put to use for mankind," so there is no moment of the Christianopolitan's day that is not also cultivated and put to use (143, 162–63). In *The Way of Light* Comenius reveals the rationalizing and levelling impulse behind the analogy when he argues that a universal language will help accelerate the plot of millennial history: "For if all men understand each other they will become as it were one race, one household, one School of God. Then the meaning of those words will be clear that 'all the world shall be turned into a plain' (Zech. 14:10)" (198). In a sense, utopian nature is no less anthropomorphic than is arcadian nature, but only to the extent that in utopia, *anthropos* has acquired a new *morphe* as a blank object of domination. Horkheimer and Adorno remark that both myth and enlightenment unify man and nature, but in opposite directions. Enlightenment demythologization "compounds the animate with the inanimate just as myth compounds the inanimate with the animate. . . . Animism spiritualized the object, whereas industrialism objectifies the spirits of men" (16, 28). Perhaps I should expand my earlier definition to say that early modern utopia is the encounter between a textual authority and a blank, displaced population in a blank, enclosed site.

The distinction between arcadia and utopia is nowhere clearer than in their attitudes toward sexuality. In arcadia the sexual ideal (if not the sexual reality) is the alignment of proper erotic sympathies in a natural setting: the pairing off of aristocratic lover and beloved, of humble shepherd and shepherdess, of fairy king and queen, in a pasture, forest, or bower. At times these various levels are themselves united in a Neoplatonic ladder of erotic emulation, with the proper love on one level providing the model for the proper love on a lower one. But in utopia, from Plato, through More, Campanella, Harrington, John Humphrey Noyes and Oneida, and Huxley, sexuality is the object of a civil experiment: the planned breeding of new human types according to a program in eugenics.

But if utopia refuses to look backward to Genesis and the garden, it also refuses to look forward to Revelation and the City of God. Or at least, it does not look immediately and exclusively toward the city. Nothing is more common in studies of utopia than an identification of the utopian imagination with a dream of the secular or sacred city. Lewis Mumford sees a dim memory of the archetypal cities of Egypt and Mesopotamia underlying the Platonic tradition of political thought. Miriam Eliav-Feldon says simply that "the utopias of the Renaissance are all visualized as cities" (12). But utopia's enlightenment impulse to universality wreaks havoc on archetypal criticism. When we turn to actual Renaissance utopias, this identification of utopia with the city becomes either banally tautologous (if we see the city as a metonym for "all of human culture") or simply false (if we see it in distinction to other cultural topoi like the monastery, the prison, the colony, the seaway, the battlefield, the cornfield). Certainly the rise of Renaissance utopia is related to the rise of the Italian city-state, the growth of metropolitan London, and the concentration of displaced populations as the urban poor. But early modern utopia is agrarian as well as urban—a dual identity that can help us understand a central paradox of *Utopia*.

As we have seen, *Utopia* is in part called into being by an agrarian revolution in England. As Raphael says, England's sheep, which "used to be so meek and eat so little ... are becoming so greedy that they will devour men themselves, as I hear" (More 14).[6] The enclosure of English commons lands for pastures may help bring England into a new market economy, but in the process it disrupts rural housekeeping and displaces rural tenants: "They leave the only homes familiar to them, and they can find no place to go" (14). But according to Erasmus, More's primary model for Book 2 of *Utopia* was England itself, and numerous concrete parallels (such as those between London and Amaurot) bear him out. How can England be the source of both the social problems anatomized in Book 1 and the solutions to them presented in Book 2?

This double identity is not altogether baffling, for *utopia* is as much the name of England's social revolution as of its social and literary correction. After all, enclosure itself is a utopian activity that creates new spaces, social groupings, and modes of production by eliminating customary and irrational uses of land like those the Utopians abhor so overseas. Consequently, we will seriously mistake More's response to the social unrest created by enclosure if we see *Utopia* as a fiction of reaction rather than a fiction of rationalization. Rather than reacting to the disruptions caused by the revolution in the English countryside by turning for relief to a dream of the garden or of the city, *Utopia* attempts to rationalize and accelerate that revolution—to the extent that every square inch of Utopian real estate has some use in a rational scheme of civil and agricultural space. We can call Utopia with equal justice an urban commonwealth with interspersed fields and a rural commonwealth with interspersed cities. Each of the fifty-four cities lies at least twenty-four miles from its nearest neighbor, with a band of farmlands at least ten miles wide surrounding it, and "no city wishes to enlarge its boundaries" (35). The city penetrates the country, for (somewhat larger) households are scattered "at proper intervals all around the countryside." The country penetrates the city, for each city house has its own garden, and blocks of houses enter into horticultural competitions with other blocks (38). The logic of the grid overrules the claim to power of any single place, or sort of place.

There are regular movements between country and city. Country Utopians visit the cities on holy days as city Utopians visit the country to help with the harvests. In fact, there is really no such thing as a "city" or a "country" Utopian, for agriculture is "the one occupation at which everyone works, men and women alike, with no exceptions" (Raphael has forgotten the exception of the scholars, though they, too, face the possibility of demotion to rural drudgery) (40). The Utopians study agricultural science in schools and take regular working field trips to farms. Each year twenty adults from each country household change places with twenty city Utopians. *Utopia* responds to the social disorder created by agricultural enclosure in its early stages with a new system of enclosure and regulated movements that irons out the transitional wrinkles. Utopia is neither England nor anti-England, but an England whose historical tendencies (as More sees them) have been accelerated and rationalized.

The conversion to enclosed pasture of English commons lands, forests, and waste grounds continued at least through the seventeenth century (Hill, *World* 32–45), finding an eighteenth-century echo in the controversy over the Black Act (Thompson, *Whigs*). This process followed a contradictory utopian dialectic of displacement: tenants displaced by enclosure and eviction would gather in commons lands, forests, and untilled heaths; the resulting threat of social disorder would lead to further deforestation, enclosure, and eviction. Enclosure gradually led to the disenchantment of the English countryside. A landscape that had been marked by local traditions and customary rights (of lords to their tenants' manorial or military service; of tenants to water, fuel, fish, game, and commons grazing privileges) became a homogeneous, divided, and calculable substance rationally integrated into the expanding European market economy.

This conversion brought resistances. The first persons termed *levellers* were peasants attempting to tear down hedge closes during the Midland Revolt of 1607, and there were many other such protests. According to a tenants' petition to Parliament, the cosmos itself resisted its disenchantment: when Sir Francis Englefield commenced the process of enclosure by overstocking the commons of Wootton Bassett, "the Lord in his mercy did send thunder and lightning from heaven," driving his stock away (Tawney, *Problem* 338n, 148n). But as Keith Thomas notes, enclosure had a religious ally of its own. The movement from an open-field system to a system of private plots with hedgerow closes interfered with such customary rituals as "rogation" or "charming the fields," in which a vicar would walk around the borders of his parish, accompanied by his parishioners, blessing fields, springs, and local landmarks. The disappearance of such rituals was all to the good from the point of view of Reformation (and particularly Puritan) theology, which preferred a relatively unmediated communion with an unlocalized God to such "magical" survivals of the medieval church (*Religion* 62–65).

The response of seventeenth-century Puritan writers to this rural revolution was not an arcadian critique but a utopian accommodation. Samuel Hartlib calls for the improvement of "England's hundreds of acres of waste and barren lands" (Winstanley 14). In his *Proposal of Certain Expedients for the Preventing of a Civil War,* Milton proposes the "just division of waste commons, whereby the land would become much more industrious, rich, and populous" (7.338). Gerrard Winstanley grounds his entire metaphysics and theory of culture in what he sees as the universal desire for the earth—a desire animating clergy, lawyers, lords, soldiers, and farmers alike (520, 566). The utopian communal experiment of Winstanley and the Diggers at George's Hill justifies itself with an appeal to the rational use of waste ground; Winstanly does not attack the enclosures themselves but asks that "the poor that have no land have a free allowance to dig and labor the commons, and so live as comfortably as the landlords that live in their enclosures" (260). John Eliot and his fellow New Englanders no sooner land in the New England "wilderness" (this rather strange term for the Algonquian tribal lands has had a surprising longevity in the white history of ideas) than they begin enclosing it for agriculture, and Eliot thinks it a vital part of his utopian project to fix the seminomadic Algonquians in stable, enclosed agricultural communities. As we will see, the very "foundation" of James Harrington's eternal commonwealth of Oceana is to be its agrarian legislation, which keeps the lands from falling into the hands of fewer than five thousand landholders, thus assuring the agricultural foundation of civic virtue. Harrington's electoral reform is also a sort of enclosure, for it sees the English landscape not as a repository of traditional rights but as the passive object of organizational reason. He proposes to overcome customary local political power by dividing England into fifty tribes, each tribe into twenty "hundreds," each hundred into ten parishes.

Even looking ahead to the nineteenth-century socialist analysis of capitalism, we can see utopia's interest in rationally integrating the country and the city. In the first volume of *Capital,* Marx quotes *Utopia*'s description of the effects of enclosure and eviction of tenants, tracing the process through the eviction of Highlands Scots in his own day—a process of precapitalist rationalization that has "conquered the field for capitalistic agriculture, made the soil part and parcel of capital, and created for the town industries the necessary supply of a 'free' and outlawed proletariat" (Marx 736, 728–31, 733). But as a solution to the cruel dislocations and poverty created by this inevitable historical process, Marx and Engels propose a utopian acceleration and rationalization. They argue (in tones reminscent of Winstanley, whom they did not know) for the "bringing into cultivation of wastelands, and the improvement of the soil generally in accordance with a common plan," the "establishment of industrial armies, especially for agriculture," the "combination of agriculture with manufacturing industries," and the "gradual abolition of the distinction between town and country" (Marx and Engels 105).

The true antagonist of utopian rationalization is not the countryside but custom: that sediment of traditional authorities and local memories that resists the claim of enlightenment to universal sovereignty and calculation. In Book 1 of *Utopia,* Raphael ridicules those who "take refuge in some remark like this: 'The way we're doing it is the way we've always done it, this custom was good enough for our fathers, and I only hope that we're as wise as they were.' And with this deep thought they would take their seats, as though they had said the last word on the subject—implying, forsooth, that it would be a very dangerous matter if a man were found to be wiser in any point than his forefathers were" (10). This custom is as much at home in the guilds, the municipal governments of the cities, and (as Raphael shows) the council chambers of the prince as in the manors and huts of the countryside. Consequently, utopia promises to integrate country and city in such a way as to abolish nonutopian custom and to prevent its reemergence. This integration has a symbolic importance exceeding its immediate social utility. In *The Discourses* Machiavelli advises the new prince who wishes to hold on to his new state to "organize everything in that state afresh," deposing old governors and appointing new ones, making the rich poor and the poor rich, demolishing old cities and building new ones, moving all inhabitants "from one place to another far distant from it; in short, to leave nothing of the province intact, and nothing in it . . . except it be held by such as recognize that it comes from you" (176–77). For Machiavelli this state of affairs is a hopelessly remote totalitarian fantasy, and he doubts it can ever come to pass. But a less Draconian version has become part of the fabric of Utopian everyday life, as we can see in the regular, mandatory movements between civil spaces: the rotation of persons from city to country each year and of families between houses every ten years. In Utopia, as in the new prince's state, these movements (which are a regularized version of the irrational movements of displaced populations) have a purpose as much symbolic as practical. As the scientists of Bacon's New Atlantis make tall animals short and short animals tall to flex their enlightenment muscles, so utopia encloses civil spaces and regulates movements between them to demonstrate a new locus of power in the reason of state orders. In the City of the Sun this demonstration takes the form of a strange new anticustomary ritual: the Solarians "go out into the fields with banners flying, with trumpets and other instruments sounding, equipped according to the occasion, whether to hoe, plow, reap, sow, gather, or harvest. . . . Moreover, they have armed scouts who constantly patrol the fields" (Campanella 83). Traditional agriculture merges with martial drill in a masque praising state reason.

The relation betwen arcadia and utopia is more than a logical or generic opposition; it is also a historical sequence. Readers of *Utopia* often assume that More's ideal state begins ab nihilo or through some social contract, forgetting its true origin in the violation of a pastoral: King Utopus's conquest of "barbarian Abraxa." Utopia is the violent civil negation of pastoral arcadia. As Frye observes, it is appropriate that Cain was both the destroyer of the first arcadia and the builder of

Enoch, the first city ("Varieties" 40–41). The myth of Cain's fall is a civil and political variant on the myth of his parents' primarily moral fall. In the first place it would seem that Cain, not Abel, has submitted himself to the curse on their parents, for he is a farmer who eats bread in the sweat of his face in accordance with God's decree, while Abel practices the more Edenic trade of pastoralism. So when the Lord "had respect unto Abel for his offering: but unto Cain and his offering he had not respect," his judgment seems even worse than arbitrary. In its lack of motivation it seems to embody an inevitable conflict between two economic modes of production.

The second, fratricidal fall is much different from the first. The first produces history, the second utopia. Before sending Adam and Eve out of Eden, God tells them that the seed of the serpent will bruise the heels of their seed, and that the latter will bruise the head of the former. Christian exegetes beginning with the author of the Book of Revelation interpret this mythically cryptic statement as a prophecy of the future conquest of Satan the serpent by Christ the Son of Man. The second fall is mundane by comparison; the curse the Lord lays on Cain is a repetition and an intensification of the previous curse but brings nothing qualitatively new. Cain will go into exile as his parents did, and the earth will become even harder to till. The conflict produced by this fall will lie not in a prophesied future but in a violent present, as Cain complains: "And I shall be a fugitive and a vagabond in the earth; and it shall come to pass, that everyone that findeth me shall slay me." Jehovah is uncharacteristically tractable. He moderates Cain's punishment, protecting him with a mark that threatens sevenfold vengeance on anyone who slays him. The full mythical import of this mark is not altogether clear, but it seems to be the Lord's compensation to Cain for his curse rather than part of the curse itself. Genesis links the mark with the birth of cities and technology. Cain becomes not a vagabond but a founder of the first city, which he names after his son Enoch. His descendants develop the arts and sciences: tentmaking, animal husbandry (evidently distinct from pastoralism), music, brassworking, blacksmithing, and warfare.

Unlike utopia, pastoral is a retrospective genre—an imaginative attempt to envision and regain a lost state of unfallen nature. But if we see Abel as the first pastoralist and his occupation as an attempt to regain Eden directly by forgetting or ignoring the Lord's commandment that man till the ground, then pastoral also seems doomed to underline its own impossibility. Nature will be restored to complete sympathy with man only when providential history has run its course;

between Eden and the New Jerusalem, it must remain alien to him. Here we may note the Miltonic pastoral archetype in Eve's postlapsarian farewell to her flowers, and the uncouth swain's rejection of pathetic fallacy in *Lycidas* as "frail thoughts" and "false surmise" that presume upon the larger plot of providential history. Pastoral is, in a sense, complementary to nonutopian or hermeneutical millennialism, for it describes a distant past that man can only yearn after, as hermeneutical millennialism describes a future that he can only wait for and attempt to prophesy.

But utopia focuses on the present or on the middle distance of the imminent future. Aware of man's Fall, it is nonetheless eager to turn to good use one of the Fall's happier results: the advancement of learning in civic and scientific wisdom. This advance is not altogether urban: agriculture is a true technic, and Cain is a farmer before (and, for all we know, after) he is a founder of cities. Rather than dwelling on the possibility or impossibility of envisioning the once-and-future sympathy between man and nature, utopia concentrates on the organizational detail of a restorative project. Among the more modest attempts of seventeenth-century Puritan writers to make up for man's expulsion from Eden were proposals for research in agriculture and for the reform of farming techniques, all to be taught in "colleges of husbandry" spread throughout the nation (Webster, *Instauration* 465–83). Once man has plucked a single fruit from the Tree of the Knowledge of Good and Evil, he may as well continue harvesting it in a rational manner. Even before the Fall, Milton's Adam and Eve are busy tending the garden, practicing an anticipatory georgic. Linking *Paradise Lost* with *Utopia*, Louis Adrian Montrose contrasts both sharply with the cult of aristocratic pastoral that flourished in Elizabethan England (426).

Joseph Addison's rule for distinguishing pastoral and georgic is equally useful for distinguishing pastoral and utopia: "No rules, therefore, that relate to pastoral, can anyway affect the Georgics, since they fall under that class of poetry, which consists in giving plain and direct instructions to the reader" (189). With its didactic emphasis on the concerns of the present and on the proper techniques for a transformation of the natural environment, utopia is much closer to georgic than to pastoral. In a reading of *Paradise Regained* as georgic, Anthony Low says that the hero of georgic "dwells on small, recurrent actions, often trivial or inglorious in themselves, that nevertheless converge toward a turning point in the world's history that will prove to be truly apocalyptic" (168). Similarly, even though the arrival of the millennium is imminent, the utopist insists that he and his readers continue the methodical culturing of civility. Just as the cultivated fields of Canaan mediate between Eden and the New Jerusalem, so agrarian utopia mediates between pastoral and millennialism.

Lamech and Martial Utopia

As the violent civil negation of pastoral, georgic utopia is inseparable from warfare, and the technology showing how to beat swords into plowshares is easily reversible. Lamech, the descendant of Cain and the father of Noah, paratactically links his twin inheritances of fratricidal guilt and compensatory power:

> And Lamech said unto his wives,
> Adah and Zillah, Hear my voice;
> ye wives of Lamech, hearken unto my speech
> for I have slain a man to my wounding,
> and a young man to my hurt.
> If Cain shall be avenged sevenfold,
> truly Lamech seventy and sevenfold.
> (Gen. 4:23–24)

Violence gives birth to cities and an accelerating technology of military power. Here begins the dialectic of warfare and utopia: the need to end the disorder and vagabondage generated by violence produces utopia, which in turn produces the capacity for new kinds of warfare. If war is the continuation of politics by other means, then utopia is the means by which politics returns the favor.

The section on warfare in Book 2 of *Utopia* has always been something of a critical scandal. It begins unobjectionably enough with a pious Latin pun: "They despise war [*bellum*] as an activity fit only for beasts [*belluinam*], yet practiced more by man than by any other beast" (71). Yet the rest of the chapter reveals the Utopians' practice of assassination, imperialist expansion, enslavement of war prisoners, and even genocide, forcing critics who want a consistent and univocal interpretation of More's work to confront certain antinomies: those between Raphael's denunciation of European warfare in Book 1 and his evident admiration for Utopian warfare in Book 2, between the Utopians' treatment of each other and their treatment of their antagonists, and between the Utopians' moral philosophy and the political theory implicit in their practice of warfare.

Shlomo Avineri's "War and Slavery in More's *Utopia*," published in 1962, is an excellent summary critique of earlier considerations of these problems and a pretty good prophetic critique of many later ones. He speaks first of a "traditional school," whose traditional response was either to ignore *Utopia*'s discussion of warfare altogether or simply to quote the first sentence of it. Second was a "power interpretation" that flourished in Weimar Germany, which read *Utopia*'s previously ignored celebration of communist empire as an anticipation of British or Soviet expansionism. Finally there was a "neo-Catholic" or dialogic reading of the chapter by R. W. Chambers, H. W. Donner, Edward Surtz, and others. Here Raphael becomes the spokesman for the Utopians, whose practice of warfare is as humane as human reason alone can make it, and "More" becomes the spokesman for More, who brings the perspective of revelation and rejects certain aspects of Utopian warfare.

The concept of irony helps this last group distinguish between those parts of Raphael's discourse suggesting rational alternatives to European practice and those parts suggesting the dangers of reason unaided by revelation. Donner, for instance, says that the chapter on war "is obviously ironical and such a tangible parody of contemporary European warfare that it seems well-nigh incredible that it should have ever been misunderstood. . . . This is no part of his ideal" (44–45). Elisabeth Hansot says simply that "More's treatment of war is clearly a satire on contemporary practice and not to be taken seriously" (70). Surtz is not so sure: speaking of the work as a whole, he says that "the gravity or levity of each passage must be weighed in itself and in its context to discovery if it attacks prevalent abuses or suggests practical reforms" (*Pleasure* 4). Not all of the chapter on warfare, for instance, is ironic: "The Utopians' love of peace and detestation of bloodshed, as well as their humane conduct of inevitable wars, can set a basic pattern for Europeans, who can and must improve upon it to the extent that a divinely inspired Christianity surpasses the enlightened humanism of paganism" (*Wisdom* 307). But we must be aware of the corrective ironic perspective revelation takes on certain "reasonable" Utopian practices: "It is impossible to believe that More intends to advocate among Christians the revival of the enslavement of war prisoners based on the law of nations" (*Wisdom* 270).

This dialogic approach to *Utopia*'s interpretive difficulties is like Augustine's to those of the Scriptures. In *On Christian Doctrine* he suggests a foolproof technique for handling troublesome passages: "In the consideration of figurative expressions a rule such as this will serve, that what is read should be subjected to diligent scrutiny until an interpretation contributing to the reign of charity is produced. If this result appears literally in the text, the expression being considered is not figurative" (193). Among the tropes at hand for such a transformation are antiphrasis and irony, which "imply the opposite of what is said" (103). Arrival at an interpretation consistent with the reign of charity is both difficult and inevitable: difficult because one must apply as a principle of reading that very "reign of charity" that one is reading in order to understand, inevitable because no passage can fail to signify the reign of charity.

Avineri shows that this self-confirming but still very powerful dialogic approach to *Utopia* answered a pressing need: "As More was beatified by Pope Leo XIII in 1886 and subsequently canonized by Pius XI in 1935, the preparations for the canonization coincided with the spreading of the 'German' approach, and the Church was in danger of finding a Machiavellian saint on its hands" (278). Given this context, an Augustinian approach to Utopian irony became invaluable, enabling More's dialogic readers to separate Raphael's long description of Utopia into the figurative and the nonfigurative. This approach was destined to be successful, at the cost of transforming *Utopia* into the noncontradictory expression of some unified personality we name "More"—a personality constructed perhaps on the basis of other Augustinian interpretations of his other writings.

This section will present a non-Augustinian, nonironic, "eutopian" reading of *Utopia*'s discussion of warfare. It will argue that the contradictions we sense between the moral philosophy of Raphael and the Utopians on the one hand and the Utopian practice of warfare on the other are not just "apparent problems" to be reconciled by an appeal to More's ironic intention, or a sign of the failings of reason unaided. Rather, they reveal the complex enlightenment dialectic of utopia and warfare—a dialectic with important implications for Puritan utopia.

After analyzing *Utopia*'s attitude toward warfare as part of its attitude toward medievalism, J. H. Hexter concludes that it is fiercely antimilitaristic. Going beyond the medieval criticism of knights or princes who fail to live up to the chivalric ideal, More attacks that ideal itself, along with the European warrior caste holding to it (*Vision* 50–54). Here I want to move beyond *Utopia*'s critique of chivalric warfare to its proposal of an alternative. *Utopia* is indeed critical of the feudal, aristocratic, and chivalric ideal, but only because that ideal gets in the way of a rational state organized for a new, more enlightened warfare. In Book 1 Raphael justifies his decision not to enter court service by condemning Europe's princes, most of whom "devote themselves eagerly to the study and practice of military matters, in which I have neither ability nor interest, instead of to the good arts of peace. They are generally more set on acquiring new kingdoms by hook or by crook than on governing well those that they already have" (10). Here the relation between peace and war seems to be an ethical binary opposition. But in the rest of Book 1 and in Book 2, we find that Raphael's objection is not to warfare in itself but to its premature practice: *first* master the arts of peace, *then* practice warfare.

We can see traces of this sort of argument in Raphael's hypothetical advice to a French king. Other counselors advise the king to gain an Italian possession through "royal connivings and schemings," such as stirring up nobles with rival claims to its throne or inciting neighboring nations to attack it. He concludes that he would (to no avail) advise the king to "leave Italy alone and stay at home, because the single kingdom of France all by itself is almost too much for one man to govern, and the king should not dream of adding others to it" (23–25). This criticism could originate from two distinct points of view: the first ethical and "contractive," the second prudential and "expansive." It may advocate that princes should learn to moderate their feudal lust for glory and content themselves with the proper rule of their own states. Or it may advocate a political reorganization bringing the state under the governance of more than "one man," enabling it to "dream of adding" other states to its empire. The latter is the point of view suggested by Book 2 of *Utopia*, where we see that the two necessary qualities of enlightened utopia—political stability and imperial expansiveness—must follow in sequence. We see that Raphael speaks from the second point of view when we examine his catalog of Utopian techniques for managing hostile foreign powers: bribing noble rivals or family members of a hostile king to act against him, hiring assassins to kill him, and inciting neighboring nations to attack (73). On the level of ethics this is a pure contradiction of the principles implied in Book 1, but on the level of state theory it is completely rational. Utopia's domestic polity is in place, freeing it to engage in imperial campaigns without destabilizing itself.

The Utopians lack the princely desire for martial glory and "go to war only for good reasons," but these reasons are accommodating enough for any imaginable occasion (71). They go to war to gain land for the settlement of their own surplus populations, to protect themselves from attack, to avenge the foreign injury of one of their citizens, to avenge friendly nations for past injuries or to protect them from present dangers, to liberate an "oppressed people" from a tyrant, and to avenge friends whose merchants have suffered foreign extortion (lower prices than they wanted?). Campanella's Solarians feel free to declare war when they "are attacked, insulted, or dishonored in some way, when their allies are put upon, or when they are called to liberate some city that is being tyrannized" (71). And they have a decidedly modern and antichivalric code of military conduct: "Nor do they refrain from wounding enemies who are rebels to reason and, as such, do not deserve to be called men" (69).

Utopia allows itself a distinctly noncommunist colonial empire, with Utopian Financial Factors managing large landed estates in conquered countries, where they "live on the properties in great style and conduct themselves like great personages," sending much of the proceeds back to the Utopian war chest (78). It has established a colonial buffer zone: "Some time ago the Utopians helped various of their neighbors to throw off the yoke of tyranny; and since then, these people (who have learned to admire Utopian virtue) have made a practice of asking for Utopians to rule over them. Some of these rulers serve one year, others five. When their service is over, they return with honor and praise to their own home, and others are sent in their place" (69). Similarly, the "tyrannies" liberated by the Solarians eagerly accept Solarian leaders (77). Whether or not More and Campanella are ironic, these unlikely arrangements signify an imperialist desire to see foreign populations as utterly anomic and devoid of local political traditions.

Utopia's imperial or provincial policy is remarkably similar to that of James Harrington's *Oceana*. In Harrington's terminology, Utopia is an expansive "commonwealth for increase" like imperial Rome, not a static "commonwealth for preservation" alone like Venice. It expands not by "imposing the yoke" as did the empires of Athens and Sparta (which creates a corrupting conflict between popular liberties at home and tyranny abroad) or by "equal leagues" like those of Holland and the Swiss cantons (which lack the unified sovereignty necessary to further imperial expansion and greatness). Rather, it spreads by an "unequal league" like that of the Roman empire, which brings "liberty" to surrounding peoples while maintaining unified Utopian sovereignty. The difference between princely and utopian warfare is that the first destabilizes the home state, while the second reinforces it. Utopia has no ruler to be assassinated, no rival nobles to perform the assassination, and no hostile states nearby that might be tempted to invade. It is stable and expansive, immune to its own destabilizing techniques.

In a brief but suggestive course description entitled "War in the Filigree of Peace," Michel Foucault describes a conflict in the seventeenth century between two views of the relationship between political life and warfare. The first view is closer to the tradition of political philosophy as we know it, for it speaks from "the position of the jurist or the philosopher, i.e., the position of the universal subject" (17). This model conceives of power as the unified force of the sovereign's will as expressed in the juridical order. It attempts to create for itself the role "dreamed of by legislators and philosophers from Solon to Kant: to establish itself between the adversaries, in the center of but above the fray, to impose an armistice, to found a reconciliatory order."

On the other hand, Foucault says, the seventeenth century also sees the development of a political theory of warfare distinct from political philosophy. It "turns the traditional values of intelligibility inside out because it explains things from the bottom" through detailed histories of actual armed conflicts. Consequently, it results in "the complete contrary of those traditional analyses which attempt to find beneath the accidents of appearance and surface, beneath the visible brutality of bodies and passions, a fundamental rationality, permanent and linked in essence to what is just and good." Rather, it attempts to construct its theory of warfare out of these very accidents. It also attempts to construct a martial theory of political action, for it claims that warfare "continues to rage inside the mechanisms of power" (16). It is not simply a philosophical discourse, for its students "are supposed to reactivate it, to make it come out of the mute and larval forms in which it is carried unnoticed" (17). Foucault locates this theory in the writings of Boulainvilliers and du Buat-Nancy in France, of John Selden, Edward Coke, and John Lilburne in England. But we should also look back to More and Machiavelli, for utopia and classical republic come closest together in their visions of the rational integration of civil and military life. And we should look ahead to the Puritan writers of the English Interregnum, who fervently believed that world history was drawing to a close in the final conflict between the marshaled troops of King Jesus and Antichrist.

Foucault says that when we begin to consider the importance of this latter theory of warfare, we should take care to set aside some "false paternities," primarily that of Hobbes: "What Hobbes calls the war of all against all is in no sense a real and historical war, but a play of representations" (18). This is not to say that Hobbes's fictive war is of no consequence in his political philosophy—in fact, it is vital. Because the Hobbesian state of nature cannot be preserved in written records (which develop only in civil society), we have access to it only through a supplemental form, the hypothetical history, the most familiar example of which is Hobbes's account of the origin of political society in the first book of *Leviathan* (80–84). In a state of nature each man possesses his own sovereignty but not his own property. On the one hand, this is a state of radical equality, for every man possesses and has the right to wield his own sovereign power. On the other hand, because power is so entropically dispersed, because there is no "common power" to enforce contract or law, there is no right and wrong, no justice and injustice, no thine and mine. The result is universal warfare— the "war of every man, against every man." This condition being disagreeable, men convenant together and agree to alienate their natural power to a single, sword-wielding sovereign. This sovereign ensures the honoring of this and all subsequent covenants and contracts. Henceforth, each man possesses his own property but not his own sovereignty. Because this covenant binds together only the covenanters and not the sovereign, his sovereignty is absolute (114–15).[7]

Curiously, Hobbes admits that there has, in fact, never been such a state of nature general in the world. The only analogies he can find are to the "savage" state of the American Indians, who, he says, have no government other than that of small families, and to the state of civil war, which he is somehow able to see as a universal chaos rather than a determinate struggle between parties (83). But however much he hedges his claims about the historical actuality of this original covenant, it is the essential enabling fiction of his political theory, for it allows him to speak of a prepolitical man, free of any prior discipline or political coercion, freely signing over his sovereignty (including his right to make war) and that of his posterity to an individual who will ensure the honoring of all civil convenants. Hobbes's hypothetical history has two claims on his political present. First, the capacity for this primordial warfare seems to live on inside every citizen as a repressed political id that justifies the repressive sovereignty of a monarchical superego. Second, the primordial covenant is everyman's entailment, for it exercises a juridical power upon all the descendants of the primordial covenanters. Hobbes's hypothetical history provides the extra-historical origin of civil history. As Foucault says, the movement into the first civil covenant marks the disappearance of warfare as a proper component of Hobbesian politics: "Sovereignty, whether of an 'instituted republic' or an 'acquired republic,' is established not by a fact of warlike domination, but on the contrary by a calculation which makes it possible for war to be avoided. For Hobbes it is non-war which founds the State and give it its form" ("War" 18).

In Renaissance utopia warfare is both less important and more important than in political philosophy like Hobbes's. It is less because utopia does not define itself against the background of some primordial conflict: no particular battle or covenantal truce in the past exercises any particular authority in the present. In Puritan utopian writing, populations at war are no closer to "nature" than are populations at peace. Unlike Hobbes's Indians, Eliot's Algonquians are not natural men, but "degenerate Jews" who have undergone a long decay of patriarchal civility, becoming a degraded, monarchical nation. Unlike Hobbes's civil warriors, Harrington's pre-Oceanic Englishmen are not prepolitical subjects, but a people in a state of political potentiality following the decay of one civil form and preceding the generation of another. Political philosophy moves upward to first principles, while the political theory of warfare moves laterally to actual populations and backward to historical records.

We can see this difference between political philosophy and the political theory of warfare in the difference between Hobbes's discussion of political origins, which we have just seen, and Machiavelli's. Machiavelli begins the first of his *Discourses,* entitled "Concerning the Origin of Cities in General and of Rome in Particular," by saying, "I would point out that all cities are built either by natives of the place in which they are built, or by people from elsewhere" (100). He goes on to say that cities in the first category may be founded by a single legislator (like Athens by Theseus) or not (like Venice); that those in the second category may be founded by princes or by republics, and these with a variety of motivations. In these simple, unresolved disjunctions, we see the essence of the Machiavellian plainstyle. These state origins frequently involve some sort of warfare or conquest, but Machiavelli never turns to a totalizing philosophical concept like the war of every man against every man, sovereignty per se, or an original covenant. These origins retain their complex empirical particularity.

Warfare is more important in Renaissance utopia than in political philosophy because, as Foucault says, it "continues to constitute the secret motor of institutions, laws, and order" ("War" 16). It is both an abstract principle of historical explanation and a force immanent in everyday life. Machiavelli goes on (in *The Discourses* and in his other works) to examine the ways in which warfare and civil life intertwine: the nature of a republic or a princedom is inseparable from its military capacity to defend and expand itself.

In the following two passages we can see More's linking the violent origin of Utopia to its present-day military expansion. In the first, which we have examined before, Raphael describes King Utopus's transformation of Abraxa into Utopia:

> After subduing them at his first landing, he cut a channel fifteen miles wide where their land joined the continent, and caused the sea to flow around the country. He put not only the natives to work at this task, but all his own soldiers too, so that the vanquished would not think the labor a disgrace. With the work divided among so many hands, the project was finished quickly, and the neighboring peoples, who at first laughed at his folly, were struck with wonder and terror at his success. (35)

A later passage describing the Utopian art of military fortification echoes this one strongly:

> They fortify their camps very carefully with a deep, broad ditch all around them, the earth being thrown inward to make a wall; the work is done not by workmen but by the soldiers themselves with their own hands. The whole army pitches in, except for a guard which is posted around the workers to prevent a surprise attack. With so many hands at work, they complete great fortifications, enclosing wide areas with unbelievable speed. (76–77)

The enclosed island of Utopia expands through a rational martial replication of its founding act of self-insulation. As Hobbes connects the originary state of nature with contemporary civil war, so Raphael connects King Utopus's founding conquest with Utopia's present-day military expansion. But while Hobbes makes the connection in order to justify a repressive sovereignty that will prevent the reemergence of civil warfare in the present, Raphael makes the connection in order to show Utopia's rational internalization of an expansive imperial warfare.

We can see the pervasiveness of warfare in Utopia in one of Raphael's critiques of the irrationalities of late feudalism. When a son succeeds his noble father, Raphael says, he frequently finds himself unable to support all his father's military retainers, so he turns them out into the countryside, where they become a displaced population of roving thieves and highwaymen alongside the evicted tenants (12–13). Henry VII had recently aggravated this problem by limiting the permissible number of retainers in an attempt to increase the central state powers and to limit the feudal power of local military aristocracies—

a rather Utopian program in itself. (As we will see, James Harrington views this reform as the turning point of modern English history.) But just as *Utopia* responds to the economic dislocations caused by agricultural enclosures with a program of accelerated and rationalized enclosure that makes every Utopian a farmer, so it responds to this breakdown of local standing armies with a program of rational military discipline that makes every Utopian a soldier, pushing the Machiavellian (and soon to be Harringtonian) ideal of the citizen soldier to its ultimate extreme: "On certain days, both men and women alike carry on vigorous military training so that they will be fit to fight should the need arise" (71). Campanella's Solarians follow suit (69). Utopians are encouraged (with that forceful Utopian encouragement that sounds so much like a command) to go to battle in units comprising entire extended families, "so that those who by nature have most reason to help one another may be closest at hand for mutual aid." Families tend to return from battle either as a group or not at all, for it is "a matter of great reproach" for a family member to return from battle alone. The cunning of Utopian state reason turns the bonds of the patriarchal family to its own superfamilial ends by turning family grief into civic shame (75). Similarly, the City of the Sun diverts private quarrels to a civic function in a modified feudal trial by combat: whichever party to a dispute gains the most glory in battle against foreigners is considered to be in the right (79–80).

Military discipline is at the center of James Harrington's utopian platform in *Oceana*. Between the ages of eighteen and thirty, all (male) Oceanic youth must submit to regular military drills that prepare them to participate in civil government. Harrington sees warfare as a key principle of historical analysis inhabiting all civil institutions. In the following passage he examines the European institution of parliamentary monarchy from the point of view of an empirical historian cataloging actual conflicts. At the same time he dismantles philosophy's juridical fictions of sovereignty and right:

Your Gothic [feudal] politicians seem unto me rather to have invented some new ammunition or gunpowder in their king and parliament (*duo fulmina belli*) than government. For what is become of the princes (a kind of people) in Germany? Blown up. Where are the estates, or the power of the people, in France? Blown up. Where is that of the people in Aragon, and the rest of the Spanish kingdoms? Blown up. On the other side, where is the king of Spain's power in Holland? Blown up. Where is that of the Austrian princes in Switz? Blown up. This perpetual peevish-

ness and jealousy, under the alternate empire of the prince and of the
people, is obnoxious unto every spark. Nor shall any man show a reason
that will be holding in prudence why the people of Oceana [England]
have blown up their king, but that their kings did not first blow up them.
The rest is discourse for ladies. (264)

Warfare refuses to be banished to the hypothetical origins of states, but
continues a series of civil wars in the decayed feudal Europe of the
present. Like *Utopia, Oceana* sees a dialectic of warfare and utopia. It
promises first a cure for the political violence and social disorder produced by the English monarchy, then a new martial republic capable
of a new and more universal warfare, even a millennial conquest of
the world.

John Eliot's *Christian Commonwealth* appears after the initial
defeats of the Stuart and Anglican Antichrists, and before the nation
has fully organized for (he hopes) a program of millennial world unification. Though he does not specifically mention a military expansion,
it would seem compatible with his praise of the early victories of the
Civil War. His Algonquian praying towns are first a response to the
dislocations caused by the Pequot War, then frontier garrisons that he
hopes will aid the English colonists during King Philip's War.

Even the pacific Gerrard Winstanley sees a civil/martial dialectic in
his utopia, *The Law of Freedom.* First he inverts Hobbes's hypothetical history. Whereas Hobbes sees the original covenant as the truce
ending the war of all against all, Winstanley sees it as the origin of
warfare and as synonymous with the Fall itself: "When mankind began
to buy and sell, then did he fall from his innocency; for then they began
to oppress and cozen one another of their creation birth right: as for
example, if the land belong to three persons, and two of them buy and
sell the earth, and the third give no consent, his right is taken from
him, and his posterity is engaged in a war" (511). Warfare is a principle
of historical explanation and argument in the present, as we see in
Winstanley's elegant argument against the unequal distribution of
crown and bishops' lands taken in the revolution. If the landholders
claim title to their land by some original Norman conquest, then "the
Kings are beaten and that title is undone." If they claim title by right
of the parliamentary army's victory over the king, then the poor who
made up and supported that army have an equal right to the land
(508). He prophesies that warfare will continue even if his ideal communist commonwealth comes into being: "While Israel was under this
commonwealth's government, they were a terror to all oppressing

kings in all nations of the world; and so will England be, if this righteous law become our governor" (516).

One utopia that lies outside my central focus nonetheless inspires to
some extent every midcentury Puritan consideration of the dialectic of
warfare and utopia: the Puritan New Model Army. To call the New
Model a utopia may provoke a number of instinctive protests; yet in
the terms of this study, it is arguably the most important utopian project of the Interregnum. It was the product of an encounter between a
displaced population (the revolutionary troops in need of discipline)
and a number of authority texts (the scriptural example of the Israelite
armies, reports on the military discipline of Maurice of Nassau and
Gustavus Adolphus). The Swedish discipline was an object of both
Puritan and Royalist fascination throughout the century; even Prince
Rupert was among its proponents. It disposed of customary aristocratic conceptions of warfare as sport, substituting for them the rationalizing practice of winter campaigning (an antipastoral conquest of
natural time) and of wearing uniforms. The New Model promised that
a reorganization of martial discipline could lead England into the
millennium.

Like Puritan utopia more generally, the New Model was an experiment in organizational rather than material technology. Following the
precedent of Gustavus Adolphus, Cromwell and his officers made the
New Model infantry a more mobile, aggressive, and efficient body by
encouraging soldiers to turn from cumbersome body armor and the
unwieldy pike to the musket and a new reloading drill that allowed
them to increase their firepower markedly. Similarly, New Model cav-
alry discipline allowed mounted troops to charge, fire, and regroup
more efficiently (Firth). Michael Walzer comments, "The immediate
result . . . was a centralized army, composed of small, highly mobile
units, capable in battle of rapid maneuver, attack, and orderly reformation" (*Revolution* 276). Weber argues that this new military discipline helped produce, and was produced by, a new rational subjectivity: "The ascetic principle of self-control also made Puritanism one of
the fathers of modern military discipline. . . . Cromwell's Ironsides,
with cocked pistols in their hands, and approaching the enemy at a
brisk trot without shooting, were not the superiors of the Cavaliers by
virtue of their fierce passion, but on the contrary, through their cool
self-control, which enabled their leaders always to keep them well in
hand. The knightly storm-attack of the Cavaliers, on the other hand,
always resulted in dissolving their troops into atoms" (*Ethic* 235–36n).
Discipline determines the use of military technology, and not the other

way around (*Economy and Society* 1151–52). The Protestant nations' organization of citizens in rational armies becomes the primary model for the capitalist organization of workers in rational factories (1155–56).

The New Model is the site for a utopian experiment in the integration of civil and ecclesiastical discipline, with frequent preaching by regimental chaplains adopting a millenarian/martial rhetoric, and with the singing of psalms before, after, and even during battle. Like Eliot's praying towns, this utopian project has an active press, producing reports on battles by chaplains like Hugh Peter acting as war correspondents (Firth 326n); devotional works like *The Souldiers Catechism* (1644), which provides soldiers with a rationale for the iconoclastic destruction of Anglican images, crosses, and the *Book of Common Prayer*; and *The Souldiers Pocket Bible* (1643), which organizes a number of scriptural verses relevant to warfare under several heads and, at sixteen pages, is suitable for carrying into battle. The New Model reproduces in small the contradictory theological dynamics of Puritanism, in which the promise of unity through scriptural fundamentalism dissolves into the actuality of sectarian scriptural interpretation. The New Model is a breeding ground for millenarians and "Anabaptists," and its soldiers often respond to official preaching with public disputation and preaching of their own—a model for the more secular opposition of soldiers to officers in the Leveller debates of the later 1640s (Firth 331–34). Looking back on the days of the New Model, Richard Baxter remembers it as a hotbed of antinomianism and Arminianism, which he blames on radical pamphlets by John Lilburne and Richard Overton "abundantly dispersed" among the ranks of soldiers, who "being usually dispersed in their quarters, they had such books to read when they had none to contradict them" (*Reliquiae* 1.73). Here we see the classic double bind of Puritanism: its fear of the ungovernability of "dispersed" print is in part its fear of itself, of its own insistence on the model of the unmediated encounter of conscience and Scripture.

The New Model is also a utopia in that it is a new corporate body with a complex and revolutionary relationship to the national corporate body that gave birth to it. It is simultaneously an expression of the state as the instrument of its national policy, a body withdrawn from the state and demarcated from it by a special military discipline that makes it resemble a Separatist congregation of the elect, and a regenerate body set in opposition to the still-unregenerate state, ready to complete its theocratic reformation. The New Model saw itself not just as the instrument of civil authority, but—like the utopias of Eliot and Harrington, like Puritan utopia in general—as an experimental site from which to reconstruct that authority. We can see the imaginative appeal of this martial utopia in an anonymous tract of 1659 entitled *The Armies Vindication of this last Change,* which attempts to inspire its readers with the millenarian fervor of the early days of the Commonwealth, when the New Model was young. In response to those who would make the army the tool of a civil sovereign (whether king alone, king in Parliament, or Parliament alone), it states that God is now "pulling down all worldly constitutions" (20) and that the people organized in an army are themselves the sovereign power of the nation: "The army are the people in an active body; not in a bulky, heavy, sluggish heap; but the people gathered up into heart and union, filled with spirit and life, for work of their generation" (5–6). The "generation" of this "active body" is an assault on custom:

> Our condition at present is not a fixed station, but a posture of direct motion; we are upon our march from Egypt to Canaan, from a land of bondage and darkness, to a land of liberty and rest. . . . Being full of spirit and vigor, enlarged in love and kindness, separated from the old forms and customs of the world, so that while the Lord leads us in a troublesome wilderness, in dark and rough paths, amidst wild beasts and enemies on every side, how comfortable is it to all good people to be led by the hand of an army in the ways of justice and freedom. (20)

The writer brings this martial ideal into line with a millennial project through a typological shift linking Israel with England: "The Lord seemed to sleep in former days, suffering his people to lie under oppression, but now he awakes, cutting Rehab, and wounding the Dragon, breaking the bands, and bringing his people from under Egyptian burdens. This cannot be done but by an army" (20). The New Model Army is simultaneously a negation of monarchy and custom and an organizational means to the millennial conquest of Antichrist's English and European allies.

Nowhere more clearly than in the New Model, we can see that alongside the history of liberty in the Puritan revolution lies a history of discipline—a history we will examine throughout this study and particularly in the final chapter. Summarizing New Model Army discipline, Firth says it produced "a compact, well-organized body, working like a machine, and directed by a single will" (67). He quotes a contemporary account of the discipline of a Scots regiment: "You would think a whole regiment disciplined as this was, were all but one body, and of one motion, their ears obeying the command all as one, their eyes turning all alike at the first stroke given, their hands going to execution as one hand" (93). Inextricably linked with the Puritan ideal of religious and political freedom centered on the conscience of the individual, there is a martial ideal of corporate unanimity centered on the disciplinary collective. The enlightenment technic of the printing press articulates both ideals: "Liberty, equality, and fraternity found their most natural, if their least imaginative, expression in the uniformity of the revolutionary citizen armies. They were not only exact repetitions of the printed page, but of the assembly line. The English were much ahead of Europe in nationalism as in industrialism, and in typographical organization of the army. Cromwell's Ironsides were in action a hundred and fifty years before the Jacobin armies" (McLuhan 223).

In *Discipline and Punish* Foucault argues that a "military dream of society" coexists in Enlightenment France with the philosophes' dream of juridical reason (169). The model of Rome serves as an analogy for both dreams: "In its republican aspect, it was the very embodiment of liberty; in its military aspect, it was the ideal schema of discipline. The Rome of the eighteenth century and of the Revolution was the Rome of the Senate, but it was also that of the legion; it was the Rome of the Forum, but it was also that of the camps" (146). The typological model of Israel has a similar complexity for Puritan utopia: the Israel of the seventeenth century and the Puritan Revolution is the Israel of the Sanhedrin and of apostolic egalitarianism, but it is also the Israel of Joshua's hosts and of the rider on the white horse, leading his armies from heaven to the conquest of the world.

The Body Politic and the *Rex Absconditus*

Perhaps the chief problem in opposing the civic and the institutional to the organic and the anthropomorphic is that civic fictions can themselves be anthropomorphic. The foremost medieval political metaphor, the body politic, envisions the entire state unified in a single, hierarchical body. Ernst H. Kantorowicz has studied the Hebraic, classical, and medieval genealogy of this metaphor. It generated an enormous volume of ecclesiastical and civil law designed to explain the continuity of the mystical body of the nation in time, despite the recurrent deaths of kingly heads. Kantorowicz argues that this political fiction even entered into Renaissance tragedy. In Shakespeare's *Richard II,* for instance, Shakespeare shows Richard turning traitor to the mystical body of the nation he heads when he hands over his crown to Bolingbroke/Henry IV, thus justifying in part the transition from the House of Plantagenet to the House of Lancaster. Like pastoral, the metaphor of the body politic allows for a unified vision of political life and nature. Shakespeare builds his tragedies of political transition around it, connecting the individual body of the king with the bodies of the state and of the entire universe in order to universalize the crisis of kingly transition. The macrocosmic body of the world reflects political transitions in the microcosmic body of the state through natural portents and outbreaks of the supernatural. In this political universe, J. G. A. Pocock says, political power is "held together by correspondence with the order of the universe itself and, should it disintegrate, the universe will by some terrible judgment restore it" ("Introduction" 21). This political fiction was still at work in the rhetoric of the Civil War. In the fourth chapter of *Eikon Basilike,* John Gauden's "King Charles" blames the tumults of the people in London and Westminster on the rebellious Long Parliament, comparing the crowds to an earthquake, the raging sea, and an ague (Gauden 14).

Utopia has a distant kinship with the political tragedy of transition. Both attempt to visualize the state as a rational totality, and both attempt to account for political transition in historical and symbolic terms. But here again, utopia distinguishes itself as a genre through its critique of anthropomorphism. The body politic was an ailing concept in the seventeenth century, beginning even with Shakespeare. When the metaphor is given only lip service, as in the Rome of *Coriolanus,* Shakespeare moves from tragedy's world of kingly analogy to satire's world of republican balance (Holstun). Michael Walzer observes that the rising Puritan classes and their parliamentary representatives made use of the metaphor only in passing, if for no other reason than to argue that the Stuart state was sick and required drastic physic. But they found the full metaphor unwieldy, for it suggests some earlier and so presumably monarchical time of political health (171–82). David Hale sees a shift in the seventeenth century from organic analogy to arguments about political contract (108–30).

Opposing political models developed—among them the revived classical republicanism of Italy—which entered into the political languages of the English sixteenth and seventeenth centuries, overlapping with and even criticizing models of absolute monarchy (Huffman). More's Utopia itself is a republic, with balanced powers of a one, a few, and a many (Fink 21–22). Each group of thirty families elects a phylarch, and each ten phylarchs are ruled by a head phylarch. All two hundred phylarchs choose a prince from among four candidates nominated by the people as a whole. Pocock argues that a theory of mixed republican government predominated in the political languages of the mid-seventeenth century, even among Royalists (*Moment* 333–400). The republican balance promises no natural political continuity. It "may be held together by careful adherence to the customs and usages which prescribe the proper working of its parts, or by rigorous enforcement of the basic principles on which it was founded . . . but if it disintegrates . . . the natural order, to which it does not appeal, cannot be expected to restore it" ("Introduction" 21). James Harrington's appeal to a dynamic and revitalized organic analogy shows just how feeble the static medieval model has become, for his Oceana is a nonhierarchical body that is, for all practical purposes, headless. The perpetual rotation of rulers through its bicameral state legislature is like the circulation of the blood (recently discovered by William Harvey) through the two chambers of the heart (287). We will see that republic and utopia come together in the writings of Harrington and even in the writings of Eliot, who makes no overt reference to the republican tradition.

Puritan utopia envisions new corporate entities built according to a new organizational detail from the bottom up, as opposed to the monarchical body politic unified from the head down. For radical Puritans this latter hierarchical model is a type of the doomed idol of Nebuchadnezzar's dream, whose shaky feet, half iron and half clay, portend the eventual downfall of all earthly monarchy. Monarchy in this organic sense, with its political vision of cure, balance, and restoration, has no place in Puritan utopia, which attempts to construct a radically new unity based on number, timetable, and discipline. Its object is not some idealized body but a newly rationalized organization of bodies. Whereas the monarchical imagination sees displaced populations such as the followers of Jack Cade in *Henry VI, Part II* as a case of political monstrosity—as a diseased limb or the "beast with many heads"—the Puritan utopian imagination sees them as the very raw material of utopia. We can see utopia's vision of the body in a chilling passage of Campanella's *City of the Sun*: "Also admirable is the fact that among them no physical defect justifies a man's being idle except the decrepitude of age, at which time of life he is still useful as an adviser. If a man is lame, his eyes make him useful as a sentinel; if he is blind, he may still card wool or pluck the down from feathers to stuff mattresses; if he has lost his hands, he can still serve some purpose. If he has but one sound limb remaining, he gives service with that" (67). In utopia the body of man is not an organic whole serving as an analogical model for the entire state. It is a raw material, susceptible to painstakingly detailed disciplinary procedures, to infinite analysis into component parts and individual reflexes, and to assembly into larger and larger inorganic and nonhierarchical corporate bodies such as the congregation, the school, the troop, or the work detail.[8]

The organic model of the body politic accompanies a model of political power as a unified, personified, and absolutist faculty located in the ruling consciousness of the individual sovereign. In his study of the self-representation of Jacobean absolutism, Jonathan Goldberg shows that an important figure for this model of power is the hierarchical absolutist gaze. In such diverse media as court masques, public plays, royal processionals, commemorative statuary and medals, Jonson's encomiastic poetry, and even Donne's "private" lyrics we can see representations of the king as the source of a sovereign gaze from above seeing into and unifying his entire realm, or as the mysterious object of his people's fascinated gaze from below. The inorganic model of Puritan utopia, on the other hand, accompanies a model of political power as a dispersed, impersonal, and popular political substance, which is figured in a nonhierarchical gaze of mutual surveillance. More's Utopians constantly observe each other, for his rationally gridded commonwealth makes sure that there are "no hiding places, no spots for secret meetings" (49). Even when they think they are alone, Utopians believe themselves to be under the constant surveillance of their departed ancestors (82). By hanging lighted lanterns in all the streets, Andreae's Christianopolitans rationalize what they see as the papist fetishism of lighting sacramental candles: "What Antichrist expects from the great number of wax candles, let him see for himself; but let us not shrink back from any system which lessens the fear of a man working at night in the darkness, and which removes the veil which our flesh is so anxious to draw over license and dissoluteness" (172). Pieter Cornelisz Plockhoy proposes to extirpate Antichristian kingly power and replace it with a communist "family government" of mutual assistance and observation. Under this form there will be an improvement in child-rearing, because children "are under the eyes and inspection of many good people," and in church government, because all meet in a public meeting house "with seats rising one higher than another, that every one may be seen" (148–49, 151). As we will see in Eliot's praying towns, the Puritan congregation makes corporate watchfulness a key part of its discipline. The central political ritual of Harrington's Oceana allows every citizen to see every other citizen exercising civic virtue in a public election combining a martial drill and the casting of ballots. Utopia dissolves the theatrical gaze of monarchical sovereignty into a diffuse but highly charged field of mutual surveillance.

But antimonarchical as it may be in its final product, utopia does rely on a certain kind of king. In Book 2, Raphael tells of the origin of Utopia. The semimythical King Utopus conquered the "rude and uncouth inhabitants" of Abraxa, forcing them to submit to his rational ideal and leaving their state his name (34–35). Utopus is More's answer to the political and narrative problem of accounting for the birth of a nonmonarchical government without resorting to the political fiction of the social contract. Just as the physics and the metaphysics of the Enlightenment require a *deus absconditus,* the sacred agent of a transition from the sacred to the human and secular, so too the political narrative of early modern utopia requires a *rex absconditus,* the monarchical originator of a nonmonarchical commonwealth. The *deus absconditus* sets his universe into action and then either withdraws to contemplate its self-sufficient workings or becomes immanent in those workings. The *rex absconditus* forms his commonwealth into a self-sufficient eternal civic entity and then withdraws into his own law codes. As the miraculous fusion of philosopher and prince—a fusion whose possibility the Dialogue of Counsel in Book 1 questions—King Utopus is the essential mythical origin of More's otherwise rational state. More's narrative does not allow us to question his origin. (Is he some power-hungry noble younger brother? The questioner feels foolish) Nor can we determine the reasons for his beneficence to Abraxa. Utopia begins simply as his intention.

Utopus's main precursor is Lycurgus, the semimythical, semimonarchical legislator who sets the Spartan republic into motion. When he sees it operating efficiently, Plutarch says, he decides to make it perpetual: "Then, as Plato somewhere tells us, the Maker of the world, when first he saw it existing and beginning its motion, felt joy, even so Lycurgus, viewing with joy and satisfaction the greatness and beauty of his political structure, now fairly at work and in motion, conceived the thought to make it immortal too, and, as far as human forecast could teach, to deliver it down to posterity" (71). After making the Spartans swear an oath to observe his laws until he returns from a pilgrimage to Delphi, Lycurgus sets out to the oracle and receives her blessing on his commonwealth. He then starves himself to death, never returning to Sparta, and so leaves the Spartans under their oath for all time.

The story of Lycurgus, an important myth of premodern republican theory, illuminates and is illuminated by Freud's story of the primal horde in *Totem and Taboo,* another myth describing the origin of political culture in a distinctly un-Hobbesian transfer of sovereignty from an individual to a collective. Through collective action the brothers of Freud's primal horde are able to murder their tyrannical father, who is guilty of constant murder and incestuous rape. They then proceed to cannibalize him: "In the act of devouring him, they accomplish their identification with him, and each of them acquired a portion of his strength" (142). Yet out of the remorse born of the love they felt for him despite his tyranny, they memorialize him through a totemic animal and forbid themselves the imitative pleasures of incest and murder. This is the birth of the social order.

Freud's myth and Plutarch's demystify each other. On the one hand, Freud's insistence on a violent origin makes it possible for us to reread the story of Lycurgus's self-starvation as a self-interested Spartan fiction devised by his bloodstained and politically empowered republican successors. By making him the agent of his own death, they attempt to prevent the emergence of aggrieved political factions or of a cycle of imitative violence (Girard). On the other hand, Plutarch makes it possible for us to see that this originating conflict between individual and collective sovereignties is not necessarily the product of a prepolitical oedipal ambivalence. The ambivalence of the republican collective can be politically explained as the product of its initial dependence on the unifying intention of the founding sovereign, and its later conflict with him as a superfluous and potentially tyrannical sovereign. The myth of the *rex absconditus* is a monarchical vaccine against monarchy in a republic, for loyalty to the mythical founding monarch precludes any willing subjection to a usurping tyrant. Utopus institutes the Utopian commonwealth by right of conquest, royal prerogative, and reason, but he takes the office of king with him to the grave, leaving only his name and his polity behind him. There is no formal necessity for a hereditary monarch in Utopia.

We can see variants on this peculiar self-limiting utopian kingship in other Puritan utopias. *Oceana*'s Lord Archon Olphaus Megaletor, Harrington's idealized version of Oliver Cromwell, sets Oceana into motion and then steps down from his archonship. In John Eliot's view, Moses himself initiated a body of workable civil law whose universal application he did not live to see fully realized. For the theocratic Fifth

Monarchists in general, the *deus absconditus* and the *rex absconditus* become one so far as they see the foundation of a holy commonwealth based on scriptural principles bringing a return of Christ to earth either in his own person or in his immanent presence in the working of his laws (Capp 131–56). Puritan discipline as a whole (church, military, educational, and political) aims to move past the immediate rule of an authority to the individual's rule of his own ascetic conscience.

This vestigial presence of monarchy in utopia may be somewhat surprising, but it is by no means a mere oversight by the utopists. We may see in the figure of the *rex absconditus* a transition from the great-man theory of history to a more modern history of social collectives and superpersonal processes, but we should note that Renaissance utopists were still unable to conceive of the transition without the control of a single, unifying intelligence. Machiavelli discusses the mechanics of such transition in *The Discourses* 1.9, entitled "That it is necessary to be the Sole Authority if one would constitute a Republic afresh or would reform it thoroughly regardless of its Ancient Institutions." He says that Romulus was justified in his murder of Remus (again, we have a fratricide at the birth of a city) because a legislator must have undivided authority when he seizes an occasion and imposes civic virtue: "Rarely, if ever, does it happen that a state, whether it be a republic or a kingdom, is either well-ordered at the outset or radically transformed *vis-à-vis* its old institutions unless this be done by one person." At this moment of legislation the people must be silent, even though they are its ultimate judges: "Though the many are incompetent to draw up a constitution since diversity of opinion will prevent them from discovering how best to do it, yet when they realize it has been done, they will not agree to abandon it" (132). Dictatorship is permissible only because it is provisional. Romulus reserved only a limited authority to himself, and after the expulsion of the monarchist Tarquins, this authority was vested in two consuls appointed annually. The founding father should have only the good of his community in mind, not that of his own family, so he should pass on his unified organizing intention in a code of laws, not in a dynasty.

Machiavelli goes on to mention Moses, Lycurgus, and Solon—the other heroes who founded states on the basis of civil codes rather than hereditary successions. He focuses on the story of King Agis of Sparta, who assumes absolute power and is killed by the Spartan ephors, or magistrates, who assume he intends a tyranny. But after his death, his successor Cleomenes discovers Agis's writings, which reveal that Agis intended only the protection of the rights of the many against the encroachments of the few. He wanted only to assume a temporary dictatorship so that he could restore Sparta to its Lycurgan purity. Cleomenes then institutes Agis's reforms (132–33). Agis's nontyrannical and provisional monarchical intention remains behind in writing, so despite his execution, he can still become immanent in the laws of his state. Here utopia is obliquely related to another didactic literary genre, the cyropaedia, or prince-book. Like the prince-book, it gives advice to a ruler, but the core of that advice is that the virtuous ruler should find some way to make himself scarce.[9]

The masses are to be molded by the Puritan utopist and his ideal legislator—possibly for their own good, perhaps for their own liberty, but molded nonetheless. They are not yet the proletarian subject of history, only the subject matter of the utopist, who speaks not *for* any particular group but *about* the alignment of a displaced population with an organizing utopian text. The formal necessity for this unifying utopian intention helps us understand the seeming paradox of Winstanley's and Plockhoy's addressing their communist utopias to so unpromising a patron as Cromwell. Even Harrington (who also dedicated his utopia to Cromwell), the Puritan utopist with the most carefully worked-out discussion of the historical development of the conditions that make his utopia both possible and necessary, has no conception in *Oceana* of a revolution in class consciousness underlying or resulting from the revolution he sees in the distribution of land. He is painfully aware of both the necessity for an agent of transition from individual to corporate political sovereignty and the problems such an agent poses: "The change of a person, with what loss soever, is yet a less change than the change of a government; the former is a change from a thing that was known to another that is known; but the latter must be a change from a thing that hath been known in this nation, to a thing that was never known in this nation." He compares the situation of the English people groping for a government in 1659, after the death in 1658 of Oliver Cromwell, with that of a man walking in the dark: "A man that walketh treadeth with almost equal boldness his next step, if he see it, though it be in the dirt: but let it be never so fair, if he see it not, he stands stock still." If there is not at least one guide who does see, if this political transition is not present to the consciousness of the legislator, it cannot come to be (780).

Given this idealist legislative determinism and the fact that Puritan utopia conceives of itself as a form of writing, it should be no surprise that the utopist frequently identifies himself with his legislator. In the following chapters I will, for the most part, forgo biographical treat-

ment of the Puritan utopists—partly to save space, partly because I'm
unable to add anything to existing biographies, partly because I'm
more interested in corporate than in individual fictions. But there is a
sense in which utopian writing is autobiographical—a sense we will
misunderstand if we see the utopist's identification with the legislator
of his ideal state as a wish-fulfillment fantasy allowing him to gain
absolute imaginative power. Frank and Fritzie Manuel, for instance,
see Renaissance utopia as compensatory autobiography. King Utopus
is More; the leader of the scientists in *New Atlantis* is Bacon (an identification that allows Bacon to make up for his feelings of oedipal and
social victimization); and "it seems obvious that Harrington fancied
himself as the Lord Archon" (254, 243–50, 365). But the *rex absconditus* is not the mere compensatory projection of the utopist's clerkish
ressentiment. Rather, both are self-limiting and self-effacing creators.
Again and again in Renaissance utopia, we see the utopist submitting
himself to the very fantasy of utopian discipline he creates. The
medium of this self-submission is the utopian theme of writing and
print, which leaves the utopist as much written on as writing. Puritan
millennial utopianism, like millennialism more generally, is an essentially scriptive practice, with the millennial scribe communicating to
his audience through his writing rather than through his voice
(McGinn 5). The multiplication of writing through print makes it possible for the early modern utopist to identify the reproductive power
of his medium with the expansive universality of the millennium. In
his identity as a catalytic millennialist, the utopist writes not about the
Scriptures but from within them, as part of a typological series of millennial scribes. Comenius's proposal for the construction of a "temple" of pansophy in his *Reformation of Schooles* implicitly places him
in a series of scribes through whom God communicated the pattern of
his temple, including Moses, Nathan, David, Solomon, Ezekiel, and
John of Patmos (78–80). He comments, "God sent (by the prophet
Nathan, as is probably held) the pattern of the Temple, and all the
parts thereof to David, who delivering it to Solomon, charged him not
to depart from the form thereof, protesting thus to him, 1 Chron.
28:19, 'All this the Lord made me understand in writing by his hand
upon me, even all the works of this pattern'" (79). In the identity
Comenius creates for himself here, we can see a self-effacing megalo-
mania we will find characteristic of utopian writing: he is bold enough
to add himself to a series of biblical kings and prophets and to propose
the way to a complete reformation of the entire world, but only by

becoming part of a series of blank pages on whom God inscribes his pattern.

To the extent that the utopian traveler represents the utopist, he begins by being abased, not by assuming power. True, Andreae begins his *Christianopolis* with an overt claim to an imaginative totalitarianism: "For inasmuch as other people (and I myself also) do not like to be corrected, I have built this city for myself where I may exercise the dictatorship" (140). His speaker seems still to be in control when he playfully narrates his setting sail upon the "Academic Sea" aboard "the good ship Phantasy" (142). But this authorial control disappears when the *Phantasy* founders in "the Ethiopian Sea." The speaker washes ashore on the island of Caphar Salama and becomes "the stranger." An "examiner" from Christianopolis interrogates him and concludes with a peculiar welcome: "He almost shouted out aloud. 'You are ours,' he said, 'you who bring to us an unsullied slate, washed clean, as it were, by the sea itself. It but remains that we pray God that he inscribe upon your heart with His holy stylus the things which will seem, in his wisdom and goodness, salutary to you'" (148). Here we have not altogether left behind the idea that utopian writing is a self-fashioning for the utopist; I would only suggest that this self-fashioning is a subcategory of his general attempt to fashion selves for others, and that it is possible only when the utopist is able to visualize himself as one of those others. After setting his utopian narrative into motion, the utopist becomes less like a writer in control of its progress and more like that blank displaced population he set out to write on.

Puritan utopia is an act of self-limiting power; the utopist's desire to exercise power over what he sees as a displaced population is by no means incompatible with a desire for a quietist self-domination. The Puritan utopist practices an asceticism not unlike that accumulative and self-disciplinary ascesticism that Weber finds characteristic of the Protestant prehistory of capitalism. Puritan utopian writing is an act of withdrawal in anticipation of an expansion, a personal mortification of the flesh and spirit in anticipation of a universal presence of the spirit in a rational organization of bodies. In Stanley Fish's phrase, Puritan utopia is a self-consuming artifact, for it attempts to consume itself and the self of the utopist writing it; given its connection to Lycurgus, it is a self-consuming artifact of a very literal sort. If the utopist's dream of a perfect state is well wrought, then it will be realized and there should be no need for him to write future utopias. He can then withdraw into the obscurity of utopian everyday life, or into the selflessness of the millennium. The utopist is the prospective mirror image of the retrospective epic poet: whereas the latter can write only one epic, summing up his poetic career and the history of his nation, the former can write only one utopia, marking the obsolescence of further utopian writings and of his old culture. Utopian writing is a single man's assertion of power that attempts to destroy the singularity of political power in a king and to diffuse sovereign power throughout a commonwealth. The *rex absconditus* attempts to legislate, the utopist to write himself out of existence.

3

John Eliot's
Empirical Millennialism

New English Utopia

Historians of utopian thought have not paid much attention to the religious and political texts of Puritan New England, perhaps because the history of New England seems to present no properly utopian writing, perhaps because it takes too much effort to see any connection between the Congregationalist New Israelites and the traditions of Erasmian humanism. As textual monomaniacs turning instinctively to the Bible in response to each new social problem, the early settlers seem worlds apart from More's learned wit. In *The English Utopia* A. L. Morton journeys to the Boston of Edward Bellamy's *Looking Backward,* but he remains within the insular bounds of his title when considering revolutionary Puritanism. J. C. Davis's study of English utopian writing pays some attention to Continental utopias but ignores the New World. Even Mark Holloway's history of American utopian thought makes only a passing reference to the Puritan experience in New England.

No doubt a complementary problem is that the entire Puritan errand into the wilderness seems like an integral utopian project. Its very complexity—its involvement with military, political, and religious events and production of a great number and variety of texts—makes it an unwieldy utopian subject lacking discrete textual margins. Cotton Mather makes this identification of all New England with utopia explicit: "Such great persons as Budaeus, and others, who mistook Sir Thomas More's Utopia for a country really existent . . . might now have found a truth in their mistake; New England was a true Utopia" (Bercovitch, *Jeremiad* 68). Frank and Fritzie Manuel also see New England as a true Utopia, but its unselfconsciousness makes it derivative and peripheral: "We consider . . . American utopian thought before the late nineteenth century an overflow of European types. . . . A long tradition identifies the colonies and the United States with utopia, but, curiously, those who were actually fashioning that utopia were dreaming about it in European terms. The writings of the Puritans with all their millenarian imagery . . . are extensions of European idea systems" (14). But it is not clear how any utopian practice could so clearly separate its dreaming from its fashioning or how any idea system as complex as Puritan political ideology could have a logical coherence impervious to rethinking and reshaping when it enters into radically new social practice.

The single most ambitious utopian project within the larger Puritan utopia of New England was John Eliot's work with (or perhaps on) the remnants of the Algonquian civilization in Massachusetts. Eliot has received very little attention from historians of utopian thought. For the most part he has been left to historians of Indian-white relations, religious missions, and millennialism. But no other Puritan, Old or New World, worked so long or with such concentration on a single utopian project, and no other Puritan utopist remained so committed to connecting utopian writing and practice.[1]

Eliot's utopian project has a distinctive integrity not because it sees itself as the mere colonial extension of a previously unified idea system or because it assumes the purely instrumental role of utopian writing in the establishment of a New World utopian practice, but because it obsessively charts the transformations between utopian writing and practice. The nineteen Indian "praying towns" that Eliot had established by the onset of King Philip's War grew out of his interpretation of a single chapter of Exodus.[2] The utopian practice in those towns in turn gave rise to a large body of utopian writing: grammars, translations, catechisms, dialogues, legal codes, and the Eliot Tracts (1643–

1671), a series of eleven missionary epistles by Eliot and others that solicited funding for the praying towns by describing their progress in "reducing" the Indians to "civility." Eliot is probably best known for his missionary role as "the Apostle to the Indians" and for *The Indian Bible,* his translation of the Bible into Algonquian—a work of formidable linguistic scholarship. But he was also a translator of utopia: his *translatio* of Hebrew Scripture across the Atlantic to New England reveals its previously unsuspected usefulness as political theory and helps create a utopian civil practice. This practice in turn provides the empirical basis for *The Christian Commonwealth,* a formal utopian platform translating that utopian practice back across the Atlantic to the politically torn English nation and promising the final translation of England into the millennium. Eliot's utopian project is, in fact, a translation of Old World writings into a new geographical setting, but like most translations it criticizes and transforms its original.[3]

Eliot was born in 1604 and took his A.B. from Jesus College, Cambridge, in 1622. He served briefly as Thomas Hooker's usher before Hooker fled to Holland in 1630. He emigrated to Massachusetts in 1631, where he soon became preacher to the congregation at Roxbury, a position he held until his death in 1690. He was a translator of the *Bay Psalm Book*—he may, in fact, bear the complete blame—and one of Anne Hutchinson's inquisitors. But for most of his years in New England he was preoccupied with his mission to the Indians. This work helped remove a source of continuing embarrassment to the early colonists. The charter of the Massachusetts Bay Colony asserts that "the principal end of this plantation" is to convert the native inhabitants to Christianity. The very seal of the colony reveals the typological imperative underlying this latter-day mission to the Gentiles. It shows an Indian man improbably beckoning across the Atlantic and begging, "Come over and help us," in an echo of the plea of the man of Macedonia to St. Paul in his dream (Acts 16:9). But in the early years of the Bay Colony there were no systematic attempts at conversion, only scattered individual conversions like those recorded in the first Eliot Tract, *New-Englands First Fruits.* Eliot launched the colony's first organized mission. His nineteen praying towns became the utopian sites for a regulated encounter between a people the Puritans saw as displaced and prepolitical and a scriptural pattern for civil organization. The encounter produced a new (if somewhat short-lived) human type: the Praying Indian.

Preceding Eliot's Indian utopias—making them both possible and necessary, in fact—is New England's larger project of utopian self-fashioning. The Puritans see themselves repeating the exile of the original displaced population: Israel wandering in Sinai. Looking back at the Great Migration of the thirties, William Hubbard says that the minds of the Puritan fathers approaching New England "were as *rasa tabula,* fit to receive any impression from the spirit of truth, either as to doctrine or worship" (Miller, *Seventeenth Century* 433). A committee of English ministers writing the dedication to the third Eliot Tract argues that the persecuting prelates have unwittingly initiated a diaspora to end all diasporas: "God doth shew that he had merciful ends, in this their malicious purpose . . . so he suffered their way to be stopped up here and their persons to be banished hence that he might open a passage for them in the wilderness, and make them instruments to draw souls to him, who had been so long estranged from him. It was the end of the adversary to suppress, but God's to propagate the Gospel; theirs to smother and put out the light, God's to communicate and disperse it to the utmost corners of the earth." The Great Migration was not a premature flight from the emerging regenerate commonwealth, but part of the accelerating plot of providential history: after the overthrow of the monarchy, "when providences invited their return," God "let them know it was for some farther errand that he brought them thither" (*Tracts* 28–29). So the conversion of the Indians is a vital part of the larger utopian project of New England. Bringing together the Algonquian remnant and the shaping authority of Scripture in a utopian site, the Puritans can see their flight to the New World as a millennial progress, their separation from the City of Man as a prelude and a means to the unification of the City of God.

The Puritans had an affinity for the utopian model of an ideal state that other colonies did not.[4] Bernard Sheehan argues that they found uncongenial the complementary myths of the noble savage and the New World paradise that controlled at least the early phases of the promotion, conquest, and colonization of Virginia (10). Even the New English landscape became an arcadia or Land of Cockaigne from the perspective of the Anglican libertine Thomas Morton. In his account of his colony at Merrymount and its conflicts with the Pilgrim Separatists of Plymouth, Morton says that New England occupies a geographical golden mean between the tropical South and the frigid North. Its climate produces a host of commodities: rich mineral deposits, ample timber and fruit, and fish that practically jump into the pan. New England even holds out a promise of human fertility. Aided by the aphrodisiac tail of the beaver (which is "of such masculine virtue, that if some of our ladies knew the benefit thereof, they would desire to have ships sent of purpose to trade for the tail alone") and by bacchic revels around the maypole at Merrymount, New England can expect a harvest of "reasonable creatures" to match that of "minerals, vegetables, and sensible creatures" (31–32, 82, 120–21). Just as this conservative imagination tells potential immigrants that the New World is a Land of Cockaigne, so it tells those who stay behind that it is a space of exile for "the swarms of our rank multitude" (Taylor 163). For the dystopian imagination, the New World is a space for the socially therapeutic purgation of the body politic. In his dystopia, *Another World and Yet the Same,* Joseph Hall, later Anglican bishop of Norwich and Milton's discursive antagonist, offers "Moronia" as the alternate name for the New World home of certain recent Brownist exiles, saying it is the proper abode for them and for all "heretics, sworn enemies of the public peace, and agitators" (104–05). These contradictory conservative visions of New England cohabit goodnaturedly in an English ballad of 1650, which moves from describing New England as a land of milk and honey, "Where fowls do cloud the sky in flight / Great turkeys threescore pound in weight," where the Puritan fathers keep all things in common, including their wives, to proposing that England purify itself by having "Bedlam, Newgate, and the Clink / Disgorge themselves into the sink" of New England (Scull).

But for the New English Puritans, the New World holds out not the guarantee but the precarious possiblity of an ideal state; it is a wilderness of utopian potentiality, not an arcadia of fulfillment. Cotton Mather snorts at a Jesuit catechism for the Hurons depicting heaven as a Land of Cockaigne, with fields always ready to harvest and the sun ever shining (1.572). In a defense of his fellow New Englanders, Eliot observes that they settled in a land too far north to profit from the sun's generation and ripening of gold and tobacco, and too far south to profit from the fur trade: "But we chose a place where nothing in probability was to be expected but religion, poverty, and hard labor" ("Conjectures" 23). Like the colonial expeditionary forces of More's Utopia, the Puritans seem almost to seek out waste, barren ground. Cecelia Tichi shows that the Puritan transformation of the Massachusetts landscape from a forest "wilderness" to farmland was the product of an ideological as well as a utilitarian imperative: the desire to recreate the City of God in the New World by taming nature (1–36). The site of Puritan utopia is neither an *outopos* nor an *eutopos,* but a place in which the former may be transformed into the latter—a physical wasteland that Puritan organization, labor, and social discipline can shape into a model Christian commonwealth.

Conquest and a plea of natural necessity and right draw the borders of this utopian site. William Bradford says that the Pilgrims in the Netherlands conceived of North America as an "unpeopled" country because the "savage and brutish men" inhabiting it do no more than "range up and down" like "wild beasts" (or the Book of Job's Satan) (26). In his *General Considerations for the Plantation in New England,* John Winthrop gives a thoroughly Utopian argument for colonial expansion, moving in a breath from Edenic pastoral community (which allows the Puritans to get a foot in the door) to postlapsarian georgic individualism (which allows them to claim sole ownership): "The whole world is the Lord's garden, and he hath given it to the sons of Adam to be tilled and improved by them. Why then should we stand starving here for places of habitation ... and in the meantime suffer whole countries, as profitable for the use of man, to lie waste without any improvement? ... That which is common to all is proper to none. This savage people ruleth over many lands without title or property; for they enclose no ground, neither have they cattle to maintain it, but remove their dwellings as they have occasion, or as they can prevail against their neighbors" (Alexander Young 272, 275–76). In the eyes of the Puritans a population whose civil state is thus naturally displaced can be rightfully displaced by others in turn. The Indians possess the lands only by natural right, a right superseded by the right of utopian conquest, civil division, fixed habitation, and written title.

The enclosure of New England proceeded in a fashion quite like that of England. As the enclosure of English commons grounds often began with a single large landholder overstocking the commons, turning it into private property (Tawney, *Problem*), so white expansion in New England often began with the Indians' allowing whites the use for settlement and cultivation of Indian commons grounds (Bowden and Ronda 12–13). In both cases, however, a relationship to the land defined by customary and communal usage became one defined by enclosure and exclusive ownership. The dispossessed and displaced English tenants and Algonquian tribesmen soon found that like all enlightenment technics, enclosure is irreversible. Speaking of the prototypical plantation, Nimrod's attempt to establish a new state composed of dissatisfied younger sons drawn from other tribes and subjected to his tyrannical authority, Eliot remarks, "Men of new plantations are subject to much distress and unquietness until all commons lands be divided, an humor which after nations have no occasion to see unto" ("Conjectures" 9).

One sign of this irreversibility is that, in both cases, utopia responds to the destabilizing effects of this deracinating enclosure with an act of rationalizing and self-protective enclosure. Just as Winstanley and the Diggers respond to the displacement of rural tenants by encouraging them to enclose and cultivate commons grounds such as those at George's Hill, so Eliot and his missionary colleagues work tirelessly to acquire tracts of land for Indian praying towns (Kellaway 84–87). However, it is crucial to see this not as missionary benevolence but as part of the larger effort at utopian enclosure in New England that Winthrop describes. The Indians are to have their own lands, but they are to have them on the basis of written deeds that both give them exclusive title to a certain plot of land and exclude them from the land to which they have no title. The previously free-roaming Algonquians are to be integrated into the newly gridded, enclosed, and rationalized New England landscape. Daniel Gookin, Eliot's missionary ally, is conscious of the irony of speaking of "Indian plantations" (*Collections* 179), but the term is accurate: the Indians may occupy the same space, but they do not occupy the same site, for the praying towns are to be the site of their transformation from a group of depraved "natural" men inhabiting a precivil society into model utopian individualities and collectives. In an early Eliot Tract, Eliot brings out the recurrent utopian analogy linking peoples and the land as objects of rational transformation, saying that while the emigrants thought at first that the Indians would be "dry and rocky ground" for conversion, they will soon find them "better soil for the Gospel than we can think," just as they found New England soil to be "scarce inferior to Old English tillage" (*Tracts* 15).

Eliot insists on separating the English and Indian settlements, but this is as much to keep the encroaching English outside the determinate civil space of the praying towns as to keep the Indians inside: "A place must be found ... somewhat remote from the English, where they must have the word constantly taught, and government constantly exercised, means of good subsistence provided, encouragements for the industrious, means of instructing them in letters, trades, and labors, as building, fishing, flax and hemp dressing, planting orchards, etc." (*Tracts* 81). In *A Brief Narrative* Eliot laments the effect on the praying town of Ogquonikongquameset of the contiguous English town of Marlborough (8). This isolation from the English may be perplexing at first, particularly since it seems merely to reproduce English civil procedures and occupations among the Indians. The praying towns are yet another instance of what Christopher Hill calls

"the Robinson Crusoe Situation": a state in which the Puritan individual finds himself or herself completely cut off from society, reliant
on conscience alone. Hill finds this situation in a number of texts: in
the prelapsarian Eden of *Paradise Lost,* in the solitary (or near-soli-
tary) pilgrimage of John Bunyan's Christian, in the long isolation of
Defoe's Crusoe, and in Henry Neville's proto-robinsonade, *The Isle of
Pines* (*Puritanism* 381–83).

But it is odd how often Hill's isolated Puritan individuals reproduce
the social state in the wilderness. Adam and Eve, of course, quickly
produce both human history and human culture through their Fall.
Christian flees his hometown, the City of Destruction, but encounters
its iniquities (and sometimes even its citizens) in serial form along his
path. Crusoe, through his isolation, is born again into a reformed Puritan identity, and then goes on to establish a stripped-down simulacrum
of society in his domineering fellowship with Friday and his rediscovery of the mechanical skills of English civilization. Though "Religious
Harry Neville" is odd man out in this group (he was a Harringtonian
republican who claimed to find Cicero as inspiring as Scripture), his
George Pine is certainly no exception. He and his four fellow cast-
aways (all women) are fruitful and multiply, and in his eightieth year
he has a total of 1,789 descendants. Neville reveals something of the
masculine fantasy underlying all such utopian isolation and reproduction. A German contemporary of Neville's noted perceptively that
Pines is an anagram of *penis* (Neville 38).

This isolation, which allows the foregrounding of Puritan conscience
by cutting the individual off from society, is not a state miraculously
encountered. Puritan writers seek it out, even stage it, to show the
reproductive power of society. After all, were Friday set down in the
middle of London, his "civilizing" would be the mere brute imposition
of cultural force. But his gradual anglicization on a remote island is a
paean to the transformative power of English civility, just as Crusoe's
painful rediscovery of the art of bread making celebrates the technical
sophistication that England may take for granted. In the experimental
isolation of the praying towns, Eliot has a site at which he may demonstrate the reproduction of English civility in a purer form, emphasizing civilization as a process and a technic—the making of a *civis*—
rather than an entity. As his first step in organizing a utopia, Eliot creates an artificial state of nature in these temporarily acivil islands cut
off from the English settlements. These sites allow him to conduct a
controlled experimental encounter between a displaced population
and a utopian textual authority.

The Scraped Board of Puritan Anthropology

The Puritans saw in the Algonquians precivil men cut off from any true political life. No doubt they took this attitude partly because they lacked a proper anthropology and so were unable to see the Indians' social organization as a positive cultural tradition. But the Indians' displacement was also real. Epidemics of European origin preceded full-scale European colonization, and a phase of military conquest culminating in the Pequot War of 1637 preceded the phase of utopian organization (Salisbury 35). Daniel Gookin gives a brief survey in his *Historical Collections* of the five Indian nations inhabiting eastern New England, all of which, he says are disorganized or greatly reduced in size because of epidemics or the Pequot War (147–49). Neal Salisbury and Kenneth M. Morrison question the image of Eliot and his fellow missionaries as intrepid spiritual pioneers, saying that they only followed these earlier phases of English conquest and worked with populations that had already been conquered. But utopian organization is not simply a disguised form of colonial domination; it is a distinct stage of it. In *Tears of Repentance,* an Eliot Tract largely made up of brief confessional autobiographies by Indian converts, one motif occurs again and again: those Indians who fought the English and saw their compatriots massacred take their own survival as a sign of special consideration by the English god, so they are more amenable to conversion and utopian reorganization in the praying towns. The first Eliot Tract, *New-Englands First Fruits,* records the conversion of Wequash, an Indian who survived the Pequot War. Wequash associates the English god with English artillery, extrapolating the sacred power of one from the ballistic power of the other: "And though before that time he had low apprehensions of our god, having conceived him to be (as he said) but a *musketto* god, or a god like unto a fly, and as mean thoughts of the English that served this god, that they were silly weak men; yet from that time he was convinced and persuaded that our god was a most dreadful god, and that one English man by the help of his god was able to slay and put to flight an hundred Indians" (6–7, misnumbered 6–15). According to the anonymous author, Wequash converted, became a missionary, and died when poisoned by non-Praying Indians.

The missionaries had a subtler ally in the diseases they brought with them. The Eliot Tracts contain many accounts of Indians converting because of God's special grace in singling them out for preservation amid the unprecedented epidemics devastating their kinsmen. Speaking of the effect of these plagues on the Indians of Martha's Vineyard (and with a horribly unconscious irony, of their cause), Thomas Mayhew says that "since the word of God hath been taught unto them in this place, the powwaws [religious leaders] have been much foiled in their devilish tasks, and that instead of curing have rather killed many" (*Tracts* 187). War and disease destroy the culture providing an alternative civil organization to utopia and traumatize the individual survivors, making them more malleable to utopian conversion. Like the intense anxieties about election we see among the Bay Colony's white sermonists and autobiographers, the Indians' cultural anomie provides that moment of traumatic anxiety essential to the psychology of Puritan conversion. The Eliot Tracts are almost Arminian in their implicit assumption that the Indians as a whole can choose grace without ever worrying about the election or nonelection of individual Indians. Both converts and missionaries seem to see the very fact of the English Great Migration as a sufficient sign of God's special grace to the Indians (*Tracts* 142, 219–20).

Because of the Indians' anomie, Eliot is able to sidestep possible accusations of pride of intellect in his utopian work; he can describe himself as God's "instrument," as a utopian engineer who does no more than aid God in the proper alignment of displaced populations and organizing text. In his preface for Thomas Thorowgood's 1660 edition of *Jewes in America,* Eliot describes the founding of his utopia in an image that suggests both his affinities with Plato's Socrates and his advantages over him: "For the foundation of their government, they have by covenant solemnly given up themselves unto the Lord, to be ruled in all things by the word of his mouth. . . . Briefly, my scope is to write and imprint no nother but Scripture principles in the *abrasa tabula scraped board* of these naked people, that so they may be in all their principles a choice people unto the Lord, owning none other lord or lawgiver but the Lord alone, who is the King of Saints" ("Conjectures" 27, misnumbered 23). The utopist does no more than imprint a scriptural civil pattern on the civil blank of the Indians. In his vision of his own instrumentality, Eliot has a great advantage over Socrates, who must come up with some method for wiping the civil tablet clean before he can reinscribe it with his new utopian principles.

Scripture provides the Puritans with both an anthropology that accounts for the Indians' historical degeneration and a political model that will lead to their utopian regeneration. In his preface for Thorowgood, Eliot develops a variant on the fairly widespread Renaissance theory of the Hebraic origins of the American Indians—a theory

that will take us on a brief detour. This theory brought together travelers' tales, scriptural exegesis, political agitation, and international
diplomacy, producing one of the most fascinating episodes in early
modern millennialism. Lee Eldridge Huddleston documents the sixteenth-century origins of the theory and its flourishing during the years
of the Commonwealth after the 1644 report of a Portuguese Jew
named Lodwick of Monterinos, or Antonio Montezinos, who claimed
to have visited a colony of Jews secluded in the Ecuadoran Andes.
Rabbi Manasseh ben Israel, another Portuguese Jew and a scholar living in Amsterdam, circulated his story. Manasseh's report attracted the
interest of John Dury, an English clergyman, a supporter of the Commonwealth, and an advocate of Eliot's missionary work. Dury put
Manasseh in touch with Thomas Thorowgood, who had a study of the
American Indians as Jews in manuscript and published it in 1650 with
an appendix in which Manasseh presented Montezinos's story. Manasseh published a study of his own entitled *Spes Israelis* in 1650; an
English translation (by Milton's friend Moses Wall) entitled *The Hope
Of Israel* appeared that same year. Peter Toon examines these discussions of Jews in America in the context of Commonwealth agitation
to readmit the Jews officially into England for the first time since their
exile by Edward I in 1290. Among those advocating such a policy to
Cromwell was Manasseh himself, along with many Puritan clergymen
of the Society for Propagation of the Gospel in New England. Richard
Popkin examines the strange and strained ecumenical appeal of this
anthropological fiction, which was essentially eschatological: the
reunion of Israel was to have been a sign of the imminent arrival of
the millennium (for Christians) or of the Messiah (for Jews).[5]

These millennial speculations energized the New England missionaries and their supporters. Roger Williams notes with interest that in
both Indian and Jewish culture, men quarantine women with the
"monthly sickness" (1.84). In an Eliot Tract dedication, Edward Winslow seconds him on this, noting in addition "their manifold daily
expressions bewailing the loss of that knowledge their ancestors had
about God and the way of his worship, the general deluge, and of one
man only that ever saw God, which they hold forth to be a long time
since ... which certainly I believe to be Moses" (*Tracts* 73). In an
appendix for the same tract, John Dury develops his theory of the Indians as the descendants of the ten lost tribes of Israel (93–98). Gookin
reviews the various theories on the origin of the Indians in the opening
pages of his *Historical Collections of the Indians in New England* (144–

47). In an Eliot Tract of 1651, Eliot delivers a version of the argument he was to expand for Thorowgood (*Tracts* 119–20).

Eliot's attitude toward the Indians is thoroughly shaped by the millennialist fervor of the Interregnum. While his conceptions are no less ethnocentric than those of the Puritan and Pilgrim mainstream, he does not insist on seeing the Indians as an intrinsically satanic race, and at least during the relatively pacific period between the Pequot War and King Philip's War, the Bay Colony tolerated and even encouraged him in his theories. Rather than seeing the Indians as demonic Tartars or sons of Ham, he sees them as "the first and chief materials" in the organization of the praying towns (*Tracts* 124). His reading of Genesis in his preface for Thorowgood—a reading no less eccentric and exorbitant than his interpretation of Exodus 18 in *The Christian Commonwealth*—allows him to account for this historical objectification that has produced his utopian raw materials. After the Flood, Noah and his sons hold a council and divide all the world, with Japheth and Ham moving westward and Shem moving eastward. With the passage of time, diverse cultures proliferate. One such culture was the result of a political innovation. Nimrod ("Rebel") gathered together "a crew of young fellows like himself that were as weary of government as he . . . and he took upon them to be their captain, their leader, and monarch, changing that form of government which had been in force ever since the world began, and was still in force, namely, paternal government" ("Conjectures" 7). When Nimrod builds the Tower of Babel to consolidate his power, God punishes him by multiplying languages among his subjects and dispersing them.

The Indians, however, are the descendants of Eber, a descendant of Shem. Eber and his race move eastward through Asia in a complex utopian dialectic of enclosure, population growth, and plantation, settling India, China, Japan, and America. Eber's name means "passing over" (the Tigris) (5). He names his son Peleg, or "division" (11). Peleg names his son Reu, or Regnu, which "signifies consociation or confederation among the divided" (13). These archetypal pilgrims, therefore, are both the actual ancestors of the Indians and the Old Testament types of the emigrating and planting Congregationalists.

For Eliot the Indians represent not some race of natural men radically other to Western men but a missing link in scriptural history and anthropology. The discovery and the conversion of the Indians signify an ultimate (or penultimate) unity of peoples and of history, not a static logical binary between nature and civility. Puritan anthropology, sketchy as it may be, is thoroughly historical. Its most pejorative and racist descriptions of the Indians show their historical connection to the English. Again and again Eliot refers to the Algonquins as a "degenerate" people who must be "reduced" (literally, "led back,"though the military connotation is close at hand) to civility.[6] Similarly, in an image originating with Thomas Hooker, taken up by the anonymous author of the first Eliot Tract, and repeated by Eliot on the first page of his *Indian Grammar* and again by Cotton Mather in his biography of Eliot, the Indians are "the very ruins of mankind."

It is true, as Ronald L. Meek points out, that the New World Puritans and the seventeenth century in general did not possess the eighteenth century's elaborately worked-out systems of staged human development. But Eliot's discussion of his missionary work does reveal a fairly complex moral history of humanity. The first human type, the *unfallen saint,* appeared only in Adam and Eve; had they remained unfallen, they would have founded the perfect polity based on a perfect identification of paternal and civil rule. The Fall initiates the reign of *degenerate man,* whose "natural" state is, in fact, a state of decayed civility. Many repetitions of the first Fall aggravate this degeneracy: the fall of the Tower of Babel is a type of the monarchical and anti-Christian barbarism of Europe in both its pagan and Roman Catholic phases. All succeeding elaborations of human reason and civility in the gentile monarchies sink man deeper into degeneracy. Degenerate man becomes *civil man* to the extent that he can throw off monarchical rule and establish a popular government through Protestant discipline. The regenerate *civis* becomes the site for the production of the final human type, the *regenerate saint,* who will close out human history.

The Indians in North America are a historical mirror for the British, as Thorowgood says, showing them their own degeneracy in the days of Augustine's missionary expedition to the British Isles (2). But they are also a challenge to the British, for their purer form of civil degeneracy is less ossified and codified than that of the gentile "nations" who suffer under the depraved civility of kingly and prelatical authority. Noble savagism enters into Puritan conversion literature when the malleability of these Indian converts becomes a reproach to the stony-hearted English. Eliot moves into prophecy: "The Lord shall be their lawgiver, the Lord shall be their judge, the Lord shall be their king, and he will save them; and when it is so the Lord reigneth, and unto that frame the Lord will bring all the world ere he hath done, but it will be more difficult in other nations who have been adulterate with their Antichristian or human wisdom; they will be loth to lay down their imperfect own starlights of excellent laws, in their conceits, for the perfect sunlight of the Scripture, which through blindness they cannot see" (*Tracts* 127). The Indians are not anti-Christian and anticivil like popish Europe and prelatical England; they are pre-Christian and precivil. When organized into a rational, scriptural polity, they, like More's Utopians, will undergo a rapid and rational conversion to Christianity.

This rapid transformation of the Indians from degenerate men to regenerate saints, with a brief mediating phase as civil men, is not to be just a repetition of European history; it will also be an accelerated epitome of that history prophesying what Europe has not yet become: a regenerate millennial community. Eliot puts his missionary work into an explicitly millennial context when he compares the Lord's ability to "find these lost and scattered Israelites" with his ability to "gather the scattered and lost dust of our bodies at the Resurrection" (*Tracts* 120). In an afterword to this tract, Henry Whitfield warns the English that these Indians may even "rise up in judgment against us and our children at the last day . . . and leave us in Indian darkness" (146–47). In an attempt to stir up a "holy jealousy and emulation," Richard Mather warns that God may transfer his favor from the English to the Indians as he once transferred it from Jews to Gentiles (*Tracts* 224–25).

In their conversion of the Algonquians, the Puritans play the role of the pillar of fire bearing the Scriptures in an ark of cedar to the virtuous pagans of Bacon's New Atlantis. The New World becomes the appointed site for the millennial encounter of clockwise and counterclockwise Israelites: the Indian descendants of Shem and Eber bearing themselves eastward, their civil tabula rasa more and more degenerate, but uncorrupted by gentile civility; and the Puritan Israelites bearing westward the Hebrew Scriptures, with their heretofore undiscovered models for regenerate civility.

Utopian Scripture and Jethro's Judges

Perry Miller downplays the utopian authority of the Bible in Puritan theories of civil government, saying that politics "was one important human art on which the Puritans said the Bible was *not* an absolute and imperious lawgiver." The Puritans allowed for more play of human invention in civil than in church government, thinking that God demanded only that there be some kind of civil authority without specifying for all times and all men the precise form that authority should take (*Errand* 142–43). Certainly, Puritan writings on politics do not conflate civil and church government; and the forms championed by various New World Puritans do run from monarchical to aristocratic to democratic. But to claim that this diversity of forms and opinions shows the basically secular nature of Puritan political thought is to underestimate the contradictory power of the Bible as a textual authority. For the Puritans, the Bible does not mark off its own limitations but claims jurisdiction over both church and civil government. The irreducible tension between church and civil government is not the conflict between faith and reason; it is internal to Scripture, as old as the space between the two tablets of the Decalogue, between man's duty to God and his duty to other men. John Cotton writes in a letter to Lord Saye and Sele that although church and civil government are "not confounded," both are "God's institutions." Whenever possible, it is appropriate that the civil commonwealth be established according to Scripture principles, which give "full direction for the right ordering of the same" (Miller and Johnson 209).

But simply because all Puritan theories of government are fundamentally theocratic, we are not at all justified in assuming that they are fundamentally the same. *Theocracy* refers not to any particular form of government as do *monarchy, aristocracy,* and *democracy,* but to a form of political rhetoric that attempts to draw all its authority from an interpretation of Scripture. Given that God seldom intervenes in the details of day-to-day civil administration, the question to pose of any state called a theocracy is, Who determines the voice of God on civil matters—a godly prince, an aristocratic Sanhedrin, a democratic assembly of the saints, or a republican balance of the three? Theocracy is compatible with any of these. Cotton, for instance, finds scriptural ground for attacking democracy: "Democracy, I do not conceive that ever God did ordain as a fit government either for church or commonwealth. If the people be governors, who shall be governed?" (209–10). Cotton went on to write *Moses His Judicials* (published in England as *An Abstract of the Lawes of New England*), a code of law founded on Scripture, which he proposed for Massachusetts. The Fifth Monarchist William Aspinwall later urged it on the colony as a Magna Charta (Maclear 237–40).

Thomas Hooker's political theory was no less anchored in a reading of Scripture, though opposite to Cotton's in political orientation. When Hooker and his followers emigrated to the Connecticut River valley, they left behind them not only the Bay Colony and its Puritan aristocracy, but also the royal charter establishing the colony. Their settlement then became a much different experiment in the civil application of church government. Emphasizing the responsibility of magistrates to those who choose them and the people's capacity to determine law and limit the powers of magistrates, they were able to translate the more democratic aspects of the church discipline of Congregationalism into the civil sphere, formalizing their efforts in *The Fundamental Orders* of 1639. In "Thomas Hooker and the Democracy of Connecticut," Miller faults earlier interpretations of Hooker as a democratic critic of the Bay Colony's theocracy by noting the theocratic strains in Hooker's thought and in the government of Connecticut. Miller admits that Connecticut's government was more democratic than that of Massachusetts Bay but insists that this was no real difference because "both policies grew out of the original body of Congregational thought. . . . It was simply that in each case the emphasis lay at a different point, and the discrepancies did not yet indicate an antagonism of fundamental points of view" (*Errand* 41). This is an excessively genetic argument: the entire lengthy history of Christian religious and political controversy seems to show that fundamentally opposed ideologies may debate inside a shared "theocratic" rhetoric. Miller seems to believe that there is a necessary antagonism between theocracy and popular government of any kind whatever.[7]

Eliot did not follow his former pastor to Connecticut, of course, but he too emphasized the more democratic aspects of Congregationalist discipline in the civil and church governments of his praying towns. Largely as a result of his missionary work, he viewed the relation between civil and church government not as a logical comparison and opposition but as a sequence. In response to the perennial complaints about the small numbers of Indians he was converting, he insisted on a mediating stage of civility and demanded more funding to establish praying towns: "As in nature there is no progresses *ab extremo ad extremum nisi per media,* so in religion such as are so extremely degenerate must be brought to some civility before religion can prosper. . . . It's hard to look upon the day of small things with patience enough. I find it absolutely necessary to carry on civility with religion" (*Tracts* 15, 88). Here Eliot quotes from the vision of Zechariah, a perfect emblem text for his utopian georgic of minute organizational detail. An angel tells Zechariah, "The hands of Zerubbabel have laid the foundation of this house; his hands shall also finish it; and thou shalt know that the Lord of hosts hath sent me unto you. For who hath despised the day of small things?" (Zech. 4:9–10). Conversion is not an instantaneous event but a methodical disciplinary procedure in a utopian site.

In a defensive description of his techniques, Eliot appeals again to the image of the Indian tabula rasa and defends his methodical civil inscription. Critics of the slowness of conversion, Eliot says, "know not the vast distance of natives from common civility, almost humanity itself. . . . If we would force them to baptism (as the Spaniards do about Cusco, Peru, and Mexico, having learnt them a short answer or two to some popish questions) . . . we could have gathered many hundreds, yea thousands it may be by this time, into the name of churches; but we have not learnt as yet that art of coining Christians, or putting Christ's name and image upon copper metal" (*Tracts* 15). Utopian civil procedures are a Protestant critique of the more sacramental and instantaneous Roman Catholic conversions. There is "no necessity of extraordinary gifts nor miraculous signs alway to convert heathens . . . for we see the spirit of God working mightily upon the hearts of these natives in an ordinary way" (*Tracts* 17). This ordinary way is a civil procedure based in scriptural detail. The kairotic moment of Augustinian conversion establishes the meaning of the life narrative of the convert by briefly lifting him out of secular time into a moment of the *nunc stans* of eternal time. But praying-town conversion turns this moment into a narrative by breaking it down into stages. Utopian conversion is a reorganization of secular time according to a civil procedure that will lead in time to full participation in the procedures of church fellowship.[8]

This utopian emphasis on the priority of civility in the task of conversion had notable advantages over the Jesuits' use of icons and sacraments in their conversions of the northern Indians. James Ronda shows that the icons the Jesuits used as ceremonial aids proved to be equally effective as symbols uniting the Indian opposition. Because the Jesuits habitually baptized those on the verge of death from smallpox, the Indians began to associate their deaths with the sacrament. One Huron, acting on a somewhat garbled but oddly compelling interpretation of the Eucharist, accused the Jesuits of bringing a plague-infected corpse with them to the New World (72–75).

In 1651, after gaining title to a tract of land on the Charles River eighteen miles southwest of Boston, Eliot founded Natick, the first of his praying towns. In the Eliot Tract entitled *Strength out of Weaknesse,* Eliot describes the auspiciousness of this first formal encounter between the Indians and his prize passage on civil organization from Exodus. The first organization "will be as a pattern and copy before them, to imitate in all the country, both in civilizing them in their order, government, law, and in their church proceedings and administrations." Like Vasco de Quiroga, Eliot finds that "the order of proceeding with them is first to gather them together from their scattered course of life to cohabitation and civil order and government, and then to form them . . . into visible church-state" (*Tracts* 171).

But like all utopists, Eliot aims to construct civil conscience, not just civil order. The Indian communities must be in some measure self-governing, for he is weary of holding all power himself: "Besides, all or many of their differences and causes they usually brought to me, which was not convenient, and I was willing to avoid: themselves also found great need that some should be over them, to judge their causes, and end differences, and much desired it" (171). The cure for this burden and the beginning of regenerate civility is to be found in Exodus 18. Eliot continues: "They had a great meeting, and many came together from diverse parts . . . where, with prayer to God I read and expounded to them the 18th of Exodus (which I had done several times before) and finally they did solemnly choose two rulers among themselves, they first chose a ruler of an hundred, then they chose two rulers of fifties, then they chose ten or tithing men. . . . And lastly for that day's work every man chose who should be his ruler of ten, the rulers standing in order, and every man going to the man he chose, and it seemed unto me as if I had seen scattered bones go, bone unto his bone, and so lived a civil political life, and the Lord was pleased to minister no small comfort unto my spirit, when I saw it" (171–72).

Exodus 18 is a peculiar utopian textual authority. It has none of the eschatological resonances of the Puritans' favorite political texts, the books of Daniel and Revelation. Even for Exodus, this chapter is something of a pedestrian interlude: in chapter 17, by contrast, Moses presides over the conquest of Amalek with the rod of God in hand and draws water from the rock; in chapter 19 he ascends Sinai for a colloquy with God the Father. But in chapter 18 he merely listens to some sound (but unsolicited) advice from his father-in-law, Jethro. Noticing how weary Moses gets when sitting as judge for the litigious Hebrews from dawn to dusk, Jethro suggests that he appoint a judicial bureaucracy: "Thou shalt provide out of all the people able men, such as fear God, men of truth, hating covetousness; and place such over them, to be rulers of thousands, and rulers of hundreds, rulers of fifties, and rulers of tens. And let them judge the people at all seasons: and it shall be, that every great matter they shall bring unto thee, but every small matter they shall judge: so shall it be easier for thyself, and they shall bear the burden with thee." The comfort Eliot takes from the institution of these utopian groupings suggests a somewhat immodest parallel between himself and Moses, for it compares his own weariness from riding circuit among his scattered converts with Moses' tribulations in Sinai. But this is a peculiarly utopian self-aggrandizement, for Eliot aims to institute procedures that will make his own authority unnecessary. He insists that the praying towns become self-governing, with their own internal government of Indian preachers and magistrates. He envisions his own role in the founding of the towns as that of the *rex absconditus,* the measure of whose success in initiating a utopian practice is his ability to withdraw from it and contemplate it from a distance. Moses is a precursor of unique authority, one who left behind him (in Eliot's view, at any rate) a workable code of civil government, gaining for himself only a Pisgah sight of Palestine, its destined site of utopian realization.

Theory to Practice: Praying-Town Discipline

The founding of Natick and of the praying towns that followed in succession, moving westward into Nipmuck country, began the crucial second phase of the Puritan conquest of New England: a phase based not on immediate military force but on the utopian organization of social detail. And yet the Puritan intention embodied in this conquest has proved perplexing to most readers of the missionary literature, who have a hard time keeping its political and religious aspects in simultaneous focus. Starting with Daniel Gookin in his *Historical Account of the Doings and Sufferings of the Christian Indians in New England,* they have contrasted what they see as Eliot's basically altruistic work with the rabid Indian hating of the other colonists. These other colonists, the argument runs, were blind to the distinction between the Praying and the non-Praying Indians, and their racism and impiety led to murmurings against Eliot and Gookin, to barbarities practiced against the Praying Indians during King Philip's War, and to the destruction of all but four of the praying towns. This tradition of simultaneously praising Eliot's piety and lamenting white military violence runs from Gookin through Cotton Mather, Convers Francis, and Ola Winslow to Alden Vaughan's influential account of Eliot's work in *New England Frontier.*

Henry W. Bowden and James P. Ronda's introduction to Eliot's *Indian Dialogues* gives a sophisticated variant on this interpretation:

"The key to understanding the cultural impact of Puritan missions is a theological one, an emphasis on sanctified living that had to follow regeneration as part of the salvation process. . . . In pursuing such an evangelical program, missionaries helped destroy native cultures, but they did not direct converts' lives in new directions for economic benefit or for their colony's political advantage. Eliot and his confreres were basically religious agents who sought to enhance the salvation of souls and a gradual achievement of Christian perfection" (36). One may dispute this interpretation on a factual basis, showing more or less mediated economic and political advantages the praying towns brought the Puritan settlers. But even granting Bowden and Ronda their distinction, it is difficult to account for the sheer bulk of the missionary literature, the intense transatlantic interest in the praying towns, and the considerable financial support that interest generated simply in terms of the actual progress of conversions. Even though the praying towns set themselves the goal of converting the entire degenerate race descended from Shem and Eber, the number of converts remained disappointingly small. If the key to understanding Eliot's intention is theological, then we need to reconstruct that theology on its own textual terms, not on the basis of a more modern definition that begins by polarizing the realm of the spirit and the realm of the state.

In *The Invasion of America* Francis Jennings takes a much different attitude toward Puritan theology. He sets the missions squarely inside the history of Puritan political maneuverings and the conquest of the Indians, documenting the Bay Colony's use of the missions in its competition for funding with the Narragansett Bay Colony and Samuel Gorton, and as frontier outposts during King Philip's War. Jennings tries to use these aspects of the missions to debunk Eliot's saintly reputation, saying that "to provide a basis for propaganda in England, Eliot's mission had to appear as an altruistic outpouring of religious benevolence. If seen as a mere maneuver to recover lost influence, it would not make headway against the critics" (238). Jennings's argument is in part persuasive, and it is certainly a valuable corrective to the Whig interpretation of the history of genocide. But the praying towns produced a rather small political and economic payoff for all the money and effort invested in them. Their military importance was finally quite negligible; the Puritan conquistadores of King Philip's War did not for the most part follow Eliot's and Gookin's advice on using the praying towns as forts and the Praying Indians as guerrillas. Instead, they professed a great deal of difficulty in distinguishing Praying from non-Praying Indians. They were so hostile to Eliot and Gookin that at one point Gookin feared being lynched (Lincoln 41). While it is true that the praying towns aimed to transform the Indians' mode of economic production, it is also true that they were not designed to, and never did, turn a profit. Cotton Mather observes that whereas Roman Catholic missions were "but a sort of engine to enrich Europeans with the treasures of the Indies," the Puritan missions "expect nothing from their Indians" (1.573). This is bigoted and self-serving but largely true. The missions depended on English financial support throughout their existence, and Eliot's aggressive fund-raising drives brought him a certain notoriety. Civil discipline was not a means to economic production; if anything, it was the other way around. In a letter to William Steele, president of the Society for Propagation of the Gospel in New England, Eliot speaks of the usefulness of offering work and wages to Indians who are initially reluctant to submit to praying-town worship and discipline, complaining that "it is no small care to have so many ways on foot as to employ every man prudently in that which [he] may be capable to do" (Eliot, "Letters of the Rev. John Eliot" 296).

These conflicting interpretations of Eliot's mission come together in their belief that theology and politics are somehow, in the final analysis, incompatible—that the true intention of texts that clumsily muddle the two must be assigned to one or the other. But neither the theological nor the political aspect of Eliot's practice is a mere tool in the service of the other, for the goal of the praying towns was not efficiency in a familiar social function, whether conversion or conquest, but an unprecedented integration of religious and political life. At midcentury, radical Puritans on both sides of the Atlantic were finding it increasingly difficult to distinguish sacred history from the sequence of contemporary events. Amid the rising millenarian speculation, the imaginative appeal of the praying towns lay not in their missionary or political utility, but in the purity of their experiment in utopian discipline. By reorganizing Algonquian social life according to a new utopian scheme of social space, time, and procedure, Eliot intended the disciplinary production of two radically new subjectivities: the corporate subjectivity of the self-governing, self-policing praying town and the individual subjectivity of the melancholic Praying Indian with the right to enter into civil and church covenant. Congregational church discipline becomes utopian when it becomes a tool for the millennial conversion of an entire culture.

The formation of a disciplinary utopia in Natick required first a division and an organization of space. In a characteristic combination of providence and practicality, Eliot recalls his discovery of the spot in the woods that was to become Natick: "The Lord did both by his providence then, and by after more diligent search of the place, discover that there it was his pleasure we should begin this work" (*Tracts* 138). The converts laid out two long streets on one side of the Charles River and one street on the other (177). This scheme seems to have had no justification except as a small-scale symbolic conquest of nature. It required the construction of a bridge linking the two sides of the river, which Eliot superintended: "There is a great river which divideth between their planting grounds and dwelling place, through which, though they easily wade in summer, yet in the spring it's deep and unfit for daily passing over, especially of women and children; therefore I thought it necessary that this autumn we should make a footbridge over against such a time in the spring as they shall have daily use of it" (138). Utopian intention has foresight and spans seasons; this bridge survives the spring floods even better than do some English bridges downstream (178). A material structure helps detach the Praying Indians from seasonal cycles and move them into a new economy, for all of them (women and children, too, one assumes) can now practice year-round agriculture.

The spatial organization of Natick proceeded, allowing for the formation of a new collectivity: the disciplinary congregation. Gookin describes this new group coming together as a chastened and modest body arranged according to sex, age, and degree (*Collections* 183). Even the material structure housing this congregation has utopian importance. Eliot says the Indians have become so adept in carpentry that they can build their own meetinghouse, and he draws a surprising conclusion: "But now being come under civil order, and fixing themselves in habitations, and bending themselves to labor, as doth appear by their works of fencings, buildings, etc., and especially in building without any English workman's help or direction a very sufficient meeting-house of fifty foot long, twenty-five foot broad, near twelve foot high betwixt the joints, well sawen and framed (which is a specimen, not only of their singular ingenuity and dexterity, but also of some industry), I say this being so, now my argument of delaying them from entering into church estate was taken away" (*Tracts* 227). Rectilinearity implies election. The New Jerusalem, which "lieth foursquare, and the length is a large as the breadth" (Rev. 21:16), finds a humble type in New England—one that will aid in the millennial conversions queuing up the future inhabitants of the sacred city itself.

Eliot's utopia was not, as Bowden and Ronda assert, Puritan collectivity's assault upon Indian individuality (6–7, 38). At least it was not merely this, for in its very spatial organization it constructed new sorts of individuality. In an early, pre-Natick Eliot Tract, Thomas Shepard relates Eliot's discovery of the lack of "privacy" in Algonquian social space and his attempts to supply this privacy through a hybrid Indian/ English architecture. The wigwams at Noonanetum are made quite large, Shepard says, "the rather that they may have their partitions in them for husbands and wives together, and their children and servants in their places also, who formerly were never private in what nature is ashamed of, either for the sun or any man to see. It's some refreshing to think that there is (if there was no more but) the name of Christ sounding in those dark and despicable *Tartarian* tents; the Lord can build them houses in time to pray in, when he hath given unto them better hearts" (*Tracts* 61–62). A place for everyone, and everyone in his or her place: this is the spatial ideal ruling utopia's distribution of bodies. The darkness of the Tartarian tents is not an absolute darkness but a contamination of private spaces—their becoming too public. Natick pushes even further this quest for privacy and the formation of Praying Indians according to an English model of social space: the living space adjoining the streets is enclosed by fences and subdivided into plots of land for individual, English-style dwellings, which are themselves divided into walled rooms inside.

The Puritans' antipastoral conquest of seasonal time through the spatial structures of their praying towns provided the essential critical component of their reorganization of time; their Sabbatarianism provided the positive component. Samuel Eliot Morison records with some amusement a discussion between a member of the Massachusetts General Court and the tribe of the sagamore Kutshamakin:

MEMBER: You are not to do unnecessary work on the Sabbath.
INDIANS: That will be easy: we haven't much to do any day, and we can well take our ease on the Sabbath. (290)

Most of the humor of this exchange, however, is visible only from within a culture thoroughly acclimated to clock time and wage labor. The transition in time sense produced in Eliot's utopia was not a movement from idle freedom to industrious necessity. It was a disciplinary redistribution of free and unfree time. E. P. Thompson, in his

"Time, Work-Discipline, and Industrial Capitalism," shows that the transition into the capitalist mode of production was also a transition from one way of structuring social time relying on natural cycles and the demands of the individual task, to another relying on the clock and the more rational and gradated time of wage work. Moreover, "Puritanism, in its marriage of convenience with industrial capitalism, was the agent that converted men to new valuations of time" (95). Christopher Hill sees a new Calvinist theory of time taking shape in the seventeenth century—a theory emphasizing a regular and rational alternation between workdays and the weekly Sabbath. This scheme of time comes into conflict with the conservative model of time based on the observance of traditional saints' days as holidays (*Society* 145–218). We might even call this second model of time a polytheist time, since it dotted the year with celebrations of various saints whom the Puritans regarded as little more than papist idols, even going so far as to commemorate pre-Christian survivals like May Day. Puritan Sabbatarianism grew out of a desire to oppose the Anglican hierarchy fixing saints' days, to discipline the unruly crowds that gathered to celebrate them, and to integrate these crowds into a weekly routine of industry and rest. We can see the disciplinary (as opposed to the strictly theological) importance of Puritan Sabbatarianism in *Robinson Crusoe:* well before he undergoes his traumatic spiritual rebirth, the castaway Crusoe begins building an industrious personality for himself by maintaining his post-and-notch calendar, taking care lest he "forget the Sabbath days from the working days" (Defoe 52).

The transformation of times in New England was a greatly accelerated version of the English transformation. Whereas the resistance of the saints' days to a Sabbatarian conquest had the considerable weight of Anglican tradition and political power behind it in England, the New England Sabbath rapidly overrode the Indians' division of time into "sleeps, moons, and winters" (Dunton 114). Eliot resisted the celebration of holidays, even Christmas, and struggled to maintain Sabbath discipline in the praying towns (Mather 1.532). The most mechanical of the Ten Commandments in its analysis of the week, the order to keep the Sabbath becomes an important means of regeneration (*Tracts* 51–52). In Eliot's fictionalized *The Indian Dialogues* a recent convert named "Anthony" calls the Sabbath "the chief hinge" of all the other commandments: "By a religious keeping of the Sabbath, we act our obedience to all the commands." The Sabbath is implicitly democratic, for it brings together high and low, rich and poor, woman and man in a weekly collective. And it divides the week between the Lord (or the disciplinary collective) and man, making possible a weekly turning away from the self and, by extension, a weekly return to the self and a concentration on individual and family industry, fixed agriculture, and a market economy (147–49).

This rigorous Sabbatarianism would seem to be a transitional step to the possessive individualism of the seventeenth century, which Macpherson defines as a reconceptualization of the individual as the *owner* of himself, as "the proprietor of his own person or capacities" (3). The worker's voluntary alienation of his labor to a wage-paying employer makes it possible to think of labor as a commodity rather than an integral part of his personality. Similarly, the saint's voluntary Sabbatarian alienation of one-seventh of his time to God makes it possible to reconceptualize his relation to time in general (both that time alienated and his "free" time) as a relationship of ownership. In Eliot's *Indian Dialogues,* when King Philip questions the need for the Sabbath, Anthony responds, "Will ye rob God?" (148). The praying-town Sabbath is an enclosure of time that, like its enclosure of space, draws borders for and helps to define new collectivities and new individualities.

Neither spatial nor temporal organization, however, is sufficient for Eliot's program in revolutionary Puritan discipline. Indeed, an overemphasis on the spatial aspects of utopia is a form of idolatry. Eliot says that Nimrod's monarchical overemphasis on architectural hierarchy led God to become the first Protestant iconoclast: "The very plot and policy he used to establish his kingdom was the very way and means to bring it to utter ruin, insomuch that his kingdom lasted but a few years: where the foundations are laid without God, the building is unstable" ("Conjectures" 9–10). The organization of discipline in the praying towns was more a matter of the adjustment of individual and civil space and time according to utopian procedures.[9]

The corporate procedures of the praying towns grew from the Indians' election of officials and entry into civil covenant. This created an autonomous corporate identity informing all of the towns' civil procedures. From his early missionary work in the 1640s to his attempts after King Philip's War to reassemble the scattered pieces and persons of his praying towns, Eliot worked to construct this civil autonomy. In a letter of 1673, he gives his reasons: "Their national customs are connatural to them. Their own nation trained up and schooled unto ability for the work, are the most likely instruments to carry on this work, and therefore a few schools among themselves, with true-hearted governors and teachers, is the most probable way of advancing this work" ("An

Account" 128). Accordingly, there were Indian schools, magistrates, judges, and, as of 1673, Indian church officers in six of the praying towns. Eliot even attempted to train Indian missionaries, whose more or less fictionalized exploits we can see in *The Indian Dialogues*. Indian magistrates, with some English supervision, were entitled to hear and decide court cases according to the municipal law codes that Eliot and the leaders of the Praying Indians began drawing up in 1646. These codes range from a five-shilling fine for all Indians caught killing lice between their teeth ("This law though ridiculous to English ears yet tends to preserve cleanliness among Indians") to prohibitions of polygamy and Sabbath breaking to threats of death for adultery or bestiality (*Tracts* 20–21, 39–40).

The first law in the first legal code orders that "if any man be idle a week, or at most a fortnight, he shall pay five shillings"—a punishment that forces a discontinuation of the offense (*Tracts* 20). Regular, universal labor was to be a central fact of praying-town life. The fixed utopian site of the praying towns solidified the transformation between modes of economic production that Eliot described even before the founding of Natick: "They begin to grow industrious, and find something to sell at market all the year long." They sell the crops of spring, summer, and fall at those seasons' markets and their indoor handicrafts in the winter (*Tracts* 59). In a late tract, one Indian's confession reveals the economic nature of conversion: "I did greatly love hunting, and hated labor: but now I believe that word of God which saith, 'Six days shalt thou labor,' and God doth make my body strong to labor" (*Tracts* 246).

Complete economic autonomy, however, remained permanently out of reach, and the praying towns required outside funding throughout Eliot's lifetime. The precariousness of the Indians' civil autonomy (praying-town government was never more than a municipal authority under the control of the Bay Colony) became clear during King Philip's War, when the towns were summarily disbanded. Puritan procedural discipline was more successful on an individual level, for Bay Colony political power was in no way threatened by the new individual the praying towns produced: the melancholic Praying Indian.

From the very beginning, this disciplinary formation of new individuals proceeds through pedagogical dialogue: an exchange of questions and answers between Puritans and Indians on the Sabbath, the traditional day for Puritan instruction, in the praying town's closest approximation to a Congregationalist meetinghouse. Eliot bluntly describes his method when visiting the wigwam of "Waaubon," or

"Waban," an Indian who was later to become a leader of Natick: "Having thus in a set speech familiarly opened the principal matters of salvation to them, the next thing we intended was discourse with them by propounding certain questions to see what they would say to them, that so we might screw by variety of means something or other of God into them" (*Tracts* 4). In a later tract Eliot expands on this, laying out his Congregationalist disciplinary supplement to group prayer under four headings: preaching, catechism, answering questions, and admonition and censure (*Tracts* 53–55). Regarding preaching, Eliot's aim was to train a body of Indian preachers who could touch Indian listeners more closely: "As for my preaching, though such whose hearts God hath bowed to attend can pick up some knowledge by my broken expressions, yet I see that it is not so taking and effectual to strangers, as their own expressions be, who naturally speak unto them in their own tongue" (Francis 178). The remaining three procedures, though supervised by Eliot and his English coworkers, were increasingly performed by Indian preachers.

Catechism uses monotonous repetition to create a new memory. Analyzing manuals of seventeenth-century catechists, Stanley Fish finds recurrent images of didactic inscription with a stamp or a seal like those we have seen applied to the Indians: "While the metaphors vary, the picture they project is consistent: the catechist labors long and hard to work alterations in materials that are at once resistant and passive, and because they are resistant and passive, the tools he employs will be blunt and crude" (*Temple* 18–19). The missionaries encounter some resistance to their attempt to inscribe Christian doctrine in the conscience of the Indians, but they characterize this resistance not as the opposition of an alternative reason but as the recalcitrance of an inanimate raw material that can be overcome by mere repetition. In *Historical Collections* Gookin says that Eliot framed two different catechisms, one for children and another for adults. Both were gradated, "a few questions at a time, according unto their capacity to receive them." Eliot would first go through the simple catechism for children, combining instruction with delight by rewarding the children with "some small gift as an apple, or a small biscuit, which he caused to be brought for the purpose." This helped the children "to get into their memories the principles of the Christian religion." The children's catechism would prepare the adults present for their more complicated catechism that followed (169).

Eliot's catechisms go beyond the education of an individual child or a lapsed sinner in the proper catechetical questions and responses to the transformation of an entire cultural memory. Neal Salisbury argues something similar in his "Red Puritans," saying that "until now this program had dealt with English, generally Puritan children. Applied to the Indians, however, it acquired a radically new purpose—the inculcation of Puritan cultural and religious values in adults and children for whom these values were utterly foreign and meaningless" (42). But this inculcation had a considerable success, and values that were originally "foreign and meaningless" to the Indians became in some measure their own. The English program was barbaric not because it could not have succeeded but because it did—because it created new subjects with a new conscience and extirpated the remnants of a previous cultural identity. It seems unlikely that the anomic Indians and their children were any further from full Puritan subjectivity than were white newborns. Cathechism makes present a sacred history previously hidden from the Indians, including "all other principles about the creation, the redemption by Christ, etc., wherein also the aged people are pretty expert, by the frequent repetition thereof to the children, and are able to teach it to their children at home, and do so" (*Tracts* 53). Eliot aims to implant not just the proper answers but the entire catechetical mechanism.

We will examine Eliot's third disciplinary procedure—answering Indian questions—in the next section. In the fourth procedure, the praying-town practice of admonition and censure, we can see most clearly a new individual being molded to fit a new collective. Admonition and censure is a public Puritan ritual that takes the place of the private Roman Catholic confessional. It is administered in the presence of the entire congregation and requires a full publication and confession of private sins and doubts by the person admonished. Eliot and Mayhew's *Tears of Repentance* contains a lengthy record of the confessions of Praying Indians before Indian elders and assemblies of fellow converts (*Tracts* 229–60). In an earlier tract, Eliot tells of the public humiliation of one man named Wampoowas, who condemns himself for having beaten his wife, which "in former times . . . was very usual." And he sees to it that the rebellious son of a sachem repents in public by insisting that the sachem openly confess to the sins that gave rise to his son's rebellion (*Tracts* 53–54). Even though the rise of Puritanism may have contributed to the formation of an important variety of early modern paternal rule, it is important to note that the final arbiter of discipline was the congregation, not the father, and that "the long-term tendency of Calvinism was to limit the extent of paternal power by setting the family within a larger disciplinary system" (Walzer, *Revolution* 50). By 1673 the Indians have internalized this self-discipline, as Eliot's response to an English questioner shows:

Q: Whether brotherly watch is observed among them according to Matt. 13, etc.

A: Yes it is so, and one is under admonition at this day, yea they are so severe that I am put to bridle them to moderation and forebearance. ("An Account" 125)

This preaching, catechism, encouragement of questioning, and admonition and censure combine to create the melancholic Praying Indian. His appearance is neither incidental nor unexpected, for the Puritan utopist does not just anatomize melancholy—he seeks it out and even produces it. One convert is so deeply affected, Eliot says, that his weeping "forced us also to such bowels of compassion that we could not forbear weeping over him also; and so we parted greatly rejoicing for such sorrowing" (*Tracts* 14). After the public admonition of one of Eliot's servants, Thomas Shepard writes that the man cried so many tears that "the dry place of the wigwam where he stood was bedirtied with them, pouring them out so abundantly. Indians are well known not to be much subject to tears, no not when they come to feel the sorest torture, or are solemnly brought forth to die; and if the Word works these tears, surely there is some conquering power of Christ Jesus stirring among them, which what it will end in at last, the Lord best knows." The Lord knows best, but Shepard has a hunch: he sets this power of the Word to elicit tears in the context of Brightman's interpretation of the Book of Daniel, the return of the Jews to Palestine, the prophecies centering on the year 1650, and "the song of the Lamb" (*Tracts* 60). This is millennial melancholy.

On a somewhat more modest plane, Eliot sees that some of the more "ingenious" Indians are "naturally sad and melancholy (a good servant to repentance), and therefore there is the greater hope of great heart-breakings, if ever God brings them effectually home, for which we should affectionately pray" (*Tracts* 17). Salisbury is no doubt correct to see the Indians' melancholy originating in their loss of their previous collective and individual identities (50). But this melancholy acquired a positive function in the formation of new identities. Public confession and weeping become signs of regeneracy and so a way to praying-town status. Waban tearfully confesses his previous sinful and prideful desire to be a sachem or powwaw, which Eliot takes as a sign of sufficient regeneracy for him to continue as a ruler of fifty, one of the highest political positions in Natick (*Tracts* 231–32). A confession of kingly pride solidifies the alternative power of the godly magistrate.

Enlightenment and the Sachems

Perry Miller's remarkable reconstruction of the intellectual history of colonial New England makes it more difficult to argue that a hostility to secular reason defines the New England mind. By examining New England's intellectual debts to Scholasticism, Humanism, Calvinism, and Ramism, its failure to sense any dire incompatibility between its dogmas and the scientific revolution of the seventeenth century, and its tendency toward a form of rationalism—even in the writings of the most orthodox Puritan theologians—Miller's study helps complicate the Age of Faith/Age of Reason binary retrospectively formulated by the methodizers of enlightenment.

What Miller does not note is that for New England, as for the Puritan Baconians of Commonwealth England, an interest in an advancement of learning went hand in hand with an interest in the millennialist advancement of Christ, and that this intellectual program could help to animate a distinctly nontheoretical social project like Eliot's utopia. Praying-town discipline, which aims both to disenchant this world and to institute the next one, suggests the compatibility of secular enlightenment and theocratic millennialism. The Eliot Tracts have all the occidental fixations of more secular utopian writing. A favorite text for the missionaries (both *The Glorious Progress* and *The Indian Dialogues* use it as an epigraph) is Malachi 1:11: "For from the rising of the sun even unto the going down of the same my name shall be great among the Gentiles; and in every place incense shall be offered unto my name, and a pure offering: for my name shall be great among the heathen, saith the Lord of hosts." Even the titles of the tracts offer a progressive solar plot: *The Day-Breaking, If Not the Sun-Rising of the Gospel with the Indians in New-England; The Clear Sun-shine of the Gospel Breaking Forth upon the Indians in New-England; The Light Appearing More and More towards the Perfect Day.* The anonymous author of the first Eliot Tract, which combines a missionary report in its first half with a report on the founding of Harvard College in its second, links millennialism with an enlightenment idea of progress: "God means to carry his gospel westward, in these latter times of the world . . . as the sun in the afternoon of the day still declines more and more to the west, and then sets; so the gospel (that great light of the world) though it rose in the east, and in former ages hath lightened it with his beams; yet in the latter ages of the world will bend westward, and before its setting brighten these parts with his glorious luster also" (10–11, misnumbered 18–19). Of course, this equation of the gospel with the light of the sun is as old as the prologue to the Gospel of John, and it offers no immediate link to a definition of enlightenment that begins with anticlerical philosophes. But using Bacon's trinity of printing, gunpowder, and the magnet, early modern utopia envisons the universality promised by John's prologue as a geographical and historical possibility. The advancement of Christ goes hand in hand with the advancement of learning and of European conquest.

Consequently, it is no surprise to find in the history of the missions both the language and the goals of enlightenment according to Bacon and Comenius. The parliamentary directive that eventually led to the establishment of the Society for the Propagation of the Gospel in New England (the organization that in its pre- and post-Restoration avatars provided much of the funding for Eliot's utopian missions) links secular and sacred enlightenment in distinctly Baconian language as it orders the preparation of an ordinance "for the encouragement and advancement of learning and piety in New England" (*Tracts* 71). R. F. Young maintains that the first two Indians educated at Harvard College learned Latin from Comenius's *Janua Linguarum Reserata* and that Comenius himself maintained an active interest in their educational progress. Cotton Mather says that Comenius thought New England so auspicious a site for the progress of knowledge that the younger John Winthrop was able to win his tentative agreement to become president of Harvard College, though Comenius later changed his mind (Mather 2.14). Eliot's earliest surviving letter (1633) is also the earliest proposal for the establishment of a college in the Bay Colony; he solicits Sir Simonds D'Ewes for an endowment, saying, "If we nourish not learning, both church and commonwealth will sink" (Everett Emerson 106). Eliot maintained an active correspondence with Robert Boyle, who was for a time president of the society, telling him of such New England natural wonders as a fish kill ("A rare work of God") and new diseases (Boyle 1.ccv). In an early tract Eliot proposes a mutually beneficial exchange of medical knowledge between the Indians and the English, with the former sharing their knowledge of local medicinal herbs and the latter sending over money and teachers of anatomy, thus helping to undermine the Indian reliance on the magic of the powwaws (*Tracts* 56–57). In his *Brief Narrative* of 1671, Eliot proposes a Comenian pansophic project among the Indians:

"And while I live, my purpose is (by the grace of Christ assisting) to make it one of my chief cares and labors to teach them some of the liberal arts and sciences and the way how to analyze and lay out into particulars both the works and word of God, and how to communicate knowledge to others methodically and skilfully, and especially the method of divinity" (23).

But in addition to a positive increase in knowledge, enlightenment requires a critique of idolatrous false knowledge, whether a belief in an anthropomorphic, pastoral nature or a belief in organic monarchy. The Puritans carried out the first stage of their critique of the Algonquian pastoral on a material level in their conquest, division, and enclosure of the Indian "commons" lands: such a divided landscape cannot enshrine a polytheist genius loci. Eliot conducts the second stage of the critique on the more abstract level of theological dialogue.

As we have seen, one of Eliot's four primary disciplinary procedures is answering Indian questions; the other side of getting the Indians to give the right answers to catechism is getting them to ask the right questions. This procedure was by no means without its setbacks, for the Indians often seem more interested in swapping myths than in a Socratic/Christian dialectic whose object is a unified and universal truth. Gookin relates with some distaste a story of his encounter with the mythopoeic savage mind, in the form of the Indians' "diverse and fabulous" myths of origin:

> Some of the inland Indians say that they came from such as inhabit the seacoasts. Others say that there were two young squaws or women, being at first either swimming or wading in the water. The froth or foam of the water touched their bodies, from whence they became with child, and one of them brought forth a male, and the other a female child. And then the two women died and left the earth, so their son and daughter were their first progenitors. Other fables and figments are among them touching this thing which are not worthy to be inserted. These only may suffice to give a taste of their great ignorance touching their original. (*Collections* 146–47)

The very multiplicity of the stories shows the Indians' benighted and degraded state; that at least one of these stories describes a feminine Genesis probably does not help matters much from Gookin's point of view.

We can see implicit clashes between Indian and English religions in some of the questions the Indians ask Eliot. He complains about an early discussion with the tribe of Kutshamakin, in which the Indians ask him about the causes of the thunder, the ebb and flow of the sea, and the wind (*Tracts* 4–5). At times, because Jesus College, Cambridge, did not provide him with a curriculum in natural science, the Indians force Eliot to fall back on an appeal to first causes. When they ask him to explain how it came to pass that "the sea water was salt, and the land water fresh," Eliot can say no more than "'tis so from the wonderful work of God, as why are strawberries sweet and cranberries sour, there is no reason but the wonderful work of God that made them so" (*Tracts* 11).

The most appealing voice of Indian resistance in the Eliot Tracts is that of the "malignant drunken Indian" named George, who hears enough questions and answers about cosmogony and origins to parody them in an irreverent and pointed query: "Mr Eliot ... who made sack? Who made sack?" (*Tracts* 47). In a later incident George constructs another critique of English colonialism by once again inserting into an English symbolic system a scandalously inappropriate but thoroughly English subject matter. Eliot reports that George tried to sell Harvard College what he claimed to be a moose (which he had presumably hunted and skinned), though it was, in fact, a cow rustled from the English in Cambridge (*Tracts* 55). George attacks the English distinction between hunting and husbandry—a distinction between technics with all the ritual importance of that between the Raw and the Cooked. The Eliot Tracts even bring us one brief but fascinating glimpse of the Indians' questioning the antimythological mythology of the English, whose compulsive effort to disenchant the world becomes so obsessive that it reverts to a mythical attack on nature. Eliot reports an unnamed Indian asking him, "Why do Englishmen so eagerly kill all snakes?" (130). While the Indian mythology of polytheism and place distinguishes snakes according to their kinds and their relation to a natural environment, the unified myth of Christian enlightenment conflates all snakes, making them subconscious representations of satanic evil. Eliot does not record his answer.

But despite these resistances, praying-town discipline was quite successful in the long run. George's fellow tribesmen are far enough along in their conversion to ridicule his question about sack and call it "a papoose question" (7). When George is called before an Indian assembly after attempting to sell the skinned cow, he is brought to confess his action, and Eliot presents the whole incident as an instance of "the power of God awing a wicked wretch by this ordinance of admonition" (55). The Indians gradually begin to ask more pedagogically productive questions, such as "How may we come to know Jesus Christ?"

(*Tracts* 4–5). In his record of the examinations of the Natick Praying Indians before their establishment as a self-governing congregation, he records the disappearance of their mythological narratives in favor of the Christian first cause:

> *Q:* How cometh it to pass that the sun riseth and setteth, that there is winter and summer, day and night?
> *A:* All are the work of God. (*Tracts* 281)

Long lists of Indian questions about Christianity constitute much of the Eliot Tracts. Thomas Shepard presents them to his English readers as "part of the whitenings of the harvest" (*Tracts* 47). These lists of questions without answers are the best evidence for the progress of conversion, for they show that "their souls be in a searching condition" (*Tracts* 86).

Though we sometimes encounter the voice of Indian resistance in these questions and even more frequently in the semifictional *Indian Dialogues,* we should not interpret this simply as Indian culture asserting itself despite the best efforts of the Puritans to repress it (Ronda 22). These recorded acts of resistance are also a sign of the power of Puritan writing to contain and rationalize Indian resistances. Again and again *The Indian Dialogues* show the non-Praying Indians (even "King Philip") moving from a perceptive critique of the English to a more or less uneasy acceptance of their religion through the ministrations of Praying Indian missionaries. In these, as in all dialogues, one colloquist has the last word. Stephen Greenblatt's analysis of the compulsion to record Indian questions in a sixteenth-century English exploration narrative is also relevant to the Indian questions recorded in Puritan missionary literature: "The recording of alien voices, their preservation in Harriot's text, is part of the process whereby Indian culture is constituted as a culture and thus brought into the light for study, discipline, correction, and transformation" ("Bullets" 51). These questions that Eliot records catch the Indians in the process of transformation. One of the Indians poses a question to Eliot that William Empson has indignantly addressed to Milton's God: "If God made Hell in one of the six days, why did God make Hell before Adam sinned?"(*Tracts* 85). Eliot does not bother to record his answer, but that makes no difference: this is a paradox, but one addressed from within Christian dialectic. "Whatever myths the resistance may appeal to, by the virtue of the very fact that they become arguments in the process of opposition, they acknowledge the principle of dissolvent rationality for which they reproach the Enlightenment. Enlightenment is totalitarian" (Horkheimer and Adorno, 6).[10]

Eliot's Puritan version of enlightenment is perhaps most totalitarian in its assault on polytheism. He recounts an early, pre-Natick attempt at conversion: "We knowing that a great block in their way to believing is that there should be but one god (by the profession of the English) and yet this god in many places, therefore we asked them whether it did not seem strange that there should be but one god, and yet this god in Massachusetts, at Connecticut, in Quimipeiock, in Old England, in this wigwam, and in the next everywhere." The Indians do indeed think it strange, and in response, Eliot resorts to the central metaphor for utopian universality: "Whereupon we further illustrated what we said by wishing them to consider the light of the sun, which though it be but a creature made by God, yet the same light which is in this wigwam was in the next also . . . and everywhere at one and the same time the same; much more was it so concerning God" (*Tracts* 7–8). The sun is the means by which nature disenchants itself.

In *The Indian Dialogues* a powwaw appeals to a cultural relativism born of polytheist custom to fend off the rationalizing, totalizing force of Puritan theology: "You tell us of the Englishman's god, and of his laws. We have gods also, and more than they. And we have laws also by which our forefathers did walk, and why should not we do as they have done? To change our gods, and laws, and customs, are great things, and not easily to be obtained and accomplished. Let us alone, that we may be quiet in the ways which we like and love, as we let you alone in your changes and new ways" (87). The English respond to this argument with an anticustomary, antimythological, unified theology. The Indian gods are not local gods with local habitations and names, but universal devils masquerading with the help of Indian names as local gods. The Indians "have ever sat in hellish darkness, adoring the Devil himself for their god" (*New-Englands First Fruits* 1). Eliot accounts for the apparent powers of the Indian powwaws by accusing them of "having fellowship with the old Serpent, to whom they pray, and by whose means they heal sick persons" (Hutchinson 399–400). The Puritans in New England practice a myth criticism like that Milton practices in the second book of *Paradise Lost,* with its parade of fallen angels and its lists of the names they will assume as they take their places in the gentile pantheons.[11]

Thomas Hutchinson quotes a story by Eliot about his trip to Pawtucket in spring 1653. At a Sabbath meeting, seeing a woman wearing around her neck a brass idol that she worshiped as her god, Eliot preaches against idolatry and offers her a half crown in exchange for it so that he can take it away and destroy it. She refuses; Eliot seizes the idol and gives her a half crown, which she accepts reluctantly. But when he leaves the village, "the woman girt up her loins and ran after me; when I perceived it, I asked her whither she went, she answered, whither I went, and she would not leave me so long as I had her god about her" (397n). An Indian idolatry that locates God in a single material object contiguous with its worshiper refuses to be bought off by an English idolatry of half crowns, which sees its currency like its God as a medium of universal exchange. Eliot returns with her to the village, enlists the support of Praying Indian allies there, smashes the idol, and blames its presence on Pawtucket's contact with northern Indians contaminated by idolatrous French papists.

But the foremost weapon in the Puritans' epistemological conquest of the Algonquians is printing, the first person of Bacon's technological trinity. Kenneth M. Morrison writes, "The Indians could not integrate themselves into the mainstream of Massachusetts-Bay life because they were a people without a written history" (88). Whether or not the distinction between cultures with writing and cultures without is so absolute, Puritan rhetoric certainly made much of the division. Cotton Mather ridicules the Algonquians' language and juxtaposes their lack of reading and writing with their lack of "any traditions worthy of our notice" (1.559). After reviewing the various historical theories of the Indians' origin, Gookin decides that the investigation cannot move beyond conjecture: because the Indians are "ignorant of letters," they have no history. Further, he suggests that "the changing of the language of a barbarous people, into the speech of a more civil and potent nation that have conquered them, hath been an approved experiment, to reduce such a people unto the civility and religion of the prevailing nation." He proposes that this experiment be performed upon the Indians as it should have been upon the Irish (*Collections* 146, 221–22).

But like his anthropology, Eliot's linguistics attempts to bridge the gap between the Algonquians and the English. His answer to the linguistic conflict between the two cultures is still English domination, but he proposes a domination through the rationalizing utopian technics of historical linguistics, grammar, and translation, not through forced imposition of English. Responding in 1664 to Robert Boyle's request for a grammar of the Indian language, Eliot suggests a reduction much different from Gookin's: "My purpose is, if the Lord will and that I do live, to set upon some essay and beginning of reducing this language unto rule; though there be corners, and anomalities full of difficulty to be reduced under any stated rule, as yourself know better than I, it is [so] in all languages" (Boyle 6.510). The product of this reduction was *The Indian Grammar Begun* (1666). Here Eliot subjects the Algonquian tongue to analysis in tables of declension and conjugation. He says that this grammar was itself made possible by an earlier reduction: "I taught our Indians first to lay out a word into syllables, and then according to the sound of every syllable to make it up with the right letters. . . . They quickly apprehended and understood this epitome of the art of spelling, and could soon learn to read" (*Grammar* 250–51).

Eliot's returning the Indians' own language to them in this fashion recalls the apparent paradox of his setting up fixed plantations for them on their own ancestral lands. Just as he transformed the Indian lands into a utopian site through enclosure and written contract, so he transforms the Indian language into a different language by reducing it into syllables and reassembling it in writing. Just as that transformation reproduced English civil space on the Algonquians' lands, so this one reproduces the English Scriptures in their language. The very movement into English characters implies a contract: in return for the English utopian technics of writing and print, the Indians are obliged to enter into a program of writing and reading by using the translated catechisms and Scriptures and by teaching others to read and write. Given this implied contract, it seems more than a coincidence that Eliot's two paradigmatic verbs in *The Indian Grammar* are *wadchanonat* (to keep) and *paummuonat* (to pay), and that the latter is a loan word from English (*Grammar* 275; Williams 181).

We can glimpse the historical aspect of Eliot's reduction of the Algonquian tongue in one of his offhand grammatical comparisons: Algonquian nouns are not "varied by cases, cadencies, and endings: herein they are more like to the Hebrew" (255). In "The Learned Conjectures" he writes, "It seemeth to me, by the little insight I have, that the grammatical frame of our Indian language cometh nearer to the Hebrew, than the Latin or Greek do" (19). *Reduction* is literally a historical "leading back": an attempt to trace the Algonquian language back to its Hebrew roots.[12] Eliot's interest in the origins of Algonquian is closely related to his interest in the utopian reunification of the world, for the world's diverse polities and its tongues originated at the same moment in the chaos at Babel. A universal paternal government (such as existed before Nimrod and will exist again under the millennial reign of Christ and God the Father) is possible only if there is a universal language, and this universal language can be restored only after man has submitted himself to a dialectical history of linguistic multiplication, dispersion, and reunification. After God's curse of linguistic multiplicity, Nimrod's followers "were necessitated not only to be quiet from the great diversions that were among them, because they could not understand each other's language, but now they were by a divine hand prepared to be sent out with quietness into all parts of the earth, to possess, and subdue the same" ("Conjectures" 10). The Old Testament katabasis of linguistic and cultural dispersal is a prerequisite to the imminent millennial anabasis.

At the conclusion of world history, the original unifying language of the world, Hebrew, will be restored to all men. In a letter of 1663 to Richard Baxter, Eliot praises Hebrew because it is capable of an infinite multiplication of words: "It had need be so, for being the language which shall be spoken in heaven, where knowledge will be so enlarged, there will need a spacious language." Hebrew seems to be the linguistic analogue of the infinitely expandable form of government Eliot works out in *The Christian Commonwealth*; in the long run it may be that the Algonquians along with the rest of the world can be restored to their linguistic birthright. In the meantime we should "make ready for Heaven in this point" by establishing Hebrew as a universal language on earth, and Eliot proposes Hebrew as an alternative to [Walter?] Charleton's proposal of a universal language in symbols. This return to Hebrew can even be part of a pansophic project in which "all arts and sciences in the whole encyclopaedia" will be translated into Hebrew, leaving out "all paganish and profane truth" so that "all the world would become a divine college" (Baxter, *Reliquiae* 293–95). Here Eliot seems to be proposing a version of the philosophical project called "encyclopaedia" or "technologia": the Puritan intellectual's attempt to reconstruct God's necessarily unified and rational scheme for the universe by using Ramist logic as a program to methodize and unify all the seemingly disunified arts and sciences. Perry Miller discusses the formulation of this project in the writings of such Ramists as Frederic Beurhusius, William Ames, and Alexander Richardson, noting the important part it played in the intellectual life of American Puritanism (*Seventeenth Century* 160–80). Eliot brings out what is only implicit in Miller's analysis: the potential this program in Puritan enlightenment has for coalescing with millennial expectations.

Of more immediate interest to Eliot is the practical utopian technic of linguistic universality: translation. Translation is "a sacred and holy work" (*Tracts* 121), and as Jehovah is the translatable god, so he is, in a sense, the god of translation. One of Kutshamakin's tribesmen asks Eliot if the English god can understand prayers in Algonquian. Eliot's first response, of course, is to assure him that he can (*Tracts* 5–6). His long-term response was *The Indian Bible,* finally printed in 1663 after Eliot's long years learning the language, questioning Indians about vocabulary in order to find Indian equivalents for biblical idioms, and corresponding with England to get a press, printer, additional type, and funding.

The transformability of the English religion into Scripture and this Scripture's translatability into any language are central to Eliot's reorganization and conversion of the Indians. In *The Indian Dialogues* Eliot allows an unconverted Indian "Kinsman" to deliver an unusually straightforward and persuasive critique of English religious ideology: "May we not rather think that English men have invented these stories to amaze and fear us out of our old customs, and bring us to stand in awe of them, that they might wipe us of our lands, and drive us into corners, to seek new ways of living, and new places too? And be beholding to them for that which is our own, and was ours, before we knew them?" (71). This opposition of Indian custom to English custom masked by religious ideology might have left the Indians and the English at an ethical (though not a military) impasse. But Eliot moves outside English custom as he moves outside purely English civility into the authority of Scripture: "The Book of God is no invention of English men." The written word preceded the conversion of the English, for they were once as ignorant and savage as the Indians themselves, says the converted Indian "Piumbukhous." He tells "Kinsman" that this "book is given to us as well as to them, and it is as free for us to search the Scriptures as for them. So that we may have our instruction from a higher hand, than the hand of man" (71).

Eliot's justification for colonial domination moves beyond the linguistic racism practiced by many of the earlier colonists, who claimed either that the Indians spoke only gibberish or that there were no serious linguistic barriers between them and the Europeans (Greenblatt, "Learning"). In *A Further Accompt* Eliot simply says that, "Their idiom to them is as ours is to us" ("Postscript," n. pag.). On the level of epistemology, this theory of translation erases all cultural hierarchy in an appeal to transcendent meaning. But on the level of social practice—who translates, what is translated and to what end—it becomes another instrument of English domination. Races without written language are to be restored to the fraternity of the Book by a painstaking application of the utopian technics of translation and analytic grammar to their spoken language, but the particular textures and oral traditions of that language evaporate in the process.

Furthermore, the written word will restore the memories of the wandering tribes of Shem and Eber. Eliot's fictional converted Indian Anthony describes the restorative power of writing in an argument recalling that of the Egyptian god Theuth in Plato's *Phaedrus:* "And this is a great benefit to us, to have God's will and word written. For a word spoken is soon gone, and nothing retaineth it but our memory, and that impression which it made upon our mind and heart. But when this word is written in a book, there it will abide, though we have forgotten it. And we may read it over a thousand times, and help our weak memories, so that it shall never be forgotten" (*Dialogues* 139–40). The printed word, which makes possible an exact iteration of Scripture, is an essential part of praying-town discipline, for it reengraves the effaced memories of the Indians and restores them to the course of scriptural history.[13]

Perhaps more surprising, Eliot's utopian thought also includes an enlightenment attack on the anthropomorphism of monarchical rule. The more radical and democratic Puritans in the New World found themselves faced with a peculiar problem: how does such an ideology as radical Puritanism, which has defined itself from its inception by its negation of tyranny and prelacy, define itself in a New World unvisited by tyrants and prelates? Of course, the long history of political and religious controversy in Puritan New England suggests part of the answer: the familiar quarrels reproduced themselves within the Puritan community and its more or less democratic or aristocratic interpretations of Congregationalist church discipline. But another part of the answer lies in the relations between the Puritans and the Indians they encountered, for the English found their only truly monarchical and prelatical antagonists in the remnants of the resisting Algonquian tribal government and religion.

It may be true that in their total conquest of the Indians, the New World Puritans enjoyed a considerable advantage over their English brethren, whose inclinations toward nascent capitalism were opposed by vestigial systems of monopoly and feudal land tenure (Bercovitch, *Jeremiad* 18–19). I myself have argued that Puritan military superiority allowed the colonists to see the North American continent as utopian raw material ripe for molding and the Indians as prepolitical subjects of utopian discipline. But it is also true, however contradictory, that the English Puritans found familiar antagonists in the New World. The Anglican Thomas Morton says that the Algonquians are *"sine fide, sine lege, and sine rege"* (21). But Roger Williams parses their culture differently and with great familiarity in *Key into the Language of the Indians of America:*

| Powwáw | / A Priest |
| Powwaûog | / Priests |

| Sâchim-maûog | / King, Kings |
| Sachimaûonck | / A Kingdom, or Monarchy. (151, 162) |

Priests, not presbyters or ministers; *kings,* not magistrates or judges: just as the Indians' religion is no separate dogma but a benighted form of devil worship, so their civil and church government are merely heathenish monarchy or prelacy.

So far as Eliot stands in as a founding monarch of the praying towns peopled by tractable and educable Indians, his utopias have an internal tendency gradually to supersede his monarchical function through self-government. But so far as Eliot and his allies meet resistance from Algonquian tribal government, his utopian project becomes more actively and externally antimonarchical, for he depicts that resistance as the resistance of tyranny to enlightenment. New England did not so much bypass the European shift between modes of economic and political organization as accelerate that shift. The antimonarchism of the Eliot Tracts is not merely transatlantic sympathy with the struggles of the English saints; the Algonquian sachems and powwaws stand in for the Stuarts and the Anglican prelates.

Eliot's radical Fifth Monarchism invades his missionary reports when he attacks "that Anti-Christian principle for man to be above God, whether the pope in the church, or monarchs in the common-wealth. . . . He that is above the law is above the word; and he that is above the word is above Christ; Christ reigneth not over such as be above his law" (*Tracts* 120). In his missionary work Eliot and his allies also attempted to place "kings" under "the law." Neal Salisbury has shown that the missionaries tried particularly hard to convert the sach-ems, thinking this would bring the conversion of many of their follow-ers. But Puritan political ideology was as much at work as was practical evangelism. Gookin says of the Algonquians, "Their government is generally monarchical, their chief sachem or sagamore's will being their law" (*Collections* 154). Gradually the sachems discovered the full political implications of Protestant conversion: "At length the sachems did discern, that religion would not consist with a mere receiving of the word; and that practical religion will throw down their heathenish idols, and the sachem's tyrannical monarchy" (209).

Eliot uses a familiar critique of monarchy when describing the sachems' opposition to his missionary work: "They plainly see that religion will make a great change among them, and cut them off from their former tyranny; for they used to hold their people in an absolute servitude, insomuch as whatever they had, and themselves too were at his command; his language was, as one said, *omne meum;* now they see that religion teaches otherwise, and puts a bridle upon such usurpations." Previously, Eliot says, the sachems extorted money from their people by tyrannical force, but "now if their sachem so rage," the Praying Indians respond with industrious Puritan piety: "Instead of seeking his favor with gifts (as formerly), they will admonish him of his sin; tell him that is not the right way to get money, but he must labor, and then he may have money; that is God's command" (*Tracts* 139). In the conquest of New England, as in the conservative polemics in Commonwealth England, antimonarchical freedom is a matter more of property rights than of natural rights; the praying-town citizen is a possessive individualist.

Eliot presents the encounter between the democratizing gospel and the Indian monarchy in a more idealized form in his *Indian Dialogues.* Here, four years before "his" war, a fictionalized King Philip enters into discussions with William and Anthony, two Praying Indians. After assuring Philip that there is no necessary conflict between what belongs to Caesar and what belongs to God—that he need fear no diminution of his *rightful* political authority under Christianity—they hedge their promise by telling him that even if his conversion should bring the defection of non-Praying Indians from his tribe, he will gain new allies in the other Praying Indians and the English. Philip sounds like an English prelate or presbyter when he objects to the social implications of congregational church discipline, in which the "poor and rich are equally privileged" and the "vote of the lowest of the people hath as much weight as the vote of the sachem." However, though he complains that "this bringing all to an equality will bring all to a confusion," the two Indian missionaries respond that this levelling is indeed an effect of right worship and must be submitted to (127–28). Sachems are to be subordinate to congregational discipline and may even be admonished. When Philip argues that the new religion will fill his subjects with "new light and notions, which withdraws them from our obedience," William compares him with "a certain people who are called Papists" who make similar arguments against the Scriptures

(134–36). Elsewhere, Eliot preaches that sachems must imitate Christ in his rejection of the kingdoms of the world (*Tracts* 141).

The modern editors of *The Indian Dialogues* show a remarkable empathy with Eliot here: "The preacher reminds Philip that Christianity is indeed a leveler among men because God is no respecter of persons. This must have struck the proud chieftain the same way it has threatened aristocracies around the world in all ages, but the missionary is firm. In religion sachems enjoy no privileged status, although salvation does not threaten their political role (Bowden and Ronda 48–49). The editors seem to share in Eliot's enlightenment vision of a universal struggle between tyranny and right reason. But to say that Christianity does not threaten established political forms is a claim that not even Eliot and Gookin would have made; certainly the death of King Philip four years later would seem to indicate otherwise.

Horkheimer and Adorno's discussion of enlightenment's attitude toward science is also relevant to its political philosophy: "For enlightenment is as totalitarian as any system. Its untruth does not consist in what its romantic enemies have always reproached it for: analytical method, return to elements, dissolution through reflective thought; but instead in the fact that for enlightenment, the process is always decided from the start. . . . In the anticipatory identification of the wholly conceived and mathematized world with truth, enlightenment intends to secure itself against the return of the mythic" (24, 25). And fails. The instinctive Puritan classification illuminates the structure of revolutionary Puritan discipline, suggesting that it is a version of enlightenment in which prelacy and monarchy function not as superseded precursors but as structurally necessary antagonists. This capacity to fit an antagonist into a universal frame of reference is no less necessary for Eliot in his relatively peaceful utopian project than for the white conquerors of King Philip's War. Part of the remarkable imaginative power of enlightenment is its ability to recognize its mythical enemy wherever it goes. The final conflict with this enemy is always, and necessarily, deferred. But the binary opposition itself has the present function of authorizing certain "rationalizing" projects in the hinterlands. As the thoroughly solar political rhetoric of the 1980s reminds us, enlightenment is able to conceptualize all local or North-South conflicts as mere manifestations of a universal and underlying East-West conflict.

In *The Christian Commonwealth* Eliot turns his praying-town experiment with the congregational disciplining of sachems into a model utopia promising revolution-torn England a complete democratic transformation that will protect it against the return of any sachemic rule except that of King Jesus. Eliot's New World utopian practice becomes a mirror reflecting a modified vision of enlightenment back to its Old World source.

Practice to Theory: *The Christian Commonwealth*

The Christian Commonwealth: Or, The Civil Policy of the Rising Kingdom of Jesus Christ inhabits a utopian site seldom trodden even during the political and religious migrations of the Interregnum: the crossroads of theocracy and democracy, of a strict biblical literalism and a radically popular political program based on near-universal manhood suffrage. The radical implications of Eliot's political thought remained more or less hidden to his contemporaries so long as he took "savages" as the object of his experiment in regenerative anthropology. But when he took the entire English nation as the object of an experiment in millennial political organization, he came into conflict with opponents who could write back, and his political radicalism became apparent. Eliot turns the results of his western experiment in antimonarchical civility into political theory for the benefit of the English Israelites, who threaten to turn back to a Stuart Pharoah or turn aside to some King Saul of a Lord Protector.

Eliot's radicalism has received little notice from his biographers. Cotton Mather has the excuse of English censorship. A long passage in his 1691 biography of Eliot describes Eliot's denunciation of Anglican prayers and rituals. Mather excised it when he included the biography in his *Magnalia Christi Americana,* which was published in London (Smith). But Convers Francis, who faced no such censorship when writing his biography of 1836, finds it difficult to credit the Restoration denunciations of *The Christian Commonwealth* as "seditious," even though he himself lacks a copy of the tract (215). Even with a copy, Ola E. Winslow comments, "The word 'seditious' applied to gentle John Eliot is occasion for a later smile" (197).[14]

One of Eliot's first public actions in the Bay Colony, however, was a challenge to established executive authority. After Governor Thomas Dudley and his advisers undertook the Pequot Treaty of 1634 on their own authority alone, Eliot denounced them from his pulpit in Roxbury, saying that they should first have obtained the consent of the people. This boldness quickly brought Eliot a delegation of his fellow ministers, including John Cotton, Thomas Hooker, and Thomas

Weld, who admonished him and gained his retraction. The Eliot Tracts themselves are full of at least general attacks on monarchy and blessings on the work of the revolutionary saints. And as we have seen, Eliot and his allies see their missionary work as part of a unified enlightenment project in antimonarchical regeneration. In *The Christian Commonwealth* Eliot attempts explicitly to fit England into this project.

Since Philip F. Gura's recent study of Puritan radicalism in New England, it has become easier to rethink the relation between the New England tradition of conservative, nonseparating Congregationalism, which Perry Miller saw defining the New England mind, and the Separatists, radical spiritists, "anabaptists," and millenarians it came into conflict with. Gura shows the New England way was not just a logically unified orthodoxy excluding a host of peripheral heresies and heretics, but a complex ideological system that helped generate those heresies and was shaped by them in turn. John Eliot's career as both the pious pastor of Roxbury and the radical millenarian author of *The Christian Commonwealth* shows clearly the tensions inhabiting the New England way.

Eliot wrote the tract in 1651 or 1652, in the closing days of the Commonwealth. J. F. Maclear speculates that Eliot may have entrusted the tract to the Fifth Monarchist and accused antinomian William Aspinwall, who sailed from New England to England in 1653 (254).[15] Whoever Eliot's English agent or correspondent was, he delayed publication until 1659. After Oliver Cromwell's death in September 1658 and the coup by the General Council that essentially overthrew his son Richard, England was possessed by a frantic search for a political settlement that was not unlike the one holding sway when Eliot had written, and his utopia joined the flood of millenarian, army, Harringtonian, and Presbyterian platforms of government issuing from the presses (Woolrych). But the "Server of the Season" who takes credit for having brought Eliot's tract to print was no server of Eliot; his tyrannicidal rhetoric was bold enough in 1652 but almost suicidal in October 1659, only seven months before Charles Stuart landed at Dover.

Another result of its delayed publication was that the political debate that had provided its rhetorical point of departure—the Engagement Controversy—had long since disappeared. On October 11, 1649, acting in response to the Levellers, who had been questioning the popular basis of the political authority of Parliament, the Rump passed a resolution entitled "Resolves of the Parliament Touching the Subscribing to an Engagement." The resolution called upon all men of influence in England (later, all men whatsoever) to swear that they were "true and faithful to the Commonwealth of England, as it is now established, without a king or house of lords" (Wallace, *Destiny* 48). The controversy generated outlived the political influence of the Levellers, who were already in decline. John Wallace and Perez Zagorin have chronicled the course of this debate, which was conducted in a series of pamphlets by such Engagers as Anthony Ascham, Francis Rous, and John Dury, and such anti-Engagers, or Nonscribers, most Presbyterian, as William Prynne and Edward Gee the elder (Wallace, "Controversy"; Zagorin, *History* 62–78, 121–31). The controversy was of great scope, attracting writers as diverse as Gerrard Winstanley in his *England's Spirit Unfoulded* (Aylmer) and (Quentin Skinner has argued) Thomas Hobbes in *Leviathan*.

The Engagers argued that there is no absolute distinction between the possession of political power and the right to exercise that power, and that a subject might respect the office rather than the person holding it, rightly obeying even a usurper when he exercises power according to constitutional tradition. The Nonscribers refused to sign what they saw as an unlawful social contract undercutting England's traditional monarchy and their own loyalty to the rightful heir of the executed king, both of which were formalized in the still binding *Solemn League and Covenant* of 1643. Wallace examines this controversy from the point of view of a new casuist articulation of the loyal subject's relation to political power. In 1654, after the Protectorate's consolidation of power, the resolution was repealed as a needless irritant, but the theoretical discussions of power, contract, and right it had prompted were to come in handy at the Restoration and again in 1688 *(Destiny)*.

Eliot entered (or thought to enter) the debate obliquely, criticizing and adopting arguments of Engager and Nonscriber alike from the perspective of his own peculiar utopian radicalism. He writes explicitly in response to Edward Gee's *Plea for Non-Scribers* (1650), an important attempt to refute the arguments for Engagement. Eliot wastes no time in declaring his radical credentials, for he dedicates his utopia to "the chosen, and holy, and faithful who manage the wars of the Lord against Antichrist in Great Britain" (*Commonwealth* 129). But he quickly moves beyond such saintly name-calling into a more sophisticated political arguement. He begins by chastizing the Engagers, who numbered among them many of his once-and-future missionary supporters and the authors of introductions and appendixes for the Eliot

Tracts, including Dury, Stephen Marshall, and Joseph Caryl. Though it distresses him to see Gee writing against the recent "glorious work of the Lord Jesus in casting down Antichrist, and setting up his own kingdom foretold in Scripture," still his arguments are more firmly grounded than are those of the Engagers. In the entire controversy over political authority, the Engagers "have so missed the principles on which the cause standeth . . . as that the answerers have clearly the upper grounds of them in many things" (129–30). Like Gee, Eliot utterly rejects the idea that right follows in some sense from the de facto possession of power. Conservative Presbyterian and radical Congregationalist come together in their insistence that all proper political power has its basis in the actual consent of the governed, even though Gee opts for a social contract underlying the Stuart monarchy and Eliot proposes a radically new social contract with its roots in the ancient Hebrew commonwealth.

Zagorin actuely observes that Gee's arguments (in other tracts) against the Rump are in some ways more democratic than the arguments for the Engagement by the Rump's apologists (*History* 77). In *A Plea for Non-Scribers* Gee writes that it is "a great wonder to us" that the Rump, while claiming that all power comes originally from the people and that Parliament does no more than represent this power, nonetheless insists that when it comes time to establish a government, "it should be these men's part to found and constitute it, the people's only to receive, submit, and engage homage to it: by this means (in the first act or being of government), the channel communicates to the spring, the branch to the root, the superstructure to the foundation" (61). Gee argues, reasonably enough, that the Rump may be the prevailing party without being the people's party.

Gee, however, pushes his critique of the Rump even further, in an antidemocratic direction reminiscent of John Cotton's query, "If the people be governors, who shall be governed?" Gee says that "a political self-created power is like an idol, that is, nothing in the world, a mere nullity, it is without all legitimation or warrant." Such a power is a logical absurdity because the "same persons cannot be the creator and the creature, the conveyor and receivers of dominion" (28). As we have seen, the logical absurdity that Gee sees here is the center of Eliot's utopian discipline, which aims at making all persons with the franchise both the conveyers and the receivers of dominion, both the creators of the individual rulers of the praying towns and the creatures of praying-town discipline. All the same, Eliot does not explicitly contradict Gee's logic of dominion as do, for example, the Levellers, with their appeal to natural rights and the human capacity for self-fashioning. Instead, Eliot makes a theocratic appeal to a prior authority: "No oaths or convenants of God's people are against Christ, but in subordination to him, and to the advancement of his kingdom. If, therefore, these great changes are carried up to that head, that is the true scope and end of those vows and promises. It were not lawful to terminate such a vow or convenant as that is upon any person, family, or creature. It were idolatry; nor was it so, nor is it now broken, by breaking all creatures in pieces that stood in the way of obtaining the true end thereof, namely, the advancement of the Lord Jesus, and his kingdom" (*Commonwealth* 140–41). Eliot picks up Gee's critique of idolatry (one of the seventeenth century's most portable rhetorical figures) and moves it toward an iconoclastic defense of tyrannicide.

To understand the peculiar originality of Eliot's utopia and the reason a millenarian tract should be considered a utopia in the first place, we should first consider what it shares with the Fifth Monarchist millennialism of its own day. At least two of Eliot's contemporaries linked his tract to the Fifth Monarchists (Winslow, plate 11; Hubbard 575). Eliot's bookseller was Livewell Chapman, the leading publisher of Fifth Monarchist tracts. Since Maclear's excellent study of New England millennialism, the connection between the Fifth Monarchists of the Old World and the New World has become much clearer. Eliot's fear of the threatened secular predominance of Cromwell and the Rump Parliament was common among the Fifth Monarchists, who viewed them (and later the Protectorate) as a usurpation of Christ's political power on earth. Nonscribers with a vengeance, the Fifth Monarchists attacked the Protectorate furiously. B. S. Capp quotes the retort of Anna Trapnel to a Protectorate soldier who was questioning her: "The Lord Protector we own not; thou art of the army of the Beast" (133).

More important than these external links, however, are the rhetoric and the formal structure of Eliot's work. The first part of his theoretical and polemical preface is ruled by biblical apocalyptic, particularly by the Fifth Monarchists' favorite text, the Book of Daniel. Eliot begins with a typological reading of the confused state of English politics, comparing it to "black and confused clouds," in whose confusion nonetheless "they whose eyes the Lord hath begun to open, to see Christ coming in power and in great glory, according to his promise, do also see the other part of his word verified, namely, that the coming of Christ is in the clouds of darkness" (*Commonwealth* 129).

Eliot follows the Fifth Monarchists in his entirely conventional reading of the second chapter of Daniel. Here Daniel interprets Nebuchadnezzar's dream of a great idol made of gold, silver, brass, and iron, with feet of iron mixed with "miry clay." Nebuchadnezzar sees a great mountain strike the idol upon its composite feet, bringing it to ruin. Daniel reveals that the various metals represent various earthly kingdoms and the destruction of the idol their destruction by the coming kingdom of God. Eliot calls this dream and interpretation "an epitome of all the monarchies, governments, and polities of men who have had their human glory in this world." The feet of mixed iron and clay represent Roman Catholic Europe, in which "that dirty Roman religion" is contaminated even further by its mingling with civil powers based in human reason, not Scripture (131). It seems that these shaky feet have taken a stand in Britain, too, for "the faithful brethren in Scotland gave the first blow at the dirty toes and feet of this image" (132). Since the iron of the civil state sticks fast to the miry clay of prelacy, they must fall together.

In *A Brief Description of the Fifth Monarchy* William Aspinwall identifies the reign of Charles I with the fourth monarchy and goes on to predict that "the uttermost durance of Antichrist's reign, will be in the year 1673, as I have proved from Scripture in a brief chronology, ready to put forth" (16). But Eliot does not attempt to prophesy, forgoing any precise periodization of kingdoms based on the metals of the idol or the chronology of future events. Even though such calculations are worthwhile, they would be "a work rather for a treatise than a preface" (*Commonwealth* 132). For Eliot the millennial passages in Jewish and Christian apocalyptic have no more than a negative function. They signify the appearance of *room* for a utopian practice: "The prayers, the expectations, and faith of the saints in the prophecies and promises of holy Scripture, are daily sounding in the ears of the Lord, for the downfall of Antichrist, and with him all human powers, polities, dominions, and governments; and in the room thereof, we wait for the coming of the kingdom of the Lord Jesus" (130).

The waiting that Eliot proposes, however, is far from passive, and it is here that we can begin to see Eliot's millenarian tract move toward utopia. The room created in England by the downfall of the Stuarts is the Old World equivalent of the anthropological tabula rasa of Massachusetts, and it demands a corresponding utopian project to inscribe it with a new polity. Eliot proposes a large-scale repetition of that organization of the praying towns he has already determined experimentally to be possible. Eliot offers this utopian tract with a double authority: the scriptural authority of Exodus and Daniel and the empirical authority of his work in the praying towns. Even as early as 1652, *The Christian Commonwealth* is a distinctly American hybrid: a cross between millennialism and empiricism, ready for export to the unenlightened.

As he moves into his positive proposal, Eliot begins with Socratic false modesty, demurring that he is "no statesman, nor acquainted with matters of that nature, but only spend my time in the study of the holy book of God." But he cannot help noticing certain similarities between the situations of the Indians and the English. In New England he encountered the "poor, blind, and dark Indians" who "desired to leave their wild and scattered manner of life and come under civil government and order." Their anomie put them in a state of remarkable utopian potentiality, for only in such a state of political shapelessness can one choose an ideal polity unconstrained by human nature. Eliot vowed to the Lord that "they being a people without any form of government, and now to choose, I would endeavor with all my might to bring them under the government of the Lord only" (135).

Similarly, "England being in a capacity to choose unto themselves a new government, and in such deep perplexity about that great question, where to set their foot in peace," they have turned in desperation to the Babel of gentile political forms and "have wearied themselves with differences" (138).[16] England must turn to a scriptural pattern instead; otherwise, "we should derogate from the sufficiency and perfection of the Scriptures" (134). Seeing Eliot's scriptural model, they "will gladly all concur together to set open the door to let in the Lord Jesus . . . who hath been all this while knocking" (138). To those participants in the Engagement Controversy ransacking feudal law and constitutional theory to determine rights, duties, and precedents, Eliot offers the simplifying and unifying power of utopian Scripture: "It is the holy Scriptures of God only that I do urge to be your only Magna Charta, by which you should be ruled in all things; which being, Christ is your king and sovereign lawgiver, and you are his people ruled by him in all things" (140). The scriptural Magna Charta is to be found not in the cryptic passages of Old and New Testament apocalyptic and prophecy, but in the modest proposals of Jethro for a government of tens, fifties, hundreds, and thousands.

Eliot has irreproachable precedents for his system. The Hebrews, of course, chose such a polity for themselves. But there is also evidence that "the angels of heaven are governed by this order of government, according as it is appliable to their condition." This is no more than one would expect, for "as hell is a place of confusion, so heaven of order" (136). Because the number of angels in heaven is so great, Eliot theorizes that heaven's polity is formed according to multiples of a thousand: 10 thousands, or myriads, are the smallest grouping, followed by 50 thousands, 100 thousands, and millions. When Christ comes to judge, his army of saints will queue up in such ranks. He even dropped numerical hints of this while on earth: "It is not nothing that when Christ fed the people miraculously, he set them down by hundreds, and by fifties (Mark 6:40) as if Christ delighted in that order" (137n). Eliot is no less inclined than the prophetic millenarians to see the Scriptures through numerological glasses, but he searches to find evidences of political order, not secret correspondences and prophecies.

Eliot's ideal state is unquestionably a theocracy. The dispossessed Prince Charles is not the rightful heir to the throne, but one of a long line of usurpers. Eliot advises his readers to "set the crown of England upon the head of Christ, whose only true inheritance it is, by the gift of his father. . . . Let him be your judge, let him be your lawgiver, let him be your king! . . . Be not behind in bringing Christ to the throne of England!" (139, 141). But as we have seen, *theocracy* is the name of a political rhetoric, not a form of government. The Fifth Monarchists' appeals to theocracy give them a way to avoid the opprobrium of any association with democratic ideals even while they attack the Stuarts and Cromwell as monarchical pretenders. Their pleas to let Christ rule function within a monarchical rhetoric of precedent and hierarchy as an antimonarchical rhetoric of revolution. But this by no means implies that Fifth Monarchist radicalism is necessarily democratic. Capp observes that in keeping with their Calvinist backgrounds, the Fifth Monarchists generally advocated an oligarchic dictatorship of the regenerate over the unregenerate (138). Aspinwall, for instance, questions Parliament's claim to the delegated power of the people by asking whoever gave the people such power in the first place (9–10).

Eliot's utopia is a remarkable Fifth Monarchist work, for while it never appeals to any overtly democratic principles—neither to theories of traditional or ancient liberties nor to the Leveller theory of natural rights—still it describes the foundation of a thoroughly democratic state. Millennial theocracy can also be democratic because, for Eliot, Christ is virtually present on earth when men are governed by his laws alone: "His kingdom is then come amongst us, when his will is done on earth, as it is done in heaven" (*Commonwealth* 131). This Christ is the supreme example of the *rex absconditus,* "who by his divine wisdom, power, government, and laws, given us (although hitherto sealed up in a great measure) in the holy Scriptures, will reign over all the nations of the earth in his due time . . . not only in church government and administrations but also in the government and administration of all affairs in the commonwealth" (130). Civil administration is not a mutable matter left by God to take different forms for different men at different times. Its ideal form has been hidden in Exodus all along, in all its mathematical rigidity. All Christ requires is a methodical exegete who will break the seals and reveal, not the threat of apocalyptic retribution, but the bureaucratic organization of Jethro's judges.

In chapters 1 and 2, Eliot defines the electoral subjects who will be the building blocks of his utopia. His definition of the franchise is, for all practical purposes, the same as that of Harrington and the Levellers (Thomas, "Levellers"). All economically self-sufficient males are entitled to vote. Women, children, and "servants, or sons living with their parents, as in the condition of servants" are all "virtually comprehended in their father's convenant" (Eliot, *Commonwealth* 145–46). Eliot's theocratic democracy is composed of numerous small paternal states.

Each qualified male heading a household may come together with a group of nine of his choosing, for "God hath commanded that ten men should choose unto them a ruler of ten. . . . By that one act of choosing his ruler of ten and subjecting himself unto him, he doth choose, and subject himself unto all the superior orders, under whom his ruler of ten is ruled" (145–46). In this initial choice we can see two aspects of Eliot's unacknowledged democratic leanings. First, he answers Gee's question about how one can be both the creator and the object of dominion, for this first choosing generates all subsequent power and simultaneously obliges the individuals choosing their ruler of ten to obedience. Michael Walzer remarks, "Social discipline was the purpose of Eliot's system, in which a tenth of all adult males (excluding servants, a category he seemed to define very narrowly) would become magistrates. Strange utopia which needed so many governors!" (*Revolution* 232). This is indeed utopian but not so very strange, since the ideal of utopian government is a movement away from a single system of hierarchized sovereignty to a universal distribution of political power. Walzer even underestimates the total number of governors: under Eliot's system of congregational political discipline, every man is the governor of every other man and of himself.

Second, it gives us yet another example of Eliot's lifelong and seemingly unconscious democratic misreading of Exodus. (We will see that James Harrington misreads the same passage in the same way to much the same end.) Jethro clearly tells Moses to *appoint* the rulers of the various groupings: "Thou shalt provide out of all the people able men, such as fear God . . . and place such over them, to be rulers of thousands, and rulers of hundreds, rulers of fifties, and rulers of tens." Eliot blithely transfers the monarchical authority of Moses to the people as a whole, allowing them a self-interested middle voice to "choose unto them a ruler." Even in the praying towns Eliot transfers the appointive power of Moses to the Praying Indians. It seems that he sees Moses' monarchical authority passing into Scripture after his death and becoming relatively democratized. Anyone willing to submit himself to scriptural discipline acquires a certain measure of political power in turn.

From this first election, all others follow. The ruler of ten joins with four others like himself to choose a ruler of fifty, this ruler with another like himself to choose a ruler of one hundred, this ruler with nine others to choose a ruler of one thousand. Eliot also attempts to build in the capacity for a numerical individuality: the ruler of ten may rule over as many as nineteen; the ruler of fifty, as many as nine orders of ten; the ruler of a hundred, as many as three orders of fifty; and the ruler of one thousand, as many as nineteen orders of one hundred. But like the family grouping of More's Utopia, these groups must split up and regroup when they reach their maximum permissible size.

In chapter 3 Eliot adds a temporal element to this biblical structure, setting his commonwealth into judicial motion. He decides that the rulers of ten should have their courts of eleven every week, the rulers of fifty their courts of six every month, the rulers of one hundred their courts of three every three months, and the rulers of one thousand their courts of eleven twice yearly. This schedule allows a prompt and regular ascent of appeals form court to court; speedy justice, a perennial ideal in early modern utopia, is the backbone of the Christian Commonwealth. Eliot's orrery of justice presents neither pure state determinism nor unfettered voluntarism, but a contractual machine bringing together free political assent and bound judicial ascent.

The entire mechanism of decentralized political authority is Jethro's answer to Moses' inability to handle all the cases of the people. It corrects the structural deficiencies of monarchy, the "overburdensomeness of the work of government" for one man. But even after the formation of this judicial bureaucracy, Moses finds that the extraordinary cases brought to him still make an excessive demand on his time. God's solution is to found the Sanhedrin, a group of seventy elders whom Moses picks out and whom God invests with Moses' spirit. But for Eliot this only compounds the problem of Moses' monarchy with the problem of a divinely ordained oligarchy, for the model of the Sanhedrin was the classic Presbyterian precedent for models of oligarchic church and civil government. Eliot has a democratic solution: the people as a whole are to take over God's function and elect a chief ruler equivalent to Moses and a Supreme Council equivalent to the Sanhedrin.

Interestingly, Reverend Eliot specifies that most of the members of this council will be civil elders (153). It will be in perpetual session as the final court of appeal of the land (153–54). Not only does Eliot transfer the appointive authority of God and Moses to the people as a whole, but he does so in such a way that he limits the power of the higher reaches of the courts of three and eleven to become an independent oligarchy at the remove of several electoral levels from the people. In other words, the Christian Commonwealth is a democratic republic, with the people as a whole electing a many, a few, and a one. Eliot goes on to describe the formation of a "Superior Platform" of government that, on the model of angelic government, multiplies the numbers of persons in the single platform by one thousand; but I will abbreviate his discussion here because, as he says with typical self-effacing immodesty, "God's method is plain" (161).

In the Christian Commonwealth, Scripture is both Alpha and Omega: the state is built on strict scriptural principles, but it also contains within its orders an institutional mechanism for defining Scripture and determining precisely what it has to say on a certain law case or political controversy. Any case appealed from one level to a higher and then to a higher is finally decided "when it hath passed the circuit of God's polity, and received its final determination according to the Scriptures, unto which not to submit is capital presumption" (155). The Supreme Council, the highest court of the land, will "search the Scriptures with all faithfulness, to find the pure mind of God, impartially and sincerely to apply the cause propounded thereunto, to declare the will of God in the case, and so return it to the court of eleven whereto it apperaineth" (157). Eliot suggests that "it were a work worthy the labors of the best divines, and the best of men" to submit all the laws of England to this scriptural review (142). Further, the records of the courts' decisions will be carefully recorded and preserved to guide future court decisions and men's behavior (163). There is no need for immediate divine intervention; like the United States Constitution, Scripture in the Christian Commonwealth is to be an authority that constantly adds to and redefines itself.

Eliot's object in his utopia is civil government, but church government is never far from his thoughts. The utopian discipline he proposes is a development of the Congregationalist discipline practiced in the praying towns and in the Bay Colony at large. The exorbitance of Eliot's proposal is that it so confidently pictures the division and the reunification of all England on the model of the individual church congregation. In *The American Jeremiad* Sacvan Bercovitch discusses the Bay Colony theory of church government, of which Eliot's is a variant. The Bay Colony Puritans inherited two antagonistic strains of Puritan thought. The first, which followed in the tradition of the Marian martyrs and exiles, saw England as an elect nation in need of secular reform and loyalty. The second, which followed in the tradition of the English Separatists of the Netherlands and Plymouth, saw England as a depraved nation containing some few elect saints who should band together in small congregations and remove themselves from such depravity. The Bay Colony combined the two strains in its vision of the elect church-state of New England acting as a model for the complete transformation of the civil and church government of all England: "In short, they were children of an improbable mixed marriage—Congregationalists on a historic mission for mankind. . . . They proceeded as though godliness could be truly detected, institutional forms could guarantee eternity, and the covenant of fraternity could be made one with the covenant of heaven" (38, 45). We might say that the Bay Colony participates in the utopian oxymoron of expansive withdrawal: like the praying towns it contained, New England was to be the insular site of an experimental rehearsal for the transformation of England and the world as a whole.

In *Visible Saints* Edmund Morgan argues that the New English Puritans were notorious among their more conservative English allies for believing that their rigorously exclusive congregations of the demonstrably elect had overcome the Augustinian opposition between the invisible church of those saints predestined for salvation and the visible and relatively impure institutional church of gathered communicants. We will see in the next section that Eliot parts company with this New English orthodoxy in some regards, but the orthodoxy's faith in its own institutional procedures for determining election helps explain why Eliot spends so little time discussing the spiritual qualifications of his utopians, moving instead right into their organization in groups. In a moment of unusual Calvinist rigor, he sternly warns that "sin will grow apace, like ill weeds, if it be not always watched," but he moves on directly to suggest an institutional cure for this innate human depravity: weekly meetings to air grievances among the members of the groups of ten (*Commonwealth* 149). He even goes so far as to claim that the individual's citizenship and spiritual regeneracy imply each other, offering an institutional cure for the Puritans' chronic predestinarian anxiety. Proper citizenship will be a civil sign of spiritual election for the English, just as it was for the Indians in the praying towns: "A willing subjection of a man's self to Christ in this covenant is some hopeful sign of some degree of faith in Christ, and love to God; and as a good preparative for a more near approach to Christ in church fellowship and covenant: he that is willing to serve Christ by the polity of the second table civilly is in some degree of preparation to serve him by the polity of the first table ecclesiastically" (144).[17] In a further integration of millennium and utopia, Eliot's Hebraic form of civil government may hasten the millennium by encouraging the Jews to return to England and convert, just as it helped restore the descendants of Shem and Eber to Christendom in the praying towns (136).

Eliot's secularization of Congregationalist church government by mutual surveillance produces his only discussion of utopian space. Each order must "cohabit together as near as may be, because that doth tend to facilitate both the watch and the word of the Lord's government." Everyone changing habitations must first obtain the permission of the rulers of the area he is moving to, "lest by such unstable changes as some may affect, they may slip out from under the government of the Lord, at least from under the watch and use thereof . . . and lest by the confluence of unruly persons to a place more remisly governed, the government of the Lord should be undermined and scandalized" (149). In the Christian Commonwealth, as in More's *Utopia*, there are to be no vagrant populations, "no hiding places, no spots for secret meetings" (More 49). Even in so fundamentally democratic a political system as Eliot's, free persons in free spaces raise the specter of wandering chaos.

Eliot's utopia is quite unlike the encyclopedic utopias of Plato, More, Andreae, Bacon, and Campanella. There is precious little consideration of the texture of life in this state, only a direction for the "well ordering" of religion, commerce, occupations, and education (155). There are no considerations of topography, no verbal diagrams of cities, streets, or houses. Eliot even denies himself a discussion of new codes of punishment (151), a topic dear both to Puritan theocrats such as John Cotton (whose *Moses His Judicials* is a fantasy of Levitical rigor) and to utopists such as More and Campanella. Instead, his utopia depicts a pure, political determinism. His very silence about matters religious, economic, cultural, and scientific indicates that these are merely superstructural and will take care of themselves once the proper political system is in place. The characteristic utopian concern with matters of detail—which in the praying towns turned bodies into disciplinary subjects through the minute organization of new utopian procedures of time and space—becomes here the transformation of bodies into purely electoral subjects who come together in precisely defined and counted groupings, at precisely defined intervals, to elect other groupings and to debate and decide individual cases according to scriptural law. In Eliot's theoretical utopia, the utopian detail of the praying towns survives only as number and timetable.

The key to Eliot's platform of government is its easy expandability. It operates, as indeed Eliot's occasionally stultifying prose operates, according to a millennial algebra. It is always open to further expansion, to incorporating larger and larger numbered masses of persons. Its capacity to generate new political structures far exceeds Eliot's ability to visualize precisely what they might do: "The causes which properly belong to the court of five myriads are such as fall out betwixt the parties of the several myriads under them" (161). This is a theoretical utopia whose free-floating abstraction promises the establishment of a unified world government. Eliot ventures that "yea, it seemeth to me, that this is that form of government by which Christ meaneth to rule all the nations on earth according to the Scriptures" (136). He sees Jethro's expanding bureaucracy with all of Nebuchadnezzar's rapture and all of Daniel's sense of millennial totality. In its infinite expandability, he hopes that it will become a political monolith, like "the stone that smote the image," which "became a great mountain, and filled the whole earth."

Retractions, Extinctions, and Transformations

Puritan utopia attempts to produce a universal political transformation through an obsessive attention to social detail. This transformation always lies just outside the reach of the utopist manipulating these details, promising but never delivering their full significance, promising but never allowing their final assembly into the immutable polis or the foursquare New Jerusalem at the end of time. Yet these details themselves and the utopian technics invented to produce and organize them have a surprising longevity. They often outlive the millennial fantasies that call them into existence in the first place.

In a certain sense, Eliot's utopian practice and writing simply ceased at the Restoration. Plans for a millennial reunion of Old and New World Jews, of English and New English saints, suddenly lost their solidity, and the hermeneutical millennialists returned to the books of Daniel and Revelation to recalculate the millennium's date of arrival. The year 1666 seemed a good bet, for it was the sum of one thousand and the number of the beast, and when it arrived, it was accompanied by the portents of the plague and the Great Fire of London. But the human and textual products of Eliot's utopian practice were subject to a more complex afterlife. One of the first results in New England of the Restoration was the suppression of Eliot's utopia. After the vague but violent uprising in January 1661 of Thomas Venner and his English Fifth Monarchists (Venner, like Aspinwall, was a former New Englander), millenarian radicalism fell into particularly low repute (Capp 199–200). In March 1661 the magistrates of the Massachusetts General Court, eager to demonstrate their loyalism, seized upon Eliot's utopia and labeled it "in sundry passages and expressions thereof . . . justly offensive, and in special relating to kingly government in England." They condemned it, directed that all copies be either delivered to the magistrates or destroyed, and ordered Eliot to retract his opinions. This he did, but with a masterful display of truculent equivocation and ambiguous pronoun usage: "I do hereby acknowledge . . . such expressions as do too manifestly scandalize the government of England by king, lords, and commons as antichristian, and justify the late innovators. I do sincerely bear testimony against, and acknowledge it to be, not only a lawful but an eminent form of government. All forms of civil government deduced from Scripture either expressly or by just consequence, I acknowledge to be of God and to be subjected unto for conscience sake. And whatsoever is in the whole epistle or book inconsisting herewith I do at once for all cordially disown" (*Records of the Governor* 5–6). This was evidently enough to satisfy both the court and Eliot's conscience. There could be no more telling evidence than this incident that the utopian discourse of the Puritans is not a hypothetical as-if fiction but a positive speech act with its own materiality: not only does it move out into political life, but when the nature of the political life changes, it must be forced back nearly into nonexistence.[18]

But Eliot, never one to abandon his utopian vision easily, came back in 1665 with his *Communion of Churches,* the ecclesiastical counterpart of his civil utopia. His proposals for the reform of church government are remarkably similar to those he offers for civil government; the main difference is that the various councils and synods he proposes are based not on groups of ten but on "the gospel measuring reed by the number twelve" (6). His earlier attacks on monarchy and kings become attacks on episcopacy and bishops (13,22). The Engagers and Nonscribers of the Engagement Controversy arguing over civil authority become Congregationalists and Presbyterians arguing over church polity. To end this argument, Eliot offers a combination of Congregationalist democracy and Presbyterian unity. He begins with the single, particular, visible congregation (the equivalent of the civil group of ten), which elects two representatives to a council or synod of twenty-four representing twelve congregations. This council in turn elects two representatives to a higher council, and so on, until (with the help of missionaries) the entire world is united under a single democratic church government. Once again, Eliot formulates an organizational solution to a political problem.

He took care to have the tract privately printed in Massachusetts—the first tract printed thus in North America (Winship, *Press* 275). He also took care to ask on the title page that any criticisms of his arguments be referred directly to him and not to any higher authorities. At times he seems to have learned his lesson, for he states clearly that his proposals for church reform have no bearing on civil government. But his utopian enthusiasm for unified authority occasionally gets the better of him: "For God is so well pleased to see his people in order, as that he will dwell in that place, and call it by his own name, *Jehovah-Shammah;* especially when they are civilly as well as ecclesiastically in good order represented before him" (*Communion* 8).

In a transatlantic correspondence lasting twenty-six years, Eliot and Richard Baxter discussed this system (along with other mutual concerns), and Baxter praised it as a model that could at one time have reconciled English Presbyterians and Congregationalists—a matter of some concern during the Protectorate quest for a religious and civil settlement (Woolrych 34–35). But Baxter and Eliot disagree sharply on three points: on the nature of fellowship in the visible particular church, on the nature of baptism, and on the procedures for determining church members and officers. In each case we can see Baxter's anti-utopian insistence on the priority of virtuous individuals over virtuous institutions, and Eliot's utopian insistence on the reverse.

Edmund Morgan notes that in both his missionary work and his theory of church government, John Eliot spent an unusual amount of time for a New England cleric worrying about those sinners outside the church (124). In sharp contrast with both Baxter and the New England orthodoxy, who propose to exclude from church fellowship those who have not yet given clear signs of justification, Eliot argues for a relatively liberal standard of admission to membership in what he calls "reforming parochial assemblies" (Baxter and Eliot 159). Only the "ignorant and profane and scandalous" should be excluded from these assemblies, leaving both the merely civil professors and the visible saints in communion with each other "so as to keep the whole heap of chaff and corn together" (160). Inside this communion the "godly saints" may hold a smaller voluntary communion with their minister, but this communion should also work to benefit those who have not yet given clear signs of justification. Eliot says that this system would be for the English what his praying-town discipline is for the Indians: just as Indian converts are encouraged to become the nuclei of gathered Indian churches rather than separating from their people and joining English congregations, so the visible English saints should continue in their congregations and "keep Sabbath and worship together and the strong help the weak" (159). Indeed, Eliot even proposes a utopian ecclesiastical colonization utterly opposite to the withdrawing and purifying New England way, saying that his ecclesiastical councils should "transplant and remove (in a way of advice and persuasion) godly and fit instruments from one parish to another where they may be of use to reform the parish into a church state" (175). Here we see the utopian priority of institutional over individual virtue: the guarantor of virtue and grace is not the virtuous individual who withdraws into a congregation of those like himself, but the individual parish along with the missionary system that connects it to others that will produce virtuous individuals with a clear sense of spiritual justification.

Second, as opposed to Baxter's claim that baptism is an essentially spiritual ordinance, the seal of an individual's union with the invisible catholic church of the elect, Eliot says that it may be simply a sign of his union with this reforming parochial assembly of those not necessarily elect. Baptism is "a political ordinance," and "as the dispenser, so the party to whom it is dispensed must be in political order, which is only found in visible church state" (173). The baptized person may in time discover signs of God's grace working in him, and so evidence that he is one of the elect, but in the meantime he is part of a visible ecclesiastical order. Just as Eliot's civil government precedes church government, so the political and visible aspect of church government necessarily precedes its spiritual and invisible aspects.

Third, Eliot disagrees with Baxter on the procedures for the choice of church officers and members. On the second page of the *Communion of Churches,* Eliot argues that the people of a congregation have the power to choose church officers. Baxter answers, "More fully and properly the officers have power to call them to be a church. . . . The people never gave that authority which constituteth an officer of Christ" (Baxter and Eliot 160–61). Eliot responds by gently attacking Baxter's notion of a clerical aristocracy: on matters of admission to church fellowship, he says, church officers should consult with the congregation as a whole because "believers are not like ordinary people, they are kings and princes in all lands," adding that "God and man will have more respect to the judgment of a sound believer than of an ungodly officer" (165). In chapter 4, we will see James Harrington's utopian polemic against the consolidation of power by a clerical aristocracy; it is remarkable that we see here a similar polemic coming from one of New England's most revered and outwardly orthodox ministers. But like *The Christian Commonwealth* in England, the *Communion of Churches* had little influence in New England. In response to Baxter's query about the reception of Eliot's tract, John Woodbridge, Jr., of Connecticut writes in 1671 that "truly, sir, I think it better took with himself than with any of his brethren, not because of his pride, I suppose you know him better, but the peculiar cut of his genius; while some were smiling at it, others whispering about it, the book, as I understand, was called in again and now none of them seen walking abroad" (Stearns 578).

When Charles II returned to power in 1660, Parliament voided the act that had set up Eliot's English funding operation. After the more Cromwellian members of that group had been purged and after certain other political maneuverings, it was rechartered under the governorship of Robert Boyle as the Company for Propagacion of the Gospell in New England, or, as it came to be known, the New England Company; it survives to this day in Canada. Eliot reached enough of a reconciliation with the line of Antichrist to allow the dedication of *The Indian Bible* (or at least those few presentation copies sent to England) to King Charles ("Dedications"; Kellaway 41–61).

Though the rhetoric of the Eliot Tracts became less overtly revolutionary Eliot was still capable of rising to a millenarian cadenza in his private correspondence. In 1663 he tells Richard Baxter of the coming millennial transformation of worldly government, to Baxter's distinct discomfort (Baxter, *Reliquiae* 293–97). Writing in 1670 to Henry Ashhurst, treasurer of the New England Company, Eliot sympathizes with the tribulations of the English saints but prophesies that "the time is at the door when the kings shall be converted, and the stone (Christ) shall be hewn out of the mountains" (Ford 38). Eliot's faith in his civil scheme for the praying towns persisted, too. Responding in 1673 to a questioner who asks him about praying-town government, Eliot speaks with dogged Mosaic defensiveness:

> *Q:* Whether as to their civil government, they are wholly conformed to the English, or have any particular ordering of their own whereby they are ruled?
>
> *A:* Conformed is a great word; we are expressly conformed to the Scriptures, and to that form of government which we find Israel was under at the first and never quite lost, to have rulers of ten, of fifty, of an hundred, we have yet gone no higher. ("An Account" 128)

About two years later, however, the praying towns suffered the devastating setback of King Philip's War, in which the intercultural status of one Praying Indian played a catalytic role. In 1664 Eliot writes to the commissioners at Hartford, describing the missionary activities of one of his converts: "And if you please to order the worshipful commissioners of Plymouth to give encouragement to John Sosoman, who teacheth Philip and his men to read, I think it will be an action of good prudence, and a means to put life into the work; for human and rational means are to be used in promoting God's works among mankind; though this work hath had this divine stamp upon it, that God himself is the beginner of it in every place" (Eliot, "From Rev. John Eliot" 484). John Sosoman (or Sassamon) was a Praying Indian who acted as Philip's interpreter, moving among the towns of the unconverted Indians, the praying towns, and the English towns. In 1675 Sassamon (according to Drake) got wind of Philip's plans to attack the English and reported them to the English at Plymouth. When word of this betrayal reached Philip, Drake speculates, he ordered Sassamon killed. In any case, the English found his body under the ice of a pond, arrested a number of Indians (including one of Philip's sons) for the deed, and hanged them.

Gookin calls Sassamon the first Christian martyr of King Philip's War, but he was by no means the last (*Account* 440). The war these killings precipitated brought the virtual elimination of the non-Praying tribal structures in Massachusetts and the deaths of perhaps half the Indians. Moreover, it brought the disbanding of the praying towns. Eliot had long seen their military potential, describing one as "a strong *palizado*" and soliciting a stock of "guns, powder, shot, swords, etc. We will make us slings, bows, and other engines, the best the Lord will please to direct us for our safety" (*Tracts* 143). During the war Eliot and Gookin suggested that the Praying Indians be armed and sent on guerrilla raids against their non-Praying fellows. But they were largely ignored. Instead, the governor's council passed two laws regarding the Praying Indians that form a macabre Catch-22 when taken in combination: the first, in August 1675, said that any Indian found outside the praying towns was subject to summary execution; the second, in June 1676, offered amnesty to all loyal Praying Indians willing to walk to Boston (Segal and Stineback 201–03).

The Praying Indians of Natick and of other towns became displaced populations once again when the English moved them to a concentration camp on Deer Island, where many starved or died of disease. Eliot and Gookin counseled them to accept their "fates" with Christian equanimity. Here we see another phase in the dialectic of utopia and warfare: utopia may begin in an attempt to organize populations displaced by warfare, but it may wind up simply allowing them to be displaced in a new, more efficient fashion by yet another war. From the colonial point of view, this displacement shows both the failure and the success of utopian discipline: a failure because it destroys the millennial promise generated by the experimental isolation of the praying towns, a success because the tractability of the Praying Indians aids in the English project of holy genocide.

The war brought Eliot and his allies into disrepute. He reports that when he, Gookin, and several others were on their way to Deer Island to tend to the Praying Indians there, an English ship near their boat suddenly swerved and ran them down, "whether wilfully or by negligence, God he knoweth." Eliot nearly drowned ("Rev. John Eliot's Records" 197). Eliot's attempts to intercede for the Praying Indians captured during the fighting were largely unsuccessful. Eliot mounted the scaffold with a captured Praying Indian named Wattasompanum, or Captain Tom. His report is a poignant epitaph for the praying towns in general: "I accompanied him to his death. On the ladder he lifted up his hands and said, 'I did never lift up my hand against the English, nor was I at Sudbury, only I was willing to go away with the enemies that surprised us.' When the ladder was turned, he lifted up his hands to heaven prayer-wise, and so held them till strength failed, and then by degree they sunk down" (413). In a letter to the Bay Colony governor and council—one much like Vasco de Quiroga's letter to the Spanish court 141 years before—Eliot pleads to no avail that the captured Indians not be sold into slavery, arguing with an outmoded missionary zeal that "the design of Christ in these last days is not to extirpate nations but to gospelize them. He will spread the gospel round the world about. Rev. 11:15" (Segal and Stineback 204). After the war Eliot pulled the remnants of the Praying Indians together into four towns, but although they retained something of their identity for some time, they never regained their antebellum millennial promise.

This genocide brought a transformation in the missionary literature. We can see traces of this transformation even in Eliot's lifetime. His last published work (excepting some reprints of earlier works) was *The Dying Speeches of Several Indians* (1680). This collection, like *New-Englands First Fruits,* focuses on the individual Indian. It is more concerned with the speeches themselves and with the authenticity death brings them than with the function of conversion and confession in creating a millennial community of the elect, the concern of the Eliot Tracts of the 1640s and 1650s. We might even see here a precursor of "the song of the dying Indian," a genre of retrospective American poetry that was to enjoy a great eighteenth- and nineteenth-century popularity paralleling the continuing white effort to give actual Indians ample opportunity to sing such songs (Farley).

Eliot's translations and *The Indian Grammar* underwent an interpretive transformation. As persons capable of speaking the language Eliot had so painstakingly learned and preserved in his translations became fewer and fewer, his works acquired a new retrospective function. Roger L. Emerson says that the eighteenth-century Scots writing on the origin of language all turned to Eliot's works to supply them with examples of the peculiar features of "primitive" languages (219). *The Indian Bible* and *The Indian Grammar,* both originally instrumental texts within a prospective project aimed at establishing the utopian universality of Scripture and ushering in the millennium, become antiquarian texts within a retrospective project in historical linguistics aimed at showing the linguistic advance of the West over a murdered people.

4

James Harrington's Commonwealth for Increase

Oceana and England

James Harrington's *Commonwealth of Oceana* (1656) lacks two modes of idealization we usually associate with utopias: it contains neither the romantic motif of an imaginary voyage nor an imaginative movement out of secular time into a golden age. Its scanty allegorical apparatus is all too thin a cloak for the England of Harrington's own day: his Oceana, Marpesia, Panopea, and Emporium refer immediately and with a lack of imaginative connotation to England, Scotland, Ireland, and London. The heroic founding legislator of Oceana, the Lord Archon Olphaus Megaletor, is a two-dimensional but still recognizable portrait of the Lord Protector Oliver Cromwell. Consequently, Harrington scholars have tended to group *Oceana* with acknowledged utopias either uneasily or not at all. G. P. Gooch says that its utopian form is a sop to Protectorate censorship, masking a work "which is in reality one of the earliest examples in political thinking of the historical method" (251). Echoing H. F. Russell-Smith (12), R. H. Tawney says that "utopia" is "a misnomer for a work whose purpose is not to paint a picture of a state laid up in Heaven, but to point a moral from English history" ("Interpretation" 207). J. G. A. Pocock argues persistently and convincingly for the millenarian qualities of *Oceana* but denies that it is a utopia. Harrington's work describes a state that is "all but immediately present." Unlike the utopias of Andreae, Plattes, and Campanella, which are located "in distant seas too ideal to have been ever caught up in the cycles of fortune," it has no imaginary locale and is intimately involved in a consideration of secular time ("Introduction" 74).

This distinction between utopias and nonutopias has two problems. First, it casts a shadow over what we might call the Oceanic aspects of canonical utopias: their concern with the social production of a new kind of citizen through the rational secular reorganization of space and time. We have seen that More's *Utopia,* for instance, rationalizes and accelerates the process of England's agricultural enclosure, separating agricultural from civic space, the household from the commons hall, the hospital at the outskirts of the city from the marketplace at the center. Furthermore, it organizes the minutiae of social time, apportioning each individual's day among the mandated six hours of labor, eight hours of sleep, and ten hours of "free" (but self-improving) leisure time. Though Andreae's *Christianopolis,* Plattes's *Macaria,* and Campanella's *City of the Sun* begin, like More's work, with the geographical fiction of a voyage, they also follow its enclosure and manipulation of social space. Though they do seem to exist in a millennium or golden age at some distance from secular history, they also consider the organization of secular time at *Utopia*'s detailed and disciplinary level.

Second, this distinction disguises some of the more imaginative and "utopian" aspects of Harrington's work. True, like, Eliot's Christian Commonwealth, Winstanley's ideal state, and Comenius's reformed classroom, Oceana is close at hand in both time and space. As a fiction it seems almost atemporal in its identity with contemporary England, atopic in its lack of a proper imaginative geography. But utopian distances can be deceptive: Harrington's England is as far from his Oceana as barbarian Abraxa is from Utopia, as far as the Canaan that Moses sees from Pisgah is from Joshua's Israel, or as far as the preconquest Massachusetts "wilderness" is from John Eliot's Natick. The transformation that will turn England into Oceana is imminent but total: this may rob *Oceana* of certain romantic qualities, but it also invests the details of the transformation itself with a utopian importance all out of proportion to their apparent innate significance. Harrington promises that a legislative transformation of England's social space and time will turn it into the utopian commonwealth of Oceana.

Like Eliot, Harrington has the utopian obsession with matters of arrangement and order: "As in houses not differing in the kinds of their offices, the orders of the families differ much; so the difference of form in different governments consists not in the kinds or number of the parts, which in every one is alike, but in the different ways of ordering those parts" (839). He believes that by organizing the displaced English people on a utopian site in accordance with the dictates of "the ancient prudence" (the textual records of the Hebrew, classical, and Italian republics), he can reveal the hidden potential of people, site, and texts alike for a utopian immortality. First, he believes that the anomic people of Interregnum England are the tractable materials of the utopian imagination that, when settled on the land in accordance with the models offered by the ancient prudence, will gain a millennial immortality. Second, he promises that the agricultural space of present- and future-day England, when submitted to the agrarian legislation of the ancient prudence and settled with a body of citizen-soldiers, will gain an organic immortality of its own. Finally, he predicts that the immortal authority of the ancient prudence will appear when the utopist shows how to use it to organize persons and places into a millennial utopian state. When Oceana's agrarian legislation has assured a rationalized inheritance of land, the nurturing of families, and a distribution of military power, and when its electoral legislation has assured a proper and perpetual circulation of persons into and out of positions of political power, then England will have gained a dynamic stability that will allow it to embark on a millennial conquest and unification of the world.

But alongside this utopian optimism lies something foreign to Eliot's utopian writing: a consideration of the means by which this utopian republic will come into being. Whereas Eliot constantly represses his own voice, assuming that he is the catalytic "instrument" of God who merely brings his materials into alignment with scriptural models, Harrington forces himself to confront the difficulties inherent in legislating his utopian commonwealth into existence. Much more than Eliot's utopian writing, Harrington's writing attempts to educate and produce the perfect legislating prince. While Eliot addresses his utopia somewhat vaguely to the British opponents of Antichrist, Harrington addresses his to "His Highness, the Lord Protector of the Commonwealth of England, Scotland, and Ireland" (155). Nowhere in Renaissance utopia outside the "Dialogue of Counsel" in More's Book 1 do we see a more painful awareness of the Platonic problem of making princes of philosophers, or philosophers of princes. Harrington sets himself the task of bridging the gap between two kinds of politician: the student of the wisdom of the ancient prudence (Harrington) and the interim dictator in possession of de facto political power (Cromwell). If he is successful, he will create the ideal legislator, the Lord Archon Olphaus Megaletor, who sets the Oceanic polity into motion and then abdicates his dictatorship. Harrington's awareness of this problem of means lies alongside his utopian optimism, pushing him into new strategies, new attempts to articulate his program in more persuasive and immediately usable ways.

The surviving records of Harrington's life are sparse and extraordinarily unhelpful for explaining his utopian radicalism (Pocock, "Introduction" 1–5). He was born in 1611, the eldest son of Sir Sapcote (or Sapcotes) Harrington of Northamptonshire and Lincolnshire. He attended Oxford without taking a degree, perhaps spending some time at the Middle Temple, perhaps serving briefly with one of the English regiments in the Netherlands before traveling to Denmark, Germany, France, and Italy. In 1647 he became one of the four gentlemen of the bedchamber to King Charles, and there are reports that he was on the scaffold when Charles was executed. He published some translations of Vergil, a treatise on biological metaphysics *(The Mechanics of Nature),* and seventeen political works. Of these last, the first *(Oceana)* appeared in 1656 and the last *(A Letter unto Mr. Stubbe)* in 1660. One other work, *A System of Politics,* survives only in the edition of his collected works published by his first editor, John Toland. After a physical and mental decline, perhaps brought on and aggravated by his months as a political prisoner of Charles II, he died in September 1677.

Since all of Harrington's political works are attempts to condense, expand upon, or defend the orders of *Oceana,* I will frequently refer to Harrington's political writing as a unified corpus. All the same, there are some significant modifications. Harrington's very repetition of content and alteration of form are rhetorical facts of some significance, as we will see.[1]

Harrington is often defensive about the discursive tedium of the thirty "orders" that institute Oceana. After proclaiming them, the Lord Archon says, "Show me another entire government consisting but of thirty orders." A certain initial complexity is essential, for "if you will have fewer orders in a commonwealth, you will have more, for where she is not perfect at first, every day, every hour will produce a new order, the end whereof is to have no order at all, but to grind with the clack of some demagogue" (337). All the same, the complexity of these orders pushes Harrington into attempts to simplify them, even in his first work. The Lord Archon himself sums up the orders in "The Epitome of the Whole Commonwealth" (333–37). The following summary of *Oceana's* orders is directed toward my discussion of Harrington as a utopist.

1. All men are divided according to the following criteria:
   a. Freedom as political subjects
      (1) Children under 18, women, lawyers, clergy, physicians, servants
      (2) Freemen
   b. Age of the freemen
      (1) Under 30: the youth or the marching army
      (2) 30 or over: the elders or the standing army
   c. Wealth of the freemen
      (1) The foot: those with a yearly income under £100
      (2) The horse: those with a yearly income of £100 or over
2. All Oceana is divided into 50 tribes, each consisting of 20 hundreds, each consisting of 10 parishes, for a total of 50 tribes, 1,000 hundreds, and 10,000 parishes.
3. All elections are to be held according to the method of the ballot of Venice, which is secret and can be managed by illiterates.
4. Early each year the elder freemen of each parish assemble and elect one-fifth of their number as the deputies of the *"primum mobile."*
5. One month later the deputies of each parish meet at the rendezvous of the hundred. Here they elect the members of the "list of the Nebulosa," four of the horse and three of the foot, who will conduct the government of the hundred for one year.
6. One month later the deputies of the parishes meet at the rendezvous of their tribe.
   a. On the first day they elect the members of the "list of the Prime Magnitude," six of the horse who will conduct the internal government of the tribe for one year.
   b. On the second day, they elect the members of the "list of the Galaxy," consisting of two "knights," chosen from the horse, and seven "deputies," three chosen from the horse and four from the foot. No one is eligible for this list who has not been away from national government for at least three years.
7. One month after the balloting of the tribe the newly elected knights and deputies of all 50 tribes, who are to be paid out of public revenues, take their places in the capital city of Emporium (London).
   a. The 100 newly elected knights take their places in the senate, replacing those knights elected three years before. All 300 knights

of the senate elect its officers and its representatives from this new group to the councils of state, war, religion, and trade to replace those who have just left. They also elect Oceana's ambassadors, who cannot be members either of the senate or of the prerogative tribe. The senate may debate and recommend legislation to the prerogative tribe but may not vote on legislation.

   b. The 350 newly chosen deputies take their places in the prerogative tribe, replacing those deputies elected three years before. All 1,050 deputies of the prerogative elect officers from this new group to replace those who have just left. The deputies and all the people may debate privately for six weeks any legislation that the senate recommends, but when the deputies assemble in the prerogative, they must vote ("give the result") with no debate at all. The prerogative also possesses the power of supreme judicature.

8. The youth of Oceana muster in arms at the levels of the parish, the hundred, and the tribe, holding elections and exercises that are the martial equivalents of the civil divisions, collections, and elections of their elders. Certain of them are to be sent to the provinces of Marpesia (Scotland) and Panopea (Ireland) for a period of three years as members of the provincial army. In wartime, this marching army of the youth combined with the standing army of the elders is to be under the command of the senate's council of war and the "lord strategus" elected by the senate.

9. There is to be a national congregational religion, with each parish deciding whether or not to accept a pastoral candidate sent to it on probation by one of the two national universities. There is to be freedom of religion for all except idolaters, Roman Catholics, and Jews; no religion disqualifies any other citizen from any civil office.

10. The agrarian law of Oceana specifies that henceforth, all landholders whose property brings them an income of more than £2,000 yearly must distribute it among their heirs so that no single heir receives a yearly income greater than £2,000, or so that any surplus is evenly distributed among all heirs. No daughter may receive more than £1,500 in dowry. There is to be no confiscation of property; if there is only one heir, he may receive everything. Oceaners may own specified values of conquered foreign territories.

From *Oceana* to *A System of Politics,* all of Harrington's writings propose these orders, with some minor modifications. That they persist through Harrington's works while the overtly utopian apparatus of *Oceana* disappears might lead us to assume that Harrington was never truly a utopist in the first place. But we would be wrong on two counts: First, the utopian form of *Oceana* has a distinct relationship to both its historical moment and Harrington's desire to create an ideal utopian legislator; that form disappears only when Harrington's utopian intention has altered. Second, even Harrington's less overtly utopian works, even this skeletal outline of the "orders" they attempt to defend, are part of a utopian project and carry with them a utopian intentionality, as we can see when we look more closely at the construction and function in Harrington's work of so seemingly innocent and self-evident a concept as "the people."

Fortuna as King People

This section proposes a redefinition of the role of "the people" in Harrington's political writing. It will argue that Harrington speaks of the people not (or not only) as the spokesman for a rising class speaks for that class, nor as a Leveller democrat speaks for the possessor of natural rights, nor as an aristocrat speaks of an unmanageable population. The voice in Harrington's writing that criticizes these other voices and puts them into context is the voice of a utopian artificer. Harrington conceives of the people of England not as any single class but as a raw material made up of the entire English nation. But since Harrington's attitude toward the people is extraordinarily complex, defining itself as much by the political rhetorics it abstains from as by those it employs, I will have to examine its modification of contiguous class rhetorics, particularly those of the Levellers and Machiavelli.

Harrington's concept of the English people figured prominently in the great polemic of the 1940s and 1950s over "the rise of the gentry." For R. H. Tawney, Harrington wrote on behalf of a rising English middle class that was in the process of displacing a landed nobility. His *Oceana* was "partly a social history" of this rise, "partly a programme based on it" ("Rise" 36). H. R. Trevor-Roper, on the other hand, saw Harrington as the spokesman for a declining class of "mere gentry"— the reactionary rural squires victimized by the Tudor and Stuart formation of a court nobility and by the Price Revolution. Harrington became the "self-hypnotized poet" of these "impoverished squires" when they, by some regrettable quirk of fate, gained control of the nation during the Puritan Revolution (quoted by Hexter, "Storm" 22–23).[2]

This discussion of economics and class interest set the stage for much of the subsequent discussion of Harrington as a political thinker. In *The Political Theory of Possessive Individualism,* C. B. Macpherson sees Harrington as the spokesman for a new "nobility" comprising the declining English aristocracy and the rising bourgeois gentry—an alliance that dominates the yeoman "people," who are nonetheless free to make "nobles" of themselves in the idealized market economy of Oceana (172–74). Christopher Hill sees a similar division but uses a much different terminology to characterize it: Harrington's "people" (which for Hill include the gentry) are an ascendant class of proto-bourgeois whom he sets off from their disenfranchised tenants and from the wandering poor. True, Harrington does champion what he calls popular government, but "when all this has been said, one still feels that Harrington wanted safeguards against too much democracy. . . . Though one object of Oceana was to establish a constitution which would protect the gentry from an absolute monarchy or military dictatorship, another was to protect 'the people' from the poor, from 'Robbers or Levellers'" (*Puritanism* 308, 307).

Various though these positions are in emphasis and in substance, they agree that political writing necessarily expresses the interests of some preexistent social class. At its worst, this argument can degenerate into a claim that we can explain an author's work by determining the economic status of his or her family; Tawney, Trevor-Roper, and Hill make some efforts in this direction. To criticize this theory of the expressive or "representative" nature of all political writing (which is just as attractive to Tory as to socialist historians), I will examine, first, some of the striking sympathies between Harrington and the Levellers (a group of political writers and actors actively claiming to "represent" a social class quite a bit lower in the chain of degree than the Harringtons of Lincolnshire) and, second, the fundamentally distinct conceptions of "the people" arising from the Levellers' democratic rhetoric and Harrington's utopian rhetoric.

We can begin handily with Hill's rather economical citation of Harrington's saying "Robbers or Levellers," which might reasonably lead us to think that Harrington is an aristocrat who associates Leveller democracy with thievery; indeed, Hill uses this same quote elsewhere to make just this point (*World* 98; *Experience* 195). Such denunciation of the Levellers by Republicans was certainly no rarity. In his chapter on the Levellers in *The Case of the Commonwealth of England, Stated,* Marchamont Nedham gathers a learned compendium of demophobic commonplaces. He calls the Levellers and the "rude multitude" they claim to represent a tumultuous rabble of ungrateful, resentful, ambitious malcontents. He even makes the common (and frequently willful) mistake of tying the Levellers to the "True Levellers," or Diggers, saying that "from levelling they proceed to introduce an absolute community . . . that like the old Parthians, Scythian nomads, and other wild barbarians, we might renounce towns and cities, live at rovers, and enjoy all in common" (110).

But in the passage Hill quotes, Harrington is speaking in the voice of the Lord Archon Olphaus Megaletor of Oceana, who is responding in turn to a speech by Epimonus de Garrula, *Oceana*'s aristocratic comic relief. Epimonus has characterized the multitude whom the Lord Archon proposes to enfranchise as a base rout of ale-swillers, football players, bear-baiters, and natural-born thieves. The Lord Archon responds that an economically motivated war of all against all is an aristocratic calumny, for there would then be "more thieves than purses." So the prospect that a "whole people should turn robbers or levellers is as impossible in the end as in the means" (292). Similarly, in *The Prerogative of Popular Government,* Harrington says that "by levelling, they who use the word seem to understand: when a people rising invades the lands and estates of the richer sort, and divides them equally among themselves; as for example—nowhere in the world" (360).

W. K. Jordan writes that Harrington feared the "anarchy" and "mob rule" of the theocratic saints (3.289), but nowhere in his writings does Harrington spend any time warning against the dangers of an anarchic people, except in a subordinate clause or two introducing the greater saintly danger of a Presbyterian or Fifth Monarchist oligarchy. He seems constantly to be assuring an aristocratic audience of the English people's trustworthiness. In this he is not unlike the Levellers themselves. In *A Manifestation from Lieutenant Col. John Lilburne, Mr. William Walwyn, Mr. Thomas Prince, and Mr. Richard Overton,* the authors proclaim that "we never had it in our thoughts to level men's estates, it being the utmost of our aim that the commonwealth be reduced to such a pass that every man may with as much security as may be enjoy his propriety [property]" (Wolfe, *Manifestoes* 391). Harrington even constructs a theory explaining the Levellers' possessive individualism along with his own: because most income arises not from rents on a piece of land but from the "industry" (economic activity of any sort, including farming) conducted on it, and because a people attempting to steal and subdivide the land would bring about the disruption of this industry, therefore "though some nobility . . . may be found to have been levellers, yet not any people in the world" (840). Harrington's physiocratic metaphysics prevents him from conceiving of a class revolution aimed at anything other than a redistribution of real estate. A theory of history as a progression of economic modes of production never enters into his writing.

So Harrington has some unexpected sympathies with the Levellers. Pocock comments, "Harrington was a republican—an aristocrat because he was a democrat; and on the democratic side of his thought he was nearly a Leveller" ("Introduction" 53). Yet, if we define a democrat as one whose rhetoric appeals to ancient liberties or natural rights in order to argue for the rule of the many, then Harrington is not really a democrat, not even on one side of his thought. His suggestion that some nobles may have levellers, a characteristically dialectical move, begins to suggest his differences from the Levellers. To shield the people from the epithet "Leveller," Harrington deflects it from them toward their rulers and toward the political orders containing and shaping them both. He transforms *leveller* from an antidemocratic pejorative to an aristocratic honorific in the process: "Levelling was never introduced but by the wisdom of some great man, as a Moses, a Joshua, or a Lycurgus; or by some accident, or accidents, bringing a nobility unto ruin, as the laws of Henry the Seventh and the ways of Henry the Eighth in England" (631). As Marx and Engels show that the communist "specter" haunting Europe is the product of an earlier bourgeois revolution that transformed the mode of production and produced the revolutionary proletariat (*Manifesto* 78), so Harrington shows that the "levellers" haunting the Protectorate are the product of an earlier levelling by so unlikely a revolutionary as King Panurgus (Henry VII), who first began to "open those sluices" of the new distribution of land, producing the independent freeholders who became the revolutionary armed citizenry of the Civil War (197). Panurgus was the unwitting republican legislator who produced the revolutionary material conditions that the Lord Archon must stabilize in a utopian polity. The balance of property has already passed into the hands of the people, and so also the balance of military power that property can support. As we will see, Oceana's agrarian legislation will attempt to stabilize this condition.

The Leveller leader John Lilburne speaks about the people of England by speaking about himself, becoming a representative of all Englishmen by forming legal test cases around the actions of "Freeborn John." He self-consciously dramatizes the conflict between civil power and individual rights, integrating autobiography and political agitation (Joan Webber 53–79). The identity and the writing voice of the Leveller leader arise from his opposition to juridical power—from his defense of the Englishman's traditional and natural rights against the encroachments of the law. Leveller writing is governed by a concept of *representation:* it begins with the fiction of a fully formed political subject who possesses sovereign political power that he is free to delegate to a representative and take back again at will. Further, it is the writer's task to represent this power of the individual in his own conflicts with the state.

But Harrington's ideal of government is not representative. His spokesman Publicola observes the monarchists also claim that the king is "nothing else but the representor of the people and their power," so that "the people's power at that rate comes to the people's slavery" (785). He faults the Levellers' *Second Agreement of the People* for proposing a parliament whose "representatives have sovereign power, save that in some things the people may resist them by arms."[3] This is no more than "downright anarchy. Where the sovereign power is not as entire and absolute as in monarchy itself, there can be no government at all. It is not the limitation of sovereign power that is the cause of a commonwealth," but a perfect adjustment of state reason and interest so as to ensure equilbrium (657–58). Power must be constructed by the legislator and the utopist who counsels him, for the popular "material" of a commonwealth has no political being or power before its organization: "In the institution or building of a commonwealth, the first work (as that of builders) can be no other than fitting and distributing the materials. The materials of a commonwealth are the people; the people of Oceana were distributed by casting them into certain divisions, regarding their quality, their ages, their wealth, and the places of their residence or habitation" (212). With his architectural metaphor, passive verb, and analytic demographics, Harrington could not be much further from the Levellers.

An important (but tricky) indication of Harrington's nondemocratic utopian rhetoric is his conception of the franchise, since it brings the vote to a proportion of the populace remarkably large by seventeenth-century standards, but without ever appealing to native liberties or the customary rights of the freeborn Englishman. Hill claims that Harrington, as the proponent of a rising bourgeois class, excludes all servants from the franchise and that the class of "servants" in the seventeenth century included all wage laborers (*Puritanism* 181). Macpherson agrees (181, 282–86). But Keith Thomas shows that servants were often more narrowly defined as those utterly dependent on a single employer and living in his household. Even the Second and Third Leveller Agreements of the People disqualified servants defined in this narrow sense, presumably because their votes would not be free from the influence of their masters. Thomas refers to Eliot's *Christian Commonwealth* for this definition, showing that Eliot seems to equate servants and sons living at home as political dependents, neither capable of exercising a free vote ("Levellers"). Similarly, Harrington says that if servants "attain unto liberty, that is to live of themselves, they are freemen or citizens" (212).[4] Neither Eliot nor Harrington makes any appeal to natural rights theory when discussing the franchise. For both, man is the political animal, and the criterion for classifying men is their independence as political subjects, not their innate rights. Both deny the franchise to household servants, women, and children because of their political dependence—a denial, of course, that strengthens and perpetuates that dependence. The conception of the franchise in both Eliot and Harrington shows that they are advocates of popular government without being democrats.

The other side of Harrington's utopian refusal to see the people as repositories of natural rights is his refusal to see them as the vessels of natural anarchic corruption; this brings us into a Machiavellian context at least as complex as the context of the Levellers. J. C. Davis sees Harrington as utterly antagonistic to popular liberty and somewhat repelled by the people considered en masse, for despite his unusually inclusive franchise, he constrains the native liberties of the people inside an electoral mechanism. Davis attacks what he calls *Oceana*'s utopianization of the Machiavellian classical republic, which he says denies the full moral worth of the individual and of the people as a whole by restricting their opportunities for making moral choices: "Those who debate the creation of the perfect and immortal commonwealth in *Oceana* seem to assume that 'it is the duty of a legislator to presume all men to be wicked'" (*Utopia* 208). Both in Davis's book on utopia and in his earlier article on Harrington, this quotation appears so often that it becomes the key prop of his argument that Harrington is a closet totalitarian. The speaker, once again, is Epimonus de Garrula, who is speaking to the Lord Archon on the question of the franchise: "Now everbody knows that the lower sort of people regard nothing but money; and you say it is the duty of a legislator to presume all men to be wicked, wherefore they must fall upon the richer as they are an army. . . . And so, the silken purses of your senate and prerogative being made out of sows' ears, most of them blacksmiths, they will strike while the iron is hot and beat your estates into hobnails" (290).

The deliberative delay of a debate is a structural necessity for the realization of Harrington's utopian state, for just like its day-to-day business once established, its genesis must be tested by the debate of the learned before receiving the result of the people. Therefore, Harrington introduces Epimonus de Garrula, whose name seems to mean Garrulous Delayer. But he hardly serves as a reliable spokesman for Harrington or the Lord Archon. The Lord Archon responds to this railing with a list of the heroic smithies of the ancient prudence in Israel, Athens, and Rome, calling them "smiths of the fortune of the commonwealth, not such as forged hobnails but thunderbolts" (291). He says that "the maxim of legislators which holdeth all men to be wicked" refers not to men in general but only to those particular men who presume to hold themselves apart from the commonwealth as individuals or parties pretending to its whole interest—that is, to would-be monarchs or oligarchs. In fact, highwaymen are more likely to be "such whose education hath pretended unto that of gentlemen" (292). The fact that the "you" Epimonus refers to above as the source of the quotation is not the Lord Archon but the Machiavelli of *The Discourses* (111–12), and that Machiavelli asserts this maxim with much less qualification than does Harrington, does not prevent Davis from arguing that Harrington's utopian modification of Machiavellian classical republicanism is a result of his more pessimistic view of human nature.

In some ways the conservative Puritan Richard Baxter is a better reader than Davis is of Harrington's utopian revision of Machiavelli. Baxter is fearful of the inclusiveness of the Oceanic franchise: "He knoweth not what prudence and piety are, or knoweth not England or mankind, that knoweth not the major part of the vulgar are scarcely prudent or pious men. . . . And he knowth not Oceana . . . that knoweth not that the ignorant and ungodly rabble are made the lords and rulers of all" (*Baxter* 86–87). He reminds Harrington with some distaste that even his godless teacher Machiavelli refers to the people as corrupt, asking, "If Machiavel be become a Puritan to him, what is Mr. Harrington to us?" (93).[5] Baxter refers here to Machiavelli's discussion of the process of civil corruption in *The Discourses*. This quasi-natural decline of the state begins almost imperceptibly, perhaps with a moral failing of the people, perhaps with the corruption of their leader, and spreads throughout the body politic. By the time its debilitating effects are noticeable, it is too late to restore the republic to health through normal legislation. Machiavelli suggests that the only hope may be a temporary dictatorship, but he admits that history offers little evidence of success for even this drastic cure (*Discourses* 153–64). Corruption is the ineradicable susceptibility of the republic to *fortuna*.

But as Baxter implies, Harrington has a different idea, disagreeing with Machiavelli on this point in unusually explicit terms. The people are corrupt not because of some moral contagion but simply because their condition as property holders is out of alignment with the political orders they live under, and "corruption in this sense signifieth no more than that the corruption of one government (as in natural bodies) is the generation of another; wherefore, if the balance [of property] alter from monarchy, the corruption of the people in this case is that which maketh them capable of a commonwealth" (202). As with *leveller,* Harrington redefines his received terminology dialectically, offering a structural definition to replace Machiavelli's organic and moral definition of corruption and a progressive history (or a movement out of history) to replace his organic cyclic history of civic rise and decay (Pocock, *Constitution* 146). For Harrington, a people's corruption is not degenerative but generative. If there is no imperfection in the generation of the new commonwealth, there is no reason for it ever to become corrupt.

Harrington's ability to see Interregnum England as politically formless and its citizens as anomic building materials allows him to become a utopist where Machiavelli was not. *The Prince* describes the legislators of the ancient prudence as the leaders of utterly displaced peoples, like Moses' enslaved Jews or Theseus's dispersed Athenians (50–51). Writing on this section of *The Prince,* Pocock describes these "legislators" as ideal republican types of the larger Machiavellian category of the political innovator, of which the new prince is a less ideal type: "To attain the ideal type, therefore, we must suppose a situation in which the matter has no form, and above all no previously existing legislator. It was therefore a logical necessity that each hero should find his people in a condition of total anomie" (*Moment* 169). Machiavelli finds no contemporary Italian opportunities for such legislation. All of Europe, in fact, seems politically overdetermined, with overlapping states, loyalties, and traditions. But in *Oceana* Harrington claims to see the appearance in modern England of an anomic people bearing the fingerprints of no previous legislator, and so also the reappearance of the true legislator in the figure of Olphaus. Harrington's astonishing ability to overlook the continuing popular appeal of the ancient constitution and traditional loyalties allows him to conceive of all Englishmen as building material. The Lord Archon addresses his council, saying, "My lords, the children of Israel were makers of brick, before they were builders of a commonwealth; but our brick is made, our mortar tempered, the cedars of Lebanon are hewed and squared unto our hands" (257). Here the classical republican becomes the utopist.

Harrington maintained this utopian attitude toward the people throughout his career as a political writer despite the shifting position of his opponents. Whereas in his earlier writings he defended the people from charges of anarchic levelling, he found himself more and more forced to answer charges such as Milton's in *The Ready and Easy Way to Establish a New Commonwealth* that they are a "misguided and abused multitude" lusting after monarchy.[6] But in *A System of Politics,* which he may have written even after the Restoration, Harrington seems still to be defending the incorruptible people when he says that during a state of "privation of government," then "the matter or foundation of a good orderly government is ready and in being, and there wants nothing to the perfection of the same but proper superstructures or form" (837). William Sprigge, Harringtonian commonwealthsman and member of Harrington's Rota Club, addresses a utopian invitation to the High Court of Parliament in his *Modest Plea, For an Equal Common-wealth, Against Monarchy* of 1659: "God hath put the nation like wax into your hands, that you may mold and cast it into what forms your honors please; we are now *rasa tabula,* and your honors may write what you please upon us. I hope it will be holiness to the Lord, that we may for the future be truly termed a holy commonwealth" (A2). The people of Oceana in Harrington's eyes, like the Algonquians of Massachusetts in Eliot's, are prepolitical and premoral raw material waiting to be shaped into an ideal polity. So long as we are looking for an imaginative geography or a movement out of secular time, we will find Harrington a disappointing utopist. But as soon as we see that he practices what he calls "political architecture" and that the materials of this architecture are human bodies, then his organizational utopian imagination moves into focus (609).

All the same, Harrington's proposed orders create a distinct hierarchy in the inequality of the horse and the foot. But since the distinction he makes between the two groups, and the related but not identical distinction he makes between the senate and the prerogative tribe, are much more elaborate than would be necessary to bolster some class interest, it is worthwhile to reexamine his reason for these divisions.

Unfortunately, he gives us several reasons, and they are not altogether compatible. In *Oceana* he draws an analogy between the divisions of a civil government and those of an army, saying the "in truth an army may as well consist of soldiers without officers, or of officers without soldiers, as a commonwealth (especially such an one as is capable of greatness) of a people without a gentry, or of a gentry without a people" (183). The analogy is anything but arbitrary, for the "greatness" Harrington refers to here is the imperial expansion of the republic under the conquering armies of the "horse" and the "foot" of the youth. But Harrington carefully distinguishes the hereditary orders of Rome, which were "the occasion of her ruin," from Oceana's horse and foot, saying that the title of horse is to be "no otherwise hereditary than a man's estate" (216). Just as the gentry and the sons of the gentry may fall into the ranks of the foot if their yearly income diminishes, so the foot may rise into the ranks of the horse on the strength of their industry or inheritance. Indeed, Harrington seems to think such movements will be frequent, since generations tend to alternate industrious and idle (353).

In two further analogies Harrington complicates the rationale for this division rather than clarifying it. In the first he compares Oceana's agreement to have a bicameral legislature composed of a debating senate and a resolving prerogative with the agreement between two girls who want the same piece of cake that one will divide the cake and the other will have the first choice, thus assuring an equal division: "That which great philosophers are disputing upon in vain is brought unto light by two silly girls: even the whole mystery of a commonwealth, which lies only in dividing and choosing" (172). Even he admits the inadequacy of this analogy, for unlike the division of roles between the senate and the prerogative, the division of roles between the two girls requires no previous qualifications for debating and choosing (416).

In the second analogy, he compares the division of the two houses of state with the hypothetical formation of government among a group of twenty men. He claims that of the twenty, six will appear as a natural aristocracy, better able to debate and consider, and will receive the natural deference of the duller fourteen, "not by hereditary right, nor in regard of the greatness of their estates only, which would tend unto such power as might force or draw the people, but by election for their excellent parts, which tendeth unto the advancement of the influence of their virtue or authority that leads the people" (173). But this fails to explain why a natural aristocracy should also hold great estates. Harrington uses "virtue" here in an uncharacteristically class-conscious sense, for it is not typically a criterion for distinguishing debate from result, but a product of their legislative integration: "That which was reason in the debate of the commonwealth, being brought forth by the result, must be virtue" (170). The role of a naturally virtuous gentry in Harrington's political thought becomes even more problematic when we look more closely at the opening of the paragraph in which he speaks of the appearance of this natural aristocracy: "A commonwealth is but a civil society of men. Let us take any number of men, as twenty, and forthwith make a commonwealth. Twenty men, if they be not all idiots—perhaps if they be—can never come so together, but there will be such difference in them that about a third will be wiser, or at least less foolish than all the rest" (172). Not only does he fail to reconcile the conflicting claims of an aristocracy of merit and an aristocracy of wealth, but his appeal to a hierarchy of idiots does not seem calculated to stroke any aristocratic egos. Harrington even gives the workable but mundane explanation that the members of the horse tend to have more leisure time to study the public interest than do the members of the foot (259).

However important these distinctions between horse and foot, between senate and prerogative tribe, they do not form the only relationship of power in Harrington's writing, and in a certain sense they tend to drop out. It is a remarkable fact, and one that has escaped the attention of those critics who assume that Harrington must be writing on behalf of some preexistent class, that all his proposals for the legislator's reshaping of his human material apply to the future horse as well as the future foot. Both classes vote as a group in all elections, and both are obliged to contribute to the extent of their ability in time of war. Harrington's agrarian legislation, which can apply only to the horse, aims to prevent the excessive concentration of wealth in a few hands. A fundamental flaw in Macpherson's analysis of Harrington as a possessive individualist is that it underestimates the extent to which his one, few, and many are exotic, anticustomary Machiavellian imports, not reflections of certain customary or protocapitalist English class groupings. If Harrington writes "on behalf of" any certain class or classes, they are classes that he hopes to write into existence.[7] While we should acknowledge the aristocratic element in Harrington's thought, we should also note certain aristocratic roads not taken. As we have seen, Harrington has the classic utopian distaste for the notion of rule by a naturally virtuous aristoi: "'Give us good men and they will make us good laws' is the maxim of a demagogue, and exceedingly fallible" (205). When he begins developing his peculiar form of political faculty psychology, we can see his utopian mixture of aristocracy and counteraristocracy.

Government, Harrington says, "is no other than the soul of a nation or city" (170). Like the soul of man, this soul "is the mistress of two potent rivals, the one reason, the other passion, that are in continual suit; and according as she gives up her will to these or either of them, is the felicity or misery which man partakes in this mortal life" (169). Remarkably, Harrington resists identifying the aristocratic few with reason and the mind, and the many with passion and the body—an indentification stretching back at least to *The Republic.* Rather, the reason of the commonwealth combines the senate's invention and the prerogative's judgment; it is the wisdom of the few expressed in debate and brought forth by the interest of the many in the result (170, 659).

This separation is essential: "The wisdom of the few may be the light of mankind, but the interest of the few is not the profit of mankind, nor of a commonwealth" (173). The few are just as capable of passion as the many, but they are even more dangerous when exercising it in the form of an oligarchic rule. Like Eliot, Harrington is less exercised by the prospect of levelling democracy than by the "base itch of the narrow oligarchy," which he calls "that foul beast" (744–45, 787). Once we see that the interest of the many is the vital complement to the wisdom of the few in the construction of state reason, the function of the prerogative tribe becomes clearer. They are, in effect, an organic version of common law: an accumulated or traditional reason or "interest" against which the propositive reason or "wisdom" of the senate may be tested without the odious mediation of lawyers, for whom Harrington has a classically utopian distaste. He anticipates objections: "An assembly of the people sovereign! . . . Why sure, it must be a dull, an unskilful thing. But so is the touchstone in a gold-smith's shop. . . . Yet without this would even the master be deceived" (676). Harrington quotes the title of Machiavelli's *Discourses* 1.58 in *Oceana* and as an epigraph to *The Prerogative of Popular Government)* "La multitudine è più savia e più costante ch'un principe [The multi-tude is wiser and more constant than a prince]" (Harrington 281, 389).

Even Pocock makes Harrington a more traditional aristocrat than he is, saying that the debate of the few informs the result of the many as the soul informs the body ("Introduction" 149). He seems aware of the counterevidence but persists in this reading: "Though the reflective intelligence or 'wisdom' of the few and the collective judgment or 'interest' of the many constituted the rational soul in politics, the rela-tion between them corresponded to that between the soul and the body" ("Contexts" 27). Pocock's first clause is indisputable, but in combination with the second, it forms a logical conundrum of which

Harrington is innocent: nowhere does he suggest that the many form the body or the few the soul of Oceana. The entire populace is the body in relation to the ideal informing soul of debate and result. Indeed, both the senate (the few) and the prerogative (the many) are elected by the entire body of the people, though the senate consists of the horse alone and the prerogative is a mixture. In Harrington's formulation, they are not so much the representatives of separate classes as distinct governing faculties that combine to form the soul of a single body.

In *A System of Politics* Harrington writes that when the people are in a state of "privation of government," they are an inanimate body awaiting the infusion of a soul. All classes in England are part of this undisciplined mixture of horse and foot, this "herd" and "rout." But unlike a human body without a soul, which is "a dead thing out of pain and misery," this "body of a people, not actuated or led by the soul of government, is a living thing in pain and misery." The only persons who are like the soul of this inanimate body are the student of the ancient prudence and the dictator before they exercise the authority of utopian government by legislating: "Formation of government is the creation of a political creature after the image of a philosophical creature, or it is an infusion of the soul or faculties of a man into the body of a multitude" (838). When these two persons merge in the figure of the utopian legislator, they contain within them the soul of the nation for one brief moment and then infuse it into the body of the people. Harrington says that Oceana is "such a commonwealth as may be dictated in a breath" (732). The legislator becomes a second god, and the tabula rasa of his anomic people becomes a political version of the pre-Adamic clay.

Harrington's utopian republicanism lacks the tempering element of *fortuna* that we find in Machiavelli's classical republicanism. In chapter 25 of *The Prince,* we read that *fortuna* is "the arbiter of half the things we do, leaving the other half or so to be controlled by ourselves." *Fortuna* is a natural force, much like violent rivers that periodically flood and ravage the surrounding countryside. "Yet although such is their nature, it does not follow that when they are flowing quietly one cannot take precautions, constructing dikes and embankments so that when the river is in flood it runs into a canal or else its impetus is less wild and dangerous" (130). For Machiavelli *fortuna* is primarily a matter of temporality. On the one hand, it brings the political innovator (whether new prince, established prince, or legislator) his moment of opportunity for innovation—his *occasione.* On the other hand, it exposes his new princedom to various destabilizing threats.

He may in time face a revolt from within by citizens who remember their ancient liberties or by adherents to factions that he has only partially subdued. He may face an invasion from without by another prince or another republic. He may even be overthrown by an utterly unpredictable quirk of fate: Cesare Borgia is in many ways Machiavelli's model new prince, but although he exercises a nearly superhuman *virtù,* he falls victim to *fortuna* in the form of his own illness and the death of his father and principal ally, Pope Alexander VI (54–61). Marchamont Nedham, Harrington's contemporary, is close to Machiavelli on this point. Republics may be the best bulwark against *fortuna,* but they are mortal organic bodies; like plants, animals, and men, they are ruled by the "decree of Nature, who in all her productions, makes the second moment of perfection the first toward their dissolution" (*Case* 1). *Fortuna* is to republican political theory what the seasons are to pastoral: a natural cycle that sets absolute limits to purposeful human activity.

Harrington simply seems uninterested in limiting his account of the rational progress of history with a concept of the unpredictable and unintelligible. In his most extended use of *fortune,* in "The First Part of the Preliminaries" to *Oceana,* he does at first seem to be invoking the Machiavellian relation between *virtù* and *fortuna,* for he opposes the external goods of fortune to the internal goods of the mind. But he also seems to be moving toward a more modern usage: "The goods of fortune are riches" (163). In speaking of the thousand-year stability of the government of Venice, he reduces *fortuna* from a positive force at work in history to the mere absence of *virtù.* Venice's perpetuity must be due to her organization and not to *fortuna,* "for the effects that proceed from fortune (if there be any such thing) are like their cause, unconstant . . . wherefore this must proceed from some other cause than chance" (276).

Harrington even appropriates Machiavelli's metaphor for *fortuna,* using it to argue for the dynamic immortality of the state rather than for its susceptibility to temporal change. Harrington's Anglican antagonist Matthew Wren has jeered at the orders of *Oceana,* saying that "this libration is of the same nature with a perpetual motion in the mechanics" (*Considerations* 67). Harrington does not deny the mechanical metaphor but distinguishes two kinds of mechanism, comparing Wren with the yokel in Horace who imagines that a river must stop running because his spigot eventually does: "The mathematician must not take God to be such an one as he is. Is that of the sun, of the stars, of a river, a perpetual motion? Even so *one generation goeth, and another cometh.* 'Nature (saith Galen) hath a tendency to make her creature immortal, if it were in the capacity of the matter on which she hath to work,' but the people never dieth" (431). The people, then, are not simply an inert rubble but contain an internal reproductive energy.

The unique quality of this "matter" allows Harrington to assume the role of an auxiliary God in forming his polity: "This motion of theirs is from the hand of a perpetual mover, even God himself, in whom we live and move and have our being; and to this current the politician addeth nothing but the banks, to which end, or none, the same God hath also created human prudence. Wherefore there is not anything that raiseth itself against God or right reason, if I say that it is in human prudence so to apply these banks that they may stand as long as the river runneth" (431). Harrington has literally *popularized* Machiavelli's temporal concept of *fortuna*. Temporality is no longer a threat, not even half the time. There is no pressing need to calculate the precise moment of legislative opportunity, the *occasione,* because the balance of property assures that England will become a republic: "Streams that are stopped may urge their banks; but the course of England into a commonwealth is both certain and natural" (660). The flowing of the river is no longer an emblem of *fortuna*'s threat to civic stability, but a promise of the dynamic perpetuity of a people organized inside the banks of utopian legislative orders.

To rationalize and control this reproductive movement of the generations, the legislator need only build the banks of his agrarian and electoral legislation. The legislator's action distinguishes him from the Hobbesian sovereign, who sees political power as the will of a single sovereign individual, and from the Levellers, who see it as a necessary evil against which native liberties must be defended. For Harrington sovereign political power is to be disseminated through the state, shared with as many citizens as possible. It is like gunpowder, which is "at once your safety and your danger, being subject to take fire against you as for you" (229). Yet when properly distributed, it becomes a rational force that can be exploited: "How well and securely is she by your galaxies so collected as to be in full force and vigor, and yet so distributed that it is impossible you should be blown up by your own magazine." He asks those who would question the possibility of such a confined or distributed sovereignty to tell him "whether our rivers do not enjoy a more secure and fruitful reign within their proper banks, than if it were lawful for them, in ravishing our harvests, to spill themselves?" (229–30). When legislation channels the people's political and reproductive potential, they come themselves to occupy the site of sovereign power. After the institution of Oceana's orders, they become a corporate entity that, like the mystical body of the king in the corporate fiction of the body politic, "never dieth" (431). The prospect of this immortality allows the lord orator Hermes de Caduceo to proclaim before the mustered ranks of the Oceanic tribe of Nubia that "this freeborn nation . . . is herself King People" (229).

Foundation, Superstructure, and Utopian Discipline

In the first part of "The Preliminaries" to Oceana, Harrington formulates his peculiarly economic definition of "equality": "An equal commonwealth is such an one as is equal both in the balance or foundation and in the superstructures, that is to say in her agrarian law and in her rotation" (180). This formulation of the state as a combination of an agrarian foundation and an electoral superstructure built upon it practically demands comparison with the Marxist formulation of society's economic base and cultural (legal, political, religious, aesthetic) superstructure. As Harrington's agrarian legislation encourages the ownership of the land by those who actually till it, so Marx's proletarian revolution encourages the control of capital by those who have labored to produce it. As Harrington's electoral legislation removes the dangerous disequilibrium between the material conditions of land distribution and the political superstructures that no longer reflect them, so the proletarian revolution will remove the alienating conflict between the oppressive conditions of production in bourgeois society and the various cultural strata that provide them with an ideological cloak or alibi.

When socialist historians discovered Harrington early in this century, these parallels encouraged them to read him as a bourgeois political theorist working toward a Marxist theory of the economic foundation of political history. Eduard Bernstein emphasizes Harrington's materialism, saying that he "came as near to a scientific conception of history as was possible in the seventeenth century. In his frequent references to *property* as the sole basis of political and other institutions, he makes it clear that his conception of property is sufficiently elastic" (206). Bernstein then stretches Harrington's conception of property as real estate to one of property as capital, which allows him to see Harrington's history of property holding as a history of the modes of production. R. H. Tawney calls Harrington "the first great English thinker to find the cause of political upheaval in antecedent social change" ("Interpretation" 200).

Later Marxist studies of Harrington have been more analytic and less genealogical. Christopher Hill criticizes the strangely ahistorical approach of his predecessors by noting the absence of a conception of mass political activity in Harrington's theory of revolution, arguing that he is "what Marxists call an economic determinist: he conceived of economic change as a blind impersonal force which somehow produced political change of its own accord" (*Puritanism* 312). C. B Macpherson's study of Harrington in *The Political Theory of Possessive Individualism* is the product of a painstakingly methodical analysis of his writings—something of a rarity in Harrington scholarship outside Pocock's.[8] He examines the relation between Harrington's agrarian legislation and his political electoral legislation, concluding that certain ambiguities and contradictions in Harrington's usage of such key concepts as the people, the gentry, and the balance may be resolved if we see him as an undeclared (perhaps unconscious) spokesman for an ascendant bourgeois gentry. Macpherson links Harrington with Hobbes, the Levellers, and Locke as proponents of a "possessive individualism" that is a key model for human personality in capitalist society.

But there is a strange dissonance between calling Harrington a celebrant of the transition from martial feudalism to bourgeois industry, and his express purpose of creating massive new assemblies of martial horse and foot. For a prophet of nascent capitalism, Harrington spends remarkably little time envisioning revolutionary modes of production. He seems unable to envision any social activity not nourished by agriculture in some fixed site (835). Activities like commerce, which moves between sites, or finance, which may not exist in a site at all but in relations of monetary forces, appear peripheral and deviant.

Beginning in *The Ancient Constitution and the Feudal Law,* Pocock has argued that Harrington was fundamentally ignorant of or uninterested in the theories of economic history that were developing in and even before his own time (124–27). He notes that had Harrington intended to institute a revolution in agriculture, he should have encouraged the accumulation of large estates rather than attempting to divide them through his agrarian legislation ("Introduction" 62). Because land or property is a historical absolute for Harrington, differences among political forms arise from their distribution of land among their citizens, not from the uses to which those lands are put under any particular mode of economic production. In an indirect attempt to refute Macpherson, Pocock has argued repeatedly that Harrington's polemical adversary Matthew Wren—though the son of a

Laudian bishop, a supporter of the Episcopal clergy, and a proponent of monarchy—is more a possessive individualist than Harrington is ("Contexts" 26; "Introduction" 88; *Virtue* 61). Indeed, Wren says specifically that Harrington overemphasizes the role of land and underemphasizes the role of commerce and finance in modern government (*Monarchy* 24). Still, Pocock has never really engaged the details of Macpherson's analysis, and the conflict continues between Pocock's analysis of Harrington's writing as a political rhetoric and Macpherson's analysis of it as an economic theory.

This conflict shows us a major difference between a scientific and a political paradigm: whereas the former may control a host of various concepts and procedures, the latter may be only one of several different paradigms at work in a single political speech act. It seems to me that there has not yet been any satisfactory study of the relation between the paradigms of economic and political theory at work in Harrington's writing. In this section I want to contribute to such a study by introducing yet another paradigm—the utopian. I will argue that Harrington's meticulous analysis of utopian discipline shows how to breed up a citizenry that will excel in both economic industry and political virtue: the utopian *homo disciplinabile* is an object of attention both compatible with and logically prior to *homo politicus* and *homo oeconomicus.*

Harrington does have a materialist theory of history that sets him off from Hobbes, Matthew Wren, and theorists of social contract and covenant in general. This theory is based on an analysis of two kinds of contradiction. The first is an "unnatural" contradiction between the ownership of the greatest part of the lands in a state (the "balance") and the political sovereignty created by a state's political orders—a contradiction, in other words, between its foundation and its superstructures. Harrington makes intelligible the circular progression of the Polybian *anakuklōsis politeiōn,* which moves from monarchy to tyranny to aristocracy to oligarchy to democracy to anarchy and back to monarchy. Monarchies, aristocracies, and democracies become tyrannies, oligarchies, and anarchies when the one, the few, or the many lose the balance, creating a tension that can resolve itself only by a movement to a new distribution of lands or a new distribution of political power. Rather than being a quasi-natural and moral process, the Polybian cycle becomes a rational dialectical history of the relationship between foundation and superstructure. Harrington sees this history as his greatest innovation: he eulogizes Machiavelli as the "prince of politicians," but claims that his own discovery of the doctrine of the balance is "that which interpreteth him" (274, 166).

The second kind of contradiction persists even inside certain "natural" polities, such as the monarchy of Oceana before the reign of King Panurgus (Henry VII). Unlike the monarchy by arms of Turkey (Harrington's exemplar of stable monarchy), Oceana had become a monarchy by nobility—a mixture of monarchy and aristocracy, in fact. In such a state the king is actually no more than an elevated noble, liable to replacement at the will of his fellow nobles and dependent on them for control of the people. The king is elevated in order to maintain a peace among the warring nobles, but so long as the nobility retains the balance of lands, the Oceanic monarchy is, in fact, ruled by the few. When the nobles deposed Dicotome (Richard II), they "got the trick of it, and never gave over setting up and pulling down of their kings" (197). Harrington does grant the hypothetical Hobbesian war of all against all a limited historical actuality in the history of the modern prudence, which has been "no other than a wrestling match" (196).

The pivotal event of recent Oceanic history was the attempt by King Panurgus to overcome completely this dependence on the nobility that created a contradiction within a "natural" form of government (197–98). Harrington's primary historical authority for this argument is Bacon's *History of King Henry VII*. According to Bacon, Henry's statutes of retainers, populations, and alienations undercut the power of local feudal lords by limiting their armies of retainers, discouraged the displacement of rural populations by enclosures, and encouraged the rise of a healthy independent yeomanry that would form the core of England's soldiery (6.93–95). But in his attempt to overcome this contradiction within a "natural" form of government, Panurgus inadvertently created an "unnatural" contradiction between the foundation and the superstructures, for the people then held the balance of lands under monarchical political superstructures, making the Oceanic monarchy "a government which of necessity must be new modelled" (Harrington 187). This transfer of lands finally produced a Hegelian moment in which a quantitative change became qualitative, changing the people from tenants of the nobility to de facto sovereigns. In his argument in *The Prerogative of Popular Government* with Matthew Wren's Hobbesian political philosophy, Harrington describes this change, arguing that "strength" is not the possession of some philosophical abstraction like the primal Hobbesian sovereign. It lies "not in a pair of fists but in an army, and an army is a beast with a great belly, which subsisteth not without very large pastures; so, if one man have sufficient pasture he may feed the beast, if a few have the pasture they must feed the beast, and the beast is theirs that feed it. But if the people be the sheep of their own pastures, they are not only a flock of sheep, but an army of lions" (411). The balance of military power in Oceana lies in the people, because they have the balance of lands to feed and support a militia. Harrington's martial designation of his two political classes as "horse" and "foot" shows that under a popular balance, soldier and citizen are one. The people become sovereign when the same man is the exerciser of martial virtue and the owner of the lands that make that virtue possible. His agrarian legislation attempts to see to it that these two remain the same man.

With a nod to Machiavelli's discussion of the pernicious effects of Rome's agrarian legislation, Harrington admits in *Oceana* that agrarian laws "of all others have ever been the greatest bugbears"; so he stages a debate between the Lord Archon and Philautus de Garbo, the oldest of five brothers and heir apparent to an estate worth £10,000 a year (231–41). The debate runs primarily to questions of the history and the necessity of the agrarian. The fourth objection Philautus raises to the agrarian is particularly interesting, for it brings us to the recurrent utopian question of the relation between civil and family government. Harrington's agrarian legislation, like Eliot's praying-town discipline, is a reorganization of the state from below. By modifying family discipline, it promises eventually to reform and stabilize the entire state.

The agrarian, Philautus argues, "is destructive unto families" (232). The Lord Archon responds that in a sense, the agrarian legislation he proposes is not revolutionary at all, for it merely responds to a situation already in existence. Philautus's argument, he says, is "as if one should lay the ruins of some ancient castle unto the herbs which do usually grow out of them, the destruction of those families being that indeed which naturally produced this order. For we do not now argue for that which we would have, but for that which we are already possessed of" (236–37). Because of the unwitting levelling of Panurgus and his son Coraunus, Oceana has levelled her own castles and has become in effect a popular commonwealth. In response to Wren's Burkean argument that the agrarian would make war against "universal and immemorial custom" (*Considerations* 89), Harrington argues that custom is not accretive but revolutionary, that there is a new custom formed by the revolutionary distribution of lands among the people (472). Harrington even extends this typically utopian critique of custom to the matter of contract, covenant, and conscience in what would seem to be a comment on the Engagement Controversy: "The whole dispute will come upon matter of conscience, and this, whether it be urged by the right of kings, the obligation of former laws, or of the oath of allegiance, is absolved by the balance" (203). The materialist doctrine of the balance cuts the casuist Gordian knot (Hill, *Experience* 193).

But England has not yet attained the fixed balance of Oceana: just as the English balance changed from monarchical to popular in the fifty years separating Henry VII and Elizabeth, so the Roman balance changed from popular to monarchical in the less than fifty years "between the lives of Scipio and of Tiberius Gracchus" (664–65). The balance of lands, even though it is the foundation of the electoral superstructure, contains no assurance of stability without agrarian legislation to fix it—a sign that we are some distance from the irreversibility characteristic of Marxist history. So the Lord Archon proposes a way out of the cycle of civic mutability: with the total yearly rent of Oceana calculated at £10,000,000 and individual holdings more or less limited by the agrarian to a yearly rent of £2,000, he claims that England's lands cannot pass into the hands of fewer than 5,000 holders, making a return to the rule of a one or a few impossible. Of course, this legislation may be revoked by future generations (Harrington has no Hobbesian notion of immutable contract), but he is confident that it will breed up new citizens who will see the reason in these laws and (what is nearly the same thing) the advantage that they may gain from them (665). Oceana's agrarian utopianism is conservative with regard to the present and radical with regard to the future, promising a Fabian reformation of family life and breeding through a gradual change in patterns of landholding.

In his discussion of the relation between the family and the state, the Lord Archon also addresses those political philosophers who see patriarchy as a natural model for monarchy. Here utopian eugenics comes together with the seventeenth-century radical critique of primogeniture (Thirsk). The Lord Archon reminds Philautus first of all that the agrarian law proposes no confiscation of estates, only their more equal division among sons. He argues that attempts to defend monarchy by appealing to the family must finally admit that the model of family government they invoke appeals in turn to monarchy. The Lord Archon's hypothetical example describes Philautus's situation exactly: "A man hath five sons; let them be called. Would they enjoy their father's estate? It is divided among them; for we have four votes for one in the same family, and therefore this must be the interest of the family; or the family knoweth not her own interest. If a man shall dispute otherwise, he must draw his arguments from custom and from greatness, which was the interest of the monarchy, not of the family; and we are now a commonwealth" (237). Similarly, in *The Art of Lawgiving* Harrington observes that the patriarchist apologists for monarchy have acknowledged only one form of family government, though it "may be as necessarily popular in some cases as monarchical in others." With a courageous disregard for anticommunist calumny, he describes an alternate family government uniting some six or ten households in family groupings not unlike those proposed by More, Quiroga, Winstanley, and Plockhoy (602–3). Just as "government whether popular or monarchical is equally artificial" (564), so family government of any sort is already a political choice, and political philosophy cannot appeal to it as the natural basis for kingship. To the traditional royalist analogy between the marriage contract and the social contract, which claims that both are voluntary but eternally binding once entered into, Harrington responds with a Miltonic defense of divorce on the grounds of withdrawn consent (indicated adequately by adultery or by other means): "There is an imperfection or cruelty in those laws which make marriage to last longer than a man in humanity may be judged to be a husband, or a woman a wife" (541). In his refusal to take the analogy as an unequivocal given, Harrington participates in that seventeenth-century debate over marriage contract and social contract analyzed by Mary Lyndon Shanley: "The course of the argument between Royalists and Parliamentarians illustrates the ways in which an analogue—initially introduced to support one argument—may itself become a focus of debate" (80).

The agrarian will revolutionize family life, which now treats its children "as we do our puppies: take one, lay it in the lap, feed it with every good bit, and drown five!" (Harrington 237). The Lord Archon tells of a friend who wonders why younger brothers do not rise up against their older fraternal oppressors. He contrasts the form of monumental immortality promised by the modern prudence of feudal England with that promised by the revived ancient prudence of Oceana: "Really, my lords, it is a flinty custom! And all this for his cruel ambition that would raise himself a pillar, a golden pillar for his monument, though he have children, his own reviving flesh and a kind of immortality." While feudal primogeniture is static, totemic, and subject to decay, the Oceanic agrarian is dynamic, phallic, and immortal.

In this reform of family life, the maternal earth couples with the paternal agrarian legislation. Like the female body, the earth is naturally fecund, able to generate rents without diminishing its own substance: "The earth yieldeth her natural increase without losing her heart; but if you come once to force her, look your force continue, or she yields you nothing" (410). Like the natural reproductive power of the people, the power of the land needs only to be harnessed by the utopist. Harrington modifies the Machiavellian metaphor for fortune once again: "The land through which the river Nilus wanders in one stream is barren, but where he parts into seven, he multiplies his fertile shores by distributing, yet keeping and improving, such a property and nutrition as is a prudent agrarian unto a well ordered commonwealth" (237–38). He changes *virtù* from its Machiavellian ideal of mastery and control to an ideal of generation and propagation: "If a river have but one natural bed or channel, what dam is made in it by this agrarian? But if a river have had many natural beds or channels, to which she hath forgotten to reach her breast and whose mouths are dried up or obstructed, these are dams which the agrarian doth not make but remove; and what parched fortunes can hereby hope to be watered by theirs only, whose veins having drunk of the same blood, have a right in nature to drink of the same milk?" (468). Machiavelli's *virtù* and *fortuna* are antagonistic: young men are more likely to succeed in asserting their *virtù,* for "fortune is a woman and if she is to be submissive it is necessary to beat and coerce her" (*Prince* 133). In Harrington, *virtù* becomes the act of rational legislation, and *fortuna* becomes the capacity for human and agricultural fertility. The former, "masculine" faculty is still dominant, but it is no longer a rapist. To nurture a new commonwealth, the Lord Archon's agrarian legislation aims to marry *virtù* and *fortuna* in a mixture of blood, milk, and earth.

Harrington's feminizing the land of Oceana finds a corollary in his objection to prostitutes, whose bodies are a land withdrawn from proper production. In one of his few forays into utopian social legislation, he condemns female wantonness—not because of its innate immorality but because it runs counter to the agrarian: "Such women as, living in gallantry and view about the town, were of evil fame and could not show that they were maintained by their own estates or industry, or such as, having estates of their own, were yet wasteful in their way of life unto others, should be obnoxious unto the animadversion of the council of religion, or of the censors" (354). Prostitutes or wanton women are not tied to the land and either generate money with no visible industry or (like financiers or Jews, in Harrington's eyes) live parastically on the industry of others.[9] Under Oceana's agrarian legislation, women will be like the land itself in that they will be strictly appraised by the father passing them along: no daughter will receive more than £1,500 in dowry (231). As the agrarian regulation of the sons' inheritances will encourage agriculture and industry, so this regulation of the daughters' dowries will encourage romantic love and fertility: "We shall at length have the care of our own breed. . . . The marriage bed will be truly legitimate, and the race of the commonwealth not spurious" (240). Harrington proposes to encourage this reproduction by taxing citizens with fewer children at a higher rate (226). The resulting increase in population is essential, for "populousness is that without which there can be no great commonwealth" (469). Women, like Oceana's industry and militia, are to be settled on its rationalized domestic enclosures of land so that Oceana may, in fact, become a commonwealth for imperial increase.

Harrington's utopian reform of family government through the regulation of inheritance and dowries is milder than the reforms proposed by Plato, More, Campanella, and Winstanley. Whereas Plato proposes to break down family ties completely by denying the reality of physical parenthood through the noble lie, Harrington proposes only a reform of inheritance that will prevent the accumulation of estates through primogeniture. Whereas Raphael condemns agrarian legislation as a mere stopgap on the way to the Utopian abolition of private property (More 31), Harrington makes it the foundation of a more efficient distribution of private property. Whereas Campanella proposes a program in positive eugenics that will improve the race directly, Harrington proposes only the removal of artificial strictures that hamper natural marital fertility. Whereas Winstanley metaphorically extends the theme of fraternal oppression (Cain's of Abel, Esau's of Jacob) to the oppression by the rich of the poor, Harrington seems concerned only with the actual younger brothers of wealthy families. But Harrington comes together with this utopian tradition in identifying customary primogeniture and dynastic patriarchalism as fundamental enemies of utopian rationality.

The legislator's reform of Oceana's agrarian foundation promises a gradual change in its family life; his reform of its political superstructures promises an immediate change in its civil and military discipline. The first stage in this political reform appears in the four divisions that constitute the first four orders of Oceana. We have seen the first three: the initial classification of persons according to their freedom as political subjects, their age, and their wealth. But this initial division also includes a division of electoral space that is to be immediate, unlike the spatial divisions that the agrarian will bring about in the future. In the fourth order the Lord Archon directs the apportionment of the land by a corps of surveyors into fifty new "tribes," one thousand "hundreds," and ten thousand "parishes." In Harrington's political dialogue, *Valerius and Publicola,* Valerius objects that the people of England, weary of political and religious divisions, "will never make a new division" of this sort. Publicola responds, "Why, then, they shall never have an equal commonwealth" (784). This is a typically utopian proposal: as a solution to the problem of spatial and ideological divisions plaguing the Protectorate, Harrington offers an accelerated and rationalized system of divisions. In this division of space as in the agrarian legislation, the land is analogous to the people—a raw material that legislation can infuse with a soul only through a rational utopian division. Commenting on the fourth order of *Oceana,* Harrington says, "For except the people be methodically distributed, they cannot be methodically collected, but the being of a commonwealth consisteth in the methodical collection of the people" (214). In utopia, dissection precedes life.

Fortuna does not disappear from Oceana altogether, for the Lord Archon's orders incorporate an element of the arbitrary in both the ballot and the rotation of office, making fortune both predictable and functional. The elections at the levels of the parish, the hundred, and the tribe replicate the division between the debating senate and the resolving prerogative, but the electoral divisions are unequivocally arbitrary. All elders blindly reach into an urn and choose one metal ball. The few who choose gold balls become the proposers of candidates for high office (and so the equivalent of the senate), while the many who choose silver balls become the voters for those candidates (and so the equivalent of the prerogative). Harrington gives both rational and providential arguments for this lottery. On the one hand, it makes the outcome of elections less predictable and thus less open to manipulation by factions. On the other hand, it stands in as God's representative in political determinations: God operated through the lot in the division of Canaan among the Hebrews and in the choice of Matthias over Barsabas as Judas's successor among the disciples (164, 544).

The rotation of office in Oceana is also a kind of rationalized fortune. *Rotation* is akin to fortune in its description of a constant alternation of political power and in its figurative and etymological associations with the *anakuklōsis politeiōn* and the *fortunae rota.*

Antagonists as diverse as Richard Baxter, John Milton, and the Fifth Monarchist John Rogers are willing to see Oceana's ballot and rotation as irrational and arbitrary. Baxter says that "the whole scope of the design is by the ballot and rotation to secure us from the danger of a probability of being ruled by wise or honest men" (*Baxter* 86). But Harrington's rotation is a circular movement in the service of a progressive, linear history. In his near oxymoron, it is an "equal vicissitude" (181, 473). The ideal of rotational government is not representation but near-universal participation; the deputies and knights serving "are less representatives in the proper sense than citizens taking their turn at participation and service" (Pocock, *Moment* 393). Fully one-fifth of the elders of each parish are present at the musters of the hundred and the tribe, and all the youth who are excluded from the franchise will in time be admitted to it (Harrington 842–43). Harrington's utopian republicanism, like Eliot's utopian Congregationalism, works for the maximum dissemination of paternal sovereignty.

Oceana, Harrington says, is governed by "an annual, triennial, and perpetual rotation" (228). The officers of all governing bodies will be elected yearly. The entire membership of those bodies will change every three years through rotation. Because this rotation is only partial, with one-third of each house retiring each year, those bodies will have a perpetual life, never disbanding completely as do the successive Parliaments of England: "For in motion consisteth life, and the motion of a commonwealth will never be current, unless it be circular" (248)[10] Once again, Harrington returns to the river as a metaphor for the dynamic immortality of Oceana. The senate and the prerogative tribe "are perpetual, not as lakes and puddles, but as the rivers of Eden; and are beds made, as you have seen, to receive the whole people, by a due and faithful vicissitude into their current. They are not, as in the later way [of successive parliaments] alternate. Alternate life in government is the alternate death of it" (264).

J. C. Davis calls Oceana "a dead society, a human machine, programmed forever for the repetitious performance of the same function; the epitome of the totalitarian state" (Utopia 239). But Davis's metaphor is much more appropriate to the political automaton that Hobbes introduces in the opening paragraph of *Leviathan*. Oceana's perpetuity is organic: the senate is like an orange tree, "having blooms, fruit half ripe, and others dropping off in full maturity . . . such as is at the same time an education or spring, and an harvest too" (Harrington 264). It is like a man, who though he "wears the same flesh but a short time, is nevertheless the same man and of the same genius" (265).

Harrington's fluvial and organic metaphors come together when he compares the rotation of office in the republic to the circulation of the blood discovered by William Harvey: "So the parliament is the heart which, consisting of two ventricles, the one greater and replenished with a grosser store, the other less and full of a purer, sucketh in and gusheth forth the life blood of Oceana by a perpetual circulation" (287). This is Harrington's resuscitation of organic metaphor—not as a hierarchical and static body politic but as a dynamic political organism reconceptualized from the cellular level. Davis observes that although Harrington seems to model his system of local government on that already in place in England, he makes one crucial change: no national officials serve at the local level (*Utopia* 226). Because political power is immanent in the entire body of the citizenry, neither a Tudor head nor a Hobbesian sovereign nor anyone representing them is anywhere to be seen.

Like Eliot's system of tens, fifties, and hundreds, Harrington's system of ballot and rotation is a disciplinary means to the creation of a new corporate subjectivity. As he moves into a discussion of the necessity of martial discipline, he gives us one of his rare meditations on human nature: " A man is a spirit raised up by the magic of nature; if she do not stand safe and so that she may set him to some good and useful work, he spits fire and blows up castles; for where there is life, there must be motion or work, and the work of idleness is mischief . . . but the work of industry is health. To set men unto this, the commonwealth must begin early with them, or it will be too late; and the means whereby she sets them unto it is education, the plastic art of government" (298–99). In the twenty-sixth order and the Lord Archon's commentary on it, Harrington proposes a system of free education administered at the tribal and national level. But Oceanic education goes beyond schooling to embrace the totality of civil life. The education of an individual is analogous to the legislative formation of a state because neither can achieve perfection unless shaped properly from the very first. The Lord Archon quotes Cicero: "*Ut male posuimus initia, sic caetera sequuntur.* What ever was in the womb imperfect as to her proper work, comes very rarely or not at all to perfection; and the formation of a citizen in the womb of the commonwealth is his education" (303–4). The legislator's disciplinary virtue informs the womb of the commonwealth; it can then bring forth *homo politicus.*

Oceanic education proceeds in a number of sites: in the schools, the universities, the trades, the professions, and, preeminently, the army. In his proposal for a civilian militia, Harrington follows in the tradition of *Utopia*. In Book 1 Raphael criticizes the idea of a standing army by pointing out its relative ineptness in times of war and its dangerous idleness in times of peace; one of the displaced populations threatening England is the horde of thieving soldiers who have been cashiered during peacetime (More 13–14). *Oceana* rationalizes the movement between warfare and civil pursuits in two ways: in the periodic muster of all citizens and in the natural maturing of citizens from youth to elders at age thirty. From the ages of eighteen to thirty, all citizens must attend the yearly musters at the levels of the parish, the hundred, and the tribe. Some of them go on rotation to occupy Marpesia and Panopea. This phase of regular martial discipline is a preparation for civil political life that will help "breed men of as good parts as no such matter. . . . He is very heavy who cannot perceive that in a government of this frame, the education must be universal or diffused throughout the whole body" (495). The entire nation becomes a school.

Harrington's proposals constantly suggest the convertibility of civil political life and military discipline. Eliot's distinction between civil and church government generates most of his utopian sequences, contrasts, comparisons, and resolutions; he barely hints at the role of military discipline. But Harrington's key generative distinction is that between the civil government of the elders and the military discipline and rituals of the youth, with church government reduced to a function of a single council of civil government. In a late tract Harrington appeals to the people's capacity for undergoing military discipline to defend them from charges that they have an inveterate predisposition to monarchy: "It is not a multitude that makes an army, but their discipline, their arms, the distribution of them into troops, companies, regiments, and brigades. . . . If they march, if they halt, if they lodge, if they charge, all is according unto orders. . . . It is no otherwise in the ordering of a commonwealth. Why say we then that the people are not to be trusted, while certain it is that they can have no other motion than according unto the orders of their commonwealth?" (738). The "orders" of *Oceana* are legislative proclamations and acts of arrangement, but they are also military commands. Man undisciplined "spits fire and blows up castles"; under *Oceana*'s martial/civil disciplinary orders, he spits fire on command and blows up designated castles.

This disciplinary formation of the citizen does not wither away; the martial discipline of *Oceana*'s youth persists even among the elders in the senate and the prerogative. The Lord Hermes de Caduceo praises the tribe of Nubia for having mastered the ritual of the ballot: "We have this day solemnised the happy nuptials of the two greatest princes that are upon the earth or in nature: arms and councils, in the mutual embraces whereof consisteth your whole commonwealth; whose councils upon their perpetual wheelings, marches, and countermarches, create her armies, and whose armies with the golden volleys of the ballot at once create and salute her councils" (228). The two houses undergo a perpetual rotation not because Harrington believes there is an inexhaustible supply of able leaders, as Gooch claims (Gooch 253), but because that rotation is itself a school of state. In the prerogative the three successive years of office are the first, second, and third "classes" (267). In the leading councils of the senate, there are to be "three forms (as I may say) in the school of state." In the first form the newly elected member undergoes a "novitiate" during which he is simply an auditor. The second year he begins speaking in the debates. In his third and final year he is capable of being a "very able leader." This rotational education is essential to Harrington's dehierarchized body politic, for "flesh must be changed or it will stink of itself; there is a term necessary to make a man able to lead the commonwealth unto her interest, and there is a term that may enable a man to lead a commonwealth unto his interest" (494).

Harrington's unusually inclusive franchise—he does not forbid the vote to defeated royalists, as do Milton, the Levellers, and even Winstanley—is an indication of his faith in the pedagogical powers of his orders. Government has a responsibility to overcome parties and factions, and "they of all the rest are the most dangerous who, holding that the saints must govern, go about to reduce the commonwealth unto a party" (204). Any who refuse the oath of loyalty are to be granted a three-year grace period on the assumption that their resistance will fade (227). Harrington shows Oceana's royalists gradually becoming strong supporters of popular government (350–51). In a late tract he addresses once again the dispute over whether virtuous men produce virtuous orders, or the other way around. Like Comenian education and Eliot's praying-town discipline, the Oceanic school of state promises a gentle and gradual conversion. Harrington warns the "saints" not to set about any ideological purges, for the disciplinary orders of a rational commonwealth will eventually produce new citizens and eliminate factions, "not through any force, as when cold weather kills flies, but by the rising of a greater light, as when the sun puts out candles." These predictions of disciplinary transformation are demonstrable by reason, but "suit better with the spirit of the present times, by way of prophecy. England shall raise her head to ancient glory, the heavens shall be of the old metal, the earth no longer lead, nor shall the sounding air eternally renounce the trumpet of fame" (745). But before this martial and millennial transformation of the world, whose foundation is an agricultural revolution, the utopist must have submitted himself to the rigors of a textual georgic.

Conversations with Particular Commonwealths

A somewhat perplexing provision of Harrington's proposed political reforms in *Oceana* is his excluding physicians from the franchise along with divines and lawyers. In *The Art of Lawgiving* he explains that divines are "inveterate enemies of popular power" and that lawyers are "feathered and aimed like sharp and sudden arrows, with a private interest point-blank against the public" (660). But he airs no parallel grievances against physicians. He does not even indulge in the traditional Protestant humanist critique of the physician as an "empiric," or quack, perhaps because the physician he wishes to exclude is not some journeyman medical mechanical but that more august physician whose university training (like that of divines and lawyers) must keep him from the yearly military musters whose discipline prepares the rest of the youth for political life as elders (309).

In any case it is unlikely he would have attacked them as empirics, for, as Matthew Wren argues, Harrington himself is a political empiric. Wren's anti-utopian raillery illuminates Harrington's approach to writing political theory. His principles, Wren says, are "merely effects and consequences of government, that is, no principles at all. . . . New models of government may be contrived with as much ease as a French tailor invents new fashions. It is the foundation of government upon undeniable principles, and the deduction from them, which render politics a complete science, without which the greatest conversation with particular commonwealths can but at most make men empirics in policy" (*Monarchy* 90). *Empiric* is a complexly derogatory term: it suggests one who fails to follow proper philosophical method and bases a presumptuous claim to knowledge on merely personal experience, not true learning. In particular, an empiric is a quack physician whose medical knowledge has been gained not at the universities (Wren was associated with the Oxford clerics and mathematicians) but through an immediate, unsavory, and possibly illicit practice on healthy, ailing, or dead bodies.

Harrington's utopian textual practice is a political empiricism that attempts to establish such contact with the bodies of ancient states. In the preface to the third book of *The Art of Lawgiving,* he contrasts a natural philosopher with a medical empiricist (here, an anatomist). The natural philosopher readily produces easily understood discourses on the body. He begins with general first principles, such as the claim that all bodies are composed of fire, air, earth, and water. The conclusions he draws from these may have a superficial persuasiveness about them, for anyone can see that a man's body returns to the earth when he dies.

Anatomy, on the other hand, is particular, immediate, and complex. It requires a meticulous and detailed knowledge of actual bodies, and its complexities are difficult to communicate: "The fearful and wonderful making, the admirable structure and great variety of the parts of a man's body, in which the discourses of anatomists are altogether conversant, are understood by so few that I may say they are not understood by any." Harrington's own political theory is like anatomy: "Certain it is that the delivery of a model of government (which either must be of none effect, or embrace all those muscles, nerves, arteries and bones, which are necessary unto any function of a well-ordered commonwealth) is no less than political anatomy" (656). Political anatomy is both more mechanical and more difficult than political philosophy.[11] It differs from political philosophy as Eliot's use of Scripture differs from hermeneutical millennialism, for it depicts itself as an act of pointing and arranging rather than an act of interpreting (though, of course, it is the latter precisely because it is the former). It designates and pieces together a model for a commonwealth from the texts of the ancient prudence, previously overlooked but now ready for immediate political application. In Harrington's utopian thought, the textual models of the ancient prudence have a materiality that transcends history as do the people and the land they will organize. The English in England are subject to the same organizing texts and principles as the Hebrews in Canaan, the Spartans in Lacedaemon.

At the same time, political anatomy, like Eliot's praying-town discipline, is a painstaking utopian georgic. It demands a self-disciplined and scrupulous attention to the organization of detail. As Eliot attempted to become God's "instrument" by immersing himself in the minutiae of translation, catechism, questioning, and admonition, so Harrington attempts to acquire the disinterested objectivity of a political scientist by immersing himself in the writings of the ancient prudence. Then, Frankenstein-style, he must anatomize the textual bodies of these ancient republics in order to construct an ideal soul of utopian orders that he can infuse into the suffering soulless body of the English people.

Wren's critique of this method is that it relies too much on "particular commonwealths," paying inadequate attention to "undeniable principles." His own philosophy of interpretation and deduction from first principles clashes with Harrington's empiricist political anatomy, and the two create distinct ways of writing political theory. Political philosophy like Wren's or Hobbes's begins with the passage from a state of nature to civil society in order to show the claims that political origin continues to make on contemporary political life. It closely associates *principles* with an originating historical moment (an *in principio*). The Hobbesian hypothetical history about the covenantal birth of sovereignty in a state of nature is the very foundation of his argument about present-day sovereignty.

At the beginning of *Oceana* Harrington critiques Hobbes's history, accusing him, in effect, of constructing a mystified theory of the origin of state power in the delegation of a "natural" (because prepolitical) power:

> Leviathan . . . hath caught hold of the public sword, unto which he reduceth all manner and matter of government; as where he affirms "the opinion that any monarch receiveth his power by covenant, that is to say upon condition, to proceed from want of understanding this easy truth, that covenants, being but words and breath, have no force to oblige, constrain, or protect any man, but what they have from the public sword." But as he said of the law that without this sword it is but paper, so he might have thought of this sword that without an hand it is but cold iron. The hand which holdeth this sword is the militia of a nation; and the militia of a nation is either an army in the field, or ready for the field upon occasion. But an army is a beast that hath a great belly and must be fed; wherefore this will come unto what pastures you have, and what pastures you have will come unto the balance of property, without which the public sword is but a name or mere spitfrog. (615)

At first it would seem that Harrington has simply adopted Hobbes's method, attempting only to go him one better by designating the balance of property as the extrahistorical origin of history that gives rise to sovereign power and then to law. This would mean little more than that an idealism of property had replaced an idealism of power. H. R. Trevor-Roper objects to such a materialist idealism in Harrington (50). So does Matthew Wren when he writes (at least temporarily in a Hobbesian vein) that political power necessarily precedes the distribution of land (*Monarchy* 19–20). In *Considerations* he accuses Harrington of a mystification of the concept of property: "If it be truly asserted that government is founded on property, then property consists in nature before government, and government is to be fitted to property, not property to government" (81–82).

Harrington's response to Wren, however, protects him from charges of an idealism of property and reveals that he practices a completely different political theory: "Whereas I nowhere deny property to derive her being from law, he insinuates that I presume property to be in nature. . . . Whereas in natural and domestic vicissitude, I assert empire is to follow the legal state of property, he imposeth as if I had asserted that empire must follow the natural state of property" (467). Harrington has turned political philosophy's search for extrahistorical origins into a circle of causes: he claims with Hobbes and Wren that government and laws proceed from covenant and that covenant proceeds from power. But he adds that this power is not a philosophical abstraction like the Hobbesian sovereign sword, but the concrete reality of a militia. The nature of this militia, in turn, depends on the distribution of lands. This distribution arises from an earlier law. Like Machiavelli, Harrington refuses to make the Hobbesian move out of recorded history into a hypothetical history of the state of nature, preferring to remain within a textualized political reality that he calls the "universal series of story" (183). He refuses to argue that any aboriginal covenant binds all the posterity of the covenanters; so far as the past has authority in the present, it is only through those orders that the political anatomist can draw up on the basis of his study of ancient states. Before the origin of any polity lies another polity, possibly less popular, possibly more, but always premarked with political form.

Harrington dramatizes this conflict between political philosophy and political anatomy in *Valerius and Publicola,* in which Valerius proposes the method of Wren, Hobbes, and the Levellers:

VALERIUS: Come, I will have you try something of this kind, and begin upon some known principle: as this, all power is in the people.

PUBLICOLA: Content. But the diffusive body of the people (at least in a territory of this extent) can never exercise any power at all. . . . Hence is the necessity of some form of government. (784)

Valerius catches on, adding, "The people, of themselves being in a natural incapacity of exercising power, must be brought into some artificial or political capacity of exercising the same." The "diffusive body of the people" is not a hypothetical population at the origin of political life, but a historical population at a particular moment in political history, in a state of "privation of government" like that of the English people during the Protectorate. Power does not derive from them but will be brought to them through a utopian encounter with Oceana's orders, which come in turn from textual models. As we will see, while Hobbes shows the birth of individual sovereignty from the death of popular sovereignty in a hypothetical past, Harrington shows the birth of popular sovereignty from the death of individual sovereignty in a hypothetical future.

Harrington begins his battle with Hobbes at the beginning of the first section of *Oceana:* the theoretical essay entitled "The Preliminaries, showing the Principles of Government." In response to Hobbes's claim that a law is but paper without a sovereign sword to back it up he claims that sovereign power is itself the product of a concrete legal system. He then generalizes his criticism: "But of this kind is the ratiocination of Leviathan ... throughout his whole politics, or worse; as where he saith of Aristotle and of Cicero, of the Greeks and of the Romans, who lived under popular states, that they 'derived those rights not from the principles of nature, but transcribed them into their books out of the practice of their own commonwealths, as grammarians describe the rules of language out of poets.' Which is as if a man should tell famous Harvey that he transcribed his circulation of the blood not out of the principles of nature, but out of the anatomy of this or that body" (162). Again, Harrington opposes the "nature" seen by political philosophy, which is an extrahistorical moment, to the "nature" seen by political anatomy, which lies in the common form of the republics of the ancient prudence. Like Harvey, Harrington discovers truths long hidden in nature with an empirical method based on an inductive study of particulars, not on "undeniable principles."

But unlike the practice of Harvey, and of Cicero and Aristotle as Hobbes describes them, Harrington's practice is both historical and prescriptive. It is a historical empiricism that claims the bodies and souls of ancient commonwealths are immediately present to the scrupulous reader, who can enter into conversations with them and the writers describing them. It offers these ancient states as models for national imitation and their legislators as models for individual heroic emulation. In his proposal for the education of Oceanic citizens, Harrington reveals his view of history as an assembly of political models by comparing travel in time with travel in space: "No man can be a politician, except he be first an historian or a traveller; for except he can see what must be, or what may be, he is no politician. Now if he have no knowledge in story, he cannot tell what hath been; and if he hath not been a traveller, he cannot tell what is; but he that neither knoweth what hath been, nor what is, can never tell what must be or what may be" (310). Indeed, a trip to Venice (such as that Harrington took in his youth) is the equivalent of a trip to the past or to the texts that preserve that past, for Venice alone among modern states "hath had her eye fixed upon ancient prudence and is attained to a perfection beyond her copy" (161).

In his conversations with the Scriptures, Harrington assumes a complex relation to radical Puritanism. On the one hand, his defense of scriptural authority against oral or interpretive authority seems consistent with that of the Independents. He repeatedly attacks the English translators of the Bible for having disguised its advocacy of popular government (175, 217, 618, 642). And his analysis in the second book of *The Art of Lawgiving* of the decline of the Israelite commonwealth from a scripturally based popular government to an oligarchy and a tyranny based on oral authority will also sound familiar to students of Puritanism. The "Commonwealth of the Hebrews" or "Elohim" was founded on written principles of popular orders such as those groupings initiated by Moses and Jethro in Sinai. It practiced ordination by the popular method of *chirotonia,* or the showing of hands, as in an election.[12] The later "Commonwealth of the Jews" or "Cabala" was founded on an oral law promulgated by the Jewish oligarchs. It consisted of "certain traditions by them pretended at the institution of the Sanhedrin to have been verbally delivered unto the seventy elders by Moses for the government of the commonwealth" and later codified as the Talmud (645). It practiced ordination by the aristocratic and monarchical *chirothesia,* or the laying on of hands, as in the Roman Catholic, Anglican, and Presbyterian hierarchies. Harrington traces this degeneration from chirotonia to chirothesia in the Hebrew commonwealth and in the early history of the Christian church, underlining his polemical point by calling the oligarchic practitioners of chirothesia "presbyterians" who "may pretend that . . . to be in Scripture, which neither is nor ever was there" (534).

But at the same time Harrington's philological conversations put him into conflict with radical Puritans such as those who propose the abolition of the universities: "We are commanded . . . to search the Scriptures; and whether do they search the Scriptures that take this pains in ancient languages and learning, or they that will not, but trusting unto translations only, and to words as they sound unto present circumstances (than which nothing is more fallible or certain to lose the true sense of Scriptures), pretend to be above human understanding, for no other cause than that they are below it?" (306–7). In his study of the Bible as a political document, Harrington never abandons this philological and anatomic method. Just as he resists the movements of Hobbes and Wren out of the "universal series of story" into philosophical first principles and hypothetical histories, so he resists the interpretations of radical Puritans who rely on a distinction between the letter and the spirit of Scripture and who recode the events of the Bible according to typological history. The utopist's reading produces an anatomic complexity of the surface that takes the Scriptures as a catalog of political models and lessons with contemporary applications, rather than a hermeneutical complexity of depth, which would take the Scriptures as the progressive cancellation of obscurity and revelation of truth. The utopist sees no radical division between Old and New Testament: the New Testament does not tear away the veils, but only stages the evangelical encounter of the Judaic and Hellenic versions of the ancient prudence.

Oceana's political polemics and history end, and its political fiction begins at the end of "The Second Part of the Preliminaries" with an act of reading—with a dramatized practice of political anatomy. The political chaos of the Oceanic parliament troubles Olphaus Megaletor, the general of the army of Oceana. His response (Olphaus is never further from Oliver) is to turn to books for guidance, among them Machiavelli's *Discourses*. He "happened upon" the second chapter of the first book, where he learned that all great commonwealths have been instituted in one action by single legislators. Inspired by the example of Sparta and emulous of its founding legislator, Lycurgus, he calls the army together and tells them his legislative plans. They unanimously appoint him sole legislator, or Lord Archon, and he deposes the sitting parliament.

But after gathering all power into himself, he immediately disperses it by gathering together a group of fifty "legislators," who begin "to assist him by labouring in the mines of ancient prudence, and bringing her hidden treasures unto new light" (207). Nine of them are chosen by lot to study the state organizations of the ancient prudence. When they are done, all fifty meet with the Lord Archon, and they debate the merits of various republics before coming to an agreement on the ideal orders for Oceana. In summary, Harrington offers "three remarkable testimonies" drawn from the reports on three independently formed republics: the Hebrew, the Spartan, and the Roman (210–12). The debaters discover certain remarkable parallels in "the Israelite divisions into rulers of thousands, of hundreds, of fifties, and of tens, and of the whole commonwealth into tribes; the Laconic into *obai, morai,* and tribes; the Roman into tribes, centuries, and *classes;* and something there must be of necessity in every government of like nature, as that in the late monarchy [of Oceana/England] by counties" (214). These parallel republican divisions indicate that the ancient prudence is a unified text, "first discovered unto mankind by God himself in the fabric of the commonwealth of Israel, and afterward picked out of his footsteps in nature and unanimously followed by the Greeks and Romans" (161).

Both Eliot and Harrington construct unified anthropologies, free from any need for an utterly savage or natural "other" to European man. But they reach this unity by very different routes. Eliot constructs a unified scriptural narrative. He produces a single, diffusive history in which all world cultures, including the Algonquian, originate at the fall of the Tower of Babel and the diffusion of peoples and languages following. Harrington reaches unity through a comparative study of various sections of the Bible and various gentile writings, dividing different cultures and different periods of the same cultures from each other and comparing them to see how God has formed the universal principles of human nature and the "universal series of ancient prudence" (174). This series is for Harrington what the course of the gentile nations is for Vico, for whom "uniform ideas originating among entire peoples unknown to each other must have a common ground of truth," a truth with its origin in human nature, which is in turn providentially formed and guided (Vico 22). The political anatomist constructs a synoptic text of the ancient prudence, one revealing the utopian reason underlying all republics and waiting for perfect and complete realization in the utopian present.

Harrington's consideration of the ways these republics divide their people and settle them on regularly apportioned enclosures of land is never very far removed from a consideration of the warfare these divisions and settlements make possible. The political anatomist examines the records of ancient republican warfare and then looks up from his texts to propose a revolutionary distribution of lands and sovereignty that will lead to an unprecedented form of warfare in the future. After examining the battle-scarred bodies of previous commonwealths, Harrington proposes not a political means of avoiding warfare but a transformation of England into a utopian state whose civil and military organization have become one. When Harrington's utopia comes closest to a secular imperialism it is also closest to a peculiar variety of millennialism.

Popular Erastianism and Secular Millennialism

John Eliot would no doubt have been disconcerted by the use to which Harrington puts his prize utopian textual authority, Exodus 18. Though both use the passage to support their proposals for the utopian division of persons and for the formation of popular government, Eliot goes to Exodus to get away from all secular political wisdom, whereas Harrington sees Moses as a student of gentile political wisdom like himself. Harrington defends his own study of the political learning of pagan Sparta and Rome and papist Venice on the grounds that Moses followed the advice of Jethro, a gentile Midianite, when forming his orders of ten, fifty, a hundred, and a thousand (177, 305, 496, 547, 629). We seem to have here an absolute distinction between textual methods, with Eliot attempting to exclude all merely human prudence and Harrington attempting to incorporate it.

But for Harrington, human prudence is never merely human: "Human prudence, in the first cause, is a creature of God, and in the second as ancient as human nature" (616). Neither the Fall nor any subsequent event in scriptural history changes this divine formation of man's nature as a political animal, which is therefore precisely the same for Hebrew, pagan, and Christian. Harrington can claim both that there were popular commonwealths in Midian and Canaan even before the founding of Israel as a popular commonwealth (616–17) and that "the heathen politicians have written, not only out of nature, but as it were out of Scripture: as in the commonwealth of Israel, God is said to have been king, so the commonwealth where the law is king is said by Aristotle to be the kingdom of God" (178). The transfer of the principles of the ancient prudence from gentile to Hebrew government, and from both to the Christian commonwealth of Oceana, is not a change in kind but a "transcription" (652). Though Eliot seems not to know that certain pagan and papist states were governed by non-monarchical principles, he and Harrington come together in their view of the universal and binary nature of the struggle between political forms. For both, popular government is the rule of written law, and monarchy the rule of men alone. We cannot distinguish between them as between theocrat and secular politician, for both see the Hebrews' election of King Saul as a triumph of merely human over divinely ordained political forms.

Each sees the same utopian relation between civil and church government, between the formation of the citizen and of the saint. Eliot's praying-town discipline begins from the assumption that civil man must be constructed before he can be turned into a regenerate saint. As we have seen, he reverses Fifth Monarchist custom by saying that rather than making visible sainthood a prerequisite for participation in civil life, such participation should be taken as a sign of spiritual election. Even the sequence of Eliot's *Christian Commonwealth* (which does not refer to any previously constructed church government) and his *Communion of Churches* (which relies on a prior civil authority) indicates that his theocratic political theory has a "secular" component. Harrington insists on a similar sequence: "Now as of necessity there must be a natural man, or a man indued with a natural body, before there can be a spiritual man, or a man in capacity of divine contemplation, so a government must have a civil part, before it can have a religious part" (678). Quoting gentile Jethro against the theocratic oligarchs, Harrington says that "the saintship of a people as to government consisteth in the election of magistrates fearing God and hating covetousness, and not in their confining themselves or being confined unto men of this or that party or profession" (204–5).

Harrington bases his defense of a state church on the integration of church and civil government in Israel. In matters of religion most people naturally give themselves over to public leadership, so that to deny them a state church would be the same thing as denying "liberty of conscience as to the state" (678). Still, toleration of all religions not "Popish, Jewish or idolatrous" is to be vigilantly protected, and no remaining dissenters are to be disqualified from civil office. This, too, has a scriptural precedent, for Israel, "though her national religion were evermore a part of her civil law, gave unto her prophets the upper hand of all her orders. . . . Democracy pretends not to infallibility, but is in matters of religion no more than a seeker" (218, 846). Harrington's language here is either careless or courageous, for it links him to such radical sectarian Seekers as Milton, Roger Williams, and John Saltmarsh (Hill, *World* 148–85).

But Harrington complains that "there is nothing more usual among divines that make mention of me than to call me madman or atheist" (759). If one thesis has united Harrington's readers, past and present, it is that if not an atheist or a madman, then he is at least a fundamentally secular thinker. Hill says that like Hobbes, Harrington has a "coldly secular attitude towards religion" (*Puritanism* 308). Arthur Barker calls *Oceana* "the product of secular and sceptical reasoning" (268). W. K. Jordan says Harrington took a secular point of view, though he fell in with the custom of his times by cloaking it in a theocratic rhetoric (3.282). Judith Shklar says Harrington's "paganism" was fundamentally incompatible with Puritanism and that his main aim was to remove God from politics ("Ideology" 684). Felix Raab agrees with Harrington's contemporary critics (Baxter, John Rogers, and even Cromwell, according to Bishop Alexander Burnet) on the matter of his "godlessness," with the slight reservation that for Harrington, the important thing about God is his irrelevance rather than his nonexistence (204). J. C. Davis denies an apocalyptic or theocratic element in Harrington's thought, saying that "his secular history of secular social processes is entirely compatible with the view that God, approving of government, had left men at liberty to devise its forms" (*Utopia* 211).[13]

There is some justice to Davis's claim, for Harrington does say that God nowhere forbids any particular form of government. Indeed, when there is a monarchical balance of land, kings are "of divine right" (574). God takes this attitude, however, not because he is indifferent to governmental forms but because he is the original republican upper house. At the beginning of the Hebrew commonwealth in Sinai, God speaks through Moses and Jethro as a utopian legislator (as he speaks, more mediately, through all legislators operating on the principles of the ancient prudence). The people may reject any law Moses proposes, "for if God, intending popular government, should have ordained it otherwise, he must have contradicted himself, wherefore he plainly acknowledgeth unto them this power."[14] When the people go against his wishes and elect Saul their king, despite the continuing popular balance of their lands, God leaves them to their folly: "This if God had withstood by his power, he must have introduced that kind of monarchy he had declared against" (525).

Like the Oceanic senate, God is a source of wisdom or authority that he embodies in proposed models of law and government, but (also like the senate) he does not exercise power in the form of the result; for Harrington, God proposes and man disposes. God's insisting that the people maintain republican orders would have put him in the awkward position of advocating popular government against the wishes of the people—a position Milton was to occupy in *The Ready and Easy Way*. Harrington's propositive God resembles much more closely God the Father in Milton's *Paradise Lost,* who created man "Sufficient to have stood, though free to fall" (3.99). To remove man's freedom of choice, God says, would be to unmake man:

> I formed them free, and free they must remain,
> Till they enthrall themselves: I else must change
> Their nature, and revoke the high decree
> Unchangeable, eternal, which ordained
> Their freedom: they themselves ordained their fall.
> (*Paradise Lost* 3.124–28)

Because of his conception of God's self-restraint, we seldom see in Harrington the uncompromisingly theocratic language we see in Eliot's exhortation to the saints to "set the crown of England upon the head of Christ, whose only true inheritance it is" (*Commonwealth* 139). True, the Lord Archon does define a commonwealth in good Fifth Monarchist fashion as "a monarchy, where God is king." But he explains that this is so only inasmuch as "reason, his dictate, is her sovereign power" (338). Harrington is close here to Winstanley's identification of "God" with "Reason." But God forms only the propositive part of the state reason of Oceana, for he must leave the result to the people. Furthermore, after the degeneration of the Israelite theocracy, God became no more than a *rex absconditus,* leaving all of his propositive wisdom behind him in Scripture.

Harrington's reliance on Scripture for his models of government explains in part his defense of a state church, for in addition to establishing "freedom of conscience" for the new corporate subjectivity of Oceana, his Erastianism has a philological function. Christ has commanded us *"To search the Scriptures,"* but "the immediate gift of tongues is ceased; how should skill in tongues be acquired but mediately, or by the means of education?" (679). Oceana must make "the best application of her reason unto Scripture," so the nation must have national universities, which entail a state religion (218)—Harrington doesn't say exactly why. Where the Puritan proponents of the universities in Old and New England argue that rational textual study is necessary to produce a godly clergy, Harrington seems to argue the converse. The universities provide philological wisdom on the proper meaning of the Scriptures and also (it seems reasonable to assume) the secular scriptures of the gentile ancient prudence. Because Oceana is itself a transcription of the ancient prudence into modern times, it requires an institutional means of assuring the accuracy of the copy.

In Harrington's odd form of popular Erastianism, church government is both parallel to and subordinate to civil government. The senate's council for religion consists of twelve knights, who see to it that state clerics perform their duties, that the two universities run properly, and that all benefices in the country maintain a yearly rent of £100. When a religious controversy arises, the council submits it independently to the two universities, each of which assembles a debating convocation of all resident clerics forty or older. After debate, each university sends its opinion to the council by means of two or three emissaries, who deliver its opinion and depart at once. The council then prepares the question for the debate of the entire senate and the eventual result of the prerogative. This indirection is necessary so that "the interest of the learned being removed, there may be a right application of reason unto Scripture, which is the foundation of the national religion" (251). In this separation of wisdom and interest, the universities are to the council of religion in church government what the senate is to the prerogative in civil government.

Similarly, after a parish petitions one of the universities for a new vicar, the university proposes a young cleric as a probationer for one year. At the end of that time the parish resolves either to keep him on as a vicar or to request another probationer. It is true, as Perez Zagorin says, that the established church of Oceana is "entirely under state control" (*History* 141). But this seems totalitarian only if we forget that "the state" reserves the result for the people—in this case, the individual parish. Harrington comments, "The universities, by proposing unto the congregation in every parish, do the senatorian office; and the people, thus fitting themselves by their suffrage or ballot, reserve that office which is truly popular, that is the result, unto themselves" (681). Here, too, Harrington attempts to preserve the interest of the many from the interest of the clerical few, while preserving the clerics' indubitable wisdom in matters of scriptural learning and education.

There are notable differences between Harrington's and Eliot's concerns in the reform of church government. As a practicing cleric, Eliot is more interested in resolving a dispute between preexisting Congregationalist and Presbyterian forms of church government, while Harrington proposes to abolish all church government above the level of the parish and to reconstruct it in a completely new form. Harrington is more adamantly anticlerical than Eliot is, for he forbids the clergy any role whatever in civil life. Harrington inveighs against church synods such as those forming the very core of Eliot's *Communion of*

Churches because of their tendency to encourage church interference in civil matters (308).

But the utopian similarities of their proposals are more striking. Eliot performs Harrington's corrective retranslation of the English Bible by returning to the Greek original of Acts 14:23 *(cheirotonēsantes de autois . . . presbuterous)*. Whereas the Geneva Bible gives us "And when they had ordained them elders by election," and the King James "And when they had ordained them elders," Eliot translates, "By holding up hands made them elders," and proceeds to elaborate his platform of popular church government *(Communion* 2). Rather than discussing the necessary moral qualifications of their clerics or the content of the ideal church doctrine, each organizes the details of a form of church government that will tend to produce virtuous clerics and an efficient determination of doctrine; doctrine is implicit in discipline. As Harrington attempts to harness the wisdom of the clerics without allowing their self-interest a role in civil life, so Eliot specifies that the pair of elders elected by each congregation must include a lay elder whose likely tendency toward a levelling democracy will temper the teaching elder's tendency toward prelacy—an implicitly republican balance between the inherent interests of a lay many and a clerical few *(Communion* 4–5). Eliot grants a greater independence to his church government, but he and Harrington share a utopian desire to prevent the establishment of any autonomous Episcopal hierarchy. All political power comes from below via an electoral assembly, not from above via an ordaining hierarchy. Harrington is, if anything, even more congregationalist than Eliot, since both his church and his civil government rise from the fundamental building block of the parish; Eliot builds his Christian Commonwealth from the strictly civil groupings of ten.

Harrington's primarily republican rhetoric is the utopian obverse of Eliot's primarily millenarian rhetoric. Nothing could be more out of place among Eliot's calls for universal submission to King Jesus than an appeal to Polybius or Machiavelli, but his distribution of sovereignty among various civil authorities (including a theocratic many, few, and one) and his reform of secular time according to the ritualized meetings of his civil groupings of individuals are essentially republican. Harrington's constant battles with the oligarchic Presbyterians and Fifth Monarchists and his praise of secular learning might lead us to overlook the millenarian side of his political thought, but the Lord Archon moves directly from proclaiming his thirtieth and final republican order into a lengthy millenarian exhortation (320–33). All of

Oceana leads up to this passage, which proposes an imperial campaign of world conquest and unification.

The Lord Archon produces the stable expansiveness of Oceana's millennialism by combining the virtues of two previous, nonmillennial republics: stable Venice (a "commonwealth for preservation") and expansive Rome (a "commonwealth for increase"). Venice is the republic that, before Oceana, most nearly attained the ideal political balance, with no internal cause of dissolution. By means of its orders, it has remained constant for one thousand years—a fortuitous period that Harrington lets speak for itself: "Whatever in nature is not sensible of decay by the course of a thousand years is capable of the whole age of nature; by which calculation, for any check that I am able to give myself, a commonwealth rightly ordered may for any internal causes be as immortal, or long-lived, as the world" (321). Venice is to Harrington's utopian proposals what the praying towns are to Eliot's: a successful experiment in an enclosed site demonstrating the practicality of utopian orders.

But Venice is not itself a millennial commonwealth. Though it has attained a seemingly perpetual stability, it lacks the complementary millennial attribute of organic imperial expansiveness. A government like Oceana's, the Lord Archon says, "is a commonwealth for increase. Of those for preservation, the inconveniencies and frailties have been shown; their roots are narrow, such as do not run, have no fivers [fibers], their tops weak and dangerously exposed unto the weather; except you chance to find one (as Venice) planted in a flowerpot, and if she grow, she grows top-heavy and falls too. But you cannot plant an oak in a flowerpot; she must have earth for her root, and heaven for her branches. 'Imperium Oceano famamque terminet astris' [Its empire is bounded by the ocean, its fame by the stars]" (320).

Harrington's quote from *The Aeneid* shows the imperial destiny hidden in Oceana's name all the while it suffered under the modern or "Gothic" prudence. Like Venice, it will be an equal and balanced commonwealth, but like Rome, it will be an imperial commonwealth for increase. Harrington denies that Rome's expansion abroad was made possible only by its class inequality and conflict at home, as Machiavelli claims. This turmoil was the accidental result of Rome's flawed and unequal birth (273–78). But "the balance of a commonwealth that is equal is of such nature that whatever falleth into her empire must fall equally, and if the whole earth fall into your scales it must fall equally; and so you may be a greater people and yet not swerve from your principles one hair" (322).

England's being an island nation brings Oceana closer to a utopia than any of Machiavelli's Italian republics could ever have come, for it creates an experimental isolation—not unlike that of Eliot's praying towns—that permits it an organizational hiatus before it embarks on its plan of world conquest. There are, for the time being, no nations lying outside waiting to invade Oceana and upset its civil experiment, only nonrepublics awaiting conquest by Oceana once it is organized as a commonwealth for increase. Just as the people of Oceana are now the passive raw materials for the legislator's organizational art, so these nations lying outside are the raw materials for Oceana's conquest.

Harrington attempts to reconcile the millenarian fiction of Christ's universal conquest at the end of the world with its more secular variants by showing the partisans of each the organizational means to their common goal of political stability and expansion. *Oceana* employs a rhetoric of reconciliation; the Lord Archon is at pains to show that nothing in his analysis of the ancient prudence is in conflict with the Scriptures. Quoting Proverbs 29:14 and then a series of other scriptural passages, he contrasts the inequality of Rome with the equality of Oceana, foretelling Ocean's imperial destiny:

> *And the king that faithfully judgeth the poor, his throne shall be established for ever.* Much more the commonwealth, seeing that equality, which is the necessary dissolution of monarchy, is the generation, the very life and soul of a commonwealth. And now, if ever, I may be excusable, seeing that "the throne of a commonwealth may be established for ever" is consistent unto the holy Scriptures. . . . These Gothic empires that are yet in the world were at the first, though they had legs of their own, but an heavy and unwieldly burden; but, their foundations being now broken, the iron of them entereth even into the souls of the oppressed; and hear the voice of their comforters: *My father hath chastised you with whips but I will chastise you with scorpions.* Hearken, I say; if thy brother cry unto thee in affliction, wilt thou not hear him? (322–23)

Here the Lord Archon uses a pastiche of biblical passages to bring saint and citizen together under the banner of the revived ancient prudence. He invokes Daniel's interpretation of Nebuchadnezzar's dream of the idol, identifying the idol with the unstable monarchies of the modern or Gothic prudence, coming very close to the millennialism of the Fifth Monarchists in the process. The idol's wobbly feet of iron mixed with clay reveal the origins of political instability in a contradiction between a state's agrarian foundation and political superstructures.[15]

He makes King Rehoboam's threat of scorpions (2 Chron. 10:11) the archetype of Hobbes's apology for the modern prudence, foretelling the increasing violence (which millenarians are free to interpret as annunciatory violence) to be expected from their attempt to hold together unnaturally mismatched agrarian foundations and political superstructures. And he puts Jehoshaphat's plea to the Lord for help (2 Chron. 20:9) into the mouths of the European sufferers under the Gothic prudence, making them (like the Indian on the seal of the Massachusetts Bay Colony) beg for English conquest.

As the Lord Archon's exhortation proceeds, Harrington's rhetoric continues to move between more millenarian and more secular perspectives on imperialism. On the one hand, the Lord Archon says that Oceana is to become "a minister of God upon earth, to the end that the world may be governed with righteousness" (323). The last three orders of *Oceana,* which establish its system of provincial rule, are the "buds of empire, such as, with the blessing of God, may spread the arms of your commonwealth like an holy asylum unto the distressed world, and give the earth her sabbath of years or rest from her labours under the shadow of your wings." He breaks into a rhapsodic pastiche of passages from the Song of Solomon, in which Oceana appears as the bride of Christ, concluding with a foray into Revelation when he asks what stands in the way of Oceana's imperial destiny aside from *"the dragon, that old serpent"* (333). On the other hand, he reinforces this apocalyptic plot from a strictly national perspective, saying that unless Oceana hurries to this conquest of the Gothic monarchies, the first European nation that "recovers the health of the ancient prudence shall assuredly govern the world, for what did Italy when she had it? And as you were in that, so shall you in the like case be reduced unto a province" (332–33).

It is true that Harrington's materialist history, with its key moment of transition in Henry VII's transfer of lands and power from the feudal nobility to the people, is some distance from the scheme of history favored by the Puritan millennialists, with its key moment of transition in the Marian persecutions and their Laudian aftershocks. But the two histories come together in their millennial vision of Interregnum Britain as an elect nation with an imperial destiny. The political allegory of *Oceana* begins just after Olphaus Megaletor has led his forces to victory in the last civil war generated by the modern or Gothic prudence. After he reforms the commonwealth according to the patterns of martial discipline offered by the ancient prudence, he proposes an unprecedented warfare that will unite *saeculum* and *millennium* and bring Oceana both "the patronage of the world" and the ability to turn the world into the "kingdom of Christ. For as the kingdom of God the Father was a commonwealth, so shall be the kingdom of God the Son; *the people shall be willing in the day of his power*" (332). If Harrington is indefinite about whether this will be a millennial or merely an imperial conquest, then he also says that the only way to settle the question is by submitting it to a trial by battle (333). In a later tract Harrington's Publicola throws down the gauntlet to the theocratic oligarchs, saying, "Let such as are truly saints but see what it is to rule the earth, and take the rule of the earth" (797). To dismiss Harrington's theocratic and millennialist language as superficial rhetorical gloss is to deny the essence of all political rhetoric: its desire to bring together a diverse audience and lead it to some course of action.[16]

So the relation between the secular and the sacred in Harrington is a matter not of either/or but of figure and ground. We can certainly pose the question, "Does Harrington sacralize politics, or does he secularize religion?" But any attempt to answer with finality one way or the other reveals more about our impulse to classify than about Harrington's writing. Davis's dispute with Pocock over whether Harrington's republicanism is to be seen as millennial or utopian arises in part from such an impulse. Pocock has argued that Harrington attempts to connect the languages of republicanism and millennialism: "Having presented the republican government as the culmination of western history, he naturally moved to presenting that history as culminating in the restoration of the kingdom of grace; and to equate republic and millennium was a climactically satisfactory solution to the problem of republican immortality" ("Introduction" 73). He shows that Harrington even had a precedent in Savonarola for claiming the identity of republicanism and millennial theocracy ("Introduction" 72n; *Moment* 102–13, 398). Because of this millennialism, Harrington's republican thought should not be considered utopian ("Introduction" 71; "Contexts" 30). Davis disagrees because (he says) millennial politics must take one of three forms: it must be the politics of saintly withdrawal, of saintly totalitarianism, or of saintly expectancy. Because Harrington practices none of these millennialisms and because he also suggests a reformation of state institutions, he must be a utopian rather than a millenarian (*Utopia* 209–12). But in my argument there is another kind of millennialism—the "catalytic millennialism" we can see in the Puritan utopists of the Interregnum, who claim that there are certain easily specifiable institutional means to the millennium. Though I agree with Davis that Harrington is a utopist, I am closer to Pocock in my reasons for doing so: Harrington is a utopist precisely because he does attempt to connect republic and millennium—because he sees a disciplinary reorgnization of time and space as the means to achieving the millennial immortality of the state and its worldwide empire.

Still, Harrington is a considerable distance from anything we could call Calvinist Puritanism. Pocock has drawn a parallel between the religious thought implicit in Harrington's political theory and that of Gerrard Winstanley. *Oceana,* which reconciles the secular and the sacred by shaping the body of the English nation with a providentially created soul of governmental orders, is like that ideal state depicted by Winstanley, in which "the restoration of social justice in the earth was coterminous with the resurrection of Christ in the body or of universal spirit in universal matter" ("England" 97). Pocock shows that this sort of thought arises in that murky ideological breeding ground the history of ideas refers to hesitantly as the English Enlightenment. He sees Harrington and Winstanley sharing a hylozoistic spiritualism that denies radical distinctions between spirit, matter, and reason.

Certainly, Harrington seems to be interested in linking spirit, matter, and reason in such a manner when he attempts to distinguish between two kinds of miracles in his *Prerogative of Popular Government:* "A continued miracle, as that the sea ebbs and flows, the sun always runs his admirable course, is nature. Intermitted nature, as that the waters of the Red Sea were mountains, that the sun stood still in the dial of Ahaz, is a miracle. To continue the latter kind of miracle were to destroy the former, that is to dissolve nature. Wherefore this is a certain rule: that no continued external act can be in the latter sense miraculous. Now government, whether in church or state, is equally a continued external act" (543). Government is a "continued external act," or "nature": the continued miracle of civil and church administration, the regular musters and elections of the youth and the elders, and the perpetual rotation of the two chambers of government. Here, Harrington seems very close to a form of deism, for he constructs a *deus absconditus* who is immanent in the continued workings of political nature.

But to initiate this continued miracle of government, Harrington relies on a miracle of "intermitted nature" that is the political equivalent of the Red Sea mountains or the sun in the dial of Ahaz. This punctive miracle, which would necessarily destroy the continued miracle of government if it persisted, is the appearance, legislation, and disappearance of Oceana's *rex absconditus,* the Lord Archon Olphaus Megaletor. His role in the creation of Oceana is the critical problem in Harrington's attempt to form a rational science of politics.

Lycurgan Oliver: Legislation as Sovereign Suicide

In this section I will argue that Harrington's practice of a historical and political writing based on heroic and antiheroic exempla accounts for the profound ambivalence of his address to Cromwell in *Oceana*. A more familiar practice of exemplary history, with some striking similarities to Harrington's, is Andrew Marvell's "Horatian Ode upon Cromwell's Return from Ireland" of 1650. A single aspect of the poem bears most directly on its attitude toward political transition: its two references to Julius Caesar.

In the first reference the recently beheaded Charles Stuart becomes Caesar and Cromwell becomes "heaven's scourge," a bolt of "three-forked lightning":

> Then burning through the air he went,
> And palaces and temples rent:
>   And Caesar's head at last
>   Did through his laurels blast.
> 'Tis madness to resist or blame
> The force of angry heaven's flame.
> (lines 21–26)

But in the second half of the poem, a young Caesar represents Cromwell as the conquering imperial hero:

> What may not then our isle presume
> While victory his crest does plume!
>   What may not others fear
>   If thus he crown each year!
> A Caesar he ere long to Gaul!
> To Italy an Hannibal.
> (lines 97–102)

The difficulty of this second reference to Caesar is that it comes into conflict with one common critical strategy for containing the poem's ambivalences. By encouraging us to link Cromwell with Charles and the first half of the poem with the second, Marvell makes it harder to claim that the poem simply dramatizes the speaker's reconciliation with Cromwell, his movement from a fearful portrait of Cromwell as regicide and Charles as martyr to a relatively sympathetic portrait of Cromwell as the virtuous civil/martial hero of the Commonwealth.

Consequently, we see a number of critical attempts to ignore or explain away the second reference. R. H. Syfret, analyzing Thomas May's translation of Lucan's *Pharsalia* (a key source for Marvell), notes many similarities between Lucan's negative characterization of Julius Caesar and Marvell's characterization of Cromwell in the first half of the poem. She suggests that Marvell models the more positive portrait of Cromwell in the poem's second half on Lucan's characterization of Pompey and Horace's of Augustus Caesar. But perhaps sensing the difficulties posed by Marvell's second reference to Julius Caesar, she denies it completely, saying that in the second half of the poem, "the analogy with Caesar is pursued no further" (168). John Coolidge follows suit, seeing a movement from a Lucan-influenced portrait of Cromwell as Julius Caesar the usurper to a Horatian portrait of Cromwell as Augustus Caesar the legitimate ruler. Annabel M. Patterson says that by offering Cromwell a choice of these two Caesarian roles, Marvell becomes a detached counselor rising above the political struggles of the Commonwealth (60–68). But neither Coolidge nor Patterson mentions this disconcertingly late reference to Julius Caesar. A. J. N. Wilson, in a detailed analysis of the Roman textures of the poem, avoids any discussion of the second reference to Caesar, perhaps because he sees the poem as an encomium to Cromwell, and "Encomium destroys itself, if it is not total, if it does not offer consistent and uniform praise of the character and conduct of the great man" (335). Elizabeth Donno simply denies the association: "The use of Caesar here [in line 101] is to be contrasted with its application to Charles in line 23" (240). Pierre Legouis agrees uneasily, saying that "Marvell is rather to be excused than praised for calling both antagonists 'Caesar' in one poem" (Marvell 1.302).

By suggesting that Marvell's Cromwell is a Machiavellian prince, Joseph Mazzeo brings us closer to an answer, though he finally fails by not being Machiavellian enough. He, too, works to distinguish the two references and, in fact, gives us two distinct reasons for doing so. The first "Caesar" doesn't necessarily refer to Julius, for the title was no more tied to a particular person than were its derivatives "Kaiser" and "Tsar." However, perhaps because relatively few of these caesars were struck down by republican tyrannicides, Mazzeo suggests an alternative distinction. Marvell is simply using historical exempla in a Machiavellian fashion, dividing exemplary personalities into collections of positive and negative traits appropriate to different arguments. Marvell is no more guilty of ambiguity than is Machiavelli himself,

who proposes Julius as a model for princely emulation in *The Prince*
and attacks him as an execrable tyrant in *The Discourses* (Mazzeo
71–72).

But Machiavelli's use of exempla in *The Prince* cannot resolve
things so neatly for us. In isolation, his exempla argue that a would-be
new prince can gain and hold political power by following certain procedures, which he proceeds to enumerate. But taken as a whole, *The
Prince* argues precisely the reverse. Because Machiavelli frequently
uses the same person to show both the successes to be gained by following a certain procedure and the defeats to be expected by failing to
follow another, he shows that the new prince is fatally dependent on
fortuna because he cannot possibly master all her contingencies. His
Boethian "Tercets on Fortune" reassembles Caesar's exemplary traits
into a unified personality:

> If then your eyes light on what is beyond, in one panel Caesar and
> Alexander you see among those who prospered while alive.
>
> From their example we well realize how much he pleases Fortune and
> how acceptable he is who pushes her, who shoves her, who jostles her.
>
> Yet nevertheless the coveted harbor one of the two failed to reach, and
> the other, covered with wounds, in his enemy's shadow was slain.
>
> After this appear countless men who, that they might fall to earth with
> a heavier crash, with this goddess have climbed to excessive heights.
>
> (*Works* 747–49)

Machiavelli offers few, if any, examples of new princes who have successfully established long-lived dynasties, but many examples of new
princes overthrown by established princes, republics, other new
princes, or impersonal quirks of *fortuna.* On this exemplary level, then,
The Prince is an obliquely republican treatise, for it reveals to the
would-be new prince his extraordinary dependence on *fortuna* and the
impermanence of the political artifact he wishes to create compared
with that of the republican legislator.[17]

Even granting Mazzeo's distinction between Machiavelli's rhetorical
intentions in the two works, the separation between Marvell's two Caesars cannot hold; for Caesar's prowess as a conquering general was not
unrelated to his ability to institute a tyranny, and this mixed nature is
equally relevant to Marvell's picture of Cromwell. As a figure of dictatorial power, Cromwell can become either the architect of a new
republic or the tyrant enslaving his state. He can be the agent either of
a progressive and millennial history or of a cyclic and backsliding

return to tyranny. Although in the final analysis Marvell praises Cromwell's martial virtue and heroic disinterestedness, he also warns Cromwell, by connecting him to Charles through Caesar, that the slayer of a tyrant may in time make himself the object of a tyrannicide.

Marvell's ambivalent portrayal of Cromwell is a fitting introduction to Harrington's lesser-known but no less ambivalent portrayal of Cromwell as the Lord Archon Olphaus Megaletor in *Oceana.* Judith Shklar says that Harrington's dedication of his utopia to Cromwell is "a puzzle, comparable to Machiavelli's dedication of *The Prince*" to Lorenzo de' Medici ("Ideology" 684). Though the comparison is apt, the puzzle is not altogether baffling: like Machiavelli, Harrington dedicates his work to a patron whom he hopes to transform in the work itself. Harrington creates in the figure of the Lord Archon a complex model for Cromwell's emulation, writing an ode in prose on the Lord Protector's dictatorial power that combines praise, exhortation, and admonition. Only Cromwell has the power that can found the rule of law in a republic, the rule of men in an oligarchy, or the rule of a single man in a tyranny. In *Oceana* Harrington directs a heroic encomium toward the abdicating Lord Archon he hopes to make Cromwell into and a muted philippic toward the self-perpetuating tyrant he fears he will become.

The moment of legislation is of such critical importance in Harrington's utopian system that it is a moment of divine grace acting in history (Pocock, "Introduction" 30; *Moment* 395–96). It is the product of a new Christian synthesis of the Hebraic and the Hellenic, for the Lord Archon is "from Moses and Lycurgus, the first legislator that hitherto is found in story to have introduced or erected an entire commonwealth at once" (Harrington 210). Harrington's description of this unified and instantaneous act of legislation is a utopian revision of the Machiavellian *ridurre ai principii,* "reduce to principles." Machiavelli describes this action as a necessary technique of republican leadership. Because the republic is a political organism, it is subject to corruption and must periodically be reminded of the value of its founding principles, whether by the threat of an outside force, by the invention of some corrective institution such as the Roman tribunate, or by the leaders' severe punishment of corrupt citizens. This return to principles is a disciplinary mnemonic that reminds citizens of the value and the power of their republican *ordini:* "Between one case of disciplinary action of this type and the next there ought to elapse at most ten years, because by this time men begin to change their habits and to break the laws" (*Discourses* 388). Any republic fortunate enough to have a regular supply of leaders who can provide such vigorous reminders can last forever (467).

But for Harrington the state is organic only in the sense that it is genetically determined at conception. He sees in England, as Machiavelli never truly sees in Italy, the possibility for an act of primal legislation. The Lord Archon responds to Machiavelli's argument with Pauline impulsiveness: "Think me not vain, for I cannot hold; a commonwealth that is rightly instituted can never swerve, nor one that is not rightly instituted be secured from swerving by reduction unto her principles" (321). The disciplinary restraint of corruption must be built into the republic's orders from the very start, not imposed from outside by the fortunate intervention of a good leader. The utopian republic requires a single good legislator, not a succession of good disciplinarians, for legislation is a single, instantaneous, and autonomous act of political poiesis: "Whereas a book or a building hath not been known to attain perfection, if it had not a sole author or architect, a commonwealth, as to the fabric of it, is of the like nature" (207). Harrington's account of the legislator's ultimate responsibility for political disorder also reveals the scope of his power: "The vices of the people are from their governors; those of their governors from their laws or orders; and those of their laws or orders from their legislators" (303). Harrington removes all the irrationalities of Machiavellian *fortuna* by concentrating all generative power in the legislator. Hill says that Harrington was an economic determinist because he described revolutionary social change without the active political participation of the masses (*Puritanism* 312). We might call him a legislative determinist for precisely the same reason. However, in attempting to preserve his ideal of rational utopian immortality from such a reliance on *fortuna,* Harrington constructs a mythological supplement to utopian rationality that is equally far removed from his ideal. This supplement appears when he attempts to account for the appearance and subsequent withdrawal of an autonomous single legislator.

Harrington's utter reliance on the legislator may seem surprising at first, for his primary modification of the Polybian theory of a republican balance of the one, the few, and the many is his discarding the claims of the one to a role in the regular operation of government. The one has only a vestigial presence in the councils and magistracies elected by the knights of the senate and the deputies of the prerogative and in the pro tem dictatorships of wartime. Pocock explains that "Harrington at no time shows signs of believing that the special virtue of a One is necessary to the republican balance, and his Lord Archon appears only in the non-recurrent role of legislator" ("Introduction" 47). But the nonrecurrence of this role does not make it insignificant. Even though Harrington's rational and predictable materialist dialectic of landholding and political power moves us away from a history focused on individuals, this very dialectic depends on the intervention of unique individuals at crucial moments of historical transition. One such intervention brought the transition from that era of history dominated by the ancient prudence (despite the presence of monarchies like that of backsliding Israel) to that era dominated by the modern prudence (despite the presence of model republics like Venice): "But as there is no appearance in the bulk or constitution of modern prudence that she should ever have been able to come up and grapple with the ancient, so something of necessity must have interposed whereby this came to be enervated and that to receive strength and encouragement. And this was the execrable reign of the Roman emperors, taking rise from that *felix scelus,* the arms of Caesar" (188). Julius Caesar is the dictator/tyrant whose military power makes possible the fundamental "translation of ancient into modern prudence" (401). Harrington's Cromwell stands at a similar historical juncture, for it lies within his power to effect the transition from the modern prudence to a revived ancient prudence, becoming Caesar's mirror image. Harrington's rhetorical purpose in *Oceana* is to see to it that Cromwell becomes Joshua or Lycurgus rather than Saul or Julius Caesar, a dictator/legislator rather than a dictator/tyrant.

The appearance of such transitional world historical figures is, from the point of view of Harrington's system, utterly unpredictable and irrational. There is no Venetian model for the legislator as there is for the ballot, for Venice has no originating heroic Lycurgus. Machiavelli himself had diagnosed the rarity of legislators in modern times: "Very rarely will there be found a good man ready to use bad methods in order to make himself prince, though with a good end in view, nor yet a bad man who, having become a prince, is ready to do the right thing and to whose mind it will occur to use well that authority which he has acquired by bad means" (*Discourses* 163–64). The Lord Archon is the mythical creator of the rational orders of Oceana, but unlike Moses, Theseus, Lycurgus, Solon, Romulus, Utopus, and Solamona, who all legislated in the misty distance of a mythical past, he must act in the historical present.

We can see that this kind of legislator is mythical even from the point of view of Harrington's political psychology. Olphaus is the only person in Oceana whose private reason and interest are identical with the public reason and interest. He has no interest outside the welfare of his nation: no family, no faction, no particular religion, no regional loyalty. Consequently, he is motivated by heroic emulation alone, not by any aspect of his relation to his contemporaries. As we have seen, the origin of *Oceana* is his reading of Plutarch's "Life of Lycurgus": "Being on this side assaulted with the emulation of his illustrious object, on the other with the misery of the nation, which seemed (as it were ruined by his victory) to cast herself at his feet, he was almost wholly deprived of his natural rest, until the *debate* he had within himself came to a firm *resolution:* that the greatest advantages of a commonwealth are, first, that the legislator should be one man, and secondly that the government should be made altogether, or at once" (207; emphasis added). As is appropriate for the individual in whom the entire sovereignty of the state temporarily resides, Olphaus alone is capable of a disinterested combination of the "debate" and the "result." But this puts him outside the conception of human nature prevailing everywhere else in Harrington's writing, making Olphaus temporarily the microcosmic embodiment of the future corporate sovereignty of Oceana.

As the debating wisdom of the knights and the resolving interest of the deputies circulate into and out of Oceana's bicameral political heart, so this initial debate and result form an embryonic heart, sending Harrington once again to William Harvey for an analogy. In his *Anatomical Exercitations concerning the Generation of Living Creatures,* Harvey describes the embryonic heart, or *punctum saliens,* of a chicken's egg as that "bloody capering point" that first begins to move on the fourth day of its incubation, initating the chick's development. This point is so small that it disappears completely during its systole, or contraction, "so slender are the first rudiments of creatures' lives, which the plastical faculty sets on foot by so undiscoverable beginnings" (89–90).

Similarly, in *A System of Politics* Harrington says that a nation without a government is like "an egg unhatched," and its legislator, or "first mover from the corruption," is its *punctum saliens* (839). Ideally, this mover should be an individual legislator, not a council: "If the *punctum saliens,* or first mover in the generation of the form be a sole legislator, his proceeding is not only according to nature, but according to art also, and begins with the delineation of distinct orders or members" (839–40). Though Harrington's political anatomy is an implicit critique of the Hobbesian myth of civil origins, he must himself turn to a myth of origin. Just as Harrington's metaphor attempts to keep us from questioning the origin of the *punctum saliens,* so it attempts to keep us from questioning the legislator's motivation for legislation. Olphaus lives only inside the closed mythical order of heroic emulation, his precursors being Moses, Jethro, Lycurgus, and God. Inspired with genial warmth by the ancient prudence, he is the mythical organic origin of the rational organic state mechanisms of Oceana; as such, he lives outside those orders.

The Lord Archon's abdication can be no more rationally explained than can his legislation. True, the model of self-denying sovereignty permeates Oceana, particularly in the rotational legislation that prevents the maintenance of political power and in the agrarian legislation that prevents the dynastic accumulation of property and so military power. But the Lord Archon's self-denial necessarily lies outside Oceana's orders; it is not the result of their constraining discipline but a precondition for their existence. The Lord Archon's continuing presence after those orders are in place would create a superfluous sovereignty or, even worse, a divided one. He would remain as an individual absolute sovereign alongside the corporate utopian sovereignty of the senate and the prerogative; and a legislator who retains his absolute legislative power for too long tends to turn into his tyrannical opposite.

To make some sense of the Lord Archon's abdication, Harrington creates a ritual of state transition in the concluding section of *Oceana,* which is entitled "The Corollary" (341–59). As the *OED* reveals, the title itself is of some interest. *Corollary* derives ultimately from the Latin *corollarium,* the money paid for a laureate chaplet, or little crown *(corolla).* In the seventeenth century it had the now-obsolete sense of "something additional or beyond the ordinary measure, a surplus, a supernumerary," and this is the sense implicitly favored by modern writers on Harrington, who have treated "The Corollary" as a baroque excrescence. Because it is the most literary passage in all of Harrington's writing, depicting dramatic events without adding anything of substance to his political theory or his analysis of English history, it has received no close attention as a formal unit. But it is also a corollary in the sense of "something that follows in natural course, a practical consequence, result" and of "something added to a speech or writing over and above what is usual or what was originally intended; an appendix, a finishing or crowning part, the conclusion." The movement beyond "what was originally intended" is the movement out of abstract political theory into a utopian political rhetoric designed to shape the course of English history. It is, in fact, the crowning part of Harrington's utopia because it is an attempt to ensure, first, that

Olphaus/Oliver will take on the essential role of legislator and, second, that he will abdicate afterward, receiving in compensation for his efforts only a symbolic *corolla* and not an actual crown. "The Corollary" of *Oceana* is a manual of state etiquette showing the people and their legislator how to behave when the former graciously show the latter to the door.

"The Corollary" proceeds on its most obvious level as an encomium to Olphaus and so an attempt to create in Cromwell an interest in the rewards of fame gained through heroic emulation. Olphaus abdicates his archonship and, Cincinnatus-style, retires to his country house. In his absence the senate debates, and the prerogative resolves upon, a way to show him proper gratitude. When he returns, they give him formal speeches of praise and three more particular honors: a yearly income of £350,000, the command of a temporary standing army that will hold off hostile nations still oppressed by the modern prudence, and the right to receive foreign ambassadors. Olphaus lives out a long life in great honor and is memorialized at his death with a gigantic equestrian statue.

But the symbolic gratitude that Oceana expresses for the Lord Archon's gift of sovereign power is also its first exercise of debate and result, and so also its first demonstration of its ability to exercise that sovereignty. The gratitude of a free commonwealth to its legislator is simultaneously a symbolic action offered in exchange for a gift of incomparable worth, and a public notice that all debts are canceled and that there will be no actual return of the gift. Alongside the narrative encomiastic plot of "The Corollary," Harrington presents a subtler consideration of the nature of republican gratitude. Though Harrington constantly tells Cromwell how much fame he will gain from his heroic legislation and abdication, he balances this with an insistence on the republic's necessary independence of its legislator and a muffled warning about the dangers of tyrannous presumption.

He constructs this ambivalent encomium by reworking Plutarch's "Life of Lycurgus." Just as Olphaus's legislation begins with his reading Machiavelli's account of Lycurgus's legislation (207), so it concludes with a Lycurgan withdrawal from power. Harrington describes the aftermath of Olphaus's legislation by beginning "The Corollary" with a lengthy paraphrase of Plutarch's tale of the final days of Lycurgus. Like Lycurgus, Olphaus takes an aesthetic pleasure in beholding "not only the rapture of motion, but of joy and harmony, into which his spheres without any manner of obstructing or interfering, but as it had been naturally, were cast." But because the full analogy between

Lycurgus and Oliver is indiscreet when pushed to its logical conclusion, Harrington attempts to limit its scope, saying that Olphaus "saw no more necessity or reason why he should administer an oath unto the senate and the people that they would observe his institutions, than unto a man in perfect health and felicity of constitution that he would not kill himself" (342). And no less? This is a strangely consanguine analogy, particularly in view of the means of Lycurgus's death; for once the Oceanic "constitution" is in place, Olphaus does indeed become redundant and, though perfectly healthy, he begins committing political suicide. The aesthetic pleasure that both he and Lycurgus take in contemplating the motions of their republican orders is in part the pleasure of self-extinction, for the artifact has replaced its artificer, the circulatory heart of the commonwealth its *punctum saliens*. Harrington cannot suggest to the Lord Protector that he emulate Lycurgus's self-starvation, but neither can he altogether ignore the political function it served.

Consequently, Harrington Christianizes Lycurgus's suicide by having Olphaus retire to his country house for a period of prayer and fasting. But in his deliberation over and announcement of his plan, we get an indication of just how great a threat he poses: "Whereas Christianity, though it forbid violent hands, consisteth no less in self-denial than any other religion, he resolved that all carnal concupiscence should die in the place, to which end, that no manner of food might be left unto ambition, he entered into the senate with an unanimous applause and, having spoken of his government as Lycurgus did when he assembled the people, abdicated the magistracy of Archon" (342). Though Harrington discreetly generalizes the Lord Archon's reflections, this carnal concupiscence and food of ambition can be none other than the Lord Archon's own.

As he leaves the senate chamber, the knights respond with a show of those "violent hands" that Christianity forbids: "The senate, as stricken with astonishment, continued silent, men upon so sudden an accident being altogether unprovided of what to say; till, the Archon withdrawing and being almost at the door, divers of the knights flew from their places, offering as it were to lay violent hands on him; while he escaping left the senate with the tears in their eyes of children that had lost their father" (342). Given that these "children" now possess the sovereignty that their "father" once had and that he who had it once might have it again, we should not be surprised at their initial silence; and their offer "as it were to lay violent hands on him" contains at least a hint of the competitive violence of Freud's primal horde. Certainly, Harrington does not presuppose any subconscious oedipal ambivalence. But the people of Oceana are at the mercy of an ambivalence of their own, one they cannot resolve through the utopian reason of their orders. They are caught between their gratitude to the Lord Archon for initiating their eternal commonwealth and their fear that he who possessed total sovereignty at one time (or someone taking him as an exemplum) might possess it again in the future. Their response is not cannibalistic, but it is oddly ritualistic.

After the Lord Archon's departure and the beginning of the senate's deliberation over the honors they will give him, Harrington begins his own consideration of the role of gratitude in political life, claiming as Machiavelli had before him that the people of a republic are always grateful to their leaders. Significantly, he does this not by listing instances of such gratitude but by arguing that certain cases of their opposition to great men should not be seen as ingratitude. The Roman people honored Camillus for his prowess in the battlefields surrounding Rome, but they rightly opposed him in the city when he opposed popular liberties. As Rome's gratitude to Camillus for his military services outside the city should not be allowed to extend inside the city, so Oceana's gratitude to the founder of a commonwealth should not extend so far as to allow a divided sovereignty inside the commonwealth he founded. Athens's ostracism of Aristides the Just should not be seen as ingratitude, for by assuming the role of "universal umpire of the people in all cases," he threatened the normal functioning of Athens's republican orders (342–43). As the Athenians were justified in banishing an admittedly virtuous man because his mere presence in the state threatened the continued integrity of its orders, so Oceana is justified in seeing to it that the Lord Archon withdraws from his archonship one way or another; for at the moment of his legislation and in his archonship, he also approaches princehood. Harrington indirectly shows the necessity for the Lord Archon's abdication by juxtaposing it with the popular resistance resulting from alternative courses taken by figures of comparable power in previous commonwealths.

By stepping down from the chair of the legislator, the Lord Archon makes it possible for Oceana to repay its debt symbolically by elevating him to a somewhat different (because not sovereign) chair. As one of the senatorial proposers economically remarks, "If this debt were exacted, it were not due; whereas, being cancelled, we are all entered into bonds." Oceana's ambivalence appears clearly in the six resolutions to honor Olphaus it resolves upon in his absence. His immense yearly income is to be for his lifetime only and cannot be passed along to his descendants, making it impossible for him to establish any hereditary archonship on its strength. His right to receive ambassadors is to be "by and with the council of state, according unto the orders of this commonwealth," as his command of the Oceanic standing army is to be "by and with the council of war," according to the same orders. The second three resolutions further temper the first three by threatening exile and heavy taxation to citizens who attempt to make "distinctions" between themselves and the rest of the commonwealth (346–47). While these warnings do not specifically mention the Lord Archon, their juxtaposition with the three orders honoring him (and the fact that before he legislated, no individual could possibly have been more "distinct" from the anomic people of Oceana than he) suggests that they have him in mind.

The rest of "The Corollary" is somewhat foreshortened. Oceana gives the returning Olphaus a tumultuous welcome, but the "lord strategus" of the senate tells him with peremptory politeness that "his highness could not doubt, upon the demonstrations given, but the minds of men were firm in the opinion that he could be no seeker of himself in the way of earthly pomp and glory; and that the gratitude of the senate and the people could not therefore be understood to have any such reflection upon him" (350). Olphaus takes temporary command of the standing army, but it disbands before the end of the second year of the commonwealth. Harrington follows with some perfunctory consideration of more limited utopian matters: taxation, the pay of the army, and the reform of the theaters. And the Lord Archon becomes a lobbyist for the agrarian legislation, which evidently requires some elaboration beyond the thirteenth order he decreed (352).

The end of "The Corollary" concludes Harrington's attempt to deal with the troublesome figure of Olphaus, a wobbly idol with one foot in the turbulent modern prudence as the general winning the last conflict it produced, and one foot in the revived ancient prudence as the legislator who reinstitutes it. Comparing Olphaus with Timoleon, who grew old among the Sicilians he freed from tyranny, Harrington says that he lives out his life with honor, reaching the antediluvian age of 116 in the fiftieth year of the Oceanic republic. But Harrington's final picture of Olphaus has an edge: the honorific inscription on the equestrian statue erected at his death is simultaneously a taboo or prohibition, for Olphaus is to be remembered as a mythical founder, not imitated as an exemplum. He is "Pater Patriae," but he is also the "sole Legislator" of Oceana (358).

Harrington's adaption of the "Life of Lycurgus" reveals perhaps the most distinctively premodern quality of his political rhetoric: the fact that it is a rhetoric based on exempla, in which Lycurgus (among others) steps directly into the seventeenth-century political arena as an object for heroic imitation and emulation. Hobbes points the way to the future of political science when he claims to found a science of politics based not on a series of heroes but on first principles. In the second part of *Leviathan,* he warns against the dangers of imitating the Greeks and the Romans. The records of the ancient prudence produce "*tyrannophobia,* or fear of being strongly governed," no less surely than mad dogs produce hydrophobia, for once young men are bitten by the accounts of ancient regicides (who call themselves "tyrannicides"), they are themselves infected with a regicidal enthusiasm (214). But we should not overlook the peculiar daring of Harrington's exemplary history: in his emulative series of Lycurgus/Olphaus/Cromwell, Harrington encourages the Lord Protector to imitate first the tyrant, then the tyrannicide.

There is no trustworthy evidence that Cromwell ever read the work Harrington dedicated to him. John Toland reports that Cromwell's agents intercepted the manuscript at the printers, taking it to the Lord Protector's residence at Whitehall. Following them to Whitehall, Harrington playfully seized the infant child of Cromwell's daughter, Elizabeth Claypole, telling her that her father had kidnapped a "child" of his own. This brought her to intercede with her father, who released the manuscript, and Harrington dedicated the work to him in gratitude. But Cromwell spurned it, saying, "The gentleman had like to trepan him out of his power, but what he got by the sword he would not quit for a little paper shot" (Toland xix–xx). However apocryphal this story, Harrington himself decided soon enough that his prince-book had missed its mark and that Cromwell had missed his chance to become Olphaus. In *Pour Enclouer le Canon,* a brief tract of May 1659, Harrington refers to Cromwell's reign as "the perfidious yoke of the late tyranny" (728)—not a state of utopian potentiality but the latest instance of the turmoil generated by the modern prudence.

But No Goose-Quill, No Scribbling

So far, we have considered Harrington's political writings as a more or less unified corpus, and this is not much of a distortion so far as their propositional content is concerned. He may allow for a simplified ballot here or for a delay in the agrarian legislation there, but for the most part he is monotonously consistent; no reader of Harrington's works would ever think of attributing his ultimate failure to any reluctance to repeat himself. Like Eliot, he is supremely confident about the coherence of his original plans, and his failure to rethink this model amid changing political circumstances has something in it of the legislator with a full-blown state in his head. Yet the nature of his political rhetoric underwent a considerable change in his three-and-one-half-year career, as we can see in his changing conception of the role of the political writer or anatomist.

The utopian form of *Oceana* allows Harrington to speak in the self-effacing voice of Raphael Hythloday rather than in the conquering voice of King Utopus. He speaks as one who has seen these orders realized in practice, not as one who wishes to impose his private model on an unsympathetic nation. Harrington can disclaim any self-assertive or presumptuous voice, for he merely comments on the orders of the Lord Archon. The long central section of *Oceana,* entitled "The Model of the Commonwealth of Oceana" (210–340), alternates between the Lord Archon's orders and Harrington's commentary on them. The former have a performative immediacy—the first order "distributing," the thirteenth "constituting," the eighteenth "appointing," the twenty-sixth "instituting." These godlike fiats are only fitting, for as "The Corollary" tells us, "In the art of man, being the imitation of nature which is the art of God, there is nothing so like the first call of beautiful order out of chaos and confusion as the architecture of a well-ordered commonwealth" (341). In a sense, the legislative imagination ruling Puritan utopia, which concentrates more on organization and order than on the details of utopian social life, brings it an immediacy that literary utopia cannot match, for we can hear its legislative architecture spoken into existence.

Because the Lord Archon is more intent on putting his model into action than into writing, Harrington follows along behind with the rationalizing voice of commentary (210). He provides explanations, historical analogies and precedents, polemical asides, and reports on Oceanic debates over certain orders. In this commentary the Lord Archon's legislation appears to be the painful institution of a new civic ritual. At first, the Venetian-style electoral machinery, with its urns, metal balls, ballot boxes, and paper pellets for casting votes, seems gamelike and trivial. Epimonus de Garrula denounces it as imported popish beadwork (243). Even the Lord Archon worries about the unavoidable complexities of describing his orders in writing (222, 265). But the people gradually become accustomed to the new civic ritual and its underlying reason, for that reason forms them into new civil subjects: "And albeit they found them in the beginning somewhat froward, as at toys, with which, while they were in expectation of greater matters from a council of legislators, they conceived themselves to be abused, they came within a while to think them pretty sport, and at length such as might very soberly be used in good earnest" (214). Harrington-as-commentator longs to have *Oceana*'s discursive complexities disappear into the instinctive movements of the rational state it prophesies.

But as we have seen, this attempt to institute a new and rational civic ritual in *Oceana* was quite unsuccessful, and only partly because of the maddening complexities of the Venetian ballot. Harrington gives vent to his frustrations at the begining of his *Brief Directions:* "There is nothing more apparent than that this nation is greatly disquieted and perplexed through a complication of two causes: the one, that the present state thereof is not capable of any other form than that only of a popular government; the other, that they are too few who understand what is the form or model naturally necessary unto a popular government, or what is required in that form or prudence for the fitting of it unto the use of this nation" (584). Consequently, Harrington followed his baroque and discursive formal utopia with a series of didactic and polemical works in different genres, from the compressed legislative platforms of *The Art of Lawgiving* and *The Rota* to the colloquial "drama" of *Politicaster* to the dialogue of *Valerius and Publicola* to the two editions of *Aphorisms Political* to *A System of Politics,* which organizes aphorisms in chapters.

This movement from one genre to another grew increasingly frantic as each proved inadequate to Harrington's didactic and propositive purpose. Though his utopian model remained basically the same, his mode of writing altered after it failed to turn the Lord Protector into the Lord Archon. We can see the beginnings of this shift in the "Epistle to the Reader" of *The Prerogative of Popular Government* (1658), Harrington's first major work after *Oceana.* He begins by insisting once again on the necessity for a single legislator, and so long as he discusses this necessity in general terms, we are on familiar ground. Because legislation is the initiating and punctive equivalent of the ongoing debate and result it will give rise to, it consists of two parts, invention and judgment. While judgment should be left to the entire people of a state, "Invention is a solitary thing. All the physicians in the world put together invented not the circulation of blood, nor can invent any such thing, though in their own art; yet this was invented by one alone and, being invented, is unanimously voted and embraced by the generality of physicians. . . . Hence, where government is at a loss, a sole legislator is of absolute necessity" (391). The situation of the legislator here seems still to be very much like that of Olphaus Megaletor at the conclusion of "The Second Part of the Preliminaries" to *Oceana.*

Yet there has been a significant change. Harrington dedicates neither *The Prerogative of Popular Government* nor any of his later works to a particular individual. *The Prerogative* has only an ironic dedication to the group Harrington takes as Matthew Wren's circle of supporters, "the university wits or *good companies,* upon condition that they laugh not always in the wrong place" (390). The "Epistle to the Reader" of *The Art of Lawgiving* (1659) begins, "It was intended that there should have been an epistle dedicatory of this book; but while reason and honesty must be . . . , it is no time for such a client to expect a patron" (600; ellipsis in original). Harrington's later writings fail to mention Cromwell as anything other than "the late tyrant." But his dictatorial power was an essential component of the Lord Archon, whose power of *invention* consisted both of Harrington's ability as a political anatomist to study the ancient prudence and construct a model and of Cromwell's ability as a military leader to dissolve Parliament and bring the people together in disciplined orders to judge the model. The people who resolve upon the Lord Archon's model have already been shaped by it; they are no longer the anomic people of Oceana, but the new corporate subjectivity of King People, assembled in civil and military muster. In *Oceana* the formal invention and proposition of a model are already an exercise of sovereign power.

In the absence of such a figure of dictatorial power, Harrington attempts to take on the role of legislator, claiming that "the duty of the aristocracy, consisting in invention, may be done by any one man and in his study" (392). All the same, the problem of legislative means looms larger, for the utopist has no power to put the anomic people of his nation into the capacity to judge. As Harrington lost a clear idea of the individual whom he hoped to turn into a legislator and took on the role himself, he became less a utopist, more a polemicist. He found himself increasingly forced to defend the virtue of the political anatomist against those who rail at the mere fact of his writing: "God, to propose his commandments to the people of Israel, wrote them in two tables; *the decemviri,* to propose their commandments unto the people of Rome, wrote them in twelve tables. The Athenians proposed in writing signed with the name of the particular inventor. After this pattern do the Venetians ... the same at this day. But no goose-quill, no scribbling; your grandees are above this. ... They are not for the Scripture, but the Cabala" (392–93). Attacking the Cabalistic tradition of oligarchic, self-mystifying power, Harrington denies any merely private ambition by an almost Puritan flight into the nurturing authority of his sacred and secular scriptures.

From the perspective of Matthew Wren, utopian writing is both too far from and too close to the exercise of political power in particular states. At best, political writing is a private hobby: "I beseech you, sir, are not we the writers of politics somewhat a ridiculous sort of people? Is it not a fine piece of folly for private men sitting in their cabinets to rack their brains about models of government? Certainly our labors make a very pleasant recreation for those great personages who, sitting at the helm of affairs, have by their experience not only acquired the perfect art of ruling, but have attained also to the comprehension of the nature and foundation of government" (*Considerations* A4r). In *Monarchy Asserted* Wren says that Harrington's private speculations on government can never be trusted "till he have spent some years in the ministry of state" (n. pag.). We assume that those who serve in the ministry are too devoted to their sovereign to waste time writing on politics while serving him, or to divulge state secrets afterward.

For the theorist of Stuart absolutism, there is between political philosophy and political practice an unbridgeable gap filled by the *arcana imperii:* the Hermetic cult of royal power that helped preserve the mysteries of absolutist rule, providing Stuart poets, dramatists, and political philosophers with a vocabulary of disguise and dissimulation (Goldberg 65–85). Robert Filmer begins his *Patriarcha* with an act of self-denial much like Wren's: "First, I have nothing to do to meddle with mysteries of the present state. Such *arcana imperii,* or cabinet councils, the vulgar may not pry into." So mysterious and overwhelming are the arcana of royal rule that they would "dazzle the eyes and exceed the capacities of all men, save only those that are hourly versed in managing public affairs" (54).

According to Wren, the utopist violates this space of mysterious political insulation by moving too close to the workings of particular states. In *Monarchy Asserted* he scoffs at Harrington's attempt to place himself in the line of Plato, Aristotle, Livy, Machiavelli, and More. Unlike those writers, who kept themselves within "general terms" and "preserved the freedom of philosophers," Harrington has written a book that is "adapted to the occasions or necessities of a particular juncture" (n. pag.). Proper political philosophy should be disinterested, removed from the play of power in political life, but *Oceana* "is not proposed with the temper and moderation becoming a philosophical opinion, but with the heat and passion belonging to a design." Furthermore, this descent into particular proposals (like the political empiric's conversations with particular commonwealths) is a descent of social station, "for though a general discourse concerning government may fairly become any gentleman, the proposing (or imposing rather) a particular model seems to relish too much of a design and wants that modesty and submission that ought to be in all private men" (110).

In *Leviathan* Hobbes sees the gentlemanly political philosopher playing two roles: the instructor of the people and the counselor of the sovereign. The former attempts to disseminate the reason of state, teaching the people "the essential rights which are the natural and fundamental laws of sovereignty" so they learn "how great a fault it is, to speak evil of the sovereign representative . . . or to argue and dispute his power; or any way to use his name irreverently" (221, 222). The counselor of the sovereign must be both experienced and disinterested. He speaks not from "examples, or authority of books" but on the basis of a long involvement with the affairs of government, with "intelligences and letters . . . and with all the records of treaties, and other transactions of state" (169, 170). He must also be disinterested, which is to say, his interests must coincide with those of the sovereign he counsels; this is "the first condition of a good counsellor" (169). This counselor rises above the particular interests and disputes of particular men, unbound by his personal relation to their struggles and their covenants. His prince occupies the sole locus of sovereignty (there can be no republican many, few, and one). The counselor takes it as his task to examine the origin, the nature, and the powers of this sovereignty and then to represent them to his sovereign in counsel. The Hobbesian counselor speaks from an autonomous site analogous to that of the Hobbesian sovereign and, in fact, consubstantial with it: "The persons counselling are members of the person counselled" (29–30).

The utopist, on the other hand, makes a self-abasing descent into particularity and conflict. As Foucault says, he "cannot occupy the position of the jurist or philosopher, i.e., the position of the universal subject. In this general struggle of which he speaks, he is necessarily on one side or the other: he is in battle; he has adversaries; he is fighting for victory" ("War" 17). Harrington defends his own defense of popular government against the attacks of Wren not by depicting it as a disinterested philosophical discourse, but by championing it as a heroic trade complementary to warfare itself: "I study not without great examples, nor out of my calling; either arms or this art being the proper trade of a gentleman" (395). In an attempt to establish an emulative series of such heroic gentleman politicians, a series parallel to that of the gentleman legislators, Harrington fights Wren for the possession of Machiavelli, who "throughout his works ... intendeth not carelessly to start some philosophical opinion, but applieth everything home and expressly unto Italy, though not without some despair, yet with the ardour (or, if you will have it so) with the 'heat and passion belonging unto' so noble a 'design'" (708).

Harrington's defense of Machiavelli is reminiscent of *Advancement of Learning,* where Bacon praises the Machiavellian form of history as a practical meditation on exempla: "The form of writing, which of all others is fittest for such variable argument as that of negotiation and scattered occasions, is that which Machiavelli most wisely and aptly chose for government; namely, observations or discourses upon histories and examples. For knowledge drawn freshly and in our view out of particulars knows best the way back to particulars again; and it contributes much more to practice, when the discourse or discussion attends on the example, than when the example attends upon the discourse" (4.56). If Harrington writes political philosophy, it is a Baconian political philosophy for use. In *Virtue, Commerce, and History* J. G. A. Pocock engages in a polemic with Marxist and other social historians that is reminiscent of Wren's with Harrington. He argues that throughout history all readers of Machiavelli and Hobbes, and so presumably all readers and writers of political theory of any kind, have been concerned only with the discursive implications of their writing, not at all with its practical consequences (14). But Harrington's utopian reading of Machiavelli as a utopist, as a political writer with an explicit "design" that can be turned to good use in England, would seem to be an exception so telling that it may well lead us to reject altogether any such absolute opposition between discourse and practice: a passionate desire to have practical political consequences animates Harrington's utopian discourse.

But the utopist must also be disengaged from public life, at least from established factions and parties agitating the rubble of the modern prudence, if for no other reason than to engage himself more securely to the corporate people whom he hopes to write into being. Otherwise, he becomes too much like the lawyer, who preserves the existing state and a place for himself within it by aggravating the complexities of its law. Harrington translates with approval Bacon's comment that detached "political persons" like himself, who have studied the public interest and the models of the ancient prudence, are better qualified to discuss politics than are lawyers, who are "obnoxious and addicted each unto the laws of their particular country," and so have "no freedom or sincerity of judgment, but plead as it were in bonds" (Harrington 697).

Of course, there is an irreducible tension in this demand that the utopist or political person be both engaged with political particulars or designs and disengaged from lawyerly political office; but it is an essentially utopian tension, which brings Harrington very close to More himself. True, Harrington distinguishes himself from More when he says that More in his *Utopia,* Plato in his *Republic,* and Bacon in his *New Atlantis* "speak higher than will fall into the capacity of practice" (697).[18] But like most of More's early modern readers, Harrington tends to identify *Utopia* with its second book, ignoring the complexities of the Dialogue of Counsel in Book 1. There the character "More" criticizes Raphael's positive proposals much as Harrington criticizes More, saying that his "academic philosophy is quite agreeable in the private conversation of close friends, but in the councils of kings, where grave matters are being decided, there is no place for it" (More 28). He advocates instead "another philosophy that is better suited for political action, that takes its cue, adapts itself to the drama in hand, and acts its part neatly and well." In response, Raphael criticizes "More" much as Harrington criticizes political counselors and lawyers, saying that any such engagement will corrupt the true philosopher; he would become like the sycophantic counselors to the king of France or the self-serving lawyer whom he once debated at the court of John Cardinal Morton. If the Dialogue of Counsel is More's unresolved autobiographical debate between his role as a detached and independent political theorist (Raphael) and his role as an engaged counselor working decorously behind the scenes ("More"), then Harrington's fiction of the utopist or political person, who writes from a site of detached independence in order to influence a potential legislator, is an attempt to resolve the debate.

As the legislator is the abdicating opposite of the self-perpetuating tyrant, so the utopist is the altruistic opposite of the self-serving lawyer, for he writes in order to lose a place, not to gain one. Like the legislator, Harrington says, he is a gentleman working against hereditary privilege on behalf of the popular government of the future: "Of all controversies of government, those in the vindication of *popular* government are the most *noble,* as that from whence all that we have that is good is descended to us (391; emphasis added). This paradoxical utopian conflict between Harrington's origin and his intention was also apparent to a Royalist named J. Lesley, who in June 1657 wrote Harrington a letter with a memorable title "A Slap on the Snout of the Republican Swine that rooteth up Monarchy" (Blitzer 3). Lesley is particularly upset by Harrington's apparent betrayal of his own aristocratic class. Harrington is a noble vindicating popular government, a bachelor writing against bachelors and fruitless marriages, an eldest son writing against primogeniture, and a former gentleman of the bedchamber to Charles I explaining why kingship is no longer possible.

So far as utopian writing attempts to enclose and manipulate displaced populations, forming them according to models of civil and church government, of military and electoral discipline, it is an exercise of sheer domination, real or wished for. But utopian writing is also an exercise in self-extinction, for it envisions no determinate position of authority within the utopian government for the utopist himself. True, he may be the only one in the commonwealth who can fully comprehend the form of its government: "In using a commonwealth, it is not necessary it should be understood; but in making a commonwealth, that it be understood is of absolute necessity" (776). Harrington claims that his own discovery of the doctrine of the balance elevates him above Livy, the Venetians, Machiavelli, and Bacon (659). This total knowledge, however, leads not to political power but to contemplation—a contemplation more Lycurgan than Platonic, as we can see when we compare the famous conclusion of Book 9 of *The Republic* with the opening of the fourth chapter of Harrington's *System of Politics:*

GLAUCON: I understand. You are speaking of the city whose establishment we have been working out—the one that can be found nowhere on earth because it is laid out only in language [*en logois*].

SOCRATES: Well, perhaps there is a pattern laid up in heaven for the man who wishes to contemplate it, and to colonize it by contemplating it. But even if this state does not now exist and never will, it is the only state whose political life he will ever participate in. (*Republic* 415–17)

There is in form something that is not elementary but divine.
The contemplation of form is astonishing to man, and has a kind of trouble or impulse accompanying it, that exalts his soul to God.

As the form of man is the image of God, so the form of a government is the image of man. (Harrington 837)

Harrington's utopianism brings him a self-consuming and Lycurgan apotheosis—a quasi-divine vision of a this-worldly form, not a Platonic this-worldly vision of a divine form.

As it became clear that there was no alternate Olphaus waiting in the wings, Harrington found the prospect for this political contemplation dimming. It is remarkable that even as his calls for a reasoned debate in response to *Oceana* brought forth ad hominem polemics and derision of his "scribbling" and "modeling," Harrington continued to defend the faculty of invention and to describe his writing as an individual act of political poiesis: "A parliament of physicians would never have found out the circulation of the blood, nor could a parliament of poets have written Vergil's *Aeneis*." And a council attempting to invent in place of a single learned utopist would produce a chaos like that of a musical consort trying to take over the role of its composer (842). Political anatomy, Harrington says, is very much like anatomy proper: true, it is an art, not a science, but it is an art founded in nature, not fancy (723). To test his scheme of popular government, Harrington challenges anyone to find an internal inconsistency with his model, saying that he will alter it for the better if possible, or admit it destroyed if not. But he repeats that it must stand or fall on its fitness as a political artifact (597–98).

In *Monarchy Asserted* Wren says that as an artist may contrive a verisimilar fiction whose parts show no internal contradiction, and as several scientists may offer internally consistent but false explanations of natural phenomena, "so in government, it is not difficult to invent variety of forms, the parts of each of which taken separately, may maintain a fair correspondence and agreement among themselves, and yet the whole be far enough from attaining to perfection" (178). Harrington supposes (not unreasonably) that the basis of Wren's objection is that the ideal commonwealth he describes exists nowhere. He responds by distinguishing between this truth ("truth of fact") and another ("truth of nature"). A political fiction may express truth of nature if it is based on principles drawn from many different commonwealths, even if they are nowhere realized in fact in a single commonwealth (693–94). Harrington claims both the authority of nature and the authority of invention for his model, for it is based on the principle that the balance of landholding determines political form, which is "as ancient in nature as herself, and yet as new in art as my writings" (411).

Still, however fundamental his discovery, the inventor or creator of a utopian model is no more a legislator than is a dictator. Even if we leave aside the question of the fit between this political artifact and the political realities of the Protectorate, its internal coherence breaks down when it comes to producing or predicting the arrival of an abdicating legislator. The relation between the utopist and the dictator whom he writes in order to influence is, in Harrington's terms, the relation between authority and power. At first this seems an ethical opposition—that between "rightful authority" and "mere power." Indeed, it had that sense in many seventeenth-century political discussions (Tuck). But Harrington characteristically veers away from a discussion of ethics. For him power is the domestic and foreign empire made possible by any given distribution of land in any government. It is by no means evil in itself, but so long as it is not fixed in a balanced, popular government, it is unpredictable and subject to decay. Power alone (which he associates with "fortune") tends to be incapable of immortality and stable imperial expansion (163–69).

The utopist brings authority, or "the goods of the mind" (163). Unlike power alone, which tends to be limited to the personal reach of the person or state wielding it, authority can extend outward in time and space to other states. The authority of a state "may govern others, as that of Athens did Rome, when the latter wrote her twelve tables by the copy of the former" (464). The utopist constructs his own authority through his political anatomy of the authority exercised by earlier republics. Authority is not opposed to power but is that which makes it capable of a millennial immortality and universality: "I come unto the principles of authority, which are internal and founded upon the goods of the mind. These the legislator that can unite in his government with those of fortune, cometh nearest unto the work of God, whose government consisteth of heaven and earth. . . . Sad complaints, that the principles of power and authority, the goods of the mind and of fortune, do not meet and twine in the wreath or crown of empire! Wherefore if we have anything of piety or of prudence, let us raise ourselves out of the mire of private interest unto the contemplation of virtue, and put an hand unto the removal of this evil from under the sun" (169). This unison of authority and power "was said by Plato . . . as 'when princes should be philosophers, or philosophers princes, the world would be happy.'" Harrington puts some English on this traditional utopian ideal: the secular/sacred coupling of "piety and prudence" and the scriptural idioms hint that this unity of power and authority is, in fact, a way to the empire of a millennial commonwealth for increase.

Yet in an earlier comment Harrington lets slip a general truth gathered from his labor in the archives of the ancient prudence that darkens the millennial prospect. Responding to Hobbes's Machiavellian observation that the reputation of prudence in a prince brings him power, Harrington responds, "The learning or prudence of a man is no more than the learning or prudence of a book or author, which is properly authority. A learned author may have authority, though he have no power; and a foolish magistrate may have power, though he have otherwise no esteem or authority" (163). In the course of a career as a political writer, the theoretical possibility of this separation was to seem more and more a description of his own situation.

In his preface to the first book of *The Prerogative of Popular Government,* Harrington responds to Matthew Wren's ridicule of private writers who attempt to meddle in government and produce no more than "pleasant recreation for those great personages" who hold actual power (*Considerations* A4r). In defense of his vocation, Harrington begins to construct an emulative series of heroic writers on politics parallel to the series of heroic legislators, but he is not so self-confident as we may have expected. He begins with Aristotle, who wrote "in the time of Alexander, the greatest prince and commander of his age ... with scarce inferior applause and equal fame." But Harrington does not show that Aristotle transformed Alexander, only that Aristotle, "being a private man, wrote that excellent piece of prudence in his cabinet which is called his *Politics,* going upon far other principles than those of Alexander's government, which it hath long out-lived." The next three exempla work in the same way: "The like did Titus Livius in the time of Augustus, Sir Thomas More in the time of Henry the Eighth, and Machiavel when Italy was under the princes that afforded him not the ear." Harrington's concluding comment on the times of Machiavelli seems to work better as support for Wren's argument than as a rebuttal of it. The authority of these writers did not "twine together" with power, but merely survived. Harrington's final example picks up the tension implicit in the unhappy example of More and Henry: "Nor have I found any man whose like endeavours have been persecuted since Plato by Dionysius." What begins as an attempt to answer the charge that princes have never heeded private writers finishes not only by conceding the point but also by adding that princes have often gone so far as to persecute them. Harrington follows with a weak plea that he be allowed to pursue his harmless trade in peace: "The magistrate that was good at his steerage never took it ill of him that brought him a card [map], seeing whether he would use it or no was at his own choice" (395).

The closest Harrington ever came to wedding power and authority may have been in Richard Cromwell's Parliament, where there was a Harringtonian party centering around Henry Neville that participated in the debate over the constitution of an upper house (Pocock, "James Harrington" 39–48). There was also, of course, a party of anti-Harringtonians. In February 1659 the conservative Puritan Samuel Gott (himself the author of a mildly utopian romance of 1648 entitled *Nova Solyma*) promised his fellow parliamentarians that "I shall not go back to times past, nor look forward to Oceana's Platonical commonwealth; things that are not, and that never shall be. We go about to grasp more, and lose that which we would have" (Burton 144). On July 6, 1659, Neville delivered to Parliament a broadside entitled *The Humble Petition of divers well-affected Persons* proposing *Oceana*'s program and drawn up (says John Toland) by Harrington. The Speaker returned the house's noncommittal thanks (Toland xxviii, 541–46).

In general, Harrington's experience with established power was even unhappier than Plato's. John Aubrey says that during his years as gentleman of the bedchamber of Charles I, "the King loved his company; only he would not endure to hear of a commonwealth" (124). We have seen the failure of his attempt to transform Cromwell. Toland printed what he says is Harrington's own account of the occasion of his writing *Oceana.* Cromwell, "having started up into the throne, his officers (as pretending to be for a commonwealth) kept a murmuring, at which he told them that he knew not what they meant, nor themselves; but let any of them show him what they meant by a commonwealth (or that there was any such thing) they should see that he sought not himself; the Lord knew he sought not himself, but to make good the cause. Upon this some sober men came to me and told me: if any man in England could show what a commonwealth was, it was myself. Upon this persuasion I wrote" (Harrington 859).

The very setting of this statement—the Tower of London—shows Harrington's experience with Charles II. After being linked with the Fifth Monarchists and other radicals, Harrington was imprisoned in 1661. During this same examination in the Tower, Toland says that Harrington had occasion to return to the series of authors he discussed in *The Prerogative,* with the understandable omissions of Plato and More: "I beseech you, my lord, did Alexander hang up Aristotle; did he molest him? Livy for a commonwealth is one of the fullest authors; did not he write under Augustus Caesar? Did Caesar hang up Livy; did he molest him? Machiavel, what a commonwealthsman was he! But he wrote under the Medici when they were princes in Florence; did they hang up Machiavel, or did they molest him? I have done no otherwise than the greatest politicians; the king will do no otherwise than the greatest princes" (859). But Charles did otherwise. From the Tower Harrington was transferred to St. Nicholas Island, a small rock off Plymouth, and then to Plymouth. After his release he went into a physical and mental decline, possibly because of the rigors of his imprisonment. He died in 1677.[19]

Well before his death, Harrington's conception of the audience he was writing for and of the nature of his authority as a utopian writer had begun to shift. Toland reports that "he used to add . . . another reason of writing this model, which was that if it should ever be the fate of this nation to be, like Italy of old, overrun by any barbarous people, or to have its government and records destroyed by the rage of some merciless conqueror, they might not then be left to their own invention in framing a new government; for few people can be expected to succeed so happily as the Venetians have done in such a case" (Toland xix). Perhaps this was Harrington's tacit recognition that the people of England were not in so anomic a state as his model assumed, and that their predisposition to kingship would be overcome only by a greater cataclysm than the Civil War. In any case, Harrington began writing for the future well before his imprisonment, submitting the model he had invented to the judgment of a later generation. At least as early as the address to the reader at the beginning of *The Art of Lawgiving* (1659), he began a program of self-memorialization: "I exhort all commonwealthsmen to seek peace and insue it, as the readiest way unto their own good; and you, reader, to bear witness that I am no incendiary nor malcontent, but have spoken with religion and reason; which if this age fail me, shall be testified by another. And so if I perish, I perish" (600). With this shift of audience from the dictator of the present to the anonymous judges of the future, his writing becomes, in the terms of this study, less utopian. Whereas in *Oceana* he sees himself as a synthesizing political anatomist, the utopian medium through whom the ancient prudence speaks to Oliver Cromwell, in his later tracts he sees himself joining the ranks of those earlier writers on the ancient prudence whose authority exercised an influence only in their futures. He leaves his own discursive republic behind him as a model for future political writers, and he begins speaking with the particular commonwealths of the future.[20]

5

Ordo Anima Rerum:
The World Turned Rightside Up

This last chapter considers some of the continuities and discontinuities of Puritan utopia at the Restoration. The first section underlines the failure of its more millenarian and totalizing claims by examining a conspicuous example of its failure to win over a noted Puritan republican, who proposes an alternative vision of history and political life that is both antimonarchical and anti-utopian. The second analyzes the satiric and "dystopian" critique of Puritan utopia, drawing an analogy between this critique and the modern criticism (and lack of criticism) of Puritan utopia that attempts to exclude it from the history of utopia proper. Section three argues that a fundamental and summary concern of Puritan utopia is to provide a disciplinary supplement to social contract theory. The concluding section shows that this disciplinary quality of Puritan utopia ties it to earlier and later utopias and even makes possible a "utopian" reading of nonutopian works.

Jeremiah versus Lycurgus: Milton's *The Ready and Easy Way*

I might summarize my discussion thus far by saying that utopian discipline is the means by which utopia produces and integrates individuality and collectivity, history and politics. On the one hand, it shows how to produce certain individualities (More's phylarchs and proto-phylarchs, Eliot's melancholic converts and rulers of tens, Harrington's deputies and knights) and collectivities (More's ideal republic, Eliot's praying towns, and Harrington's imperial King People). The very act of writing Puritan utopia is the individual utopist's attempt to gain a new identity for himself inside the utopian collectivity he imagines. On the other hand, utopian discipline attempts to integrate political activity with providential history. The disciplined political interaction of individual and collective lays the foundation for a stable and expansive era of progress, perhaps even the millennium. Indeed, for Eliot and Harrington, political life itself constitutes the millennium.

But the Puritan utopist's faith in the ability of discipline to effect these multiple integrations was by no means universal, even among his Puritan compatriots. We have already seen that during King Philip's War, the Puritans of New England preferred an act of immediate genocidal repression to Eliot's program of gradual, rational discipline. In Harrington's England we see a similar anti-utopianism in a wide array of Puritan political tracts. This section will concentrate on one such tract: the second edition of Milton's *The Ready and Easy Way to Establish a Free Commonwealth.* No tract could have a more utopian title. In it Milton proposes a republican platform of government and draws on many of the same biblical and classical precedents as do Eliot and Harrington. He even refers specifically to Harrington's program (though not to Harrington), admitting that it might be tried. But though Milton occasionally speaks in the same language as the utopists, he speaks in a different genre, for this tract is finally an anti-utopian jeremiad. It argues that the individual political writer can join a proper collectivity only by withdrawing from and denouncing the degenerate community of the present and establishing solidarity with a historical series of inspired prophets also alienated from their communities. In *The Ready and Easy Way* we can see the failure of utopian political rhetoric to overcome an alternative Puritan political (or apolitical) vision, the disappearance of faith in the transformative power of Puritan discipline, the alienation of individuality from collectivity, and the sundering of political life from providential history.

After the death of Oliver Cromwell in September 1658, England saw a bewildering succession of ruling persons and forms and a torrent of political platforms that proposed even more (Woolrych). Cromwell was succeeded as Lord Protector by his modestly qualified son, Richard. In November the Council of State decided to recall the Parliament in January 1659. Richard was persuaded to permit the formation of the General Council of Officers, which first met on April 2. On April 22 the army saw to the dissolution of Richard's wrangling Parliament, replacing it with the Council of Officers (a junta of field officers smaller than the General Council of Officers), eliminating Richard from power in the process. On May 6 the Council of Officers recalled the Rump of the Long Parliament, which had not met since April 1653. Tensions arose between the Rump and the army, however, and Generals John Lambert and Charles Fleetwood purged the Rump on October 13. Later that month the Council of Officers transferred governmental powers to the twenty-three-man Committee of Safety, which in turn appointed a subcommittee to prepare a new form of nonmonarchical government. The General Council of Officers met in December to debate this model and resolved on seven republican "principles and unalterable fundamentals." But the committee dissolved in December, and the remnants of the old Council of State recalled the Rump once again; it met on December 26. In January 1660 General George Monck began his march south from Scotland. He entered London on February 3, and on the twenty-first he restored to Parliament the predominantly conservative and Presbyterian members excluded from it in Pride's Purge of 1648. According to Woolrych, this action ensured that "however the government was settled, King Charles II would be at the head of it" (176). This old-modeled body dissolved itself on March 16 after issuing writs calling for the election of a new parliament, which met on April 25. This, the Convention Parliament, proclaimed Charles king on May 8. Charles landed at Dover on May 25. He entered London in triumph on the twenty-ninth, and by mid-October Parliament was hanging, drawing, and quartering eleven selected tyrannicides.

The ideological climate of these final months of the Interregnum is not a simple unity. It might best be described as an accelerated and self-destructive recapitulation of all the controversies of the Interregnum, for the previously submerged and mutually antagonistic political ideologies of the previous twelve years broke free and rose to the surface of a gathering ground swell of popular support for a return to the customary rule of king, Lords, and Commons. Tracts proposing ways to settle civil and church government came from the pens of Anglican loyalists, Presbyterians like William Prynne, conservative Independents like Richard Baxter, Commonwealthsmen harking back to the Good Old Cause of the 1640s, Harrington and his Rota Club republicans, proponents of army rule, remnants of the Leveller party crushed in 1649, and millenarians of various stripes. Accompanying this publication was a general and more or less uneasy awareness that the popular sentiment inclined to a restored monarchy.

In this context Milton wrote and published *The Ready and Easy Way,* his last major political tract. It appeared in two editions—the first probably in late February 1660 and the much expanded second in April 1660, shortly before the Restoration. One measure of the turmoil of the times is that Livewell Chapman, the Fifth Monarchist publisher of the first edition (he had published Eliot's *The Christian Commonwealth* the previous October and Harrington's *Oceana* in 1656) was a fugitive from the Council of State by the time of the second edition, which does not reveal its publisher.

In his "Historical Introduction" to volume 7 of the *Complete Prose Works of John Milton,* Austin Woolrych captures the critical consensus on the proper way to read the tract when he says that of all Milton's prose works, it "needs to be read in closest relation to the political circumstances in which it was composed" (177). Within this consensus there is some controversy over the tract's closeness of fit with these circumstances, but most critics deny the tract's ideal or "utopian" quality and focus their attention on the relation between its concrete proposals and the political events to which they seem to refer. Michael Fixler allows that "his model does seem utopian," but "the fact is that the immediate objectives of his proposals (as opposed to the long-range glamour with which he invested his model) were eminently practical and concerned with the shifting pattern of contemporary political realities" (206). Barbara K. Lewalski says that the tract presents the case for "Milton the practical politician, close to affairs and quite non-utopian in approach to political problems" (197). Don M. Wolfe agrees in part, saying that Milton's work is drawn more from the crises of the moment than from any classical or Hebraic models, that "Milton's proposed commonwealth was not his ideal commonwealth" (*Milton* 297). Similarly, Woolrych says that "it is not in any sense a utopia, and we should not do Milton the injustice of regarding it as his model of an ideal commonwealth" (187). But Wolfe and Woolrych agree on the tract's utter unfeasibility, raising the disquieting possibility that political theory may be impracticable without being idealist. Keith W. Stavely, sensing this same tension between the tract and its political circumstances, invokes irony to restore Milton's authority, saying that he is "wilfully and ironically utopian" in this tract because he is self-conscious about the conflict between his idealistic proposals and "recalcitrant political circumstances" (99–100). Arthur E. Barker sees no contradiction between the tract's "Platonic search for that ideal city whose pattern is laid up in heaven" and its Puritan utopianism, but he finds both to be "profoundly modified" by the political chaos just before the Restoration (288). These critics disagree on many particulars, but they come together in their definition of utopia as a realm of political ideality rather than a genre of political writing, and in their belief that Milton's tract cannot be seen as a true utopia because of its more or less conscious, more or less successful compromise with political circumstance.

I want to join this consensus that Milton's work is not a utopia, but through the back door—by drawing on my own redefinition of utopia as a genre of political writing very much concerned with its circumstances: with the displaced populations forming its subject matter, the models of government drawn from Scripture or imported from abroad, the alternative political theories that it must debate and defeat, and the signs of an approaching millennium. By this definition Milton's tract is certainly not utopian; despite Woolrych's claim, there is a sense in which it asks to be seen in isolation from its political circumstances, for it systematically cuts itself off from participation in the debate, choice, and action of the expiring English polis. We can best reconstruct its ultimate political purpose by examining its rhetoric of political abdication as well as the political circumstances it refers to.

Milton proposes a national government by a perpetual aristocratic Grand Council balanced by the local rule of the gentry and nobility. This is the antithesis of Puritan utopia, not because Milton's work is undemocratic (so is Puritan utopia, at least in its rhetoric) but because it sees the state as the embodiment or expression of a preexistent virtue, not as a pedagogical and disciplinary mechanism for the production of virtuous citizens, as in Eliot, Harrington, Winstanley, Plockhoy, and Comenius. The center of Milton's proposed government is an election sequence that finally chooses the Grand Council. A large group of "rightly qualified" voters chooses a large body of candidates. A smaller elite of these voters (a group "of a better breeding") chooses a smaller group from among these candidates, and so on, until the fourth and smallest group of voters chooses the Grand Council: "After a third or fourth sifting and refining of exactest choice, they only be left chosen who are the due number, and seem by most voices the worthiest" (Milton, *Prose* 7.443).

This is voluntarist political theory of the purest sort. The mere act of choice, seemingly disconnected from any determining interest, will automatically single out preexistent virtue. Here we see an aristocratic and exclusive form of that more democratic idealism of *Areopagitica,* where "reason is but choosing," but the choice is not confined to a single party (2.527). Milton does not say precisely how the worthy will be known, and his vagueness about whether this will be an aristocracy of birth, property, merit, or grace has exercised his readers. Perez Zagorin argues persuasively that the history of Milton's political thought is the history of his changing conception of the aristocracy and that in this tract he fell back on "the aristocracy of blood," in which "ability and social position, virtue and breeding, go cheek by jowl" (*History* 119). Because this model is aristocratic, its motivation for distinguishing and dividing persons is anti-utopian; in Milton's jeremiad we have not the utopian division and organization of an anomic population in order to produce a virtuous state (as in Eliot's tens, fifties, and hundreds; Harrington's parishes, hundreds, and tribes), but the separation of those fit to rule from the unfit and unruly.

Milton's frantic search for a principle of government even brings him to compromise his own overt support of aristocratic principles. True, in the early days of the Long Parliament, the English people did not use a democratic principle when they resisted the Presbyterian majority: "The best affected and also best principled of the people, stood not numbering or computing on which side were most voices in Parliament, but on which side appeared to them most reason." But neither did they use an aristocratic principle and seek out men they knew to be virtuous, since upright men may support bad causes, and bad men may support good causes for the wrong reason, and "who had not rather follow Iscariot or Simon the magician, though to covetous ends, preaching, than Saul, though in the uprightness of his heart, persecuting the gospel?" (7.414–15).[1] This is still an antidemocratic argument, but the association of the virtuous side with Judas and Simon Magus is likely to leave an acrid reek in aristocratic nostrils. Later, Milton adds that to abandon the commonwealth because of the imperfections of its proponents, "to betray a just and noble cause for the mixture of bad men who have ill managed and abused it," would be as bad as abandoning the Reformation itself because it is "so much intermixed with the avarice and ambition of some reformers" (7.422). Even the heroes of the Reformation and the Good Old Cause emerge sullied from Milton's defense. He attacks democracy from an aristocratic viewpoint, only to admit that there is no class of certifiable aristoi to whom the nation can turn for virtuous guidance. There is at best some unlocatable, free-floating principle of the good that his orders seem incapable of capturing and harnessing.

Arguing heroically (if somewhat vaguely) for a commonwealth of virtue, Milton self-consciously presents his tract as an anti-utopian alternative with a minimum of institutional reform, saying that it is "without intricacies, without the introducement of new and obsolete forms, or terms, or exotic models" (7.445). His primary referent here is Harrington's model in *Oceana,* which he repeatedly takes up and worries (7.433–37, 440, 444, 461). He grudgingly admits that it might be employed but never truly comes to terms with it, for he is fundamentally antagonistic to Harrington's dynamic utopian vision. Speaking of Harrington's proposal for rotational government, he says, "I could wish that this wheel or partial wheel in state, if it be possible, might be avoided, as having too much affinity with the wheel of fortune" (7.435). He worries about the English liking for such dynamic and fluvial models of government, suggesting that it is the product of an oceanic and insular sensibility, "the fluxible fault . . . of our watery situation" (7.437). Harrington's conception of government itself as a circulatory school of political virtue is simply invisible to Milton, who fears its "putting out a great number of the best and ablest: in whose stead new elections may bring in as many raw, unexperienced, and otherwise affected, to the weakening and much altering for the worse of public transactions" (7.435).

Similarly, Milton rejects Harrington's agrarian legislation on the grounds that no mere preponderance of lands could threaten the innate moral virtue of a proper governmental form (7.445). And he provides for a minimal reform of local government, proposing that local lords and gentry determine the law and judicature of each county (7.458–61). Zera S. Fink has tried to make a case for Milton's debt in this tract to Polybian classical republicanism, with its vision of the balanced powers of a many, a few, and a one; but so far as *The Ready and Easy Way* proposes any balance, it is a balance of local and national oligarchies. Milton says that the people retain military power as a check on oligarchic abuse, but he provides no means for them to muster and exercise that power (Milton 7.435). Martial virtue is not thoroughly integrated with civic virtue as it is in *Oceana.*

This tract reverses the rhetorical situation of *Areopagitica,* where Milton claimed a vision of a mighty, rising commonwealth. Now all images of potentiality, power, progress, and multiplicity conspire against Milton and his stopgap republican Grand Council. Milton's finest prose in this tract appears in his denunciation of mobs and monarchy, while his republican propositions are hedged about with qualifications and demurrers. Unlike Harrington, he cannot explain the popular inclination to monarchy, so he resorts simply to a defense of minority rule: "More just it is doubtless, if it come to force, that a less number compel a greater to retain, which can be no wrong to them, their liberty, than that a greater number for the pleasure of their baseness, compel a less most injuriously to be their fellow slaves" (7.455).[2] Defending this paradoxically oligarchical liberty, Milton moves into mere denunciation and invective: the people are the "mad," the "rude," the "inconsiderate multitude" who wish to "creep back so poorly" to the "detested thralldom of kingship" (7.427, 442, 446, 422). Nowhere in Milton's writings do we see a greater loathing of the English people. Whereas utopia opposes an organizational reason to a blank human subject matter, Milton's anti-utopian jeremiad opposes the virtuous reason of a lone prophet to the monstrous irrationality of the multitude.

The unruly popular multitude will bring in a tyrannous monarchical multitude: "There will be a queen also of no less charge; in most likelihood outlandish and a Papist; besides a queen mother such already; together with both their courts and numerous train: then a royal issue, and ere long severally their sumptuous courts; to the multiplying of a servile crew, not of servants only, but of nobility and gentry, bred up then to the hopes not of public but of court offices, to be stewards, chamberlains, ushers, grooms even of the close stool" (7.425).[3] Milton describes (somewhat inaccurately, as it turned out) Charles's future spouse as an unnaturally fecund brood queen. In this fear of multiplicity and feminine reproduction (which concludes with excremental disgust), there is something of Milton's portrayal of Sin in Book 2 of *Paradise Lost* as the mother of a teeming rout of offspring sired by her father Satan and son Death.

Harrington's rotational republic also threatens a fatal excess through the proliferation of law, for the surfeit of knights and deputies will set about "altering or repealing former acts, or making and multiplying new . . . till all law be lost in the multitude of clashing statutes" (7.434). The very persons constituting Harrington's government threaten to become one more of those displaced populations that rational government should control: the yearly movements of the deputies and the knights to and from Westminster will be "troublesome and chargeable, both in their motion and their session, to the whole land, unwieldy with their own bulk" (7.441).

As an alternative, Milton can offer only a static image of the perpetually sitting Grand Council as "both foundation and main pillar of the whole state; and to move pillars and foundations, not faulty, cannot be safe for the building" (7.434). In this late tract, Virtue is, if not cloistered, at least thoroughly architectural. And its millennialism is tepid at best: Milton says "with as much assurance as can be of human things," that his ideal state "shall so continue (if God favor us and our willful sins provoke him not) even to the coming of our true and rightful and only to be expected king" (7.444–45).

At almost every turn Milton's tract either rejects institutional solutions or qualifies them out of existence, systematically cutting itself off from the political debate of the closing months of the republic. At the level of the sentence, Milton's arguments against a return to monarchy eviscerate themselves. He begins a denunciation of backsliding by warning, "Besides this, if we return to kingship and soon repent, as undoubtedly we shall . . ."—suggesting that the return as well as the repentance may be indubitable (7.423). In a characteristically self-consuming period he writes, "I doubt not but all ingenuous and knowing men will easily agree with me, that a free commonwealth without single person or house of lords is by far the best government, if it can be had; but we have all this while say they been expecting it and cannot yet attain it" (7.429). The first half of this sentence may hint at a certain circularity (ingenuous knowledgeability and agreement with Milton typically imply each other), but we do at least begin with the reassuring assertion of a consensus. The second half of the sentence makes this consensus wishful ("if it can be had"), shifting our attention from the consensus itself to the presumed fewness of its members, a fewness that has rendered it ineffectual. Early in the tract Milton writes that his purpose is "to remove, if it be possible, this noxious humor of returning to bondage" (7.407). Lewalski writes that this tract is "an eminently practical attempt to rescue the Puritan cause, if possible, from the ever-increasing perils besetting it" (195), reproducing not only Milton's dubious and nostalgic claim that there is some such thing as a unified or "Good Old" Puritan cause, but also the very syntax in which he questions his own powers to make it prevail.

Milton's self-negation appears on a larger scale inside his positive political propositions, as we can see in his argument for the relative ease of removing an improper governor in a commonwealth. A king is "not to be removed, not to be controlled, much less accused or brought to punishment, without the danger of a common ruin, without the shaking and almost subversion of the whole land. Whereas in a free commonwealth, any governor or chief counselor offending, may be removed and punished without the least commotion" (7.426–27). This comparison operates in two realms of rhetoric at once. First, it operates in the abstract realm of republican political philosophy as a positive, even "utopian" argument for political change, offering one more reason why commonwealths are stabler than monarchies. At the same time it operates in the concrete realm of recent history as a retrospective view of the birth and backsliding death of the Commonwealth. On this historical level Milton seems almost to be speaking from the future in the voice of an apologist for monarchy, whose thesis would be precisely that the removal of King Charles brought "the danger of a common ruin" and "the shaking and almost subversion of the whole land," and that the governors of a commonwealth can be "removed and punished without the least commotion"—and should be. Milton's argument appears even weaker when we remember that for most of his audience and even for himself, the frequent alteration of rulers and governing forms was one of the most pernicious effects of the tyrannicide.

Milton's use of Scripture is characteristically anti-utopian. True, like Eliot, Winstanley, and Harrington, he denounces any return to monarchy as a typological repetition of Israel's "gentilism": its rejection of God's republican theocracy in favor of King Saul's "gentilish imitation" of other monarchies (7.424, 429). But whereas the utopists are also able to turn to the Bible when making their proposals for transforming the state, Milton is unable to find any scripturally sanctioned mechanisms for producing virtuous citizens. The iconoclast cannot become an iconographer, and the most important biblical allusions in *The Ready and Easy Way* are at the service not of utopian proposition but of the jeremiad's denunciation of backsliding.

Study of the Puritan jeremiad, which has focused on New England, began with Perry Miller's classic discussion in *The New England Mind: From Colony to Province* (27–39). Miller argues that the jeremiad was particularly important for the second- and third-generation Puritan settlers, who felt that they had declined from the moral standards of the emigrants. Whereas the first, heroic generation of emigrants had lived in strict covenant with God, later generations strayed and lost their sense of national election. The jeremiad emerged as a latter-day rite of communal self-chastisement. Miller sees the jeremiad as a transgeneric literary mode informing such diverse kinds as poetry, the election sermon, reports of ecclesiastical synods, and even Cotton Mather's massive ecclesiastical history, *Magnalia Christi Americana*. But its origin was in the fast-day sermon. On community fast days, a preacher would link together New England's past, present, and future by recalling its special covenant with God in the early days, lamenting its present-day backslidings, ordering a reformation, and prophesying the future punishments awaiting an unheeding community.

Milton's tract is much closer to the jeremiad than to the utopia, despite its generally secular tone, and it follows rather closely the form Miller describes: it celebrates God's special covenant with an earlier generation of Englishmen, what Milton calls the "wondrous acts of his providence" in the early days of the Commonwealth (7.450); then it laments the chaotic factionalism of the present day, orders a reformation, and prophesies the divine judgments of the Stuart tyranny and the Anglican prelacy awaiting an unheeding nation.

But there is a key difference between Milton's fundamentally pessimistic jeremiad and the subtly optimistic New England jeremiad. In their studies of the latter form, David Minter and Sacvan Bercovitch stress its more optimistic and self-affirming qualities. By insisting on its national iniquities, New England simultaneously insists on its special status as an elect nation. In *The American Jeremiad* Bercovitch says, "The most severe limitation of Miller's view is that it excludes (or denigrates) this pervasive theme of affirmation and exultation" (6). He sees the jeremiad not simply as a reaction to social decline but as a social rhetoric with a positive life of its own. He extends it forward into the nineteenth century and backward to such works of first-generation emigrants as John Winthrop's lay sermon *A Model of Christian Charity,* written and delivered in 1630 during Winthrop's Atlantic crossing.

The best-known passage of that sermon—its appeal to American politicians is perennial—is Winthrop's prophetic view of the Bay Colony as a city on a hill:

> He shall make us a praise and glory, that men shall say of succeeding plantations: the Lord make it like that of New England. For we must consider that we shall be as a city upon a hill, the eyes of all people are upon us; so that if we shall deal falsely with our God in this work we have undertaken and so cause him to withdraw his present help from us, we shall be made a story and a by-word through the world, we shall open the mouths of enemies to speak evil of the ways of God and all professors for God's sake. (Miller and Johnson 198–99).

Winthrop's rhetoric optimistically tempers his tone of admonition in several ways. It is explicitly communal rather than an individual rhetoric of denunciation, for the speaker presents himself as an individual speaking to a community from within that community. It is future-directed and hortatory, aimed at unifying a party in some feasible course of action. It softens the threat of divine retribution with the promise of New England's national election. And it alludes to a distinctly reassuring (and nonjeremiadic) scriptural text, Christ's Sermon on the Mount:

> Ye are the light of the world. A city that is set on an hill cannot be hid. Neither do men light a candle, and put it under a bushel, but on a candlestick; and it giveth light unto all that are in the house. Let your light so shine before men, that they may see your good works, and glorify your Father which is in heaven. (Matt. 5:14–16)

The allusion lessens the threat of those outside the community: though they may scoff at failure, they are also students of a sort, awaiting instruction and illumination. The product of Winthrop's sermon is an optimistic neurosis—that peculiarly Puritan anxiety that binds the individual, the congregation, and the colony together in the search for signs of personal and national election.

In his jeremiad Milton also quotes Christ, but to much less reassuring effect. Like Winthrop, he has a sense of the conspicuous importance of the Puritan city on a hill; unlike Winthrop, he sees that city as a lost possibility of the past:

> To creep back so poorly as it seems the multitude would to their once abjured and detested thralldom of kingship . . . and by thus relapsing to verify all the bitter predictions of our triumphing enemies, who will now think they wisely discerned and justly censured both us and all our actions as rash, rebellious, hypocritical, and impious, not only argues a strange degenerate contagion suddenly spread among us fitted and prepared for new slavery, but will render us a scorn and derision to all our neighbors. And what will they at best say of us and of the whole English name, but scoffingly as of that foolish builder, mentioned by our Savior, who began to build a tower, and was not able to finish it. Where is this goodly tower of a commonwealth, which the English boasted they would build to overshadow kings, and be another Rome in the west? The foundation indeed they laid gallantly, but fell into a worse confusion, not of tongues, but of factions, than those at the tower of Babel, and have left no memorial of their work behind them remaining, but in the common laughter of Europe. (7.422–23)

Here Milton withdraws from his community, almost merging with this nameless continental scoffer, who quotes Scripture (as we will see) and constructs typological history with the facility of Milton himself. This passage looks not toward the future but toward the early days of God's covenant with England, when it began constructing the still-unfinished tower of the Commonwealth. When we finally arrive at the long-delayed predicate of Milton's first sentence, we expect a future tense that will leave time for reform, or a conditional that will at least leave us the possibility: "To creep back will/would make us a mockery." Instead, we encounter a present tense "argues" and find that England is already creeping and contagious. And Milton associates England not with Israel as an elect nation but with Babel and Rome as a nation doomed by civic hubris.

Unlike Winthrop's scriptural allusion, Milton's does not soften his admonitory tone but stresses the pointlessness even of admonition at this late stage. Christ's parable of the foolish builder is in the fourteenth chapter of Luke:

> And there went great multitudes with him. And he turned, and said unto them, "If any man come to me, and hate not his father, and mother, and wife, and children, and brethren, and sisters, yea, and his own life also, he cannot be my disciple. And whosoever doth not bear his cross, and come after me, cannot be my disciple. For which of you, intending to build a tower, sitteth not down first, and counteth the cost, whether he have sufficient to finish it? Lest haply, after he hath laid the foundation, and is not able to finish it, all that behold it begin to mock him, saying, 'That man began to build, and was not able to finish.' . . . So likewise, whosoever of you that forsaketh not all that he hath, he cannot be my disciple."

This parable is much different from the passage Winthrop alludes to, for it advocates not stalwart commitment to a great civil cause but prudent consideration before committing oneself to it. The English should have reconsidered their plans in the past; they have nothing to gain from a renewed commitment to tower building in the present, as Milton's Babel analogy makes plain. Here Milton marks the final defeat of that glorious "spiritual architecture" he prophesies in *Areopagitica,* for which "there must be many schisms and many dissections made in the quarry and in the timber, ere the house of God can be built" (2.555). But in this later tract, the paradoxical moral of Christ's parable has an antipolitical function. Christ seems almost to be driving away the "great multitudes" following him: only those who have relinquished all worldly goods and all human ties are properly provisioned and accompanied for true Christian discipleship—not the ideal text for encouraging the political solidarity of a disintegrating republican collective.

Our understanding of the rhetorical force of the second edition of Milton's tract should begin with an acknowledgment that for Milton, it has no real audience. This is not altogether true for the first edition, in which Milton has at least the illusion of a receptive audience in the newly returned members of the Rump, who were about to call for elections to increase their scant numbers. He is presumably speaking of the Rump in the first edition when he says that "God hath yet his remnant" (7.363), and he concludes the tract optimistically: "I trust I shall have spoken persuasion to abundance of sensible and ingenuous men: to some, perhaps, whom God may raise of these stones, to become children of liberty, and may enable and unite in their noble resolutions to give a stay to these our ruinous proceedings and to this general defection of the misguided and abused multitude" (7.388).

But the elections following the first edition returned only sixteen of the sitting Rumpers to Parliament, and England was clearly on the road to a restored monarchy. In the second edition Milton's earlier reference to a remnant disappears (7.428). After his proposal for a Grand Council, he concedes that most of the nation is bent on kingship and that he writes "not so much to convince these, which I little hope, as to confirm them who yield not" (7.455). Even these unyielding few have grown deaf by the end of the tract. In the magnificent final paragraph Milton quotes Jeremiah, saying, "Thus much I should perhaps have said though I were sure I should have spoken only to trees and stones; and had none to cry to, but with the prophet, 'O earth, earth, earth!' to tell the very soil itself what her perverse inhabitants are deaf to" (7.462–63). The "abundance of sensible and ingenuous men" of the first edition now seem to be "choosing them a captain back for Egypt," and they are syntactically indistinguishable from "this torrent also of the people," whom Milton begs "not to be so impetuous, but to keep their due channel" (7.463). Milton's metaphor revises both Machiavelli and Harrington in an antipolitical direction. The people here are even more threatening than the river of *fortuna* is in *The Prince*, which Machiavelli says can be controlled at least half the time. Like Harrington, Milton sees the people themselves as a river, but here they are ungovernable, monstrous, and rash. Unlike Harrington, Milton attempts to address this popular river directly but recognizes his own inevitable failure. His exhortation of the river will likely have no more effect than King Canute's address to the incoming tides. *The Ready and Easy Way* is political oratory with no true listeners.

Still, there is a remnant of sorts, and even if Milton's jeremiad is less self-affirming than those of New England, it does have a positive purpose in its construction of an autobiographical voice of prophetic authority. As discouraging as Milton's allusion to the parable of the tower is as a piece of political rhetoric, it is at least obliquely relevant to his autobiographical purpose in this tract, for like the true disciple, Milton is in the process of cutting himself off from his community. He does not attempt to unite a community around some program of political innovation (like the Puritan utopist) or renovation (like the American Jeremiah). Rather, he creates for himself the identity of a lone prophet who withdraws from his community and stands prophesying its ruin.

Here we can see an important distinction between Harrington's identity as a Lycurgan utopist and Milton's as a Jeremiah. As we have seen, Harrington's Olphaus Megaletor is an abdicating legislator, a *rex absconditus* whose only memorial lies in the grateful memories of his political offspring, who have forever grown beyond any need for the authority of a single person. Harrington's own writing puts him into much the same position, for he writes against his own class interests and longs for the moment when the realization of his utopian propositions will put an end to his career as a utopist. Both Milton's memorial and the extinction he proposes for himself differ from Harrington's, for by addressing his tract to the returning Stuart monarchy, Milton attempts to destroy himself and pass down his own resolute opposition to monarchy as an example to future times. In the passage quoted above on the foolish tower builder, he fears that the English will have "no memorial of their work behind them remaining, but in the common laughter of Europe" (7.423); but even Milton doubts that this will be altogether the case, for his career as a prose writer has left behind a series of heroic memorials. In the autobiographical excursus of *The Reason of Church Government,* Milton indirectly prophesies the importance of his prose writings to come by emphasizing the promise of the poetic talents he is rechanneling into political polemics: he tells his English countrymen that his discriminating Italian readers had predicted, on the basis of his early poetic efforts, that "I might perhaps leave something so written to aftertimes, as they should not willingly let it die" (1.810). He simultaneously memorializes his earlier poetry and prophesies his future greatness as a prose writer.

In his Latin defenses of the English people in the 1650s, he continues this process of self-memorialization and prophecy. In the closing paragraph of *A Second Defense* (1654), he speaks elegiacally of the early days of the Commonwealth and somewhat critically of its latter days:

> If the most recent days of my fellow countrymen should not correspond sufficiently to their earliest, let them look to it themselves. I have borne witness, I might almost say I have erected a monument that will not soon pass away, to those deeds that were illustrious, that were glorious, that were almost beyond any praise, and if I have done nothing else, I have surely redeemed my pledge. (4.685)

Milton's countrymen seem always to be backsliding, always falling off from some earlier time of promise.

He goes on to compare himself with an epic poet, saying that he has celebrated those great persons and actions of the Commonwealth in his prose political epics. As he alludes to the upcoming convention of the first Protectorate Parliament, he seems to be alluding to the disheartening fable of the foolish builder:

> If after such brave deeds you ignobly fail, if you do aught unworthy of yourselves, be sure that posterity will speak out and pass judgment: the foundations were soundly laid, the beginnings, in fact more than the beginnings, were splendid, but posterity will look in vain, not without a certain distress, for those who were to complete the work, who were to put the pediment in place. . . . Yet there was not wanting one who could rightly counsel, encourage, and inspire, who could honor both the noble deeds and those who had done them, and make both deeds and doers illustrious with praises that will never die. (4.685–86)

Milton has just praised a heroic pantheon of the early Commonwealth, including Cromwell, Thomas Fairfax, Fleetwood, Lambert, and Algernon Sidney, but the greatest hero to be memorialized is the polemist who sums them all up and defends the Commonwealth with his pen.

This self-memorialization undergoes its final metamorphosis in *The Ready and Easy Way*, where Milton seeks out examples of first-generation Commonwealth virtue against which to measure the backsliding second generation. He finds only one hero worthy of explicit mention:

> Nor was the heroic cause unsuccessfully defended to all Christendom against the tongue of a famous and thought invincible adversary; nor the constancy and fortitude that so nobly vindicated our liberty, our victory at once against two the most prevailing usurpers over mankind, super-

stition and tyranny, unpraised or uncelebrated in a written monument, likely to outlive detraction, as it hath hitherto convinced or silenced not a few of our detractors, especially in parts abroad. (7.420–21)

Modestly tucked away inside all these litotes is a reference to Milton's own Latin defenses. Whereas Cromwell and Fairfax were formerly worthy of some mention, he himself has now become the only representative of the first generation worthy of explicit memorialization. Here Milton plays two of the roles we see in the American jeremiad: he is both the latter-day Jeremiah, denouncing the fallings-off of a later generation, and the sole representative of that upright emigrant first generation they fall away from. England has failed Milton. In the face of near-universal backsliding, he stands as a one-man remnant; in writing an elegy for the lost civic virtue of his nation, he writes the epic song of himself.

Here Milton ends another phase of his career, calling the concluding lines of *The Ready and Easy Way* perhaps "the last words of our expiring liberty" (7.463). His final tract appears not as political proposition in the present but as polemical defiance of the future, for he says that the model of national government he proposes "can have no considerable objection made against it, that it is not practicable, lest it be said hereafter that we gave up our liberty for want of a ready way or distinct form proposed of a free commonwealth" (7.446). Its failure is a foregone conclusion. In the act of their utterance his words memorialize themselves, and they will find their true, fit and few audience—and Milton his vindication—only in the future.

In the fiercely antimonarchical rhetoric of the second edition, published only six weeks before the Restoration, Milton seems to be making sure that his written memorial will have someone to memorialize. *The Ready and Easy Way* is a self-consuming artifact of a dangerously literal sort: not only does it undercut its own positive proposals, it also threatens the life of its author. Milton as Jeremiah pleads almost suicidally for his own execution, which will verify his prophecy about his nation's expiring liberty, and so also his own authority as a prophet. Like the Christ of the parable (whose prophetic words are accurately translated by "whosoever doth not carry his own cross"), Milton prophesies his own martyrdom: he has become the true disciple who hates his own life. The particular reason this plea went unheeded has eluded Milton's biographers. After the Restoration the Royalist pamphlet bravos eagerly proposed his execution in a number of satires, and the House of Commons actively considered him for a place on the gallows alongside his fellow tyrannicides. But something or someone saved him—perhaps the timely intercession of Andrew Marvell or William Davenant (Parker 567–76).

Milton wrote no more prose jeremiads, but the persona of the Jeremiah appeared again in his poetry. In the major poetry (and even in some of the earlier poetry) we repeatedly encounter a heroic figure who, like the author of *The Ready and Easy Way,* removes himself from political life, denounces the social collective, prophesies the downfall of the unregenerate state, and submits himself to the scourges and blessings of providential history. We meet such a figure in Book 5 of *Paradise Lost,* where the angel Abdiel alone withdraws from Satan's rebellious northern legions, and then in a few lines moves from proposing a ready and easy way for Satan to regain God's favor to prophesying his expulsion from heaven. In *Paradise Regained,* the fasting Christ rejects Satan, the kingdom of the world, and the political role of the liberating martial Messiah of the Jews, gradually coming to understand his own self-sacrificing role in providential history.

Most strikingly, we meet a Jeremiah in *Samson Agonistes,* where blinded Samson denounces both the Philistine tyranny and the unheroic Hebrew commonwealth it has enslaved. He resists the demands of those who would destroy his alienated individuality by reintegrating him into some familial or political collective, refusing in sequence the Danite Chorus's invitation to join them in bewailing the universal depredations of *fortuna,* Manoa's attempt to reintegrate him into his household, and Dalila's attempt to reintegrate him into hers. After the Chorus attempts to blame Samson for Israel's enslavement to the Philistines, however, he responds with Miltonic resentment:

> That fault I take not on me, but transfer
> On Israel's governors, and heads of tribes,
> Who seeing those great acts which God had done
> Singly by me against their conquerors
> Acknowledged not, or not at all considered
> Deliverance offered.   (lines 241–46)

The Chorus duly receives this instruction and recalls a historical series of Hebrew heroes alienated from the collectives they were to have led:

> Thy words to my remembrance bring
> How Succoth and the fort of Penuel
> Their great deliverer contemned,

> The matchless Gideon in pursuit
> Of Madian and her vanquished kings:
> And how ingrateful Ephraim
> Had dealt with Jephtha, who by argument,
> Not worse than by his shield and spear
> Defended Israel from the Ammonite.
>
> (lines 277–85)

Jephtha's lengthy and learned defense of the Hebrew people against the Ammonite king (Judg. 11:12–33) makes him the precursor of Milton, with his defenses of the English people against the Royalist attacks of Claude de Saumaise. Samson responds:

> Of such examples add me to the role,
> Me easily indeed mine may neglect,
> But God's proposed deliverance not so.
>
> (lines 290–92)

In *The Ready and Easy Way* Milton also adds himself to the role. This is not to suggest any simple identity among Samson and Jephtha and the Milton of the prose works, only that a profoundly apolitical conception of heroism informs both the poetry and the prose. Andrew Milner disagrees, arguing that while Samson's destruction of himself and of the Philistine nobility under the ruins of Dagon's temple might seem to be simply a personal act on a grand scale, it should, in fact, be seen as "genuinely political," given Milton's bourgeois individualist world view, which necessarily recodes political action in individualist terms (191). Even granting that this individualism was the only political philosophy to which Milton had access (Harringtonian republicanism and Fifth Monarchist radicalism would seem to suggest otherwise), it is difficult to characterize as political an individual's utter rejection of the collective, except insofar as any negation of politics is itself political. Like Samson, the prophetic Milton of *The Ready and Easy Way* seeks out the consolations of a providential history in which there is, at least for the moment, an absolute distinction between individual and collective, history and politics, jeremiad and utopia. Milton's tract is not anti-utopian because of its involvement with its circumstances, but because it cuts itself off from those circumstances. One of those circumstances, one of those forces "standing around" Milton as he wrote, was the material form of Puritan utopia.

Still, there are other generic points of view from which all these dis-

putes between jeremiad and utopia disappear. One of sovereign power's prerogatives is its ability to conflate its diverse antagonists into one
monstrous Other whose differences it can then see as the symptoms of
a single, underlying republican malaise.

Satire, Utopia, and the Future Imminent

*The Censure of the Rota Upon Mr Miltons Book, Entituled, The Ready
and Easie Way to Establish a Free Common-wealth* is the most pene-
trating critique of Milton's republican jeremiad; yet it was written not
by Harrington or by any other member of his Rota Club but by an
anonymous Royalist. The tract, which appeared in late March 1660,
between the two editions of Milton's tract, presents itself as the min-
utes of a meeting of Harrington's Rota Club on March 26, 1660. John
Aubrey says that this political debating society, which numbered
among its members Aubrey himself, Milton's friend Cyriack Skinner,
Sir John Wildman, Sir William Petty, Samuel Pepys, and Andrew
Marvell, had, in fact, disbanded a month before at the unexpected
southward march of General Monck. The title page of the tract clearly
announces its satiric quality by listing the clerk of the Rota as "Trun-
dle Wheeler" and its printer as "Paul Giddy ... at the sign of the
Windmill in Turne-again Lane." Still, it is not surprising that so many
bibliographers and readers have taken it as a genuine product of
the Rota Club, for it delivers a stinging Harringtonian attack on
Milton's oligarchic republicanism. In its capacity to understand
Harrington's republican principles, yet to present them inside a satiric
framework that lumps him together with Milton, *The Censure of the
Rota* demonstrates the failure of Harrington's rhetoric of utopian
reconciliation.[4]

One speaker at this fictional meeting couples an aristocratic and
most un-Harringtonian denunciation of the effect of "rhetoric" on "the
mob" with a political anatomist's attack on Milton's generality, so
appropriate to a jeremiad and so inappropriate to a utopia. He says
Milton's tract is "windy foppery from the beginning to the end, written
to the elevation of that rabble and meant to cheat the ignorant. . . .
You trade altogether in universals, the region of deceits and fallacy,
but never come so near particulars, as to let us know which among
diverse things of the same kind you would be at. For you admire commonwealths in general, and cry down kingship as much at large without any regard to the particular constitutions which only make the one

or the other good or bad" (13). He takes advantage of the monarchist populism made possible by the antidemocratic republicanism of tracts like Milton's during the closing days of the Protectorate, saying that "though you brag much of the people's managing their own affairs, you allow them no more of that in your *utopia* (as you have ordered it) than only to set up their throats and bawl . . . once in an age, or oftener, as an old member drops away, and a new one is to succeed" (14).

The concluding judgment on Milton's tract, spoken by "J. H.," is a Harringtonian critique spoken by a character satirizing Harrington as well as Milton. This speaker condemns Milton for saying nothing of the balance and the agrarian (an omission Milton was to make up for in the second edition—as a result of this critique?) and for his explicit rejection of rotation. He criticizes Milton's sloppy comparison of the senate of Rome (which excludes the people) with the Grand Council of Venice (which takes them in). And he sounds most of all like Harrington when he denounces the Protectorate as an absolute monarchy and Milton's Grand Council as an oligarchy, wondering "at what politic crack in any man's skull the imagination could enter of securing liberty under an oligarchy, seized of the government for term of life, which was never yet seen in the world" (6, 15). In an impeccably Harringtonian argument, he concludes that Milton has "really proposed the most ready and easy way to establish downright slavery upon the nation that can possibly be contrived, which will clearly appear to any man that does but understand this plain truth, that wheresoever the power of proposing and debating, together with the power of ratifying and enacting laws, is entrusted into the hands of any one person or any one council (as you would have it), that government is inevitably arbitrary and tyrannical" (16).

Yet the speaker distances himself from Harrington through his characterization of the principle of rotation, whose logic he nevertheless understands much better than Milton does: "And if you have studied this point as carefully as I have done, you could not but know there is no such way under heaven of disposing the vicissitudes of command and obedience, and of distributing equal right and liberty among all men, as this of wheeling, by which (as Chaucer writes), a single fart hath been equally divided among a whole convent of friars, and every one had his just share of the savor" (15). The nature of Harrington's orders is clear, but the excremental vision of satire, which allies itself with established and traditional state power, can dismiss them without engaging them. The authoritarian power of political satire at the Restoration derives not from analysis and debate but from a rhetoric of social and political inclusion and exclusion, a metaphor of disease and cure, and the opposition of private fantasy to public wisdom.

The modern dystopian tradition has made us familiar with a pejorative sense of the term *utopian* that is largely foreign to the seventeenth century; we will mistake the nature of the polemics surrounding Puritan utopian writing if we assume that the only possible critique of utopia is the defense of the beleaguered individual against the encroachments of the totalitarian state, in the manner of the dystopias of Huxley, Zamiatin, and Orwell. If anything, the seventeenth-century situation is precisely the reverse, for the Puritan utopist finds himself most vulnerable to a conservative critique that ridicules him as a fanciful political hobbyist. Conservative satirists attack Puritan utopists not as totalitarian enemies of the free individual but as presumptuous intruders upon the accumulated wisdom and traditional prerogatives of state authority, whether that of the king, Parliament, Lord Protector, or Council of Officers. Utopists are fanciful and vaporous dreamers, the political equivalent of the Puritan religious "fanatics" and "enthusiasts."

We have seen something of this approach in Hobbes's implicit and Wren's explicit critique of Harrington's political writing. Charles I (or John Colepeper and Lucius Cary writing in his name) set the tone in 1642 in *His Majesty's Answer to the Nineteen Propositions of both Houses of Parliament,* where he defends the integrity of his ministers against the accusations of "some persons who have now too great an influence even upon both houses, [who] judge or seem to judge to be for the public good, and as are agreeable to that new utopia of religion and government into which they endeavor to transform this kingdom" (Rushworth 1.727). We can see a similar argument during the Protectorate from Marchamont Nedham, the ideologically flexible editor of the Cromwellian state newspaper, *Mercurius Politicus.* Sensing a likely move to some sort of Cromwellian monarchy, Nedham took the opportunity to recant his erstwhile republicanism in five satiric letters from "Utopia" and "Oceana" prefacing numbers 352 to 356 of the paper (March 5, 1657 to April 9, 1657). He describes the recent attempts by "the Utopians" to cure themselves of "an infectious itch of scribbling political discourses, caused by a salt humor first bottled in the brain pan, and then breaking out at the fingers' ends" (7643). In the view of established seventeenth-century power as in that of Soviet psychiatry, political dissent becomes a symptom of some individual pathology. Nedham writes that the Utopian magistrate "gave order to put the whole society of pols into the hospital of the *incurabili,* to have their skulls opened up and searched with a long sword, and so served up with green-sauce, as a fitting punishment for presuming to break the fundamental law of Utopia, by daring to be in earnest, and appear in print so profound and serious projectors." He announces the arrival of "a jolly crew of the inhabitants of Oceana, in company of the learned author himself" for the cure (7644).

Throughout these letters the argument is against exotic models and for individual submission and engagement to established authority. Nedham speaks in the conservative voice of a romance hero, back home again, older but wiser: "Indeed ... all that we have learnt by travelling is this, how to live at home and be quiet, having gained so much experience as to know there is a necessity of a settlement, and that it matters not what the form be, so we attain the ends of government" (7674). His argument against utopia is an antiformalist critique of enthusiastic fancy: "The High Shoon, the Leveller, and the Enthusiast" think government consists of "having no landlord, no law, no religion save his own phantasy." In fact, "every form of government is a fiction or figment of the brain, which is nothing in itself, further than as it is a necessary device for putting men into a way convenient for the acting and exercising of their natural rights and judgments." And he invokes the traditional fiction of England's ancient mixed constitution, of the "three estates, as most excellent, most suiting with the genius of our people" (7691).

Nedham's relation to established authority is both self-mocking and self-serving. He mocks his own radical writings by including one "wondrous wise republican called Mercurius Politicus" among the group arriving in Utopia from Oceana for the cure (7644). He invokes More's rapprochement with established authority as a precedent: "Of him our annals say that as an eminent statesman, he had the right knack of living in the world, his motto being *Ioco-Serio, Betwixt Jest and Earnest,* which the most learned in the languages of the suburbs have translated *drolling*" (7642). Henry executed More only because he strayed from this moderate standard into presumptuous high seriousness. Nedham seems to be speaking of himself when he says that "it has been the policy of this country to retain a state droll in pension as a most necessary officer, to correct all that presume to print or dispute about models of government" (7690). The very form of these issues of *Mercurius Politicus* reveals their politic jocoseriousness, since each begins with a burlesque defense of the state against those "mangy scribblers" who criticize it and concludes with a matter-of-fact and officially licensed publication of state business and diplomatic news.

A flood of anti-utopian satire accompanied and followed the utopian platforms of the Interregnum. Eliot's *Christian Commonwealth* seems to have been unknown to the wits, but radical English sectaries and Harrington in particular drew the attention of a great deal of "curative" satire. "Republic" and "Utopia" become synonyms, allowing dystopian satirists who anticipate the restoration of monarchy to mock utopian writing with a brutal parody of the republican forms of proposition and debate. Henry More, writing as "Alazonomastix Philalethes" in *Free-parliament queries proposed to tender consciences* (1660), proposes as a topic for debate, "Whether hanging or drowning be the best ways of transportation of our late republicans to the commonwealths of Utopia and Oceana?" (Gibson 410). In the same year William Colline's *The Spirit of the Phanatiques Dissected* (given the drawing and quartering of the regicides, the title itself has a cruel ring) places Harrington in a utopian tradition through a rhetorical query directed at Milton's *The Ready and Easy Way:* "Whether his new frame of a commonwealth without readmitting of kingship, together with that fool Harrington's, ought not to be sent to *terra incognita* or Sir Thomas More's Utopia, along with the authors themselves, to frame a free state there?" (Parker 99). Sir Edmond Pierce, writing in *England's Monarchy Asserted* (1660), mocks the Oceanic method of balloting: "How doth the press labor (in this scribbling age) under the burthen which is put upon it by every wild and brainsick fancy of our republican candidates, each . . . flinging his paper mite . . . for this Utopian thing of a commonwealth, so much talked on amongst us" (Gibson 409). The anonymous author of *Democritus Turned Statesman* proposes shipping Harrington's *Aphorisms Political* to Jamaica. Samuel Butler goes him one better by proposing the same fate for Harrington (Russell-Smith 100–101). Given Harrington's actual transportation and imprisonment, and the real threat of public execution faced by Milton and the other regicides, these satires are steel-tipped. The conservative dystopian parody of utopia transforms the utopian voyage and civic ritual into a fantasy of penal transportation and public torture.

In Samuel Butler's *Characters* we can see a satire of utopian writing from a generic point of view distinct from that of the broadsheet or Nedham's jocoserious state newspaper, but no less tied to a conservative aristocratic ideal. The Theophrastian character enjoyed a great revival during the seventeenth century, in part, Douglas Bush says, because of "literary men's consciousness of aristocratic cultural standards and of the disturbing pressure of commercial, professional, and

religious groups" (198). The character book is the generic inverse of
utopia. Where utopia sees a blank, displaced population, the character
book sees a seething multitude of diverse religious, political, and economic types, the result of a sociopathological deviation from an aristocratic and conservative norm. Where utopia invites its readers to
lose themselves in the unified corporate subjectivity of the future, the
character book encourages them tò analyze and control the mob by
identifying themselves with some preexistent and so presumably non-
"charactered" ideal of custom and permanence.

Butler caricatures Harrington in "A Republican" and "A Politician." He seems to be referring to Harrington's Rota Club and to "The
Corollary" of *Oceana* when he mentions "the state quack that used to
mount his bank in a coffeehouse, and foretold Oliver Cromwell should
live so many years after he was hanged, and after dying leave the
republicans his heirs" (25). On the one hand, republicans are self-
destructive idiots who "cheat themselves with words, mistaking them
for things" (24). The Republican "has not judgment enough to observe
that all models of governments are merely Utopian that have no territory but in books, nor subjects but in hot heads and strong fancies"
(24). He calls Oceana a Laputa-esque "floating island" and democracy
"but the effect of a crazy brain; 'tis like the intelligible world, where
the models and ideas of all things are, but no things" (26).[5] On the
other hand, republicans can harm others and the state as a whole. Harrington (or the "character" that he and his Rota Club produce) is a
"state charlatan," a "state fanatic," and a "state empiric" whose political anatomy "dissects the body politic into controversies as anatomists do the body of man, and mangles every part, only to find out
new disputes" (27). So dangerous is this republican that Butler indirectly threatens him with hanging (26). Butler does not mention Eliot
directly, but he does turn his gallows irony to "A Fifth-Monarchy
Man." He says that those Fifth Monarchists who recently attempted
to establish God's kingdom on earth (the heads of the rebel Thomas
Venner and twelve of his followers had adorned London Bridge in
1661) are the heirs of John of Leyden, though they "had no sooner
quartered his coat with their own, but their whole outward men were
set on the gates of the city, where a head and four quarters stand as
types and figures of the Fifth Monarchy" (45).

If we take a genetic approach to utopia's generic identity, this Interregnum and Restoration division between utopia and satire would
seem to be an unnatural split between two essential constituents of the
utopian imagination. More's *Utopia* is supremely ambiguous in this

regard: is the Humanist punning merely ornamental that christens his ideal place a no-place, its ideal river a no-river, or is it a satiric trap laid for anyone who might think his ideal state possible? More seems to leave the question open, and many subsequent critics have taken their cue from him. Darko Suvin says this dystopian/utopian ambiguity is an essential feature of utopia and that utopia as a genre is to be judged by "the degree of integration between its constructive-utopian and satiric aspects: the deadly earnest blueprint and the totally closed horizons of 'new maps of hell' both lack aesthetic wisdom" (55). Robert C. Elliott argues that utopia and satire are inseparable because both had their birth in the preliterary festival of the Saturnalia (24).

Agreeing with Elliot (115), Suvin argues that utopia's combination of negative and positive elements makes it at home in the subjunctive mood. Suvin returns utopia to the fold of Kantian aesthetics, saying that it is "a heuristic device for perfectibility, an epistemological and not an ontological entity" (52). Michael Holquist concurs, saying that there is a "generally playful quality to be found in even the grimmest utopian literature," and that utopia exists in the "hypothetical or heuristic time" of the game, not in clock time (111–12). The game quality of utopia stakes out an imaginative domain. In More's *Utopia,* for instance, "the complex social, economic, and religious factors which are in the grip of the course of English history in reality, when reduced and stylized into counters, become accessible to the freedom of play in the utopia. The irreversibility of history is stemmed, and outcomes determined by the contingency of actual experience can, in utopia, be reversed in the freedom of the utopist's imagination. Another set of laws obtains in the utopia, arbitrary but infinitely open to recombination. Utopia is play with ideas" (119). Elisabeth Hansot, drawing on Huizinga's *Homo Ludens,* also calls utopia a form of serious play in which "utopia builders reconstruct existing social arrangements as if they were transparent to the will." If we fail to build utopias, we risk acquiescing in the less self-conscious game of politics and losing our capacity for play (201).

Speaking of More's *Utopia* specifically, C. S. Lewis clearly distances himself from any positive political reading of the work, saying that we should read it not as a "philosophical treatise" but as a "holiday work, a spontaneous overflow of intellectual high spirits, a revel of debate, paradox, comedy and (above all) of invention" (219). Harry Berger, Jr., agrees, saying that whereas criticism has tended to overemphasize the Raphaelite earnestness of *Utopia,* we should see it instead as a "green world" that provides a "temporary haven for recreation or clarification," projecting "the urge of the paralyzed will to give up, escape, work magic, abolish time and flux and the intrusive reality of other minds" (212).

Such appeals to joking, games, and play resemble the critical appeal to More's "irony" we examined in an earlier chapter. They attempt to dispose of all interpretive problems by turning all utopian contradictions into "seeming" contradictions, and to resolve all paradoxes by appealing to the controlling intention of a happy gamester we call "More." At the same time they attempt to hold off incursions from that world outside the canonical game space of utopia. When "real world" forces seem to enter utopia, they must be turned into neutral "counters" subject to the utopist's shaping imagination. When seemingly utopian works attach themselves too strongly to political rhetoric and social practice, when they seem reluctant to question adequately their own political materiality, they must be designated as nonludic, and so nonutopian. This vigilant defense of playfulness has something in it of Nedham's pensioned jocoseriousness: as Nedham maintains a position for himself as a "state droll" by defending the state apparatus from attacks by oppositional political writers, so the defender of ludic utopia maintains a position for himself as a *criticus ludens* by defending a canonical reading of canonical utopias against the difficulties posed by noncanonical works and methods of interpretation. The price of this criticism is self-censorship and the effacement of the contradictory historicity of utopia; Robert M. Adams comments perceptively on the dangers of such a reading of *Utopia:* "Calling an uncomfortable idea a joke is an easy way of cutting the great disquieting books of the past to the measure of our own parochial preconceptions" (202).

Another problem is that it is too easy a way to cut down the disquieting qualities of joking itself and its cognate concepts of irony, game, and play. Sooner or later, often despite the utopist's best efforts, the pleasure principle at work in every utopia insists on integrating itself with a reality principle. Utopia's game quality suggests not so much the wish fulfillment dreams of Freud's *Creative Writers and Daydreaming* as the repetition compulsion of his *Beyond the Pleasure Principle.* Here Freud presents us with a case history that led him to formulate a new theory of psychological adjustment. Freud noticed a seemingly irrational game played by an infant who would toss a toy attached to a string over the edge of his crib and cry *"fort!"* (gone), then reel it back in and cry *"da!"* (there). Freud comments, "The interpretation of the game then became obvious. It was related to the child's great cultural achievement—the instinctual renunciation . . . which he had made in allowing his mother to go away without protesting" (9). By repeatedly staging his mother's painful absence (*fort*) and then her return (*da*), he gains a certain rationalizing mastery over the vagaries of infantile *fortuna:* "At the outset he was in a *passive* situation—he was overpowered by the experience; but by repeating it, unpleasurable though it was, as a game, he took on an *active* part. These efforts might be put down to an instinct for mastery that was acting independently of whether the memory was in itself pleasurable or not" (10). But it is difficult to say whether the infant plays the game or the game plays the infant.

In the terms of this study, the *fort/da* game is a utopia (*fort/da* is a pretty good translation of *utopia*) and the infant a utopist. He attempts to establish control over a host of displacing, threatening particulars (the comings and goings of his mother) not by repressing them or reacting to them through a compensatory fantasy, but by repeating them in such a carefully staged fashion that he gains at least the illusion of some control over them.[6] In his *fort/da* game, the utopist defers his desire for instantaneous pleasure. Rather than fleeing from, or attempting to reverse, the oppressive and impersonal forces at work in the outer world (this would be more properly the mode of pastoral, even of satire), he seeks out an insular experimental site in which to submit himself, his readers, and his displaced populations to them. In the process he hopes to rationalize those forces, removing their threat and making them calculable, even productive. For instance, we have seen that utopia begins in reaction to irrational practices of enclosure, warfare, and customary domination and that it produces an accelerated process of enclosure, a universal warfare, and a more efficient form of domination. This impulse to mastery through rationalizing repetition is equally relevant to the structure of More's literary work, to Eliot's social practice, and to Harrington's political rhetoric. The utopian repetition compulsion is, in fact, a sort of game, but it is a game that shapes its player, for the rationalization it offers is possible only at the cost of the player's own "instinctual renunciation."

Because it seeks to accelerate history rather than reverse it and play with it, Puritan utopia is notoriously lacking in satiric wit, which requires a reflexive reversal to some preexistent standard of judgment. This lack may explain the dutiful tones in which historians of literary utopia typically refer to Puritan utopia. The Manuels, for instance, find the utopias of the English Interregnum distasteful. They are particularly upset by *Oceana*'s "dullness," calling it "as arid a work as has sprung from the mind of utopian man" (365, 361). Negley and Patrick say that Harrington's works "have hardly any interest for the general reader and not infrequently bore the scholar" (382). But the humorlessness of Puritan utopia (we could certainly rank Eliot, Winstanley, Comenius, and Plockhoy with Harrington) is an indication less of desiccated Calvinist sensibilities than of the development of competing traditions of utopia and dystopia after More. The very word *humor* holds Puritan utopia to a standard inappropriate to it, invoking as it does a genre to which the satiric dystopia has stronger ties: the satiric comedy of humors. This genre proposes restoring a balance of humors according to some essentially conservative social vision. We may see this satiric tradition in such comic dystopias as Bishop Joseph Hall's *Mundus Alter et Idem (Another World and Yet the Same)*, which uses an imaginary voyage and geography to ridicule bodily, intellectual, and political "excesses"; in *Gulliver's Travels*, whose fantastic states offer not different frames of utopian government but different perspectives from which to satirize Swift's own society; and in Hawthorne's *Blithedale Romance*, whose humane and "humourous" narrator, Miles Coverdale, ridicules the seriousness of the Fourierist utopists of Blithedale/Brook Farm.[7] The dystopist satirizes the utopist and his positive proposals, judging them according to a preexistent standard of individual moderation and social order. But since Puritan utopia offers a mechanism for the creation of new kinds of individuality and social order, it seems unfair to fault it for its lack of self-conscious and reflexive humor. And as the various satiric assaults on the utopian republics of the Interregnum show, one man's saturnalia is often (perhaps always) another man's torture.

Harrington seems to address this question of utopian humorlessness directly in the quote from Horace that he uses as the epigraph for *Oceana:*

> Tantalus a labris sitiens fugientia captat
> Flumina: quid rides? mutato nomine, de te
> Fabula narratur.

> [Thirsty Tantalus snatches at streams that flee his lips. But why do you laugh? Change the names, and the fable is told of you.]
> (Harrington 155)

Satiric whimsy is inappropriate when a universal political transformation is just within reach. Puritan utopia is urgently propositive rather than suggestively heuristic. Its proper verbal home is more a matter of tense than of mood, for it appears in what we might call a "future imminent," not in the subjunctive. It offers certain concrete proposals to inaugurate the millennium—proposals that demand to be accepted or rejected, not to be entertained. The future imminent refuses to enter into a future-contrary-to-fact construction.

The aesthetic critique of Puritan utopia's tedium is in one sense painfully true, and in another, beside the point. Writing (and reading) Puritan utopia is a disciplinary preparation for the rigors of utopian discipline, not a means for raising up and casting out superfluous humors. The Puritan utopist's fixation with ordering groups of bodies on a national level also appears on a formal level in his ordering discursive detail on the page: in the Eliot Tracts' repetitive, numbered, and meticulously organized lists of Indians' confessions, questions, and conversion narratives; in Eliot's multiplication of higher and higher levels, larger and larger groupings of persons in *The Christian Commonwealth* and *Communion of Churches;* in the ritualized rationality of Harrington's orders for the assemblies, marches, wheelings, and ballotings of Oceana's elders; and in Harrington's parallel orders for the military assemblies and drills of the horse and the foot of the youth, which prepare the marching army for their millennial conquest of the world. Neither Eliot nor Harrington shows a reluctance to repeat his utopian formulas for any reader not persuaded on the first reading. In its attempt to fashion a new self for its reader through the tedium of disciplinary repetition, Puritan utopia is much closer to catechism and meditation than to the satiric dystopian narrative. But even though it is not fundamentally a narrative genre, its textual ordering is heavy with the promise of an irreversible progress in the imminent future.

Hobson's Contract: Utopian Discipline and the Right to Make Promises

For multitude unordered, by how much the greater they are, the greater is their cumber, and unaptness to operate in order unto their end. *Ordo anima rerum.* Order is one of the beauties of heaven, and so it is of the churches: *Let all things be done in order* (1 Cor. 14:40). Jerusalem is a city compacted (Ps. 122:3), and the more orderly bodies are, the better are they compacted. Bodies that are compacted are so ordered by number and measure: the New Jerusalem is the most glorious city that ever shall be on earth, and we see that it shall be compacted by number and measure (Rev. 21:12–18).   JOHN ELIOT, *Communion of Churches*

If we study things carefully, we will discover that what preserves the entire universe, down to its smallest detail, is order, plain and simple. Order is the division and arrangement of things first and last, greater and lesser, major and minor, like and unlike, according to the place, time, number, measure, and weight proper to each. Therefore many have said *ordo anima rerum,* order is the soul of things, and quite rightly too. Whatever is well ordered is stable and permanent so long as it remains in order. But if it loses order, it weakens, wavers, collapses, and falls in ruins.   JOHN AMOS COMENIUS, *The Great Didactic*

In the formation of a commonwealth, to begin with that first which is naturally last is to invert the order, and by consequence the commonwealth, which indeed is nothing but order.

JAMES HARRINGTON, *Aphorisms Political*

John Eliot and James Harrington write in different hemispheres, in response to different social and political problems, and in different theocratic rhetorics. Yet by constructing an enlightenment critique of anthropomorphic monarchy and oligarchy, by speaking in the Lycurgan voice of self-consuming political authority, and by proposing an organizational means to the millennium, they operate within the same system of enabling and constraining conventions—a system I have been calling Puritan utopia.

Foremost among these conventions (in a sense, summing them all up) is Puritan utopia's capacity for representing the displaced population to the utopist as a raw material for his imaginative transformation. The nature of Puritan utopia as a genre of imaginative writing comes into focus only when we recognize the utopist's ability to conceive of human collectives as a blank page on which he must write. His contemporary opponent (he can be monarchist, aristocrat, democrat, or republican; Roman Catholic, Anglican, Presbyterian, or Independent) sees in the people a dangerous but reassuringly familiar enemy: the mob, which is a monstrous growth or pathological infection somehow exterior to the state proper. This mob inspires him to construct conservative fantasies of penal transportation, torture, and execution. The Hobbesian variant is only marginally different, for Hobbes transports the displaced population to prehistoric times and uses the threat of its reemergence to justify some admonitory and punitive sovereign swordplay in the present.

But the Puritan utopist sees in this population a new thing under the sun—the raw material of his managerial technic. In a rational fantasy arguably no more humane than that of his opponents, he proposes to arrange and manipulate the bodies constituting the displaced population. The Puritan utopist looks around himself and sees a state of political conflict generated by an overdetermined conjuncture of political languages, institutions, and social classes. He then blinks, looks again, and sees a postdiluvian landscape and an anomic populace awaiting utopian enclosure and rationalization. Puritan utopia promises that in a millennial moment of formal freedom, the utopist may create the soul of a thoroughly rational civil form by a methodical arrangement of persons, spaces, and procedures: *ordo anima rerum.*

Like all such formalist theories of culture, Puritan utopia fails not simply because of its indifference to the brute facts of history, but also because it overlooks the historical momentum or remanence of other cultural forms. No political writer ever finds himself brooding on a formless prima materia; rather, he is locked in conflict with alternative forms or with previous forms materialized as custom. The plans of Eliot, Harrington, the other Puritan utopists, and their fellow Commonwealthsmen shipwrecked on the Restoration's anti-utopian fictions of continuity: the conservative satire, with its railing threats of hospitals, jails, and gallows; the myth of the ancient constitution and the traditional English republic of king, Lords, and Commons (Eliot was forced to invoke it when recanting *The Christian Commonwealth*); the persistence of local electoral and agrarian traditions reluctant to bow down before a new, totalizing state reason; and the aristocratic fiction characterizing the English people as an untrustworthy and turbulent "beast with many heads." A genocidal variant on this last fiction—the Indian-hating vision of the Algonquians as accursed and demonic savages—never disappeared from Eliot's Massachusetts, and it prevailed during and after King Philip's War.

Writing long before the Restoration, Gerrard Winstanley is much less sanguine than Eliot and Harrington are about the prospect for a universal new modeling of English civility, perhaps because he writes from the point of view of a social class more conscious of the economic continuities than of the political discontinuities. In *The Law of Freedom* (1652), written after the crushing of the Digger communes, he offers an abstract model for the reformation of England, but as Christopher Hill argues, Winstanley's work is more postutopian than utopian—an attempt to understand England's failure rather than an optimistic proposal of its way to a rational settlement (*Experience* 39).

Winstanley notes that although the king has been deposed, he still reigns through his "Norman" laws of buying and selling—specifically, in the control of roads into market towns by "Norman toll takers," the rule of most of the parishes by "two or three of the great ones," the overstocking of commons lands with sheep and cattle, and the continuing demand of landlords for rents, fines, and heriots (505–6). Well before Harrington and Eliot, Winstanley registers England's failure to live up to its potential as an elect nation.

By presenting itself as the neutral instrument by which theocratic reason shapes an anomic population, Puritan utopia (like early modern utopia in general) claims to be a text without an author for a people without a text. An ideological critique of this claim should point out that it is wrong on both counts: what presents itself as a neutral and universal text is actually the instrument of a local will to power (whether white, English, Congregationalist, possessive individualist, or personal); what appears in utopia as an utterly anomic population is, in fact, a culture capable of resistance to utopian rationalization, since all peoples, even illiterate and displaced peoples, have a cultural "text" of some sort.

Still, while this ideological critique of Puritan utopia may adequately explain the failure of its global and millennialist projections, it fails to explain the considerable importance of the genre in its early modern context, and its usefulness for us in reconstructing the emergence of modern Western conceptions of individual and corporate subjectivity; that utopia fails to take into account the remanence of other cultural forms does not mean that it has no remanence of its own. The rest of this study will attempt to analyze the importance of Puritan utopia in its context and in ours by examining its relation to another genre of political writing: social contract theory.

Early modern Europe's obsession with social contract theory and voluntarist models of the state (Gough, *Contract*) is more familiar and somewhat more respectable than its obsession with utopia and disciplinary order, but the two are intimately connected. A good vantage point from which to begin examining the relation between the two is David Hume's brief, iconoclastic essay "Of the Original Contract," which sums up most of the claims of seventeenth-century contract theorists and then dismisses them as pure ideology, at least so far as they claim to describe actual origins. Hume examines the empirical records of the birth, growth, and death of actual states and asks, "Is there anything discoverable in all these events, but force and violence? Where is the mutual agreement or voluntary association so much talked of?"

(199). Furthermore, it is simply foolish to suppose that any original contract signed by some people would irrevocably bind all future generations. What passes for contract, Hume says, is in fact a pattern of habitual obedience and subjection. Most absurd of all is the Lockean idea of "tacit consent," by which a person living under some prince is said to have placed himself by implication under the jurisdiction of a social contract: "Can we seriously say that a poor peasant or artisan has a free choice to leave his country, when he knows no foreign language or manners, and lives from day to day, by the small wages which he acquires? We may as well assert that a man, by remaining in a vessel, freely consents to the dominion of the master, though he was carried on board while asleep, and must leap into the ocean, and perish, the moment he leaves her" (203). Social contract theory actually arises from the desire of certain factions to "cover that scheme of actions which it pursues" by a "philosophical or speculative system of principles" (193).

In "Varieties of Literary Utopia," Northrop Frye also sees social contract theory as "ideology," but in a less pejorative sense. In fact, it is a myth complementary to the myth of utopia: "Both begin in an analysis of the present, the society that confronts the mythmaker, and they project this analysis in time or space. The contract projects it into the past, the utopia into the future or some distant place" (25). Because the contract myth attempts to explain contemporary situations in terms of historical evidence, it tends to function more as "an integral part of social theory," whereas utopia remains fundamentally "speculative" and so more akin to fiction. In the Christian tradition the contract myth finds its archetypal home at the beginning of history in the Garden of Eden, and the utopian myth at the conclusion of history in the New Jerusalem (34).

Frye's discussion of social contract theory and utopia as myth is useful because it helps us move the study of political fictions out of the context of their referents (is it reasonable to suppose that any such contract ever did exist, or that any such utopia ever will?) into the context of human desire (what genealogical or prophetic longings do these fictions attempt to embody?). But since myth always returns to the present after being projected into the future or the past, since it always takes on, or operates inside, a material form, we may also move into a political context, asking what uses have been made of these fictions in political life. The seventeenth century and particularly the political controversy of the Interregnum produced an explosion of social contract theory: the covenant theology of Old and New England; the Leveller, Digger, and army discussions of the "Norman Yoke" and Magna Charta; Hobbes's absolutist theory of the covenantal birth of irrevocable sovereignty; Locke's more democratic theory of the original delegation of de jure authority. Now, all these may indeed be dismissed as hypothetical myths of civil genesis that can never escape their fictional origin. But the fictional becomes actual, and these theories of the nature of contract intertwine with contracts that are far from hypothetical: the civil and church covenants of the Puritan colonists, the army debates at Putney and Whitehall over the corporate nature of the New Model Army, the Solemn League and Covenant of 1643 and the Commonwealth's attempt to override it through the Engagement, the discussion of the marriage contract by Milton and others, and the political settlements of 1660 and 1688–89.

Just as the retrospective fiction of the social contract assumes a material form in the present, so too (as I have been arguing throughout this study) does the prospective fiction of Puritan utopia, which looks not just toward some distant place or imagined time but also toward the displaced populations inhabiting its political present. Because utopia and social contract theory inhabit the same political present, they assume a relation to each other more complex than one of mythical analogy. Puritan utopia simultaneously precedes, supplements, and criticizes social contract theory. It attempts to construct a prerequisite to all such contracts, one whose existence contract theory typically takes for granted: the individual with the right, the will, and the capacity to enter into contract. There is no social contract without a prior disciplinary utopia that qualifies the contractors. Whether it remains at the level of a literary work or whether it also enters into political rhetoric and social practice, Puritan utopia is animated by a disciplinary imagination.

In the words of Nietzsche's *Genealogy of Morals,* Puritan utopia sets itself the task of showing how "to breed an animal with the right to make promises" (189). In this work Nietzsche goes beyond Hume's critique of social contract theory, moving past his discovery of an ideological cloaking of pure violence to a discovery of the origins of political rationalization. Like Hume, he argues that all political beginnings are violent—that a "commonwealth" is originally nothing other than "a pack of savages, a race of conquerors, themselves organized for war and able to organize others, fiercely dominating a population perhaps vastly superior in numbers yet amorphous and nomadic" (219). We must abandon the idea of a unified political origin through a voluntarist social contract and replace it with the historical actuality of domination: "I take it we have got over that sentimentalism that would have it [the state] begin with a contract. What do men who can command, who are born rulers, who evince power in act and deportment, have to do with contracts? Such beings are unaccountable; they come like destiny, without rhyme or reason ruthlessly, bare of pretext. . . . Their work is an instinctive imposing of forms. They are the most spontaneous, most unconscious artists that exist. They appear, and presently something entirely new has arisen, a live dominion whose parts and functions are delimited and interrelated, in which there is room for nothing that has not previously received its meaning from the whole" (219–20).

Nietzsche's study is in part a celebration of this process of cultural domination, and so far as it universalizes it and sees it as the necessary relation between "organized" and "amorphous and nomadic" peoples, it participates in the Western enlightenment rhetoric of class domination, racism, and colonialism. But we can adapt Nietzsche's genealogy to a different kind of criticism. Though it does not altogether free itself from its enlightenment philosophical forebears, it does demystify the voluntarist fiction of the social contract by which enlightenment attempts to recode and master its concrete practices of domination. Nietzsche's genealogy does not simply dismiss the idea of social contract as mystifying ideology, but insists on supplementing it by moving us outside the philosophical rhetoric of sovereignty and right into the history of social discipline. For Nietzsche this is a history of instructional procedure, penal correction, and mnemonic torture aimed at producing individuals capable of entering into contract—individuals with a memory of what is to be gained by doing so and of what is to be lost through a breach of contract. This exercise of social discipline before and subsequent to all contract has "the preparatory task of rendering man up to a certain point regular, uniform, equal among equals, calculable" (190). Its final and most glorious product is the "conscience" or "bad conscience" of the individual with the right to make promises: an internal mechanism of self-discipline replacing the previous external mechanisms and constraints. The point here is not that social contract theory is a mere ideology of voluntarism cloaking some darker reality of domination. Rather, it is that contract theory is always rationally integrated with a system of utopian training that will produce human subjects who will either assent to the contract offered or be subjected to a program of discipline that will bring them to assent the next time around. Utopia sees to it that the social contract is a political version of Hobson's choice: this or none.

Nietzsche's concept of this social discipline that precedes all contract is analogous to Freud's repetition compulsion and Weber's Protestant ethic. All are demystifying concepts designed to reveal the social production of human types previously taken as natural, as philosophical données: the free political subject ready to enter into social contract, the psychological subject equipped with a conscience and engaged in a process of adjustment to the reality principle, the worldly ascetic laboring diligently in his calling because of his calculation of future economic needs and divine judgments on sloth. Speaking of the formation of this last type, Weber says, "A man does not 'by nature' wish to earn more and more money, but simply to live as he is accustomed to live and to earn as much as is necessary for that purpose. . . . Labour must, on the contrary, be performed as if it were an absolute end in itself, a calling. But such an attitude is by no means a product of nature. It cannot be evoked by low wages or high ones alone, but can only be the product of a long and arduous process of education" (*Ethic* 60, 62).

By no means did Nietzsche make social contract theory a dead letter, however, for it lives on in a certain kind of social philosophy that happily cuts itself free from the confused worlds of literature, politics, and social practice. Patrick Riley's *Will and Political Legitimacy* sees social contract theory as a unified and autonomous tradition that we can characterize as part of "the voluntarization of western social thought" (4). Troublemakers like Hume, Marx, and Nietzsche get short shrift: Riley either ignores their arguments, relegates them to footnotes, or merely records them in such a way that they do not unsettle his central discussion of a philosophical problematic defined by the works of Hobbes, Locke, Rousseau, Kant, and Hegel. With the exception of Kant, Riley says, these thinkers are hampered by their inability to formulate a sufficiently "clear" concept of the will (18). But taken as a whole, the social contract tradition has a great value in its development of "a metaphysic of morals to show why men are obligated by virtue of free acts of their own, why human will can be understood as a kind of moral causality that makes intelligible such notions as promise, responsibility, imputability, and the like" (200). It provides, in other words, a philosophical defense of established political authority and a rationale for punishment, all this without ever mentioning concrete polities and penal practices. Throughout his study Riley follows his contract theorists in attributing such abstract philosophical concepts as "will," "consent," and "obligation" to an abstract universal subject, who presumably is a fair and representative stand-in for "man-in-general." Political moral philosophy is the privileged space for discussing such philosophical and juridical universals without descending to or even acknowledging the historically diverse disciplinary processes that produce distinct human subjectivities and their distinct wills.

Renaissance discussions of social contract are certainly no less theocratic than those of Puritan utopia, but they tend to turn to different scriptural texts. The classic scriptural discussion of the relation between the individual conscience and the demands of the state is in Romans 13: "Let every soul be subject unto the higher powers. For there is no power but of God: the powers that be are ordained of God." J. H. Hexter says that "centuries before 1516 and more emphatically during the century to come, those verses were to be at the center of an intense debate on the political obligation of Christians" (*Vision* 3). They were, for instance, the central text of the Engagement Controversy. Therefore, Hexter says, it is all the more remarkable that neither *Utopia* nor *The Prince* (we might add the rest of Renaissance utopia, along with Machiavelli's *Discourses*) makes any reference to this text. This is because neither More nor Machiavelli is interested in political obligation as a living problem (9–10).[8] Each practices a political empiricism that precludes (or precedes) a consideration of the relation between individual conscience and established authority. Machiavelli analyzes the concrete histories of various political forms, not the casuistic difficulties arising from their legitimacies. The empiricism of *Utopia* is a somewhat different kind, one it shares with other utopias. In its formal being, utopia is incapable of separating contract and discipline; it has no recourse to moral philosophy's abstract moral subject, its abstract time of unconstrained deliberation, or its abstract logical space of voluntarist freedom. Even at its most legalistic and nonnarrative, utopia describes not just flat or underdeveloped characters, but disciplinary subjects moving in a rationally gridded site according to a rational timetable. Characters in utopian fiction, like persons subject to utopian social practice or considered as the objects of utopian political rhetoric, are human bodies located in disciplinary time and space and subject to certain procedures of training and correction. Utopia's vision of the blankness of human populations is an idealism, but one that nevertheless allows it to criticize moral philosophy's idealist claim to logical autonomy.

More's *Utopia* gives us the most sophisticated version of this utopian critique of moral philosophy, and we will examine it in some detail before moving on to Puritan utopia. The long section on moral philosophy in Book 2 of *Utopia* is unusual because only here does

Raphael consider some aspect of Utopian life without showing (at first) its institutional basis. He simply gives us a Utopian catalog of great ideas. Raphael's claim that "in matters of moral philosophy, they carry on much the same arguments as we do" seems distressingly accurate if we note some of their favorite topics: the nature of the good, the difference between good and bad pleasures, the relation between reason and religion. More important, I think, is that the Utopians carry on this philosophical discourse in the voice of the universal subject. They speak of such abstract universals as "pleasure," "virtue," and "nature," attributing them to a universal moral subject: "When nature prompts *us* to be kind to our neighbors. . . . By simply following *his* senses and *his* right reason *a man* may discover what is pleasant by nature. . . . What true and natural pleasure can *you* get from someone's bent knee or bared head?" (55, 56, 57; emphasis added).

But *Utopia* also critiques this idea of the universal moral subject by depicting concrete practices of social discipline that produce a complex array of actual subjects. In a sense, all of Book 2 is a Möbius paragraph on a grand scale. The sexual inequality running through Utopian everyday life shows the ideological quality of the neuter universal subject. The ceremonial robes of the priests we see in the section on religion undercut the Utopian philosophical critique of finery in dress. The Utopians' war chest and the foreign luxury of their Financial Factors complicate their claim to a philosophical contempt of gold and jewels. The point here is not that the Utopians are hypocrites because they fail to live up to their philosophical universals, but that the structure of *Utopia* itself reveals the ideological (because compartmentalized) nature of all such philosophical universals. Utopia is an ideal state not because it is animated by a single moral ideal but because it portrays an ideally aggravated conflict between universalizing moral philosophy and individualizing social discipline.

In chapter 2 we saw one instance of this idealized conflict in the discrepancy between the good medieval *contemptus belli* which opens the section on warfare in Book 2 and the martial ideal permeating the rest of that section and indeed all of Utopian life. We can see another instance of this conflict in the distance between Book 2's consideration of moral philosophy (52–62) and its consideration of religion (78–88). Despite some important continuities and redundancies between the two sections, the distance between them signifies a shift in focus from the abstract moral subject of moral philosophy to the disciplinary subject of the Utopian social practice of religion. In the section on moral philosophy, we read that "their religious principles are of this nature:

that the soul of man is immortal, and by God's goodness it is born for happiness; that after this life, rewards are appointed for our virtues and good deeds, punishment for our sins. . . . And they add unhesitatingly that if these beliefs were rejected, no man would be so stupid as not to realize that he should seek pleasure regardless of right and wrong" (54–55). This argument recalls Machiavelli's discussion in *The Discourses* of the utility of religion (139–52), but it is still safely inside a universalizing language of moral philosophy.

In *Utopia's* section on religion we find the same doctrine at work in a much different context: "Thus the Utopians all believe that after this life vices are to be punished and virtue rewarded, and they consider that anyone who opposes this proposition is hardly a man, since he has degraded the sublimity of his own soul to the base level of a beast's wretched body. They will not even count him as one of their own citizens since he would undoubtedly betray all the laws and customs of society, if not prevented by fear" (80). Here we move from the universal "they" of the first section to a normative "they" set in opposition to a deviant "him," revealing the cultural heterogeneity that moral philosophy attempts to repress. But, as always, Utopia subjects this heterogeneity to a disciplinary erasure. First, we read that this mortalist heretic is "offered no honors, entrusted with no offices, and given no public responsibility; he is universally regarded as a low and sordid fellow" (81). More goes on to say that "they do not afflict him with punishments, because they are persuaded that no man can choose to believe by a mere act of the will" (81), but this social exclusion seems close enough to a form of punishment. However, even this modest restraint disappears, and we see the "they" breaking down even further into a complex apparatus of ecclesiastical and civil discipline governing both body and soul. The priests are free to excommunicate "persons whom they find to be extraordinarily wicked," and we can only assume that this kind of heretic would qualify. Those who do believe in a judgment after death (or who regain their faith after excommunication gives them a mnemonic foretaste of that punishing afterlife) are "tortured by the fear of damnation." But the heretic has an even more immediate and pressing motivation for reformation: "Not even his body is safe for long, for unless he quickly convinces the priests of his repentance, he will be seized and punished by the senate for impiety" (84). This disciplinary state, which forms and reforms conscience through the discipline of the body, is far distant from the world of Utopian moral philosophy; yet they coexist in the same Utopian site.[9] Moral philosophy does have a certain autonomy in Utopia, but it is the structural autonomy of a discrete and enclosed social practice, not the privileged autonomy of an ethics governing and informing all social life.

Even so sensitive a reader of More as Hexter confuses the precepts of Utopian moral philosophy with the functioning of the state as a whole, concluding that an antihierarchical egalitarianism is the ideal animating Utopian justice (*Vision* 136). In this he strangely resembles the character More, who at the end of Book 1 formulates the classic conservative critique of utopia by equating antimonarchism and the community of property with egalitarian anarchy: "I for one cannot conceive of authority existing among men who are equal to one another in every respect" (32). Neither can Raphael or the Utopians: even though Utopia's communism attacks traditional fictions of hierarchy (the nobility of blood, the body politic, the chain of degree), still it shows us that "hierarchy" is only a subset of the larger category "inequality." Utopia undercuts the idea of the universal moral subject by showing a state consisting of those who have attained full subjectivity (that is, "the right to make promises"), those who are in the process of being disqualified from or qualified for it (minor males, slaves, the sick, heretics, docile foreigners), and those who are forever denied it (all females, the Utopians' Zapolete mercenaries, foreigners who resist Utopian domination). Utopian justice is not a static egalitarianism, but a dynamic process of disciplinary exclusion, qualification, and disqualification encompassing all aspects of Utopian life: its foreign policy, penology, family discipline, education, labor, medicine, religion, and military training.

Penal slavery looms large in this process—large portions of Books 1 and 2 are devoted to it—but this is not because slaves are a collection of moral pariahs who must be purged from the state in order to maintain Utopian perfection, defining it by contrast, as Shlomo Avineri argues (288). The third group listed above (that including women) would seem more appropriate for this caste, since they are permanently exiled from full Utopian civility. Slaves, on the other hand (at least males), inhabit a disciplinary continuum with the rest of the state, and just as all slaves are in the process of being requalified for Utopian citizenship, so all citizens are subject to falling back into slavery.

In Book 1 Raphael recalls a conversation on crime and punishment he had many years before at the court of John Cardinal Morton. He formulated a number of reforms that suggest a connection with both Puritan utopian discipline and the liberal ideology of penal reform analyzed by Michel Foucault in *Discipline and Punish*. Criminality,

Raphael says, is the result not of an individual moral failing but of a breakdown in social structure. It appears when society fails to provide for its wounded and cashiered soldiers and its unemployed or evicted tenants (10–20). Penalties are themselves irrationally strict, punishing theft and murder alike, so that a thief has no reason not to kill the witnesses to his lesser crime. Raphael proposes a system of punishment like that of the Polylerites, who gradate punishments to fit the severity of the individual crime (11–12). Punishment should be deanthropomorphized, directed toward restitution and the reformation of the criminal, not toward the punishment of his body; thieves, for instance, should be forced to repay their debt and then set to penitential labor (18). Because punishment should be useful, the state should hire criminals out as cheap labor. It should also establish a trustee system allowing any prisoner who reports on the planned escape of another prisoner to earn his freedom. No one should be altogether without hope of freedom "if he accepts his punishment in the spirit of obedience and patience, and gives promise of future good conduct. Indeed, every year some are pardoned as a reward for their submissive behavior." Above all, punishment is to be corrective and disciplinary rather than retributive: "Thus I've described their policies in this matter. You can see how mild and practical they are, for the aim of the punishment is to destroy the vices and save men. The criminals are treated so that they see the necessity of being honest, and for the rest of their lives they atone for the wrong they have done before" (19). Similarly, Andreae's Christianopolitans believe that "it is far more humane to tear out the first elements and roots of vice than to lop off the mature stalks. For anyone can destroy a man, but only the best one can reform" (165). Well before the liberal critique of absolutist torture and retributive punishment (which punished the criminal's body in analogical response to his assault on the corporate body of the king), we can see the Humanist dream of a disciplinary penology aimed at reforming the soul (if need be, through the discipline of the body).

The cardinal approves Raphael's plan and suggests the experimental conditions under which it might be tried out. The king might reprieve some condemned thief ("without right of sanctuary") to see if it works: "If it turned out well, then he might establish it by law; if not, he could execute immediate punishment on the man formerly condemned." With this reservation, "the experiment would involve no risk." The state acquires experimental rights over the bodies and minds of those who have lost their juridical equality, and there is no good reason a similar experiment might not be performed on other such disqualified or displaced persons: conquered nations, the sick, the old, the young, and so forth. Indeed, the cardinal goes on to suggest that vagabonds be treated in the same way, "for though we have passed many laws against them, they have had no real effect as yet." Another guest suggests that they move on to discuss the problem of the sick and the aged poor, and Morton's fool adds beggars and mendicant friars to the list (20). Given this generalizing turn to the discussion and the fact that it began with a consideration of the ways in which irrational military and agricultural organization leads to poverty and then to crime, it seems that More's consideration of penal discipline is a consideration of social discipline in general.

Utopian penal practice bears this out. The Utopians set no fixed penalties, but fit punishments to the individual crime (67). They do not set criminals altogether outside civil society. Those who submit with good grace may eventually be restored to citizenship, provided they have formed a new conscience: "When subdued by long hardships, if they show by their behavior that they regret the crime more than the punishment, their slavery is lightened or remitted altogether, sometimes by the prince's pardon, sometimes by popular vote" (67). Public honor is the other side of public punishment: "As they deter men from crime by penalties, so they incite them to virtue by public honors" (68). Utopian collective discipline produces conscience on both sides of the law.

True, the Utopian criminal or slave works under the public eye and is set off as a dramatic spectacle to warn Utopian freemen and freewomen of the dangers of crime and to shame the criminal into repentance. But this shame does not set the Utopian criminal off from the rest of the Utopians. Stephen Greenblatt has shown that almost all Utopian life is conducted in public, so that every citizen is subject to the perpetual surveillance of every other. The result is shame: a pathological fear of deviance that acts as a mechanism of social control (*Self-Fashioning* 47–51). In Nietzsche's terms, this shame is a "bad conscience" that makes the Utopians "regular, uniform, equal among equals, calculable" (Nietzsche 190).

On the other hand, as Greenblatt says, there are unavoidable moments of privacy, so the Utopians encourage a belief that their ancestors walk among them and keep them under perpetual surveillance (More 82). Freud describes a similar superstition in *Totem and Taboo*. Conscience, guilt, and civil society are all born when the individual's veneration of his ancestors succeeds in repressing his fear and hatred of them. This repression creates the pathological symptom of a belief in the perpetual surveillance of an omniscient God, who is, in fact, a version of those dead ancestors. This belief in turn becomes an internalized disciplinary mechanism and a prerequisite for membership in civil society (67–70, 147–51). But whether we call this psychological state shame, bad conscience, guilt, or worldly asceticism, *Utopia* shows that it is both the precondition for and the product of civil life. The state mechanisms of disciplinary surveillance can never wither away, for they must continue producing new citizens and reinforcing the conscience of old ones.

This discipline invades Utopian family life, which is merely one disciplinary institution among others. Lawrence Stone says that the emerging early modern family finds "ideal expression" in Utopia, where it replaces all other social institutions (135). Hexter agrees (*Vision* 40–45). But a host of disciplinary groupings modify the exclusive power of the family, including the city block, the city, the hospital, the army, and the church. And the size of Utopian families—from ten to sixteen adults in the cities and at least forty in the country—makes it difficult to see them as reflections of the nuclear family.

Rather than simply reflecting the rise of the early modern family, *Utopia* takes family discipline as both a model for and a subordinate part of state discipline. On the one hand, Utopia deploys what Foucault calls a "pastoral of power," regulating those details of dress, labor, education, and even table manners previously regulated by fathers alone. As Raphael tells us (in a comment rich with Freudian ironies), "The whole island is like a single family" (49). But, on the other hand, in every possible clash the larger family of the state overrides the smaller family of the household. As Stephen Greenblatt says, "More has, in effect, imagined a split in the family as he would have known it, so as to preserve its disciplinary power while discarding its exclusiveness and particularity" (*Self-Fashioning* 44). In an earlier chapter we saw that the Utopian state turns family loyalty to its own ends by sending entire family units into battle together. And the state can order or "encourage" the individual to leave the household and go to the public dining hall, to the hospital, to the country or city on annual rotation, to families with deficient numbers, or to foreign colonies. Raphael encapsulates the disciplinary status of the Utopian family in a discussion of penality: "Husbands chastise their wives and parents their children, unless the offense is so serious that public punishment seems to be in the public interest" (67). Unquestionably, we have a sort of paternal rule here, but the authority marking its borders is public, not private. Fatherly dominion is permissible so long as it serves the ends of the state.

No doubt the medieval monastic community provided an important model for the sort of family state ruled by a pastoral of power that we see in More (and Campanella). But because of its celibate ideal, the monastery is, in James Harrington's terms, a "commonwealth for preservation" like stable Venice, not a "commonwealth for increase" like imperialistic and overpopulated Utopia (whose excess population suggests yet another contradiction between its ascetic moral philosophy and its social practice). We see the best early modern examples of this kind of expansive family state in the patriarchal Protestant communities of the Atlantic world: in the European Protestant states, the parishes proposed by Harrington, the radical spiritist communes like those of Winstanley and Plockhoy, and the Puritan congregational communities like Eliot's praying towns. In each of these the family provides an organizational model for the larger social grouping to which it is ultimately subordinate.

If More's *Utopia* is an imaginative and theoretical consideration of the nature of a reformed social discipline, then Puritan utopia is a machine that attempts to use such discipline to manufacture civil or "bad" conscience out of anomic human raw materials. Its explicit and repetitious discussion of discipline reveals it to be popular without being democratic—a distinction that seems quite odd from the point of view of modern democratic ideologies of both the right and the left. It conceives of a postmonarchical society that disseminates sovereignty among its citizenry, but without recourse to any democratic notions of natural rights, ancient liberties, or the fundamental equality of men as moral agents. It appeals only to the unified rationalizing power of its authorities and sees men as fundamentally equal only so far as they are equally susceptible to being written on by these authorities.

Consequently, we do not see Puritan utopia concerning itself immediately with contract, conscience, obligation, or right. Eliot resists those who demand that the Indians immediately sign the contract of Christian conversion and leave their old oral religion, tribal society, and "kingly" government behind. They must submit to praying-town discipline and become civil men before they can become regenerate saints and enter into church covenant. Similarly, in *The Christian Commonwealth* Eliot rejects the arguments both for and against the Engagement, saying that men must form themselves according to the model of disciplinary order proposed by God in Exodus 18 before they can sign any such contract with particular rulers.

Harrington rejects Hobbes's hypothetical history of the covenantal birth of absolute sovereignty, saying that "the people, of themselves being in a natural incapacity of exercising power, must be brought into some artificial or political capacity of exercising the same" (784). Harrington's vision of military discipline informs his utopian vision. It is not merely a means to the attainment and the preservation of political liberty but is somehow the same thing as that liberty. The regular military musters of the youth prepare them for the regular civil musters of the elders, who retain their military designations of "horse" and "foot." The voting elder of Oceana has acquired full individuality and the right to vote. But he does not occupy the site of sovereign autonomy and subjective freedom, as his manner of voting makes clear. In liberal democracy the individual's arrival at the polling place as part of a haphazard queue of voters makes possible his self-delusive conception of his political autonomy and subjective freedom as a voter. But in Oceana the elder stands in front of the poll at the intersection of a column and a row in a quasi-military formation, voting in a prescribed fashion at a designated time, surrounded by the inescapable signs of the state's disciplinary construction of his autonomy.

Utopian discipline continues within the state as a mnemonic threat, reminding citizens of what they have to lose by abrogating the social contract. Those Oceanic citizens who refuse to submit to its disciplinary rituals after three years face exile and the forfeiture of property (Harrington 347). Eliot says that "he is beneath the condition of a stranger who shall apostatize from the government of the Lord, yea beneath the condition of barbarians who are not yet come in" (*Commonwealth* 146). The utopian citizen escapes the organic tyranny of anthropomorphic hierarchy and the dead weight of custom only to find himself occupying a point on an infinitely gradated scale of disciplinary qualification, other points of which are occupied by the youth in military muster, the vagrant in the workhouse, the child in the reformed school, the sinner undergoing congregational admonition, the Praying Indian undergoing catechism, and the prisoner undergoing correction.

Puritan utopia's obsession with the disciplinary construction of conscience through the ordering and manipulation of bodies permeates Puritanism in general. But it tends to be repressed or recoded in anti-utopian political theory, which assigns the body to civil government, the conscience to church government. In *A Holy Commonwealth* Richard Baxter first proposes that "in a true theocracy or divine common-wealth, the matter of the church and commonwealth should be alto-gether or almost the same!" (*Baxter* 80). But he goes on to qualify this claim considerably. The two types of government differ radically in their forms of administration: "The magistrate ruleth imperiously and by force, having power upon men's estates and persons. But the pas-tors have none such, but govern only by the word of God explained and applied to the conscience" (83). Furthermore, churches are more democratic than states are, for a member of a particular church should have a voice in electing officers regardless of his property, whereas pov-erty disqualifies a man from citizenship.

Milton scorns "the multitude" and restricts the civil franchise to the "well-affected" in his *Ready and Easy Way* of 1660, but he argued just as vigorously the year before in *A Treatise of Civil Power in Ecclesi-astical Causes* for absolute freedom of conscience (for Protestants). He acknowledges that the priests and Levites of Israel judged in matters both ecclesiastical and civil, but he explains that with the transition from the Old Law to the New Law, God separated the two realms of government (7.259–60). Church government differs from civil govern-ment under the New Law "because it deals only with the inward man and his actions, which are all spiritual and to outward force not liable" (7.255). This separation of absolute spiritual freedom from the neces-sary limitation of civil freedom may seem tolerant and liberal until we notice that the first attempts to justify the second. For both Milton and Baxter, this split exists inside a unified political system that offers reli-gious liberty as a compensation for oligarchic civil government.

We can see this motive at work in Milton's defense of "Christian liberty" in *The Ready and Easy Way.* He criticizes "exotic models" like Harrington's *Oceana,* saying that they propose "ideas that will effect nothing, but with a number of new injunctions to manacle the native liberty of mankind; turning all virtue into prescription, servi-tude, and necessity, to the great impairing and frustrating of Christian liberty" (7.445). In its opposition of a collectivist and impersonal "pre-scription" to an individual "virtue" and "liberty," this is a classic for-mulation of the anti-utopian critique of "totalitarianism." But Milton goes on directly to criticize Harrington's agrarian legislation, saying that his own proposal "requires no perilous, no injurious alteration or circumscription of men's lands and proprieties; secure, that in this commonwealth, temporal and spiritual lords removed, no man or number of men can attain to such wealth or vast possession, as will need the hedge of an agrarian law . . . to confine them from endangering our public liberty" (7.445). The "our" here is strategic, since Milton's platform seems to say that only those who have a good deal of property can have full public liberty. These men alone will administer justice in the courts of the local governments and elect the council of the national government. A defense of individual liberty blends perfectly into a defense of class interest. The anti-utopian claim of the possessive individualist to moral autonomy is, in fact, a claim made on behalf of a certain class interest.[10]

The distinction of Puritan utopia is that it does not resort to the fiction of autonomous conscience but analyzes the connections between body and conscience, discipline and contract, civil and church government. It is no coincidence that utopia tends to shy away from the New Testament when looking for its political models. The New Testament (particularly Romans 13) confronts the fact of an alienated theocracy; in the present there is an unbridgeable separation between Christian conscience and church polity and the civil dominion of Rome and its Greek and Jewish clients. Ancient Israel's integration of civil and church government in a single theocracy provides a much more attractive model for utopia. James Harrington may well have Milton himself as well as his late employer Cromwell in mind when he comments on this ancient unity of governmental forms: "The distinction of liberty into civil and spiritual is not ancient, but of a latter date, there being indeed no such distinction; for, the liberty of conscience once granted separable from civil liberty, civil liberty can have no security. It was the only excuse that the late tyrant pretended for his usurpation, that he could see no other means to secure the liberty of conscience" (742). As we have seen, John Eliot draws his civil model from the unified Hebrew theocracy of Exodus 18 and his ecclesiastical model from the Book of Revelation, where the unified Hebrew theocracy returns in a Christian form. In *The Law of Freedom* Gerrard Winstanley turns to ancient Israel for a model, saying that "the glory of Israel's commonwealth was this, they had no beggar among them" (524). Winstanley's materialist spiritism cannot separate the inward freedom of the conscience from the civil constraint of the body. Some say that it is "true freedom to have ministers to preach, and for people to hear whom they will, without being restrained or compelled from or to any form of worship," but this is an "unsettled freedom." All "inward bondages of the mind" are produced by "the outward bondage, that one sort of people lay upon another" (519–20). The only cure for this bondage is a reform of outward communal discipline.

For the Puritan utopist the individual subjectivity of conscience and the corporate political subjectivity of the state are equally products of civil and church discipline; it is impossible to reserve the former as a realm of absolute freedom that compensates for, and requires the protection of, a particular, oppressive form of civil government. Both Eliot and Harrington distinguish church and civil government, but their distinction is not between freedom and necessity, between the individual's rule of his own conscience and the government's rule of the individual's body. The Puritan utopist sees the discipline of the body as the means to the creation of both civil and spiritual conscience. Utopian church government parallels utopian civil government, for it specifies certain groupings, elections, and movements of bodies as the essence of the life of the spirit.

Michael Walzer stresses the voluntarism of Puritanism, saying that it multiplied theories of organization, contract, and covenant, including a new ideology of vocation, in which one's ability to fulfill contractual obligations within one's own profession became a sign of godliness. At the same time it bred its own species of the animal with the right to make promises: "The saints would come together almost exclusively in the course of their work. . . . Such relations as they then established would be contractual, that is, entered into voluntarily by formally free men, whose calling was sufficiently certain and whose activity was sufficiently sustained for them to make long-term promises and agreements" (*Revolution* 213). Walzer takes issue with Marx's view of Puritanism as one of the means by which capitalism reached into its own past and created a disciplined and docile army of wage earners, objecting that "those who entered the world of Christian discipline did so voluntarily" (230).

But it is vital to distinguish between this philosophical concept of voluntarism, which instinctively represses its disciplinary antecedents, and that determinate sequence of preparatory discipline, contract, and reinforcing discipline that we see in Puritan practice. In the first place, Puritan family discipline sees to it that certain individuals (male children) gradually acquire the rights of "formally free" individuals with the right to make promises, while certain others (female children and women) are permanently denied that right, or enjoy it in promises contingent on the promises of their fathers or husbands. That "the individual" and "the patriarchal household" are rough synonyms in Puritan utopia is possible only because of such family discipline. This family discipline leads in turn to the larger family of the Puritan congregation, which replaces the geographical and hierarchical model of the Anglican parish with a disciplinary and contractual model of preaching, catechism, self-examination, mutual surveillance, admonition and censure, and personal testimonies to conversion (Hill, *Society* 219–58). Because the Puritan congregation is not tied to a fixed and customary system of parishes and dioceses, it is no more geographically bound than utopia itself. It can propagate itself through missionary work (another mediation between discipline and contract) and even uproot itself and begin to replicate its mechanisms for constructing new wills in New England. But the imbalance of power between the individual Puritan or Puritan-to-be and the Puritan family, congregation, or state he finds himself in should temper the extent to which we see Puritanism as a radically voluntarist ideology: in his relative lack of alternatives, the Puritan voluntarist is in much the same position as Hume's hypothetical sea traveler. Six weeks after the Mayflower anchored at Plymouth, Mary Bradford, wife of soon-to-be-Governor William Bradford, "fell overboard" and drowned—in desperation at the thought of life in the New World, it is now believed (Bradford xiii).

Utopian educational discipline like that of John Amos Comenius is analogous to Congregational church discipline. In his *Analytical Didactic* Comenius insists on school discipline as a "means of furthering instruction"—an essential supplement to the subject taught and the method of teaching it (104). It should be constant, gentle, persuasive, and gradated. The teacher should drive his lessons home by establishing his authority over his class, by letting his students know they are always under his watchful eye, by encouraging friendly rivalry among his students, by instantly admonishing those who err, and by making them examples before the entire class. He compares school discipline to the tongs that hold the iron (the pupil) in place on the anvil (the teaching itself) so that the hammer (the teacher) can shape it properly (117). In a playful etymology, he shows us how little volition has to do with the creation of an enlightened will: "Thus the word *discipline* is, as it were, a *discipellina,* because by discipline an unwilling pupil is driven *(impellitur)* to learning *(ad discendum)*" (104).

There is even a utopian or disciplinary side to the anti-utopian theorists I have been defining utopia against. We have seen that Richard Baxter contrasts the realms of civil coercion and of subjective freedom, but he also describes the disciplinary formation of conscience. In *A Holy Commonwealth* he speaks of "voluntary" conversion in such rigorously disciplinary terms that one is almost tempted to suspect him of Nietzschean irony: "Though magistrates cannot force men to believe, love God, and so to be saved, yet they must force them to submit to holy doctrine, and learn the word of God, and to walk orderly and quietly in that condition, till they are brought to a voluntary personal profession of Christianity, and subjection to Christ and his holy ordinance; and so being voluntarily baptized (if they are new converted heathens, that never were before baptized) or confirmed (if they were baptized before), they may live in holy communion with the church" (*Baxter* 116). This sounds much like Eliot's praying-town discipline, and, in fact, Baxter commiserated with Eliot over their mutual missionary work with "degenerate savages"—Eliot with the Algonquians, Baxter with the lapsed Christians of Kidderminster.

Discipline may ideally be an instrumental practice ultimately at the service of doctrine, but it quickly acquires a material independence. In *Of Reformation* Milton defines it as "the execution and applying of doctrine home," but in *The Reason of Church Government* it becomes "the very visible shape and image of virtue" (1.526, 751). The latter work contains a lengthy hymn to discipline, whose capacity to master the civic wheel of fortune makes it a corporate Protestant *virtù:* "He that hath read with judgment of nations and commonwealths, of cities and camps of peace and war, sea and land, will readily agree that the flourishing and decaying of all civil societies, all the moments and turnings of human occasions are moved to and fro as upon the axle of discipline. So that whatsoever power or sway in mortal things weaker men have attributed to fortune, I durst with more confidence (the honor of divine providence ever saved) ascribe either to the vigor or slackness of discipline. Nor is there any sociable perfection in this life, civil or sacred, that can be above discipline, but she is that which with her musical cords preserves and holds all the parts together" (1.751). Overtly anti-utopian Puritans, who feel free to invoke the fiction of the sovereign and autonomous conscience when they are attempting to balance a defense of oligarchy, also feel free to show that this sovereignty is itself the product of disciplinary procedures. The utopian inhabits the anti-utopian.

Surprisingly enough, it also inhabits the prelapsarian and the postapocalyptic. Comenius argues that the Fall itself could have been prevented had God given Adam and Eve a bit more time for schooling: "It is clear that even before the Fall, a school in which man might make gradual progress was opened for him in Paradise. For although man was the first created thing, and no sooner brought forth than capable of movement, speech, and reason, still it is clear from the conversation of Eve with the serpent how ignorant she was of knowledge derived from experience. For if she had been more experienced, she would have known that the serpent is unable to speak and that some sort of deception must have been at hand" (*Great Didactic* 53–54). In Books 7 and 8 of *Paradise Lost,* Raphael proposes to Adam what is essentially a Baconian project in restorative utilitarian science well before there is anything to restore. We can see both in the countless pictorial representations of the New Jerusalem as a fortress and in Milton's *Reason of Church Government* (he is close to Eliot's *Communion of Churches* here) that discipline will not disappear even at the end of time: "The state of the blessed in Paradise, though never so perfect, is not therefore left without discipline, whose golden surveying reed marks out and measures every quarter and circuit of New Jerusalem" (1.752). Puritan utopia's imperial desire for universal discipline knows no geographical or temporal boundaries, not even those set by Man's Fall, which made such discipline necessary in the first place, and by his ultimate restoration at the end of time, which will finally reverse the Fall. I have argued in this study that Puritan utopia's rational millennialism marks out its characteristically early modern moment, for it proposes rational discipline as the means to a nonrational, customarily prophesied future state. But by invading both the lost origin and the transcendent telos of history that justify its present-day rigors, discipline becomes in a sense its own justification. It is both secular means and millennial end.

Enlightenment Comes to the Most Dull-witted

This study has been the partial history of a political moment: that brief period between the fall of one secular kingdom and the restoration of another when the Puritan saints thought the millennial monarchy of Christ was at hand, waiting only for God's Englishmen to set it in motion. During this moment the prospect of an imminent millennium sparked utopian efforts to hurry it along by a reorganization of political life on the model of the anticipated kingdom of Christ. But the Stuart Restoration put an end to the more universal ambitions of Puritan utopia, dividing millennialism from utopia in the process.

Hermeneutical millennialism has relatively little trouble in adjusting to a failed prediction. The millennium still exists somewhere in the future as an undeniable promise, and when the millenarian's projection of its date of arrival proves faulty, he can simply return to his sacred texts and commence his recalculations. But failed predictions

of catalytic or utopian millennialism face a somewhat greater difficulty, for Puritan utopia is an instrumental rhetoric in a way that hermeneutical millennialism is not. It attempts to convince its audience
to adopt certain rational organizational means to the millennium. If it
fails—if the millennium fails to arrive—the utopist must reconsider
not only his predictions but his faith in the means he has proposed.

The typical response of Puritan utopia to such a failure is not simply
a recalculation but a radical scaling down—a movement away from
programs for the unification of the world to smaller-scale social practices, more limited political rhetorics. The brief fantasy of a world
ruled by a unified enlightenment reason fades at the Restoration
(somewhat earlier for Harrington, somewhat later for Eliot), splitting
into a number of practices, ideologies, and writings that we can call
more or less Puritan, more or less utopian, more or less (usually less)
millenarian: the four Indian praying towns surviving King Philip's
War, transformed into something resembling reservations or concentration camps; the disciplinary collectives of the Independent congregations, battered by the Act of Conformity but surviving in both Old
and New England; the quietist utopias of the Quakers and the other
spiritist sects, which claimed many of the radical sectaries; institutions
of scientific learning such as the Royal Society, which preserved something of the Comenian enlightenment but in an antimillenarian form;
the political language of the neo-Harringtonians, from which the millennium has been almost completely expunged; the utopian novel or
romance (*Gulliver's Travels, Robinson Crusoe,* Henry Neville's *The
Isle of Pines,* and a host of later utopias and robinsonades); and early
factories, which put the disciplinary rationalization of time and space
to work in the interest of capital accumulation.[11]

This discontinuity creates considerable difficulty for the critical
study of utopia, for such a study frequently contains a generic imperative to continuity hardly less insistent than utopia's own. With the
death of utopian programs, it longs to celebrate the compensatory survival of a utopian spirit. The history of utopia has often been written
as a perpetual enlightenment relay race, with each utopist passing
along the dream of organizational reason to a successor, then falling
by the wayside into death, prison, or obscurity.

Unfortunately, this kind of study often has to assume precisely the
continuity it sets out to demonstrate, so the medium of continuity
becomes magical. Puritan utopia suffers particular problems here. The
forced recall of Eliot's work and the penal censorship of Harrington
put them into a long and honorable tradition of persecuted utopists,

but this did not encourage the dissemination of their programs. Other Puritan utopists fared even worse. In 1668 Comenius published his *Via Lucis (The Way of Light),* dedicating it "to the torchbearers of this Enlightened Age, Members of the Royal Society of London." But the enthusiastic millenarian rhetoric of the work so appropriate to the year of its composition (1642) was hopelessly outdated in the antienthusiastic atmosphere of Restoration England. In 1670 Comenius died an exile in Amsterdam. Gabriel Plattes starved to death in 1644, his utopia *Macaria* misattributed (probably) to Samuel Hartlib until very recently (Webster, *Revolution* 369–85). The anticommunist gentry repeatedly leveled Winstanley's Digger communes; his writings disappeared into two centuries of almost complete obscurity, one indication of which is that while Marx does refer to the Levellers and other radical sectaries of the English Civil War, he makes no mention of Winstanley, the greatest seventeenth-century English proponent of a communist materialism. Like many other radicals and ex-radicals, Winstanley probably became a Quaker (Alsop). Plockhoy's New World communism was even more forcefully repressed: the English, under Sir Robert Carr, conquered New Amsterdam in 1664 and, according to a later English account, "destroyed the Quaking society of Plockhoy to a nail" (Plockhoy 63).

In a sense, this discontinuity is a necessary corollary to that conjunctural theory of genre used throughout this study. In the first section of chapter 1, I quoted the following passage from Adorno's *Aesthetic Theory* on the utopian truth content of modernist literature, arguing that it is also relevant to that of Puritan utopia: "Unconsciously, every work asks itself whether, and if so how, it can exist as a Utopia. And the answer invariably is: through the constellation of its elements. Thus the art work transcends the immutable not merely because of its sheer abstract difference, but also because it appropriates the immutable, dismantling it and putting it together again in an act of aesthetic creation, as they say. One criterion of the truth content of art works is their ability to compose the other out of elements of the immutable" (431)—but also, we should add, their ability to calcify into a newly untrue immutability, or to shatter into nonutopian shards. A materialist theory of genre must acknowledge that even a powerful social form like Puritan utopia can be worn out, inverted, and stripped for parts.

All the same, the tendency of all utopian constellations to decompose in time is no argument against their historical reality. And Puritan utopia has another truth content that survives discontinuities such as the Restoration—a truth content that exists for us in criticism, if not for itself in the millennium. Here, as we move beyond the strict confines of Puritan utopia, we move from considering *utopia* as a genre to considering *the utopian* as a transgeneric concept. Throughout this study and most explicitly in the preceding section, I have been arguing that we can best define Puritan utopia as a genre that foregrounds the disciplinary processes by which early modern Protestantism produces various revolutionary individualities and collectivities. *Puritan utopia,* then, is a genre that proposes a particular discipline during a particular historical moment, with certain specifiable relations to other utopias and other genres contemporary with it. And the utopian aspect of a nonutopian work is its particular relation to the utopias contemporary with it—in other words, its acknowledged or assumed processes for the rational formation of individuals and collectives.

The most important quality of Puritan utopia for the student of early modern culture is that at the moment of birth of modern Western conceptions of voluntaristic democratic sovereignty, it insists on holding those conceptions face-to-face with their disciplinary supplement—a supplement that political and moral philosophy often attempts to ignore, as we have seen. We might say that the fantasy of universal discipline at the center of Puritan utopia allows us to pose a "utopian question" of other writings, rhetorics, and practices that do not seem explicitly utopian: by what disciplinary procedure has this represented person (or group or author or abstractly conceived moral or political subject) been qualified for (or disqualified from or excluded from) entering into contract (or writing or speaking or exercising political power or making moral choices)? For instance, when we examine the extraordinary discussions of ancient liberties and natural rights (two ostensibly anti-utopian political concepts) in the debates at Putney, at Whitehall, and in the Leveller tracts, we should look not only at the conceptual history of liberty and freedom but also at the way in which New Model Army discipline qualified a previously voiceless social class to enter into political debate with its officers and with the government as a whole.

Nor are we limited strictly to Puritan writings, rhetorics, and practices when posing this utopian question. Puritan utopia's insistence that discipline is an essential supplement to contract and will—a supplement that can never wither away, not even in the New Jerusalem—can help us challenge the notion that the post-Puritan civil order of

Enlightenment England (and modern culture more generally) is a post-disciplinary society founded on pure voluntarism. Michael Walzer argues rightly enough that "the study of the Puritans is best begun with the idea of discipline" ("Puritanism" 79). But because he sees discipline too exclusively as an act of revolutionary repression and not as a positive system for the formation of rational subjectivities, he also argues that discipline itself ends with the end of the Puritan revolution. After Puritanism had fashioned its worldly ascetics, Walzer says, the Enlightenment had no need of a rigorous regimen of discipline: "Liberal confidence made repression and the endless struggle against sin unnecessary. . . . The Lockeian state was not a disciplinary institution as was the Calvinist holy commonwealth, but rather rested on the assumed political virtue of its citizens" (*Revolution* 302). Even granting this reading of Locke as a theorist of pure voluntarist contractarianism (his educational theory would seem a likely spot to begin complicating such a reading), it is difficult to see "the Lockeian state" as a synonym for "Enlightenment and liberal England," as Walzer seems to do. The emerging ideal of the disciplined factory as a rational and productive corporate organism, the rise of Methodism as a theological mechanism producing docile workers for those factories, the continuing presence of radical sects practicing an oppositional religious discipline, and the rise of secular opposition from socialist groups—all these disciplinary developments suggest that the transition from Puritan to post-Puritan society required not the disappearance of discipline but a change in its forms.

The utopian question can help us open up continuities between Puritan utopia and a later literary genre that is itself crucially important in Enlightenment economic, political, and educational theory. Of all Puritan utopia's descendants, the robinsonade resembles it most. But *Robinson Crusoe*'s affiliations with the social contract tradition, natural law theory, and economics are more familiar to us than its relation to the disciplinary imagination of utopia. This is not completely surprising, for Defoe's novel lacks two key elements of Puritan utopia. First, while it does portray an alternative cultural totality, it is a quasi-journalistic fiction written for the literary marketplace rather than a political fiction written as part of a political debate. Second, while its plot is not completely secular, it is thoroughly demillennialized. Whereas Puritan utopia dreams of the imminent arrival on earth of Christ's kingdom, *Robinson Crusoe* dreams of primitive capital accumulation, as we can see in Crusoe's growing stock of tools and techniques, his growing hoard of salvaged gold and silver, and his growing store of profits from his Brazilian plantation.

Accompanying this economic plot, however, we can see a plot of utopian discipline. We might almost say that Crusoe incorporates within himself the utopian dialectic of displacement and enclosure. In the first place he is ruled by a secularized, mercantilist version of the Puritan model of life as a journey. This archetypal early modern Englishman, like so many of the Puritan utopists, is himself a displaced person. He is born Robinson Kreutznaer, the son of a merchant from Bremen. Before, during, and after his island sojourn, we see him itching to wander, explore, and establish new plantations and new dominions. He also conceives of himself as the object of a program in enclosure and rational discipline. As the Puritan utopist can move into autobiographical self-fashioning only by conceiving of himself as a member of the displaced population whose disciplinary transformation he prophesies, so Crusoe can begin his process of postshipwreck self-transformation only by conceiving of himself as a natural man subject to God's rational discipline.

Even before his traumatic conversion, Crusoe submits himself to a program in discipline, just as Eliot submits the Algonquians to praying-town discipline before allowing them to enter into church fellowship. He attempts to rationalize his own accidental enclosure on his island by creating further enclosed "islands" within it: his country house, seacoast house, bower, and secret caves. Further, he establishes a fixed work schedule for each day, divides the Sabbath from the working days of the week, and begins conquering and rationalizing the seasons. After discovering an Edenic nook stocked with wild grapes, he responds first with prudent reflection (remembering the deaths of several Englishmen who had gorged themselves on such grapes, he abstains), then with a calculating projection (anticipating the coming dry season, he plans to dry the grapes in order to have a store of raisins) (79). The sensuous pastoral present dissolves into a calculating georgic asceticism.

Though Defoe's novel lacks the millenarian promise of Puritan utopia, it does have the utopian interest in the small-scale experimental preparation for a larger-scale social transformation. After Crusoe's shipwreck has brought him to see himself as the helpless object of God's discipline, he reforms himself and is soon able to assume godlike powers over others. Like More's Cardinal Morton, Crusoe sees as the natural subjects for his experiments in civility those whom he has reprieved from execution: Friday, Friday's father, and the Spaniard (whom he saves from being slain and eaten by the cannibals); the captain of the English ship (whom he saves from the mutineers); and the mutineers themselves, to whom he proposes Hobson's contract. They can either return to an almost certain English hanging or they can remain behind on the island and repeat his own experience there. Their decision is predictable: "When they had all declared their willingness to stay, I then told them I would let them into the story of my living there and put them into the way of making it easy to them; accordingly, I gave them the whole history of the place and of my coming to it, shewed them my fortifications, the way I made my bread, planted my corn, cured my grapes, and in a word, all that was necessary to make them easy" (219). Even before the hypothetical histories of the Enlightenment robinsonades, Crusoe's experience on the island has become a repeatable course in insular discipline—a course that he himself teaches to a captive audience. With his power of life and death, Crusoe has something of an advantage over the Puritan utopists, whose readers can simply grow bored and put their books down.[12] The disciplinary experiments he has performed on himself and Friday allow him to begin the larger-scale experiment of a penal colony. He tends this experiment carefully, and several years later, after visiting "his" island, he sees to it that it will become a commonwealth for increase: "Besides other supplies, I sent seven women, being such as I found proper for service, or for wives to such as would take them" (237). The robinsonade, with its model of an experimental insular discipline, mediates between Puritan utopia and Enlightenment educational theory.

We can even produce a utopian reading of the classic texts of nineteenth-century liberalism, whose defense of individual liberties against social coercion of any kind would seem to be the antithesis of utopia's insistence on the priority of the disciplinary collective. But the liberal critique of collective coercion is always, in a more or less mediated form, a defense of one sort of collectivity/individuality against another. For instance, a program of utopian discipline penetrates John Stuart Mill's *On Liberty* despite its explicit concern with defending individual liberty against the tyranny of the majority. Mill begins his treatise by promising three successive topics of consideration: liberty of conscience and speech, liberty of tastes and pursuits, and liberty of combination among individuals (12). Our greater familiarity with the first two topics is not accidental, for Mill's argument breaks down in a curious way when we come to the third. Here, Mill encounters a dangerous threat to individuality in the oppositional movements of his day (that is, temperance leagues, labor unions, socialist organizations—collectives of the left), and he develops two strategies of containment. First is a discursive regression in which he backs down from his self-assigned sequence, returning to the first two points in a higher key by celebrating the cult of the genius, who magically rises above the faceless collective. Second is his proposal of a corporate apparatus designed (paradoxically enough) to produce masses of such individuals: a state-administered system of public education. "Liberty of combination" becomes in Mill's work the limited freedom to submit oneself to a program of state-supervised collective discipline. British colonial rule provides a global corollary, for its mission is to educate and bring to full individuality those "backward states of society in which the race itself may be considered as in its nonage" (10). What begins as an anti-utopian defense of the individual against social coercion concludes as a defense of one sort of collective discipline (centralized and imperial statism) against others (socialism and non-European nationalism). Liberalism does not simply shun or assume the disciplinary processes of collective coercion and training: at some level it also incorporates them, for the utopian inhabits the anti-utopian.

Michel Foucault, the foremost modern historian of the disciplinary supplement to rationality, has posed what I am calling the utopian question to a wide array of modern social practices. There are significant differences between the early modern dream of universal discipline formulated by Puritan utopia and the modern disciplinary apparatus developed by Foucault's liberal technicians of rational training. Puritan utopia sees itself as a revolutionary discipline set in opposition to the customary political order, whereas modern discipline, however revolutionary it may be in the long run, works within the horizon of established political order. Puritan utopia tends to see the Indian, the child, the recruit, the citizen-to-be, the vagrant, as members of the same displaced population and as subject to precisely the same disciplinary techniques, because all these bodies will ultimately be rationally assembled in the foursquare civis of the New Jerusalem. Puritan utopia has formulated neither that complex modern array of medical, military, penal, and educational disciplines analyzed by Foucault nor that equally complex array of clinical types those disciplines discover or create. Puritan utopia is a pre-Enlightenment discipline whose millenial hubris keeps it from adequately enclosing and partitioning itself. In contrast with Puritan utopia, modern discipline rationally integrates its procedures with an architecture. In *Discipline and Punish* Foucault examines the functioning of Jeremy Bentham's invention, the panopticon: an observation tower set in the center of a circular prison from which a single hidden guard can look into every cell and observe every prisoner. Because this guard can see without being seen, the panopticon can exercise a disciplinary power over prisoners even if there is no guard inside: the mere possibility that they are being watched is sufficient to modify their behavior (*Discipline* 195–228; *Power* 146–65).

Still, the panopticon operates according to the same model of dispersed, postmonarchical power we have seen at work in early modern utopia.[13] It is the architectural equivalent of the utopian *rex absconditus* (whose disciplinary intention inhabits the corporate orders he has left behind him), of the Utopians' watchful dead ancestors, and of the mutual surveillance of the Puritan congregation. Most important, Foucault's study of modern discipline reveals the continuing importance of locating the utopian supplement to social contract theory:

> The "Enlightenment," which discovered the liberties, also invented the disciplines. . . . Discipline creates between individuals a "private" link, which is a relation of constraints entirely different from contractual obligation; the acceptance of a discipline may be underwritten by contract; the way in which it is imposed, the mechanisms it brings into play, the non-reversible subordination of one group of people by another, the "surplus" power that is always fixed on the same side, the inequality of the different "partners" in relation to the common regulation, all these distinguish the disciplinary link from the contractual link, and make it possible to distort the contractual link systematically from the moment it has as its content a mechanism of discipline. We know, for example, how many real procedures undermine the legal fiction of the work contract: workshop discipline is not the least important. (*Discipline* 222–23)

In the dispersed utopias of modern culture—the prisons, factories, schools, and hospitals that Foucault calls the "disciplinary archipelago"—we see that the "contractual link" is itself indissolubly linked to discipline.

The liberal tendency to dichotomize the individual and the collective appears in a somewhat more complicated form in the twentieth-century dystopian novel. Because liberalism must, in the final analysis, deny the priority of the disciplinary collective, it must personify the totalitarian state. The dystopias of Huxley and Orwell, for instance, present inverted and demonic versions of the utopian *rex absconditus* in the sinister figures of the powers behind the scenes: Mustapha Mond for Huxley, Big Brother/O'Brien/the Party for Orwell. This effort to reduce the corporate dynamics of utopia to a conflict between powerless and empowered individuals is all that much more in need of a utopian reading that will recover the collective subtext. Huxley presents us with a conflict between the ascendant depersonalizing forces of Freudianism, Marxism, and mass culture on the one hand and an appalled aristocratic humanism on the other. Reconstructing the genealogy of Huxley's hero John Savage, who represents this humanism, Theodor Adorno remarks, "This type, incidentally, is bred at Oxford and Cambridge no less than are Epsilons in test tubes, and it belongs to the sentimental standbys of the English novel" (*Prisms* 105). We may nose yet another collective subtext (one not unrelated to the first) in the odd ubiquity of Jewish surnames in the depraved new world, and in Huxley's emphasis on the Semitic features of the despised and despicable Bernard Marx (Jew-as-resentful-malcontent?) and of Mustapha Mond (Jew-as-manipulating-mastermind?). And, of course, the beginnings of the cold war provide much of the subtext for Orwell (Howe). Fredric Jameson helps decode the peculiar use made of the term *utopian* in modern polemics: "From religious arguments about the sinful hybris of an anthropocentric social order all the way to the vivid 'totalitarian' dystopias of the contemporary counterrevolutionary tradition (Dostoevsky, Orwell, etc.), Utopia is a transparent synonym for socialism itself, and the enemies of Utopia sooner or later turn out to be the enemies of socialism" ("Islands" 3).

Of course, these enemies do not confine themselves to a literary realm. In *Dictatorship and Double Standards,* Jeane J. Kirkpatrick calls Marxism "the most influential utopian political philosophy of our times," adding that it is in fact a totalitarian variety of utopianism "which seeks moral reform ends through political means. Totalitarians use power to remake men" (102, 103). Like "More," Baxter, Milton, Mill, and the anti-utopian tradition in general, she opposes to this totalitarian model of politics a model beginning with the sovereign individual (120). Like this tradition, her individualist critique of one kind of collective discipline coexists with a proposal to institute another kind. Arguing that "the infant is very nearly a blank page in many respects most relevant to politics and government," she advocates turning American schools into factories for the production of civic virtue: "Concepts like truth, honor, teamwork, responsibility, rule of law, restraint in the use of power, respect for others, must be introduced, illustrated, and transformed somehow into habits" (238, 244). The utopian penetrates the anti-utopian.

And as the Reagan Administration's key foreign policy ideologue and its ambassador to the United Nations, Kirkpatrick has been able to package a version of this anti-utopian utopianism for export. Even after she resigned her ambassadorship, the Reagan Administration continued to base its foreign policy on her distinction between "authoritarian" (read: nondemocratic and non-Marxist) and "totalitarian" (read: Marxist) regimes. Where authoritarian oppression is partial, isolated, contingent, and susceptible to reform, totalitarian oppression is total, expansive, intrinsic, and self-perpetuating. This distinction produces a double blindness. On the one hand, there is a blindness to the capacity of customary authoritarian rule for acts of unspeakable barbarism—for example, the gradual, night-by-night murder of an entire oppositional class in El Salvador (including recalcitrant *campesinos,* students, intellectuals, nuns, reporters, labor leaders, and an archbishop) by privately controlled death squads or moonlighting members of the Salvadoran Treasury Police. This extermination is customary and contingent, and so merely "authoritarian"—less oppressive in the grand scheme of things than, say, the Nicaraguan institution of press censorship and compulsory draft laws.

On the other hand, this critique of "utopian totalitarianism" produces a blindness to the role of modern rationalization in maintaining and increasing the oppressiveness of "authoritarian" rule—for example, the U.S. training and coordination of military, intelligence, and police forces throughout non-Marxist Central America. And compare Eliot's praying towns with the contemporary disenchantment of the Guatemalan highlands in the name of an anticommunist defense of liberty. Using foreign models (the strategic hamlets program of American advisers recalling their own aborted utopias in preliberation Vietnam, the agricultural cooperatives proposed by Israeli advisers), the Guatemalan army is attempting to create utopian "model communities" for displaced Mayan Indians. These communities attempt to cut peasant links not only to their guerrilla fellows but also to their previous tribal culture and oral traditions. Like Eliot's utopia, this one operates alongside more straightforward sorts of genocide. One recent study estimates that since 1980 more than fifty thousand Guatemalans have been murdered, most of them Mayan Indians, most of them by the army and its auxiliaries (Foster).

All the same, these parallels and contrasts between Puritan utopia, on the one hand, and the robinsonade, liberal political philosophy, Enlightenment penal discipline, the dystopian novel, and Reaganite foreign policy, on the other, remain purely formal and unmediated, at least so far as I have developed them here. To construct mediations would lead me into other utopian conjunctures and constellations, and so outside the proper borders of this study. Rather than conclude by attempting to reconstruct or hypothesize some fundamental continuity between Puritan utopia and the present, I would like to measure some of the distances between Puritan and modernist visions of utopia by comparing two accounts of utopian encounters between a textual authority and a blank human subject matter. Both are by Czech writers: the first, a seventeenth-century Moravian Protestant exile, philosopher, millenarian, and associate of Interregnum English utopists; the second, a twentieth-century Jewish writer of German fiction, with no conceivable connection to the first or to Puritanism.

In an earlier chapter we examined John Amos Comenius's proposals in *The Great Didactic* for a universal and millennial reform of the state through a reform of pedagogy. In another passage Comenius claims that his discovery of the true principles of education will prove as revolutionary as the discoveries of writing and that technological trinity of printing, gunpowder, and the magnet praised by Bacon in *Novum Organum*. His new method of teaching will seem as astonishing to his European contemporaries as the art of writing seems to the American Indians or as the western voyages seemed to Columbian Europe. For this invention as for those earlier ones, the key is rational order. Like the printing press, artillery, and the sailing ship, the reformed school depends for its successful operation on the proper ordering of its component parts and procedures (94–95). The curriculum must be gradated according to levels of difficulty; the year must be divided into regular terms and vacations, the class day into set periods for particular subjects, and the pupils into groups, each of which is to be watched over by the teacher's subordinates (94–96). Comenius summarizes: "The art of teaching, therefore, demands nothing more than the artful arrangement of time, the subjects taught, and the method of teaching" (96).

In his summary chapter 32, entitled "Of the Precise, Rational, and Universal Order of Schools," Comenius reasserts his claim to have discovered a new enlightenment technic, using a disciplinary conceit that compares reformed education to printing. He coins the term *didachography* to describe such education: "In didachography the paper is the students whose minds have to be inscribed by the characters of knowledge. The type is the schoolbooks and the rest of the apparatus devised to assist in the business of imprinting minds. The ink is the living voice of the teacher, which transports the sense of things from the books to the minds of the listeners. The press is school discipline, which keeps all the pupils in order and compels them to soak up the instruction" (289). Didachography has as many advantages over conventional pedagogy as typography has over hand copying. Just as a single printer can correct all his mistakes in proof and then turn out many more copies (and those more uniform and more accurate) than a host of copyists ever could, so the reformed school will produce hordes of standardized students much more efficiently than the old schools ever did. Just as typography once mastered is a simpler skill than copying, so didachography is easier to teach than the old pedagogy, and large numbers of teachers can be quickly trained—teachers who will rely on a constant supply of standardized textbooks and books on teaching procedures (the conceit is not arbitrarily chosen).

As the printer can make use of any paper, no matter how flimsy, while the copyist must have only the finest and stiffest paper, so the reformed teacher can teach any student: "Any kind of paper may be used, yet the cleaner it is, the brighter will be the impression of the type. In the same way, our method works with everyone, yet succeeds best with the brightest students" (288–89). In the reformed schools the more talented students will become better educated, and the duller ones at least "more docile in manner, learning to obey civil magistrates and church ministers" (67).

In an earlier passage we can see that this reformed education is to be a utopian, universal means of reform, for Comenius connects the reformed school, the reformed state, and reformed religion through a classic utopian definition of man: "Nature gives us the seeds of learning, virtue, and piety. But it does not give us learning, virtue, and piety themselves. These are acquired by prayer, education, and application. Therefore man is not badly defined as the *animal disciplinabile:* without discipline, in fact, man cannot become man" (52). From the utopian perspective, this definition of man is not incompatible with other definitions (man as the animal with the right to make promises, as *zoon politikon,* as *homo oeconomicus,* as *homo faber,* and so forth), but logically prior to them. Man's essence is not any positive trait, but his capacity for transformation. As Comenius reveals in his *Reformation of Schooles,* this animal is completely at home in a rationalized and rationalizing world: "You might not improperly call the world the home of discipline" (2).

Nowhere does Comenius refer to the student as an autonomous subject or even as a being with any trace of prior individuality. He (or she—Comenius proposes the education of both sexes) is only the blank paper on which didachography prints. But the sheer repetitiveness of the printing becomes millennial: "For the moment, it is enough to have shown that our discovery of didachography or the panmethodia can multiply learned men in precisely the same way that the discovery of printing has multiplied books, those vehicles of learning; and to have shown that this is greatly to the advantage of mankind, since 'In the multitude of the wise is the well-being of the world'" (Wisd. of Sol. 6:26). And since we struggle to multiply the sum of Christian wisdom, to implant piety itself after planting learning and morality in the souls of all who are consecrated to Christ, we can hope for the fulfillment of those divine prophecies that we are commanded to hope for: 'The earth shall be full of the knowledge of God, as the waters cover the sea' (Isa. 11:9)" (*Great Didactic* 293–94). The millennial production of generic, identical scholars who will eventually fill the world is the pedagogical variant on the millennial expansiveness we have seen in the spreading of Eliot's judicial groupings of myriads and thousands of myriads, and in Harrington's exhortation for the Oceanic conquest and unification of the world. The (to modern ears) absurd clash between the modest reforms Comenius actually proposes and the millennial importance he attributes to them is a measure of two transformations of Puritan utopian discipline. First, utopian discipline since the seventeenth century has detached itself from millennialism and is no longer capable of moving from the mastery of some minuscule social detail to a vision of universal millennial order. This capacity for rapid focus, so characteristic of Puritan utopia, has disappeared amid the proliferation of disciplinary institutions, each of which stakes out its own domain, treating its own errant or "blank" disciplinary subjects with its own more or less systematized and quantified methods.

Second, accompanying the evaporation of this project's millennial ends has been the institutionalization of its utopian means. The reforms of school discipline that Comenius proclaims with the joy of discovery (a universal standardizing of the school day and year, of class periods and sizes, of instructional texts and methods) have become second nature, so much so that modern proposals for the reform of education have difficulty doing anything other than reiterating them. The sheer self-evidence of a world in which some people are writers and others written on (these identities change from different disciplinary perspectives) measures the extent to which children—like the poor, military conscripts, criminals, Third World peasants, and other displaced populations—remain disciplinary subjects even when their inscription is emptied of millennial promise.

Franz Kafka's name seldom appears in histories of utopian literature, perhaps because his allegories of modern life seem to lie outside the realist narrative we find in both the dystopian tradition of Huxley,

Zamiatin, and Orwell and the more properly utopian tradition of Bellamy, Morris, Wells, Lem, and Le Guin. Yet a considerable portion of this allegorical quality (perhaps its anagogic level) consists of our utopian recognition of a disciplinary whole in a disciplined part—our intuition that a distant staring face, an individual's reflex movement, or a perplexing bureaucratic memorandum signifies a complex and threatening disciplinary universe. Whereas the Puritan utopist delights in imagining the millennium immanent in the most trivial of organizational details, Kafka shudders to find the modern state immanent in the most trivial oddity of everyday life.

The allegorical plain style of Kafka's postutopian novella "In the Penal Colony" gives him a perspective on enlightenment didachography somewhat different from that of Comenius. Kafka begins with an objectifying device familiar to us from utopia: the dialogue between the traveler and the philosopher. An unnamed European explorer is investigating an unnamed island penal colony belonging to some unnamed nation. He is shown the sights by an officer of the colony, a fierce partisan of the previous commandant of the camp, who founded it. Though this commandant is dead and buried, his "organization of the colony was so perfect that his successor, even with a thousand new schemes in his head, would find it impossible to alter anything, at least for many years to come" (193). A reading of Kafka as a negative theologian will identify the absence of this commandant with the death of God, but we are at least as justified in seeing it as a narrative figure for the political transition from an individual to a corporate sovereignty—for the utopian birth of the modern state. His technological and organizational omniscience prompts the explorer to ask, "Did he combine everything in himself, then? Was he soldier, judge, mechanic, chemist and draughtsman?" (196). In his demigodlike founding power, he resembles utopia's *rex absconditus.* A popular superstition holds that he will rise from the dead and return the camp to its original governing principles (226).

Like the abdicating legislator of Renaissance utopia, the commandant has left behind him a rational, antianthropomorphic mechanism: an intricate machine for executing capital sentences. In fact, we see very little more of the colony than this machine. The entire dialogue between the explorer and the officer consists of a discussion of its operation and the role it plays in the camp. The machine holds the gagged condemned prisoner tight while rotating him and inscribing the actual words of the particular law he violated on his body with a "harrow" of needles. As the machine rotates the prisoner, gradually deepening the inscription and washing away his blood to keep it visible, it gradually executes him. The prisoner slated for execution on the day of the explorer's visit has been derelict in his duty and has threatened his master. His "sentence" (the English translation is felicitous) is "HONOR THY SUPERIORS!"

In Kafka's description the precise institutional nature of the penal colony blurs, making it a parody of the optimistic early modern schemes of universal discipline. It has something of the nature of a military outpost, for the condemned man was assigned as a sort of adjutant to a "captain," and the explorer comments on the colony's "military discipline" (198, 199). It seems to be a prisoner-of-war camp, for the prisoner speaks only French, the officer and the explorer some other language. But we see no one described as a prisoner sent to the colony; the condemned man has committed a crime inside the colony and is condemned by the colony's own court and judge. The executing machine itself, in its precise clinical technology, is like a therapeutic device; the officer remarks that the explorer may have seen something like it in a hospital (196). Kafka's portrayal of the machine shows the disciplinary connection of modern penality and modern medicine. Foucault notes that the physician is typically part of the "army of technicians" that has taken over the task of the executioner: "Today a doctor must watch over those condemned to death, right up to the last moment—thus juxtaposing himself as the agent of welfare, as the alleviator of pain, with the official whose task it is to end life" (*Discipline* 11). In his scrupulous solicitude, the officer combines these two roles. Finally, the unexpected presence of oddly nondisciplinary structures in the colony (a teahouse, a dockyard) makes the colony seem less like a single disciplinary site, more like a compressed insular version of a disciplinary society. The dystopian fantasy of penal transportation has become obsolete, for the state and the penal colony have become one.

We can even see the colony as a Comenian disciplinary reformed school and the condemned man as a student. The officer admits that his prisoner has been summarily condemned and has not even been told his sentence: "There would be no point in telling him. He'll learn it on his body" (Kafka 197). In the normal course of execution as the officer describes it, the typical condemned man does indeed learn: "But how quiet he grows at just about the sixth hour! Enlightenment comes to the most dull-witted. It begins around the eyes. From there it radiates. A moment that might tempt one to get under the Harrow oneself. Nothing more happens than that the man begins to understand the inscription, he purses his mouth as if he were listening. You have seen how difficult it is to decipher the script with one's eyes; but our man deciphers it with his wounds" (204). Like Comenius's duller students, Kafka's condemned "stupid-looking wide-mouthed creature" may require the repetition of his lesson and the deepening of the inscription, but he will eventually acquire knowledge and conscience through the discipline of the body. Kafka reveals the disciplinary connections between institutions that utopia may attempt to separate: the instrument of enlightenment at the sixth hour is the instrument of death at the twelfth. Not only does utopian reason write on and form bodies; it also eventually penetrates, deforms, and destroys them. The machine reveals the essential falseness of enlightenment reason's claim to have transcended utterly irrational and customary domination, for it combines the medieval iron maiden and the enlightenment printing press.

All the same, Kafka's work is not a utopia, and the dead commandant is not a utopian *rex absconditus*. His founding intention was not immortal, for factions have grown up inside the penal colony. This sort of execution, previously a festive public ritual, is now ignored. The officer attempts to enlist the aid of the explorer in his attempt to initiate a Machiavellian *ridurre ai principii* that would undercut the new commandant and restore the executions to their previous place of honor. When the explorer refuses, the officer despairs, frees the condemned man, programs a sentence for himself ("BE JUST!"), and takes his place in the machine. But the machine as well as the order of the penal colony has begun to decay. It begins throwing cogs, destroying itself and the officer in a matter of seconds. The explorer leaves the penal colony, uncertain of the nature of the news he has for Europe. In the mortality of the commandant's legislating intention, in the breakdown of the machine, and in the appearance of political factions inside the colony we can read the breakdown of enlightenment utopia's claim to sovereign omniscience. For Kafka cultural totality is always a contradictory totality.

But neither is Kafka's work part of the modern dystopian tradition. Unlike the dystopian worlds of Huxley and Orwell, Kafka's penal colony contains no figure of sovereign evil. The officer, the likeliest candidate for the role, himself longs for the caresses of the machine, as the Puritan utopist longs to disappear into the ascetic anonymity of utopian everyday life. As Puritan utopia's *rex absconditus* has become immanent in the corporate orders he has left behind him, so Kafka's commandant has become immanent in the workings of his state and the machine at its center. Kafka's view of the dark side of totalizing enlightenment forbids us to purge ourselves of dread by externalizing and personifying its will to domination.

Even when this machine is destroyed (or destroys itself), Kafka allows no hope for a move outside the disciplinary state. "In the Penal Colony" lacks the textual refuge providing the modern dystopist a humane perspective from which to satirize the state. Huxley's John Savage can measure the depravity of the feelies with his edition of Shakespeare, as Orwell's Winston Smith can measure the falsity of Oceania with his glimpse of uncensored (and therefore "true") news reports and books. But Kafka lacks their humanist faith in the saving power of print. The only texts to appeal to are the sentences written on paper (which are too ornate to read) or inscribed on the bodies of the condemned. These bodies, unlike the uniformly inscribed bodies produced by Comenius's didachography, are devoid of millennial immanence. The explorer looks into the face of the dead officer: "It was as it had been in life; no sign was visible of the promised redemption" (225). In modern culture, after the decline of Puritanism, "the rosy blush of its laughing heir, the Enlightenment, seems also to be irretrievably fading, and the idea of duty in one's calling prowls about in our lives like the ghost of dead religious beliefs" (Weber, *Ethic* 182). Modern man remains imprisoned in the "iron cage" of bureaucratic domination and discipline without the otherworldly compensations promised by Puritanism (181).

Similarly, both Huxley and Orwell give their heroes a pastoral *locus amoenus* from which to criticize dystopian society: John Savage's Indian reservation and the patch of (seemingly) unsurveyed ground in which Winston and Julia meet. But no such escape is possible for Kafka's explorer, for the uncanny, or *unheimlich,* quality of the story arises largely from the fact that the explorer sees the colony not as something distant from himself but as something strangely familiar. Like Raphael and other utopian travelers, he half recognizes this "ideal" foreign state as an accelerated and rationalized version of his own. Even in his parting revulsion we can see that he inhabits a disciplinary universe and that no escape is possible. Pursued by the reprieved condemned man and the officer's assistant, he boards his boat just in time: "They could have jumped into the boat, but the explorer lifted a heavy knotted rope from the floor boards, threatened them with it and so kept them from attempting the leap" (Kafka 227). As he flees from the spectacle of enlightened torture, he becomes a figure for the reactionary humanist critic of modern culture by assuming the stance of a medieval torturer wielding a knout. There is no other world, no alternative realm of humane freedom. The disciplinary state is no longer the longed-for promise of the imminent future but the threatening reality of the present. Man remains the disciplinable animal, but for Kafka this fact names the problem, not the solution.

Notes

Chapter 1

1. The primary and secondary literature on utopia is considerable, so I will simply flag a few works that flag many others in turn. Two recent encyclopedic studies—*Utopian Thought in the Western World* by Frank E. Manuel and Fritzie P. Manuel and *Utopia and Revolution* by Melvin J. Lasky—have extensive bibliographies; Lasky is less intent on distinguishing utopian literature from utopian political rhetoric and social practice. J. C. Davis's *Utopia and the Ideal Society: A Study of English Utopian Writing, 1516–1700* also has an extensive bibliography, one more narrowly focused on early modern utopia. Glenn Negley's *Utopian Literature: A Bibliography* is comprehensive and handily organized: entries are alphabetical by author, with a chronological index. J. Max Patrick's bibliography (in R. W. Gibson's *St. Thomas More: A Preliminary Bibliography of His Works*) is less comprehensive but includes helpful annotations. A recently issued microfiche collection, *Utopian Literature: Pre-1900 Imprints,* is invaluable despite (and because of) some eccentric omissions and inclusions; Bobby C. Wynn edited the bibliographic guide. In this study I will not attempt to present a narrative history of utopia. For efforts in that direction, see Marie Louise Berneri, Davis, Elisabeth Hansot, Manuel and Manuel, A. L. Morton, Negly and Patrick, and Vernon Louis Parrington, Jr.

2. In part, this compulsion to define utopia has a ritual function in academic life. To make room for a genre tainted with overtly political content, the self-policing literary critic must denounce badly written or superficially boring utopias as blueprints, programs, dissertations generically distinct from the literary works he or she wishes to consider, whereas the student of, for instance, epic poetry feels no compulsion to begin a study of *The Aeneid* by denouncing *The Columbiad*. Compare the situation of academic Marxism, which (at least until very recently) found itself called upon ritually to denounce bad Marxist criticism as "vulgar Marxism" (O peculiar calumny!), whereas the history of ideas or the New Criticism has faced no analogous demand. But however effective as a ritual of initiation, this act of self-denial finally proves enervating: since it must move between centers and margins, genre criticism is no less dialectical a practice than is Marxist criticism, and so it is no less vitiated by such a self-confinement to canonical texts and self-exile from the noncanonical.

3. The notable exception here is Jameson, because of his fascination with literary form and because he transforms "ideology" and "utopia" from headings in a taxonomy of works to modes of reading. A single literary work, then, is subject to both a utopian and an ideological analysis, and Jameson's entire study reveals a complex dialectic of utopia and ideology inside both literary and critical writings.

4. Pocock's introductory essay summarizes and updates his earlier theoretical arguments in *Politics, Language and Time: Essays on Political Thought and History,* which work out in more detail his adaption of Thomas Kuhn's theories to political writing. See particularly "Languages and Their Implications: The Transformation of the Study of Political Thought" (3–41) and "On the Non-Revolutionary Character of Paradigms: A Self-Criticism and Afterpiece" (273–91). In the following pages I will argue that Pocock need not exclude the study of social practices from his study of political rhetoric, but one might also make a case for literary form, the third member of my triad. Because he concentrates on the analysis of political languages and the statements they produce (langue and parole, in the Saussurean terminology he invokes), Pocock tends to scant such mediating verbal categories as the tract, the book, and the genre. His infrequent references to literary criticism tend to reduce it to a belletristic stylistics with no historical method (*Politics* 12–13; *Virtue* 9–10). All the same, Pocock's study of political languages and their transformations should be of tremendous interest to literary historians and theorists; see note 5.

5. In *James I and the Politics of Literature,* a study of the languages of Jacobean absolutism, Jonathan Goldberg also finds much of value in Pocock's study of the discursive quality of political life, but he too sees some problems in Pocock's tendency to equate political discourse with the reciprocal conversation of civic humanism. Goldberg notes that James exercises discursive power in the public theater, in his own poetry and prose, and in state proces-

sions and masques through his very silence, his refusal to enter into a reciprocal civil conversation. See, particularly, 273 n.46.

6. In my discussion of Weber, Frankfurt, and Foucault, I am indebted to
J. E. T. Eldridge's examination of the rationalization theme in the writings of
Weber and his followers (Weber, *Max Weber: The Interpretation of Social
Reality* 53–70) and to discussions of Weber and Frankfurt by Andrew Arato
(Arato and Gebhardt 191–93) and Martin Jay (258–62). Barry Smart draws
some helpful comparisons and contrasts among Weber, Frankfurt, and Foucault (123–37), as do Hubert Dreyfus and Paul Rabinow (Dreyfus and Rabinow 132–33, 165–67; Foucault, *The Foucault Reader* 26–27). *Rationalization,
enlightenment,* and *discipline* will be joined in chapter 4 by two related concepts: Freud's concept of the repetition compulsion and Nietzsche's concept of
the genealogy of morals and contract.

7. Unlike rationalization and enlightenment, Foucault's conception of
power occasionally runs the risk of replacing the critique of concrete local acts
of domination with a celebration of dynamic immanence. Foucault says that
"power is everywhere" (*The History of Sexuality* 93)—a quote that asks to be
(and has been) taken out of context and circulated as an aphoristic refutation
of class-based Marxist analyses of domination and repression. Foucault's
change in subject matter in his later work from practices of domination (psychiatry, medicine, penology, military discipline, education) to practices of self-
fashioning (the construction of sexual selves in the classical world) tends to
aggravate this problem. Edward Said remarks, "Foucault's eagerness not to fall
into Marxist economism causes him to obliterate the role of classes, the role
of economics, the role of insurgency and rebellion in the societies he discusses.
. . . The problem is that Foucault's use of the term *pouvoir* moves around too
much, swallowing up every obstacle in its path" (Said 244, 245). Foucault
addresses this problem in a late essay: "Let us not deceive ourselves: if we
speak of the structures of the mechanisms of power, it is only insofar as we
suppose that certain persons exercise power over others" (Rabinow and Dreyfus 217). But in this same essay he says that "what defines a relationship of
power is that it is a mode of action that does not act directly and immediately
on others. . . . It is . . . always a way of acting upon an acting subject or acting
subjects by virtue of their acting or being capable of action. . . . Power is exercised only over free subjects, and only insofar as they are free" and so capable
of some change in action. And he takes pains to distinguish between power
and mere violence, which "acts upon a body or upon things; it forces, it bends,
it breaks on the wheel, it destroys, or it closes the door on all possibilities. . . .
The relationship proper to power would not therefore be sought on the side of
violence or of struggle (220–21). Not only does Foucault occlude oppositional
struggle, but his very examples ("it breaks on the wheel") tend to periodize
and distance repressive violence and so to deny its present-day reality. But it
is difficult to see how (or why) we should distinguish mediated disciplinary

power from brute violence in any historical context whatever. To take only one important mode of modern violence/power: the aerial bombing of civilian populations in Indochina, El Salvador, West Beirut, Afghanistan, and Libya is no doubt an attempt to act upon the actions of those outside the blast zone by traumatizing them into inactivity, fragmenting their capacity for resistance, or inciting them to greater resistance and so bringing on an escalation of warfare. But it simultaneously exercises immediate violence upon the bodies of others: those blown up or otherwise made incapable of further action. Foucault's struggle to avoid falling into a leftist denunciation of power as a merely repressive possession leads him away from those practices of brute domination to which all power is tied. Throughout this study, we will see that utopia's relatively pacific and mediated disciplinary power is always in a dialectic with the more immediate violence of warfare and eviction. The latter produce the displaced populations that utopia takes as the subject matter of its gentle rational discipline. Utopian discipline, in turn, makes possible a more global and accelerated practice of eviction and warfare. But this is certainly not to say that warfare and eviction act upon free subjects "only insofar as they are free."

Chapter 2

1. On the displaced populations of the English sixteenth century, see Tawney's *Agrarian Problem* and Kelly's *Thorns on the Tudor Rose*. On the attempts of sixteenth- and seventeenth-century political writers and poets to characterize "the mob," see Hill's "Many-Headed Monster" (*Change* 181–204) and Greenblatt's "Murdering Peasants," a study of the ways in which Dürer, Sidney, Spenser, and Shakespeare "commemorate" the repression of peasant rebellions.

2. The following studies of millennialism have been influential or cover undeservedly neglected areas. Ernest Tuveson's *Millennium and Utopia* gives a history-of-ideas overview of millennialism, with emphasis on early modern England. Norman Cohn's *The Pursuit of the Millennium,* a study of the radical millenarians of medieval northern Europe (with some forays into the sixteenth and seventeenth centuries) has been extremely influential, in part because of the ahistorical analogy it draws between radical millenarians and Leninist revolutionaries. This analogy has a long pedigree: the *reductio ad Münsterum* has been a favorite conservative trope since the sixteenth century, allowing proponents of custom to link each new radical movement to the bloody reign in Münster of John of Leyden and the Anabaptists. Cohn's study is also marred by his willingness to take as a reliable guide to the ideologies of millenarian radicals the confessions preserved by those who tortured them to death. William Haller's *Foxe's Book of Martyrs and the Elect Nation* has had a considerable influence on historians of political millennialism on both sides of the Atlantic, including Sacvan Bercovitch *(The American Jeremiad)* and J. G. A. Pocock *(The Machiavellian Moment).* For studies of radical seven-

teenth-century eschatology, see Richard Popkin's essay, "Jewish Messianism and Christian Millenarianism"; Charles Webster's study of the millenarian affiliations of Puritan science in *The Great Instauration;* Peter Toon's collection of essays, *Puritans, the Millennium, and the Future of Israel;* and B. S. Capp's social history, *The Fifth Monarchy Men.* In *Godly Rule* William Lamont examines a wide range of seventeenth-century millennialisms, excepting radicals like the Fifth Monarchists, whom he dismisses as "cranks"; in *Richard Baxter and the Millennium,* he studies the fitful hold of millennialism over a distinctly nonradical writer. An exchange between Lamont and Capp reveals some of the controversies animating millenarian studies (Webster, *Revolution* 386–434). For studies of seventeenth-century New English millennialism, see J. F. Maclear's "New England and the Fifth Monarchy" and Philip F. Gura's *Glimpse of Sion's Glory* 126–74). Stephen J. Stein's "Transatlantic Extensions: Apocalyptic in Early New England," Nathan Hatch's *Sacred Cause of Liberty,* and Tuveson's *Redeemer Nation* carry this study into the American eighteenth and nineteenth centuries. See also the wide-ranging collection of essays, *The Apocalypse in English Renaissance Thought and Literature,* edited by Patrides and Wittreich.

3. Thomas Harriot's *Briefe and True Report of the New Found Land of Virginia,* an exploration and promotional tract of 1590, shows just such an encounter of European technology with the Indians. The Algonquians of Virgina (modern-day North Carolina) are amazed by such inventions as "sea compasses, the virtue of the lodestone in drawing iron, a perspective glass whereby was shewed many strange sights, burning glasses, wildfire works, guns, books, writing and reading, spring clocks that seem to go of themselves, and many other things that we had." They think that "they were rather the works of gods than of men, or at the leastwise they had been given and taught us of the gods" (27). Renaissance exploration literature thus makes a double discovery. It reveals a natural warehouse of raw materials for European exploitation and commerce (the bulk of Harriot's tract is a catalog of "marchantable" and other useful animals, vegetables, and minerals). And it foregrounds the imperial magic of European technology. See Greenblatt's "Invisible Bullets" on this tract.

4. This characterization of Vico as an enlightenment thinker is at odds with the readings of such critics as Hayden White, Edward Said, and Harold Bloom. Despite their considerable differences of interpretation, they all see Vico as the proponent of an anti-Cartesian, counter-Enlightenment humanism that sees the origin of culture in man's poetic consciousness, without insisting on a radical separation between the knowing subject and the object known. This characterization is true so far as it goes, but it ignores Vico's critical attitude toward that origin and his belief that man has transcended it. True, concrete poetic language preceded analytic prose, but that was only because "man in his ignorance makes himself the rule of the universe. . . . Man becomes all things by *not* understanding them" (88). Because of his ignorance, man conceives of the

world poetically, through the poetic tropes of metaphor, metonomy, synec-doche, and irony. Yet the need for these poetic tropes simply disappears when "with the further development of the human mind, words were invented which signified abstract forms or genera comprising their species or relating parts with their wholes" (90). Though Vico accords a greater importance to these ancient verbal idols than Bacon does, the two agree that they have been superseded by the abstract, conceptual language of philosophy.

5. For other examples of this verbal pattern, see Raphael's description of Utopian hospitals (46), care of the sick and dying (65), warfare (71–78), and treatment of heretics (80).

6. Richard Halpern's account of Raphael's irony here is perceptive: "Hyth-lodaeus's attack on enclosures begins with a witty metonomy: not the land-owners, but the sheep themselves depopulate the countryside. By blaming the animal victims of this process, Hythlodaeus parodies the corresponding metonomy which allows the lawyer to blame its human victim. Moreover, he then invests the sheep with a malignant *will.* Like the deracinated farmers, they used to be 'tame and cheaply fed' but now have become 'greedy and wild.' By reproducing the lawyer's logic on these dummy subjects, Hythlodaeus reveals the purely simulacral nature of their 'voluntary preference' for stealing, and thus de-reifies the lawyer's ethical discourse." Halpern's chapter on More in his forthcoming study of the relation between early modern English literature and the origins of capitalism should do much to reopen critical discussion of the relation between ethics and economics in *Utopia.* I discuss a related mat-ter—the conflict between moral philosophy and social discipline in *Utopia* and utopia—in my final chapter.

7. In "The Sovereign, the Theater, and the Kingdome of Darkeness: Hobbes and the Spectacle of Power," Christopher Pye sees a fundamental aporia in Hobbes's account of civil origins: whereas Hobbes says that men in a state of nature create the sovereign by delegating to him authority that they previously owned, he also says that the intervention of sovereign power is a necessary prerequisite to ownership of any sort. But this aporia disappears if we distin-guish between man's ownership of his own power in a state of nature and his ownership of property in civil society, possible only through his delegation of power to a sovereign.

8. Compare Edward Bellamy's utopian novel *Looking Backward* (1888), which has a cheerful vision of a future collectivist state organized as an "indus-trial army"—an army that even has an "invalid corps, the members of which are provided with a light class of tasks fitted to their strength. All our sick in mind and body, all our deaf and dumb, and lame and blind and crippled, and even our insane, belong to this invalid corps, and bear its insigns. The strong-est often do nearly a man's work, the feeblest, of course, nothing; but none who can do anything are willing quite to give up. In their lucid intervals, even our insane are eager to do what they can" (109). The last sentence is particu-larly chilling: if eagerness to work is a sign of lucidity, is laziness a sign of

insanity? In a characteristically utopian move, Bellamy fabricates his ideal future industrial army from the mangled veteran bodies populating his own post–Civil War present.

9. In his haste to separate the Puritans' radical politics from Machiavelli's, Michael Walzer says that he "relied exclusively upon the prince" when discussing the establishment of the state (*Revolution* 1–2). This overlooks the vital Machiavellian distinction (most visible in *The Discourses* but present also in *The Prince*) between the new prince and the legislator of a republic. It also overlooks the considerable importance of the godly prince in conservative Puritan political theory (Lamont, *Rule*). It is indeed possible to see Machiavelli as less absolutist than is John Winthrop or Richard Baxter.

Chapter 3

1. The studies of utopia by Davis, Holloway, Lasky, the Manuels, and Morton do not even mention Eliot. Everett Webber gives him one cursory page. Negley and Patrick decide that Eliot's *Christian Commonwealth,* along with Richard Baxter's *Holy Commonwealth,* inhabits "the outskirts of Utopia" (291). And according to their definition of utopia as a fictional work whose theme is the political structure of a particular state or community, it does not really qualify. But Eliot's utopia slips into Negley's bibliography of utopias (39) and into Patrick's (Gibson 339). Parrington does briefly consider Eliot as a utopist, but finally dismisses him as a solipsistic and authoritarian theocrat cut off from mainstream Puritan political theory. Robert S. Fogarty has no entry for Eliot in his *Dictionary of American Communal and Utopian History.* Many studies of Eliot from outside the history of utopia are helpful. See Francis Jennings and Alden T. Vaughan for contrasting views of his role in the conquest of the Algonquian nations. Bowden and Ronda analyze his missionary work. And J. F. Maclear's discussion of Eliot in the context of New England millennialism is the best introduction to his political thought. There are no recent scholarly biographies of Eliot. Ola Elizabeth Winslow's *John Eliot: "Apostle to the Indians"* follows very much in the hagiographic and ethnocentric tradition of Mather and Francis. I have been unable to examine Frederick Farnham Harling's "Biography of John Eliot, 1604–1690," Diss. Boston University, 1965. For shorter accounts of Eliot's life, see Byington, Morison (289–319), H. R. Tedder's article in the *DNB,* or "Eliot, John," in *American Authors, 1600–1900.*

2. Francis Jennings's suggestion of "The Second Puritan Conquest" as an alternative designation for "King Philip's War" is attractive, for neither King Philip nor very many of his nation were around at war's end to accept the dubious honor of its christening.

3. Eliot's published works and letters have never been collected and must be culled from a number of scattered sources. This note and the works cited refer to some of the more important works and accessible editions, but they

are by no means exhaustive. Some helpful bibliographies may be found in Weis (the most complete and accurate listing of Eliot's letters); in Winslow's biography; and in Spiller et al., eds., *Literary History of the United States: Bibliography*. The Eliot Tracts, as much as any body of utopian writing, show that utopia not only attempts to produce new corporate subjectivities but is produced by them. All but the first center on Eliot's work: some are attributed to him, others contain letters from him, and still others contain reports of his work. But some are attributed to other authors, including agents and allies of the Society for Propagation of the Gospel in New England, and the authorship of others is still in dispute. With their introductory epistles and appendixes and with the mutually supporting testimony of the various authors, they constantly attempt to construct a corporate authority rather than a unified individual authority. Tracts 2 through 8 have been reprinted as *Tracts Relating to the Attempts to Convert to Christianity the Indians of New England* in *Collections of the Massachusetts Historical Society* 3.4 (1834): 1–287. I will refer to these as *Tracts* and give the page numbers of this reprint, which I have broken down in the list below. For editions of the other tracts, see the Works Cited. All the tracts were published in London.

    1. *New-Englands First Fruits* (1643).
    2. *The Day-Breaking, If Not the Sun-Rising of the Gospel with the Indians in New-England* (1647): 1–23.
    3. Thomas Shepard. *The Clear Sun-shine of the Gospel Breaking Forth upon the Indians in New-England* (1648): 25–67.
    4. Edward Winslow. *The Glorious Progress of the Gospel, amongst the Indians in New-England* (1649): 69–98.
    5. Henry Whitfield. *The Light Appearing More and More towards the Perfect Day* (1651): 100–47.
    6. Henry Whitfield. *Strength out of Weaknesse* (1652): 149–96.
    7. John Eliot and Thomas Mayhew. *Tears of Repentance* (1653): 197–260.
    8. John Eliot. *A Late and Further Manifestation of the Progress of the Gospel amongst the Indians in New-England* (1655): 261–87.
    9. John Eliot. *A Further Accompt of the Progresse of the Gospel amongst the Indians in New-England (1659)*.
    10. John Eliot. *A Further Account of the Progresse of the Gospel* (1660).
    11. John Eliot. *A Brief Narrative of the Progress of the Gospel Among the Indians in New-England, in the Year 1670* (1671).

For editions and reprints of *The Christian Commonwealth, Indian Dialogues, The Indian Grammar Begun,* Gookin's chronicles of the missionary work and of King Philip's War, Eliot's correspondence with Baxter (under Baxter and Eliot) and Eliot's less important works and letters, see the Works Cited. *Com-*

munion of Churches is unavailable in reprint, but like all of Eliot's works published in America before 1800 (primarily his translations into Algonquian), it is available in the *Readex Microprint Corporation Collection of Early American Imprints, 1639–1800,* edited by Clifford K. Shipton and published by the American Antiquarian Society. James Constantine Pilling's *Bibliography of the Algonquian Languages* has a long section on Eliot's translations, including reproductions of many title pages (127–54).

4. Here I follow Sacvan Bercovitch's distinction between the political visions of New England and those of the colonies farther south. While Maryland and Virginia settlers saw the New World as a utopian realm of material plenty and progressive secular history, New Englanders saw it as a New Israel with a vital role in millennial history (*Origins* 137). I question his view of the strictly secular nature of the tradition of More, Burton, Rabelais, Andreae, Bacon, and Campanella, for millennium and utopia can come together in a political project (like those of Eliot, Harrington, Winstanley, Comenius, Andreae, Bacon, and Campanella) intended to produce a new human type that will populate a future phase of millennial history.

5. With the fading of millennial hopes in the Old World and the New, these theories declined. The agitation for the official readmission of Jews into England failed, largely because of the opposition of English merchants fearful of Jewish competitors (Toon 123–25). As messianic hopes faded in eastern Europe during the pogroms of the later seventeenth century, so the theories of the Jewish origins of the Indians faded after King Philip's War encouraged whites to diabolize the Indians.

6. In "reduction" we can see the dialectical relationship between utopia and warfare: Indian culture must be reduced (conquered) before the individual Indians can be reduced (led back) to civility by reducing them (gathering them together) into praying towns. The Jesuits' Indian communes in Paraguay were known as *reducciones.*

7. The Algonquians seem to be more conscious than Miller is of the contradictions implicit in a theocratic rhetoric. Some of Eliot's converts return from an encounter with Samuel Gorton's Winstanleyesque radical spiritist arguments against ministers, magistrates, and a geographically locatable heaven and hell. One asks, "What is the reason, that seeing those English people . . . had the same Bible that we have, yet do not speak the same things?" (*Tracts* 136). On Gorton, see Gura 276–303.

8. To Eliot's frustration, the Bay Colony authorities did not allow the Indians to enter into full church covenant until 1660. Eliot's utopian sequence of civility and conversion was by no means universal. His missionary colleague Thomas Mayhew tended to separate his work at conversion on Martha's Vineyard from the organization of Indian civil government (Jennings 231). Roy Harvey Pearce says that eighteenth-century missionaries abandoned Eliot's initial cultivation of civility for an immediate and total conversion (33–34). We can see here the breakdown of a utopian belief in the necessary integration

of a political and religious project under the authority of the Bible: after a series of Indian wars, the colonial policy regarding the Indians changes from utopian millennialism to evangelism supplemented by sheer, genocidal military domination.

9. Critics frequently call Eliot a writer of limited intellectual means and ambition, and he seems to have written no treatises on Ramist logic or historical studies of church polity, as did so many of his fellow ministers. But could we say that his model for civil elections and his praying-town discipline are themselves an exercise in Ramist methodizing? Eliot's practical emphasis on rational order in the praying towns does not really remove him from Ramist Puritan philosophy, which Perry Miller says was largely a matter of arrangement, ordering, and method: "The essence of the Ramist system was exactly this belief that logic is no more than the distinguishing of entities and the joining of them together, that the function of thinking is primarily discerning and disposing, not investigating and deducing" (*Seventeenth Century* 134). Incidentally, the strangest product of Eliot's presses was *The Logic Primer* (1672), a simplied Algonquian version of Ramus's *Dialecticae*.

10. J. Paul Hunter points to biographical evidence suggesting that Defoe may have been familiar with Puritan missionary literature, perhaps even the Eliot Tracts. He also notes a strong parallel between one of Friday's questions to Crusoe and a question posed by an Indian in the Eliot Tracts: "If God much strong, much might as the Devil, why God no kill the Devil, so make him no more do wicked?" (Defoe 170); "Why did not God kill the Devil that made all men so bad, God having all power?" (*Tracts* 47). Though Friday initially proves the superior casuist, forcing Crusoe to withdraw and meditate his answer, Crusoe eventually returns, satisfieds Friday, and brings him to a complete conversion. Friday's question appears in Defoe's novel not as the oppositional protest of an alternative culture or religion, but as the voice of an individual already being disciplined by Christian dialectic. As Hunter notes, Defoe, like Eliot, chose to depict Indians as neither noble or ignoble savages but as educable natural men. And in his isolation from his culture, Friday approaches the anomic state of the postconquest Indians of New England. Like the borders of Eliot's praying towns, the shores of Crusoe's island turn an ethnic Other into a disciplinary specimen.

11. Eliot owned a copy of *Paradise Lost;* it is now owned by Trinity College, Hartford, Connecticut.

12. Thomas Morton proposes a gentile and heroic variant in *New English Canaan*—by linking the Indians and the English through a common Trojan ancestry rather than through a shared millennial destiny. On the basis of a number of linguistic parallels he sees among Algonquian, Latin, and Greek, he concludes that "the original of the natives of New England may be well conjectured to be from the scattered Trojans, after such time as Brutus departed from Latium" (18).

13. The Puritan argument that the Indians had no history almost transcends

its falseness, partly because that argument aided in the conquest assuring they would have no future. Ethnohistorians today disagree on the appropriate approach to take in analyzing the primary surviving records of the Puritan conquest: the Puritan tracts. Alden T. Vaughan is untroubled, saying that the Puritans had "no reason to conceal their attitudes or actions toward the Indians" (vii). This is an extraordinary claim, even if we agree with Vaughan's assumption that the proper activity of history is the reconstruction of "attitudes" and the cataloging of "actions." Even historians sympathetic with the Indians sometimes proceed from methodologically dubious assumptions. James P. Ronda, for instance, takes Eliot's *Indian Dialogues* as an accurate record of Puritan and Praying Indian encounters with non-Praying Indians. J. William T. Youngs, Jr., says we should "probe beneath the surface of Puritan rhetoric to comprehend actual Indian experience" (241). But he relies on sympathetic and speculative "may have's" and "must have's" to reconstruct this actuality. Kenneth M. Morrison remarks that "in their aboriginal world the Indians lived incredibly rich and meaningful lives"(89), but he has understandable difficulty evoking this lost richness. My "solution" to the problem— my attempt to remain within an immanent analysis of the contradictory Puritan rhetoric of conquest and utopia—does not and cannot altogether avoid making positive claims about the Indian culture that rhetoric helped to destroy. But only an arrogant and ethnocentric immanentism would claim that all aspects of the conflict and of the Indian critique of Puritanism have been preserved. See James Axtell's review essay, "The Ethnohistory of America."

14. The "Founders Song" of Roxbury Latin School—founded by Eliot in 1645 and still holding classes—preserves this image of the gentle apostle who rises above sectarian strife:

> In the days when merry England was ablaze with civil war
> And the Cavaliers and Roundheads were at strife,
> In the wilderness of Roxbury lived a pious man of peace,
> Teaching men better ways of life.
> To the good apostle Eliot it mattered little then
> Whether King or Parliament should rule,
> For he taught both Whites and Indians to walk the narrow way,
> And he founded this ancient Latin school.

I am grateful to George D. Gopen (Roxbury alumnus) for these lines and to Eric Solomon (another) for a memorable rendition.

15. A speculation. In a letter to the Reverend Jonathan Hanmer of Barnstapel in Devonshire, dated July 19, 1652, Eliot tells of the founding of Natick: "In the year 1651 in a day of fasting and prayer, they entered into a covenant with God, and each other, to be ruled by the Lord in all their affairs civilly, making the word of God their only Magna Charta, for government, laws, and

all conversation, and chose rules of tens, fifties, and of an hundred. The plat-form of which holy government of God's own institution, I have sent over this year to Mr. Nichols [Rev. Ferdinando Nicolls, rector of St. Mary Arches in Exeter] with the reverend elders in Exon [Exeter?]. And if the Lord give you opportunity, I should gladly wish yourself might also have a sight of it, that I might receive your animadversions on it. But in my poor thoughts, I appre-hend it would be a mercy to England, if they should in this method of [?] take up that form of government, which is a divine institution, and by which Christ should reign over them, by the word of his mouth" (Eliot, *John Eliot and the Indians* 7–8). I have modified somewhat the transcription of the manuscript original (photographically reproduced in this edition) by the editor, Wilber-force Eames. Eames says (14) that Eliot is referring here to the Eliot Tract *Strength out of Weaknesse.* But timing and common sense suggest that Eliot would not have sent to England in 1652 a published copy of a tract issued earlier that year in London. It is even more unlikely that Eliot would have sent a manuscript copy, since the tract consists of two introductory epistles by the English preachers constituting the Society for Propagation of the Gospel in New England, two letters of different dates by Eliot, and additional letters from nine others. It is possible that Eliot originally sent the second of his two letters to Nicolls and that it eventually found its way to Henry Whitfield, the compiler of *Strength out of Weaknesse.* But this letter contains only a cursory descrip-tion of the Mosaic government of the Indians (*Tracts* 171–72). The letter to Hanmer specifically proposes the transformation of England and even contains some strong verbal echoes of *The Christian Commonwealth* ("Magna Charta" and "Christ should reign over them, by the word of his mouth"). And Eliot's request for "animadversions" on a "platform" would seem more relevant to a theoretical utopia than to a missionary tract. So it is conceivable that Nicolls was the recipient of Eliot's manuscript of *The Christian Commonwealth* and that he or one of his "reverend elders" became the "Server of the Season" who published the manuscript in 1659. Another candidate for the role is Hugh Peters (coinquisitor with Eliot of Anne Hutchinson). Peters returned to England in 1641, became a chaplain to the New Model Army, and was exe-cuted by the Stuart monarchy in 1660. Summarizing and quoting a letter from Eliot to Peters of October 12, 1649, Joseph B. Felt observes that "Eliot pro-ceeds to advance ideas, like those in his Commonwealth: 'The only Magna Charta in the world, is the holy Scriptures. Oh! what an opportunity hath the Parliament now to bring in Christ to rule in England. If they do that, Christ will prosper them and preserve them'" (Felt 292).

16. The allure of the myth of the ancient constitution (Pocock, *Constitution*) proves too much for Eliot, and he breaks his own rule about excluding gentile political wisdom from the discussion. He seems to have a theory that Alfred ruled England according to some such model as he proposes: "England long since had happy experience of it" (*Tracts* 127). And he chooses an Anglo-Sax-onism to name his leaders of tens: "Then they chose ten or tithing-men (so I

call them in English) for so they were called (as is reported) in England, when England did flourish happily under that kind of government" (171).

17. In this inclusiveness Eliot reverses John Cotton's more conservative interpretation of Exodus 18. Cotton argues that regenerate church fellowship is to be an absolute prerequisite for civil magistracy: "Jethro's counsel to Moses was approved of God, that the judges and officers to be set over the people should be men fearing God, Exod. 18:21" (Miller and Johnson 210).

18. In *The Puritans* Miller and Johnson make the intriguing observation that Eliot's tract was an expression of Puritan radicalism that was driven underground at the Restoration, only to reemerge in the tracts of the radical pamphleteers of the eighteenth century (xl–xli). But I have been unable to find that any later revolutionaries read Eliot. Still, Exodus 18 did provide Federalist ideologists with a biblical precedent. In a sermon he preached at Concord on June 5, 1788, advocating the ratification of the United States Constitution, Samuel Langdon compares the situation of the Israelites wandering in Sinai with the situation of America under the Articles of Confederation. The order brought by the Articles corresponds to the interim Hebrew government of thousands, hundreds, fifties, and tens, but "the great thing wanting was a permanent constitution, which might keep the people peaceable and obedient while in the desert, and after they had gained possession of the promised land." Therefore, the Sanhedrin, which Langdon calls a "Senate," was formed. The continuing organization of the Israelites in twelve tribes corresponds to the governments of the thirteen states. Like Eliot, Langdon wrestles with the oligarchic implications of the Sanhedrin, saying that "as to the choice of this Senate, doubtless the people were consulted, who appear to have had a voice in all public affairs from time to time, the whole congregation being called together on all important occasions: the government therefore was a proper republic" (8–9). America's particular republican mission will allow it to avoid the Hebrews' degeneration into anarchy, oligarchy, and monarchy. But the millennial implications of Eliot's commonwealth have nearly disappeared: Langdon promies no millennial unification of the world under this polity, only the creation of an American government that will be "the best which the nations have yet known" (48).

Chapter 4

1. Toland's edition appeared in 1700. Various versions of it appeared through the eighteenth century; the edition of 1771 was the last collected edition before J. G. A. Pocock's edition of 1977. Frank E. Manuel and Fritzie P. Manuel survey *Oceana* and proclaim it "a waterless Sinai for the present generation" (336). If so, we are a stiff-necked and murmuring generation, for since *The Ancient Constitution and the Feudal Law* (1957), Pocock has been making Harrington's works the center of his own brilliant study of political thought as the history of its languages. He has examined Harrington's writings in the contexts of Italian republicanism, seventeenth-century English political theory,

and eighteenth- and nineteenth-century British and American republicanism. Unless otherwise noted, all references to Harrington's works are to Pocock's edition of Harrington's political writings; Pocock's "Historical Introduction" is the best introduction to Harrington. See also Shklar ("Ideology Hunting") on Harrington's nineteenth- and twentieth-century critics. Liljegren's notes to his 1924 edition of *Oceana* are unsurpassed for identifying Harrington's allusions and sources. Macpherson's chapter on Harrington in his *Possessive Individualism* is a study of great skill, interest, and influence.

2. In "The Storm over the Gentry," J. H. Hexter summarizes and adds a voice to the methodological and ideological controversy. To criticize the rival economistic explanations of Tawney and Trevor-Roper, Hexter quotes Raleigh, Bacon, and John Selden on the vast changes brought about by the Tudor statutes of retainers, alienations, and populations. The nobility's loss of feudal military power, Hexter argues, brought the rising gentry a freedom and independence that culminated in the rallying of parliamentary opposition under one of their number, John Pym, and finally in the Civil War. This is to say, the "rise of the gentry" is a chapter in the history of political liberty and military power as much as, or more than, it is a chapter in economic history. Without even mentioning Harrington by name, Hexter invokes his three main authorities on English history, revivifies his theory of historical causality based on the power to make war, and reproduces his concrete analysis of Tudor history! Whether this parallel is conscious or unconscious, Hexter's analysis is witty, lucid, and persuasive.

3. Harrington pieces these words together from the *Agreement,* from the modifications to it proposed by the Council of Officers, and from his own reading of the Leveller tracts. See Harrington 657n; Woodhouse 355–67.

4. The controversy over the meaning of *servant* in the seventeenth century continues. For a recent entry and a bibliography on earlier entries, see Anthony Arblaster's sympathetic critique of Macpherson's chapter on the Levellers.

5. William Lamont has found the only surviving record of Harrington's response to Baxter. Henry Hickman "informed Baxter that his *Holy Commonwealth* had almost murdered Harrington. The thought that Baxter had quoted Herodotus to make a point about the Roman army made Harrington laugh so much that medical attention was required" (Lamont, *Baxter* 199).

6. See Harrington's tract of 1659 entitled *A Discourse upon this saying: The Spirit of the Nation is not yet to be trusted with Liberty: lest it Introduce Monarchy, or invade the Liberty of Conscience* (735–45).

7. I do not intend to deny altogether an expressive or "ideological" (Mannheim's sense of the term) quality in Harrington's writing, which would allow us to see him as a spokesman for the gentry. Certainly, his utopian orders are amenable to a gentry-dominated state and are antagonistic to the rule of other classes or persons (an absolute monarchy, an aristocracy of blood or of grace, an undifferentiated people). But an attempt to champion the interests of one

class in the present is by no means incompatible with a wish to change that class into something else. Compare Engels's argument in *The Condition of the Working Class in England* that Communism sides with a certain class (the proletarians) on behalf of a postcapitalist, postbourgeois, and even postproletarian class that it hopes this alliance will bring into existence: "Communism rises above the enmity of classes, for it is a movement that embraces all humanity and not merely the working classes" (335). The next section will examine the disciplinary quality of this embrace in Harrington's writings.

8. I will not reproduce Macpherson's argument in detail here, but I will point to two places where I think it falters. First, Harrington's conception of "equality" is more political than economic in origin: it refers not to a market economy state in which there is equality of opportunity, but to a utopian state whose "equal" orders are impervious to sedition. There is little or no criticism of the tyranny of economic custom in Harrington. Second, it seems to me that at one point Macpherson's partial quotation of Harrington creates one of the "contradictions" he analyzes, and that the complete passage is consistent with the general run of Harrington's argument. Interested readers should compare Macpherson (188–89 and 189 n. 1) with Harrington (425). This point is the keystone in Macpherson's argument that Harrington's doctrine of the balance is so self-contradictory that it lessens his claim to consideration as a systematic political theorist (so that he remains only an unsystematic prophetic theorist of capitalism). In *Virtue, Commerce, and History* Pocock continues his argument with claims by Macpherson, Hill, and others that an ideology of possessive individualism dominated the later seventeenth century because of a revolution in both economic actuality and economic theory. At times Pocock seems to be constructing a very useful critique of such theories of historical expressive causality (one not altogether incompatible with some Marxisms—Louis Althusser's, for instance), saying that there is a complex seventeenth-century dialectic among economic reality, economic theory, and theories of political authority. But at other times he seems simply to be reversing this causality, suggesting that theories of political authority were at "the center" of the debate (and theories of property at the periphery), that "the notion of property might subserve that of authority," and that "the point is that *property* was a juridical term before it was an economic one" (58, 63–64, 56). Outside of some hypothetical history, it is difficult to conceive of a juridical sphere apart from and prior to an economic one. Pocock complicates matters even more by saying that "ideas about authority and ideas about property were independent variables" (59). Here he abandons his usual object of study (the history of complexly overlapping political languages) for the more traditional study of the history of political thought (which hides the polyvalence of statements by assigning them to governing "ideas").

9. Harrington proposes an unusual conversion as a solution to the perennial millennial problem of settling the Jews. They cannot be admitted into

Oceana, for they are perpetually unassimilable, but they could be settled in underpopulated Panopea (Ireland): "Though the Jews be now altogether for merchandise, yet in the land of Canaan (since their exile from whence they have not been landlords) they were altogether for agriculture; and there is no cause why a man should doubt but, having a fruitful country and good ports too, they would not be good at both. ... To receive the Jews after any other manner into a commonwealth were to maim it; for they of all nations never incorporate but, taking up the room of a limb, are of no use or office unto the body, while they suck the nourishment which would sustain a natural and useful member" (159). See Liljegren's "Harrington and the Jews." This is Harrington's only substantial recourse to the decrepit corporate fiction of the body politic. Here, as in so many other times and places, anti-semitism provides the occasion for the ceremonial airing of atavistic political fictions. On Harrington's attitude toward the Irish, compare the words of a latter-day Archon, Arthur James Balfour, in a memorandum of 1919: "For in Palestine we do not even propose to go through the form of consulting the wishes of the present inhabitants of the country, though the American Commission has been going through the forms of asking what they are. The four great powers are committed to Zionism and Zionism, be it right or wrong, good or bad, is rooted in age-long tradition, in present needs, in future hopes, of far profounder import than the desire and prejudices of the 700,000 Arabs who now inhabit that ancient land. In my opinion that is right" (Sykes 5). The utopist need consult neither the displaced population being settled nor the settled population being displaced, whether they are Utopia's "barbarian" neighbors, degenerate Algonquians, slothful popish Irish, "unnatural" and parasitic Jews, or Palestinian Arabs ruled by their "desires and prejudices" rather than by any true sense of a history and a national identity. Each remains a blank population that neither speaks nor writes but is spoken for and written on.

10. In a similar argument for regular elections, Winstanley says that "nature tells us that if water stand long, it corrupts" (540). Plockhoy argues for a rotational government in his communist utopia, with twelve men and women ruling each household, half retiring each six months, leaving the other half behind to instruct those who replace them (143).

11. James Cotton says, "In order rightly to understand Harrington's method it is necessary to take seriously his claim to be a practitioner of the art of 'political anatomy,' and perhaps the originator of that art" (418–19), but he does not say very much about what that art entails. William Petty, later a member of Harrington's Rota Club, used the term a good deal, but he seems to have had in mind more an examination of the functioning economic totality of a modern state than a historical study of the political principles of an ancient one. Charles Blitzer examines some relevant connections between Harrington and Harvey (89–108).

12. Harrington's scrupulous political anatomy uncovers an etymology that some genealogist of the democratic ideology of freedom of choice ought to

explore: "The first signification of the word *chirotonia* imports a certain lewd action of the hand, which seemeth also, by the Greek that renders it by the same word, to have been intimated by Isaiah, 58:9" (502).

13. Before Pocock's examination of Harrington's millennialism, the only historians to see significant connections between Harrington and the Puritan theocrats were J. W. Gough ("Harrington and Contemporary Thought") and Zera S. Fink (*The Classical Republicans*).

14. Harrington quarrels with the English translators of the Bible on this point: "*Haec est lex quam Moses proposuit* (Deut. 4:44); and whereas betwixt a precept and a command there is a large difference, in places more than I can stand to number, where the Latin hath it *praecipit Moses,* the English hath it: *Moses commanded*" (618n).

15. Harrington is understandably taken with Psalm 11:3: "If the foundations be destroyed, what can the righteous do?" He uses it as an epigraph to the first book of *The Art of Lawgiving* (Harrington 602).

16. Compare the rhetoric of a later secular political thinker who uses millenarian imagery (which evokes the woman of Revelation 12 who flees into the wilderness to escape the dragon) to unite a diverse audience in a program of secular/sacred military solidarity: "O ye that love mankind! Ye that dare oppose, not only the tyranny, but the tyrant, stand forth! Every spot of the old world is over-run with oppression. Freedom hath been hunted round the globe. Asia, and Africa, have long expelled her. —Europe regards her like a stranger, and England hath given her warning to depart. O! receive the fugitive, and prepare in time an asylum for mankind. . . . *The time hath found us*" (Paine, *Common Sense* 100).

17. Harrington's aphoristic judgment on *The Prince* in his *System of Politics* reveals another implicitly republican aspect of Machiavelli's work and suggests a promising starting point for an analysis of its rhetorical force (as opposed to its propositional content): "Take a juggler and commend his tricks never so much, yet if in so doing you show his tricks, you spoil him" (853–54). Like *Oceana* and many other utopias, *The Prince* is a prince-book with a subliminal message.

18. Here Harrington is actually translating Bacon's judgment in the *Advancement of Learning* on *The Republic* and *Utopia,* turning Bacon's criticism against his own *New Atlantis* as well. So far as I have found, Harrington refers to "utopia" only in his *Brief Directions,* where he says that he fears the models of republic government he has been describing will be dismissed as "chimeras or utopias" (590).

19. Harrington imagined that his sweat spontaneously generated insects, and he devised elaborate experiments to prove his theory. William Craig Diamond, after analyzing Harrington's brief treatise on this subject, entitled *The Mechanics of Philosophy,* finds it a coherent argument in the tradition of the "spiritual mechanics" of his day. Diamond also shows some illuminating connections between Harrington's natural and political philosophies. Like the Neoplatonic

natural philosophers, Harrington had a hard time finding a role for Christ in his system. But Diamond's argument that a Hermetic and Neoplatonic "spiritus" mediates between the "body" and the "soul" of Oceana is not very convincing, partly because Harrington's few references to the "spirit" of a polity reveal no consistent distinction between it and a polity's "soul," or political orders.

20. In a curious sense, Harrington's prophecy of his own authority was realized. While his writings lost their utopian and millenarian promise, they did not lose all their republican authority, for they became important parts of the Atlantic republican tradition well into the nineteenth century. See H. F. Russell-Smith's study of Harrington's influence in France and America, particularly during their national revolutions. See also Pocock's *Politics, Language and Time* (104–47), his *Machiavellian Moment* (401–552), and his "Historical Introduction" (128–52). Davis discusses a Harringtonian tradition of "utopian" (as opposed to "republican") writing in the later seventeenth century in such works as Sprigge's *Modest Plea* and the anonymous tracts *Chaos* and *The Free State of Noland* (Davis, *Utopia* 241–76).

Chapter 5

1. In his analysis of the two editions of *The Ready and Easy Way,* Stanley Stewart hides the anguished tone of Milton's argument here by identifying the Good Old Cause with the sincere persecutor Saul (whom Stewart prematurely converts into St. Paul), and the Royalists with Judas Iscariot and Simon Magus (215).

2. John Adams provides us with forthright, sputtering republican censure of Milton's model, the oligarchic implications of which tend to be occluded by Milton's contemporary critical apologists: "Can one read, without shuddering, this wild revery of the divine, immortal Milton? If no better systems of government had been proposed, it would have been no wonder that the people of England recalled the royal family, with all their errors, follies, and crimes about them. . . . What! A single assembly to govern England? an assembly of senators for life too? What! did Milton's ideas of liberty and free government extend no further than exchanging one house of lords for another, and making it supreme and perpetual?" (565). On the other hand, Adams admired Harrington's political theory, viewing it as a prophecy of the American Revolution.

3. Is this a sneer at Harrington, former gentleman of the bedchamber to Charles I?

4. William R. Parker reproduces the tract in facsimile in *Milton's Contemporary Reputation.*

5. Butler's raillery reveals something of the political subtext of that curiously obsessive scribbling against scribbling we encounter in the satire of the Restoration and the eighteenth century. What presents itself as a semiological disgust at the "dullness" of signifying words cut free from signified things and

from any animating imagination is in part a memory of the prolific and relatively uncensored presses of the Interregnum and the proposals for political action they produced.

6. In a further development of this case history, Freud brings us even closer to utopia considered as a rationalizing response to the traumatic displacements produced by warfare. A year later he observed the boy throwing his toys away from him and saying, "Go to the fwont!"—a reference to the absence of his father, who was then fighting at the front. Maddeningly, Freud resists seeing the formal parallel to the earlier game; through an Oedipus complex flip-flop, he claims that this game represents a genuine antipathy, the result of the fact that the boy did not wish to be disturbed "in his sole possession of his mother" (10).

7. Hawthorne's romantic typology of Puritanism in *The Blithedale Romance* gives us the most direct dystopian satire of Eliot. He shows the monomaniacal Hollingsworth mounting Eliot's Pulpit, a rock formation from which Eliot was said to have preached to the Indians two centuries before, in order to preach his philanthropic, feminist, and utopian dogmas. Hawthorne's narrative corrects his utopian presumption, for he winds up firmly committed to a traditional (and unhappy) marriage.

8. Hexter also groups Claude de Seyssel's *Monarchie de France* with *Utopia* and *The Prince* in this regard. More than any other Puritan utopist, Harrington combines More's and Machiavelli's peculiar kinds of political empiricism. As far as I can tell, Harrington refers to Romans 13 only once (204).

9. The "conflict" between More the proponent of an ideal state and More the persecutor of Protestant heretics thus finds its way into his ideal state itself.

10. J. C. Davis follows Milton in his possessive individualist critique of *Oceana*. Looking at Harrington's proposals for state limitations on the dynastic accumulation of property and on parents' powers over their children's education, Davis says that they amount to an attack on "the individual," not on a particular form of patriarchal plutocracy (*Utopia* 238). His entire study of early modern English utopia, in fact, is a self-avowed defense of the "possessive individualism" that Macpherson subjects to an ideological critique. In his concluding pages Davis says, "Man in his freedom can choose to choke the human race in a sea of pollution, to destroy and squander those resources on which human life upon this planet depends. . . . The utopians will offer to save us from any or all of these fates, but only at the price of freedom of choice. . . . And in the process man as a moral agent, a possessive individual, ceases to exist" (388). By this definition those men, women, and children who lack the ability to wreck the environment on a grand scale—that is to say, almost all living persons—have no moral agency. For instance, this definition of "man in his freedom" would seem to assign greater moral agency to the Union Carbide plant in Bhopal, India, than to the thousands of Indians who had no choice but to die when the plant released a cloud of toxic vapor.

11. See Thompson's study of the disciplinary reorganization of labor time

during early capitalism ("Time") and Davis's incisive discussion of the "full employment utopia" in the England of the later seventeenth century, which charts connections between utopia and the beginnings of modern factory discipline under Bellers and the Crowleys (*Utopia* 299–367). A critique of the contemporary tendency simply to equate "utopia" with the "totalitarian" communist state might begin with a historical and comparative examination of factory discipline in the East and the West.

12. See, for instance, the intelligent annotations in a seventeenth-century hand of the copy of Comenius's *Reformation of Schooles* (1642), reproduced by the Scolar Press: the annotations stop one-fifth of the way through. The role of a bored readership in the failure of the Puritan utopists should not be underestimated.

13. J. H. Hexter calls the penal discipline of the Polyleirites of More's Book 1 "the first of those attempts to conceive a wholly rational penology of which the Panopticon of that radical of radicals, Jeremy Bentham, was to be the most notorious" (*Vision* 131).

Works Cited

Adams, John. *The Works of John Adams*. Vol. 4. 1856. New York: AMS, 1971. 10 vols.

Adams, Robert M. "The Prince and the Phalanx." More 192–203.

Addison, Joseph. *The Works of the Right Honorable Joseph Addison*. Ed. Richard Hurd. Vol. 1. London, 1811. 6 vols.

Adorno, Theodor W. *Aesthetic Theory*. Trans. C. Lenhardt. Ed. Gretel Adorno and Rolf Tiedemann. The International Library of Phenomenological and Moral Sciences. London: Routledge, 1984.

———. *Negative Dialectics*. Trans. E. B. Ashton. New York: Seabury, 1979.

———. *Prisms*. Trans. Samuel Weber and Shierry Weber. London: Spearman, 1967.

Alsop, James. "Gerrard Winstanley's Later Life." *Past and Present* 82 (1979): 73–81.

Andreae, Johann Valentin. *Christianopolis: An Ideal State of the Seventeenth Century*. Trans. and ed. Felix Emil Held. New York: Oxford UP, 1916.

Arato, Andrew, and Eike Gebhardt, eds. *The Essential Frankfurt School Reader*. New York: Continuum, 1982.

Arblaster, Anthony. "Revolution, the Levellers, and C. B. Macpherson." *1642: Literature and Power in the Seventeenth Century*. Ed. Francis Barker et al. Proceedings of the Essex Conference on the Sociology of Literature, July 1980. Essex: U of Essex, 1981. 220–37.

The Armies Vindication of this last Change. London, 1659.

Aspinwall, William. *A Brief Description of the Fifth Monarchy, or Kingdome, That shortly is to come into the World.* London, 1653.

Aubrey, John. *Aubrey's Brief Lives.* Ed. Oliver Lawson Dick. London: Secker, 1949.

Augustine. *On Christian Doctrine.* Trans. D. W. Robertson, Jr. New York: Liberal Arts, 1958.

Avineri, Shlomo. "War and Slavery in More's *Utopia.*" *International Review of Social History* 7 (1962): 260–90.

Axtell, James. "The Ethnohistory of America: A Review Essay." *William and Mary Quarterly* 3rd ser. 35 (1978): 110–44.

Aylmer, G. E., ed. "*England's Spirit Unfoulded: Or, An Incouragement to take the Engagement.* A Newly Discovered Pamphlet by Gerrard Winstanley." *Past and Present* 40 (1968): 3–15. Webster, *Revolution* 109–23.

————, ed. *The Interregnum: The Quest for Settlement, 1646–1660.* London: Archon, 1972.

Bacon, Francis. *The Works of Francis Bacon.* 14 vols. Ed. James Spedding, Robert Leslie Ellis, and Douglas Denon Heath. London, 1868–1901.

Barker, Arthur E. *Milton and the Puritan Dilemma, 1641–1660,* Toronto: U of Toronto P, 1942.

Baxter, Richard. *Reliquiae Baxterianae: Or, Mr. Richard Baxter's Narrative of the Most Memorable Passages of His Life and Times.* London, 1696.

————. *Richard Baxter and Puritan Politics.* Ed. Richard B. Schlatter. New Brunswick, NJ: Rutgers UP, 1957.

Baxter, Richard, and John Eliot. "Some Unpublished Correspondence of the Rev. Richard Baxter and the Rev. John Eliot, 'The Apostle to the American Indians,' 1656–1682." Ed. F. J. Powicke. *Bulletin of the John Rylands Library* 15 (1931): 138–76, 442–66.

Bellamy, Edward. *Looking Backward: 2000–1887.* 1888. Ed. Cecelia Tichi. Harmondsworth: Penguin, 1982.

Bercovitch, Sacvan. *The American Jeremiad.* Madison: U of Wisconsin P, 1978.

————. *The Puritan Origins of the American Self.* New Haven: Yale UP, 1975.

————. "Typology in Puritan New England: The Williams-Cotton Controversy Reassessed." *American Quarterly* 19th ser. 2 (1967): 166–91.

Berger, Harry, Jr. "The Renaissance Imagination: Second World and Green World." *Centennial Review* 9 (1965): 63–74. Rpt. as "[*Utopia*: Game, Chart, or Prayer]." More 203–12.

Berneri, Marie Louise. *Journey Through Utopia.* New York: Schocken, 1971.

Bernstein, Eduard. *Cromwell and Communism: Socialism and Democracy in the Great English Revolution.* Trans. H. J. Stenning. London: Allen, 1930.

Blitzer, Charles. *An Immortal Commonwealth: The Political Thought of James Harrington.* Yale Studies in Political Science 2. New Haven: Yale UP, 1960.

Bowden, Henry W., and James P. Ronda, eds. Introduction. *John Eliot's Indian Dialogues: A Study in Cultural Interaction.* By John Eliot. Contributions in American History 88. Westport, CT: Greenwood, 1980.

Boyle, Robert. *Works.* 6 vols. Ed. Thomas Birch. London, 1772.

Bradford, William. *Of Plymouth Plantation, 1620–1647.* New York: Modern Library, 1981.

Burton, Thomas. *Diary of Thomas Burton.* Ed. John Towell Rutt. Vol. 3. London, 1828. 4 vols.

Bush, Douglas. *English Literature in the Earlier Seventeenth Century, 1600–1660.* Oxford History of English Literature 5. New York: Oxford UP, 1945.

Butler, Samuel. *Characters and Passages from Notebooks.* Ed. A. R. Waller. Cambridge: Cambridge UP, 1908.

Byington, Ezra Hoyt. *The Puritan as a Colonist and Reformer.* Boston, 1899.

Calvin, John. *On God and Political Duty.* Ed. John T. McNeill. 2nd ed. The Library of Liberal Arts. Indianapolis: Bobbs, 1956.

Campanella, Tommaso. *La Città del Sole: Dialogo Poetico / The City of the Sun: A Poetical Dialogue.* Trans. Daniel J. Donno. Berkeley and Los Angeles: U of California P, 1981.

Capp, B. S. *The Fifth Monarchy Men: A Study in Seventeenth-Century English Millenarianism.* London: Faber, 1972.

The Censure of the Rota Upon Mr Miltons Book, Entituled, The Ready and Easie Way to Establish a Free Common-wealth. 1660. Parker, n.p.

Chambers, R. W. *Thomas More.* New York: Harcourt, 1935.

Cohn, Norman. *The Pursuit of the Millennium: Revolutionary Millenarians and Mystical Anarchists of the Middle Ages.* Rev. ed. New York: Oxford UP, 1970.

Comenius, John Amos. *The Analytical Didactic of Comenius.* Trans. Vladimir Jelinek. Chicago: U of Chicago P, 1953.

———. *The Great Didactic of John Amos Comenius.* Trans. M. W. Keatinge. 1910. New York: Russell and Russell, 1967.

———. *A Reformation of Schooles.* Trans. Samuel Hartlib. 1642. English Linguistics, 1500–1800 143. Menston, Eng: Scolar, 1969.

———. *The Way of Light.* 1668. Trans. E. T. Campagnac. Liverpool: Liverpool UP, 1938.

Coolidge, John. "Marvell and Horace." *Modern Philology* 63 (1965): 111–20.

Corbett, Margery, and Ronald Lightbown. *The Comely Frontispiece: The Emblematic Title-Page in England, 1550–1660.* London: Routledge, 1979.

Cotton, James. "James Harrington and Thomas Hobbes." *Journal of the History of Ideas* 42 (1981): 407–21.

Cotton, John. *An Abstract of the Lawes of New England* [*Moses His Judicials*]. 1641. Force, vol. 3, separate pagination.

Davis, J. C. "Pocock's Harrington: Grace, Nature and Art in the Classical Republicanism of James Harrington." *Historical Journal* 24 (1981): 683–97.

———. *Utopia and the Ideal Society: A Study of English Utopian Writing, 1516–1700.* Cambridge: Cambridge UP, 1981.

"Dedications to the Rev. John Eliot's Indian Version of the Old and New Testament." *Collections of the Massachusetts Historical Society* 1st ser. 7 (1800): 222–28.

Defoe, Daniel. *Robinson Crusoe.* Ed. Michael Shinagel. New York: Norton, 1975.

Diamond, William Craig. "Natural Philosophy in Harrington's Political Thought." *Journal of the History of Philosophy* 16 (1978): 387–98.

Donner, H. W. *Introduction to Utopia.* London: Sidgwick, 1945.

Donno, Elizabeth Story, ed. *Andrew Marvell: The Complete Poems.* Harmondsworth: Penguin, 1972.

Drake, Samuel G. *The Book of the Indians: Or, Biography and History of the Indians of North America, from Its First Discovery to the Year 1841.* Boston, 1841.

Dreyfus, Hubert L., and Paul Rabinow. *Michel Foucault: Beyond Structuralism and Hermeneutics.* 2nd ed. Chicago: U of Chicago P, 1983.

Dunton, John. "Extracts from *The Life and Errors of John Dunton, Late Citizen of London: Written by Himself in Solitude.*" 1705. *Collections of the Massachusetts Historical Society* 2nd ser. 2 (1805): 97–124.

Eliade, Mircea. "Paradise and Utopia: Mythical Geography and Eschatology." Manuel 260–80.

Eliav-Feldon, Miriam. *Realistic Utopias: The Ideal Imaginary Societies of the Renaissance, 1516–1630.* Oxford: Clarendon, 1982.

Eliot, John. "An Account of Indian Churches in New England." *Collections of the Massachusetts Historical Society* 1st ser. 10 (1809): 124–29.

———. *A Brief Narrative of the Progress of the Gospel Among the Indians in New-England, in the Year 1670.* 1671. Ed. W. T. R. Marvin. Boston, 1868.

———. *The Christian Commonwealth: Or, The Civil Policy of the Rising Kingdom of Jesus Christ. Written Before the Interruption of the Government.* 1659. *Collections of the Massachusetts Historical Society* 3rd ser. 9 (1846): 127–64.

———. *Communion of Churches.* Cambridge, Mass., 1665.

———. *The Dying Speeches of Several Indians.* Cambridge, Mass., 1680.

———. "From Rev. John Eliot." Letter to the Commissioners at Hartford,

25 June 1664. *Public Records of the Colony of Connecticut, May 1678–June 1689*. Hartford, 1859. 483–86.

————. *A Further Accompt of the Progresse of the Gospel amongst the Indians in New-England*. London, 1659.

————. *A Further Account of the Progresse of the Gospel: A Selection of the Confessions made by several Indians*. London, 1660.

————. *Indian Dialogues*. 1671. Bowden and Ronda 57–162.

————. *The Indian Grammar Begun*. 1666. *Collections of the Massachusetts Historical Society* 2nd ser. 9 (1832): 243–366.

————. *The Indian Primer: Or, The way of training up of our Indian Youth in the good knowledge of God*. 1669. Ed. John Small. Edinburgh, 1877.

————. *John Eliot and the Indians, 1652–1657: Being Letters Addressed to Rev. Jonathan Hanmer of Barnstaple, England*. Ed. Wilberforce Eames. New York: Adams, 1915.

————. "John Eliot to John Winthrop, Jr." Letter of 24 May 1675. *Collections of the Massachusetts Historical Society* 5th ser. 1 (1871): 424–26.

————. "The Learned Conjectures of the Reverend Mr. John Eliot touching the Americas." Thorowgood, separate pagination.

————. "Letters from Rev. John Eliot of Roxbury to Hon. Robert Boyle." *Collections of the Massachusetts Historical Society* 1st ser. 3 (1794): 177–88.

————. "Letters of the Rev. John Eliot, the Apostle to the Indians." *New-England Historical and Genealogical Register* 36 (1882): 291–97.

————. *The Logic Primer*. 1672. Ed. Wilberforce Eames. Cleveland: Burrows, 1904.

————. "Rev. John Eliot's Records of the First Church in Roxbury, Mass." *New-England Historical and Genealogical Register* 33 (1879): 62–65, 236–39, 295–99, 413–16.

"Eliot, John." *American Authors, 1600–1900: A Biographical Dictionary of American Literature*. New York: Wilson, 1938.

Elliott, Robert C. *The Shape of Utopia: Studies in a Literary Genre*. Chicago: U of Chicago P, 1970.

Emerson, Everett, ed. *Letters from New England: The Massachusetts Bay Colony, 1629–1638*. Amherst: U of Massachusetts P, 1976.

Emerson, Roger L. "American Indians, Frenchmen, and Scots Philosophers." *Studies in Eighteenth-Century Culture* 9 (1979): 211–36.

Empson, William. *Milton's God*. Norfolk, CT: New Directions, 1961.

Engels, Friedrich. *The Condition of the Working Class in England*. Trans. and ed. W. O. Henderson and W. H. Chaloner. Stanford: Stanford UP, 1958.

Farley, Frank Edgar. "The Dying Indian." *Anniversary Papers, by Colleagues and Pupils of George Lyman Kittredge*. 1913. New York: Russell and Russell, 1967. 251–60.

Felt, Joseph B. "Memoir of Hugh Peters." *New-England Historical and Genealogical Register* 5 (1851): 9–20, 231–94, 415–39.

Filmer, Robert. *Patriarcha and Other Political Works.* Ed. and Introd. Peter Laslett. Oxford: Blackwell, 1949.

Fink, Zera S. *The Classical Republicans: An Essay in the Recovery of a Pattern of Thought in Seventeenth-Century England.* 2nd ed. Evanston, IL: Northwestern UP, 1962.

Firth, C. H. *Cromwell's Army: A History of the English Soldier During the Civil Wars, the Commonwealth, and the Protectorate.* Introd. P. H. Hardacre. London: Methuen, 1902.

Fish, Stanley. *Is There a Text in This Class? The Authority of Interpretive Communities.* Cambridge: Harvard UP, 1980.

———. *The Living Temple: George Herbert and Catechizing.* Berkeley and Los Angeles: U of California P, 1978.

———. *Self-Consuming Artifacts: The Experience of Seventeenth-Century Literature.* Berkeley and Los Angeles: U of California P, 1972.

Fixler, Michael. *Milton and the Kingdoms of God.* Evanston, IL: Northwestern UP, 1964.

Fogarty, Robert S., ed. *Dictionary of American Communal and Utopian History.* Westport, CN: Greenwood, 1980.

Force, Peter, ed. *Tracts and Other Papers Relating Principally to the Origin, Settlement, and Progress of the Colonies in North America, from the Discovery of the Country to the Year 1776.* N.d. Gloucester, MA: Smith, 1963. 4 vols.

Ford, John W., ed. *Some Correspondence Between the Governors and Treasurers of the New England Company in London and the Commissioners of the United Colonies in America, the Missionaries of the Company, and Others Between the Years 1657 and 1712.* 1886. New York: Franklin, 1970.

Foster, Douglas. "Guatemala: On the Green Path." *Mother Jones* 10.9 (1985): 12–16.

Foucault, Michel. *Discipline and Punish: The Birth of the Prison.* Trans. Alan Sheridan. New York: Pantheon, 1977.

———. *The Foucault Reader.* Ed. Paul Rabinow. New York: Pantheon, 1984.

———. *The History of Sexuality, Volume 1: An Introduction.* Trans. Robert Hurley. New York: Pantheon, 1978.

———. *Power/Knowledge: Selected Interviews and Other Writings, 1972–1977.* Ed. Colin Gordon. Trans. Colin Gordon, Leo Marshall, John Mepham, and Kate Soper. New York: Pantheon, 1980.

———. "Structuralism and Post-Structuralism: An Interview with Michel Foucault." Ed. Gérard Raulet. Trans. Jeremy Harding. *Telos* 55 (1983): 195–211.

————. "War in the Filigree of Peace: Course Summary." Trans. Ian Mcleod. *Oxford Literary Review* 4 (1980): 15–19.

Francis, Convers. *Life of John Eliot, The Apostle to the Indians.* The Library of American Biography 5. Boston, 1836.

Freud, Sigmund. *Beyond the Pleasure Principle.* Trans. James Strachey. New York: Norton, 1961.

————. *Totem and Taboo.* Trans. James Strachey. New York: Norton, 1950.

Frye, Northrop. *Anatomy of Criticism: Four Essays.* Princeton: Princeton UP, 1957.

————. "Varieties of Literary Utopia." Manuel 25–49.

Garin, Eugenio. *Italian Humanism: Philoscphy and Civic Life in the Renaissance.* Trans. Peter Munz. New York: Harper, 1965.

[Gauden, John]. *Eikon Basilike: The Portraiture of His Sacred Majesty in His Solitudes and Sufferings.* Ed. Philip A. Knachel. Ithaca: Cornell UP, 1966.

Gee, Edward, the elder. *A Plea for Non-Scribers.* N.p., 1650.

Gibson, R. W. *St. Thomas More: A Preliminary Bibliography of His Works and of Moreana to the Year 1750. With a Bibliography of Utopiana Compiled by R. W. Gibson and J. Max Patrick.* New Haven: Yale UP, 1961.

Girard, René. *Violence and the Sacred.* Trans. Patrick Gregory. Baltimore: Johns Hopkins UP, 1977.

Goldberg, Jonathan. *James I and the Politics of Literature: Jonson, Shakespeare, Donne, and Their Contemporaries.* Baltimore: Johns Hopkins UP, 1983.

Gooch, G. P. *English Democratic Ideas in the Seventeenth Century.* 2nd ed. Cambridge: Cambridge UP, 1927.

Gookin, Daniel, the elder. *An Historical Account of the Doings and Sufferings of the Christian Indians in New England, in the years 1675, 1676, 1677.* 1836. New York: Arno, 1972.

————. *Historical Collections of the Indians in New England.* 1674. *Collections of the Massachusetts Historical Society* 1st ser. 1 (1792): 141–229.

Gott, Samuel [attrib. to John Milton]. *Nova Solyma, The Ideal City: Or, Jerusalem Regained.* 2 vols. Ed. and trans. Walter Begley. London: Murray, 1902.

Gough, J. W. "Harrington and Contemporary Thought." *Political Science Quarterly* 45 (1930): 395–404.

————. *The Social Contract: A Critical Study of Its Development.* Oxford: Clarendon, 1936.

Greenblatt, Stephen. "Invisible Bullets: Renaissance Authority and Its Subversion." *Glyph* 8 (1981): 40–61.

————. "Learning to Curse: Aspects of Linguistic Colonialism in the Sixteenth Century." *First Images of America.* Vol 2. Ed. Fredi Chiappelli. Berkeley and Los Angeles: U of California P, 1976. 2 vols. 561–80.

———. "Murdering Peasants: Status, Genre, and the Representation of Rebellion." *Representations* 1 (1983): 1–30.

———. *Renaissance Self-Fashioning: From More to Shakespeare.* Chicago: U of Chicago P, 1980.

Gura, Philip F. *A Glimpse of Sion's Glory: Puritan Radicalism in New England, 1620–1660.* Middletown, CN: Wesleyan UP, 1984.

Hale, David George. *The Body Politic: A Political Metaphor in Renaissance English Literature.* The Hague: Mouton, 1971.

Hall, Joseph. *Another World and Yet the Same: Bishop Joseph Hall's* Mundus Alter et Idem. Yale Studies in English 190. Trans. John Millar Wands. New Haven: Yale UP, 1981.

Haller, William. *Foxe's Book of Martyrs and the Elect Nation.* London: Cape, 1963.

———. *The Rise of Puritanism.* New York: Torchbooks-Harper, 1957.

Haller, William, and Godfrey Davies, eds. *The Leveller Tracts, 1647–1653.* 1944. Gloucester, MA: Smith, 1964.

Halpern, Richard. "The Poetics of Primitive Accumulation." Unpublished typescript.

Hansot, Elisabeth. *Perfection and Progress: Two Modes of Utopian Thought.* Cambridge: MIT P, 1974.

Harrington, James. *The Political Works of James Harrington.* Ed. J. G. A. Pocock. Cambridge: Cambridge UP, 1977.

Harriot, Thomas. *A Briefe and True Report of the New Found Land of Virginia.* 1590. New York: Dover, 1972.

Harvey, William. *Anatomical Exercitations concerning the Generation of Living Creatures.* London, 1653.

Hatch, Nathan O. *The Sacred Cause of Liberty: Republican Thought and the Millennium in Revolutionary New England.* New Haven: Yale UP, 1977.

Hawthorne, Nathaniel. *The Blithedale Romance.* Ed. Seymour Gross and Rosalie Murphy. New York: Norton, 1978.

Hegel, G. W. F. *The Philosophy of History.* Trans. J. Sibree. New York: Dover, 1956.

Hexter, J. H. "Storm Over the Gentry." *Encounter* 10.5 (1958): 22–34.

———. *The Vision of Politics on the Eve of the Reformation: More, Machiavelli, and Seyssell.* New York: Basic, 1973.

Hill, Christopher. *Change and Continuity in Seventeenth-Century England.* Cambridge: Harvard UP, 1975.

———. *The Experience of Defeat: Milton and Some Contemporaries.* New York: Viking, 1984.

———. *Puritanism and Revolution: Studies in Interpretation of the English Revolution of the 17th Century.* London: Secker, 1958.

————. *Society and Puritanism in Pre-Revolutionary England.* 2nd ed. New York: Schocken, 1964.

————. *The World Turned Upside Down: Radical Ideas during the English Revolution.* New York: Viking, 1972.

Hobbes, Thomas. *Leviathan.* 1651. Ed. Michael Oakeshott. Oxford: Blackwell, n.d.

Holloway, Mark. *Heavens on Earth: Utopian Communities in America, 1680–1880.* London: Turnstile, 1951.

Holquist, Michael. "How to Play Utopia: Some Brief Notes on the Distinctiveness of Utopian Fiction." *Yale French Studies* 41 (1968): 106–23.

Holstun, James. "Tragic Superfluity in *Coriolanus.*" *ELH* 50 (1983): 485–507.

Homer. *The Odyssey.* Trans. Robert Fitzgerald. With drawings by Hans Erni. Garden City, NY: Doubleday, 1961.

Horkheimer, Max, and Theodor W. Adorno. *Dialectic of Enlightenment.* Trans. John Cumming. New York: Seabury, 1972.

Howe, Irving, ed. *1984 Revisited: Totalitarianism in Our Century.* New York: Harper, 1983.

Hubbard, William. *A General History of New England from the Discovery to MDCLXXX.* 1680. *Collections of the Massachusetts Historical Society* 2nd ser. 6 (1815): 1–768.

Huddleston, Lee Eldridge. *Origins of the American Indians: European Concepts, 1492–1729.* Austin: U of Texas P, 1967.

Huffman, Clifford C. Coriolanus *in Context.* Lewisburg, PA: Bucknell UP, 1971.

Huizinga, Johan. *Homo Ludens: A Study of the Play-Element in Culture.* Boston: Beacon, 1950.

Hume, David. *Theory of Politics.* Edinburgh: Nelson, 1951.

Hunter, J. Paul. "Friday as a Convert: Defoe and the Accounts of Indian Missionaries." *Review of English Studies* ns 14.55 (1963): 243–48.

Hutchinson, Thomas. *The History of the Colony and Province of Massachusetts Bay.* Vol 1. Cambridge: Harvard UP, 1936. 3 vols.

Huxley, Aldous. *Brave New World.* New York: Harper, 1939.

Jameson, Fredric. "Of Island and Trenches: Naturalization [sic for Neutralization] and the Production of Utopian Discourse." Rev. of *Utopiques: Jeux d'Espaces,* by Louis Marin. *Diacritics* (1977): 2–21.

————. *The Political Unconscious: Narrative as a Socially Symbolic Act.* Ithaca: Cornell UP, 1981.

Jay, Martin. *The Dialectical Imagination: A History of the Frankfurt School and the Institute of Social Research, 1923–1950.* Boston: Little, 1973.

Jennings, Francis. *The Invasion of America: Indians, Colonialism, and the Cant of Conquest.* Chapel Hill: U of North Carolina P, 1975.

Jordan, W. K. *The Development of Religious Toleration in England.* Vol. 3. 1932. Gloucester, MA: Smith, 1965. 4 vols.

Kafka, Franz. *The Penal Colony: Stories and Short Pieces.* Trans. Willa Muir and Edwin Muir. New York: Schocken, 1961.

Kantorowicz, Ernst H. *The King's Two Bodies: A Study in Mediaeval Political Theology.* Princeton: Princeton UP, 1957.

Kautsky, Karl. *Thomas More and His Utopia.* Trans. H. J. Stenning. New York: International, 1927.

Kellaway, William. *The New England Company, 1649–1776: Missionary Society to the American Indians.* New York: Barnes, 1962.

Kelly, J. Thomas. *Thorns on the Tudor Rose: Monks, Rogues, Vagabonds, and Sturdy Beggars.* Jackson: UP of Mississippi, 1977.

Kirkpatrick, Jeane J. *Dictatorship and Double Standards.* New York and Washington, D.C.: American Enterprise Institute and Simon & Schuster, 1982.

Kuhn, Thomas S. *The Structure of Scientific Revolutions.* 2nd ed. International Encyclopedia of Unified Science 2.2. Chicago: U of Chicago P, 1970.

Lamont, William M. *Godly Rule: Politics and Religion, 1603–1660.* London: Macmillan; New York: St. Martin's, 1969.

———. *Richard Baxter and the Millennium: Protestant Imperialism and the English Revolution.* London: Croom Helm; Totowa, NJ: Rowman, 1979.

Langdon, Samuel. *The Republic of the Israelites: An Example to the American States.* 1788. *The American Republic and Ancient Israel.* New York: Arno, 1977. Separate pagination.

Lasky, Melvin J. *Utopia and Revolution.* Chicago: U of Chicago P, 1976.

Le Guin, Ursula K. *The Dispossessed.* New York: Avon, 1974.

Lem, Stanislas. *Solaris.* Trans. Joanna Kilmartin and Steve Cox. New York; Berkeley, 1971.

Lewalski, Barbara K. "Milton: Political Beliefs and Polemical Methods, 1659–1660." *PMLA* 74 (1959): 161–202.

Lewis, C. S. *English Literature in the Sixteenth Century Excluding Drama.* The Oxford History of English Literature 3. Oxford: Clarendon, 1954. 167–71. Rpt. as "[A Jolly Invention]," More 217–20.

Liljegren, S. B. *A French Draft Constitution of 1792 Modelled on James Harrington's* Oceana. Lund, Swed.: C. W. K. Gleerup, 1932.

———. "Harrington and the Jews." *Humanistska Venenskapssamfundet i Lund Arsberättelse* 4 (1931–1932): 65–92.

———, ed. *James Harrington's* Oceana. Heidelberg: Carl Winters Universitätsbuchhandlung, 1924.

Lincoln, Charles H., ed. *Narratives of the Indian Wars, 1675–1699.* New York: Barnes, 1913.

Low, Anthony. "Milton, *Paradise Regained,* and Georgic." *PMLA* 98 (1983): 152–69.

McGinn, Bernard. "Early Apocalypticism: The Ongoing Debate." Patrides and Wittreich 2–39.

Machiavelli, Niccolò. *The Discourses.* Trans. Leslie J. Walker, S.J. Ed. Bernard Crick. Harmondsworth: Penguin, 1970.

——. *Machiavelli: The Chief Works, and Others.* Trans. Allan Gilbert. Vol. 2. Durham, NC: Duke UP, 1965. 3 vols.

——. *The Prince.* Trans. George Bull. Baltimore: Penguin, 1961.

Maclear, J. F. "New England and the Fifth Monarchy: The Quest for the Millennium in Early American Puritanism." *William and Mary Quarterly* 3rd ser. 32 (1975): 223–60.

McLuhan, Marshall. *The Gutenberg Galaxy: The Making of Typographic Man.* Toronto: U of Toronto P, 1962.

McNeill, John T. "Natural Law in the Teaching of the Reformers." *Journal of Religion* 26 (1946): 168–82.

Macpherson, C. B. *The Political Theory of Possessive Individualism: Hobbes to Locke.* Oxford: Clarendon, 1962.

Mannheim, Karl. *Ideology and Utopia: An Introduction to the Sociology of Knowledge.* Trans. Louis Wirth and Edward Shils. New York: Harvest-Harcourt, 1936.

Manuel, Frank E., ed. *Utopias and Utopian Thought.* Boston: Houghton; Cambridge, Mass.: Riverside, 1966.

Manuel, Frank E., and Fritzie P. Manuel. *Utopian Thought in the Western World.* Cambridge: Belknap-Harvard UP, 1979.

Martyr, Peter [Pietro Martire d'Anghiera]. *The Decades of the Newe Worlde, or Weste India.* Trans. Richard Eden. 1555. Ann Arbor: University Microfilms, 1966.

Marvell, Andrew. *The Poems and Letters of Andrew Marvell.* Ed. H. M. Margoliouth, Pierre Legouis, and E. E. Duncan-Jones. 3rd ed. Vol. 1. Oxford: Clarendon, 1971. 2 vols.

Marx, Karl. *Capital: A Critique of Political Economy.* Ed. Frederick Engels. Trans. Samuel Moore and Edward Aveling. Vol. 1. New York: International, 1967. 3 vols.

Marx, Karl, and Friedrich Engels. *The Communist Manifesto.* Harmondsworth: Penguin, 1967.

Mather, Cotton. *Magnalia Christi Americana.* 2 vols. 1853–1855. New York: Russell and Russell, 1967.

Mazzeo, Joseph A. *Renaissance and Seventeenth-Century Studies.* New York: Columbia UP; London: Routledge, 1964.

Medawar, Peter. "'The Effecting of All Things Possible.'" *Listener* 82.2114 (1969): 437–41.

Meek, Ronald L. *Social Science and the Ignoble Savage.* Cambridge: Cambridge UP, 1976.

Mill, John Stuart. *On Liberty.* Ed. Alburey Castell. Arlington Heights, IL: AHM, 1947.

Miller, Perry. *Errand into the Wilderness.* 1956. New York: Torchbooks-Harper, 1964.

————. *The New England Mind: From Colony to Province.* Cambridge: Belknap-Harvard UP, 1953.

————. *The New England Mind: The Seventeenth Century.* Cambridge: Belknap-Harvard UP, 1939.

Miller, Perry, and Thomas H. Johnson, eds. *The Puritans: A Sourcebook of Their Writings.* Vol. 1. 1938. New York: Torchbooks-Harper, 1963, 2 vols.

Milner, Andrew. *John Milton and the English Revolution: A Study in the Sociology of Literature.* Totowa, NJ: Barnes, 1981.

Milton, John. *Complete Poetry and Major Prose.* Ed. Merritt Y. Hughes. Indianapolis: Odyssey, 1957.

————. *Complete Prose Works of John Milton.* Gen ed. Don M. Wolfe. 8 vols. New Haven: Yale UP, 1953–1983.

Minter, David. *The Interpreted Design as a Structural Principle in American Prose.* New Haven: Yale UP, 1969. 50–66. Rpt. as "The Puritan Jeremiad as a Literary Form." *The American Puritan Imagination: Essays in Revaluation.* Ed. Sacvan Bercovitch. Cambridge: Cambridge UP, 1974. 45–55.

Montaigne, Michel de. *Essays.* Trans. J. M. Cohen. Harmondsworth: Penguin, 1958.

Montrose, Louis Adrian. "Of Gentlemen and Shepherds: The Politics of Elizabethan Pastoral Form" *ELH* 50 (1983): 415–59.

More, Thomas. *Utopia.* Trans. and ed. Robert M. Adams. New York: Norton. 1975.

Morgan, Arthur E. *Nowhere Was Somewhere: How History Makes Utopias and How Utopias Make History.* Chapel Hill: U of North Carolina P, 1946.

Morgan, Edmund S. *Visible Saints: The History of a Puritan Idea.* New York: New York UP, 1963.

Morison, Samuel Eliot. *Builders of the Bay Colony.* Boston: Sentry-Houghton, n.d.

Morris, William. *News from Nowhere: Or, An Epoch of Rest, Being Some Chapters from a Utopian Romance.* 1891. New York: Vanguard, 1926.

Morrison, Kenneth M. "'That Art of Coyning Christians': John Eliot and the Praying Indians of Massachusetts." *Ethnohistory* 21 (1974): 77–92.

Morton, A. L. *The English Utopia.* London: Lawrence, 1952.

Morton, Thomas. *New English Canaan: Or, New Canaan.* 1637. Force, vol. 2, separate pagination.

Mumford, Lewis, "Utopia, The City and The Machine." Manuel 3–24.

Nedham, Marchamont. *The Case of the Commonwealth of England, Stated.* Ed. Philip A. Knachel. Charlottesville: U of Virginia P, 1969.

————. *Mercurius Politicus* 352–56 (March 5, 1657–April 9, 1657). *The English Revolution III, Newsbooks 5, Volume 15:* Mercurius Politicus, *1657.* Ed. Peter Thomas. London: Cornmarket, 1971. 37–116.

Negley, Glenn. *Utopian Literature: A Bibliography, with a Supplementary Listing of Works Influential in Utopian Thought.* Lawrence: Regents P of Kansas, 1977.

Negley, Glenn, and J. Max Patrick, eds. *The Quest for Utopia: An Anthology of Imaginary Societies.* New York: Schuman, 1952.

Neville, Henry. *The Isle of Pines.* 1668. *The Isle of Pines, 1668: An Essay in Bibliography.* Ed. Worthington Chauncey Ford. Boston: The Club of Odd Volumes, 1920.

New-Englands First Fruits. 1643. Samuel Eliot Morison. *The Founding of Harvard College.* Cambridge: Harvard UP, 1935. 418–47.

Nietzsche, Friedrich. The Birth of Tragedy *and* The Genealogy of Morals. Trans. Francis Golffing. Garden City, NY: Anchor-Doubleday, 1956.

Orwell, George. *Nineteen Eighty-Four.* 2nd ed. Ed. Irving Howe. New York: Harcourt, 1982.

Paine, Thomas. *Common Sense.* Ed. Isaac Kramnick. Harmondsworth: Penguin, 1976.

Parker, William R. *Milton's Contemporary Reputation.* 1940. Folcroft, PA: Folcroft, 1969.

Parrington, Vernon Louis, Jr. *American Dreams: A Study of American Utopias.* 2nd ed. 1947. New York: Russell and Russell: 1964.

Patrides, C. A., and Joseph Wittreich, eds. *The Apocalypse in English Renaissance Thought and Literature: Patterns, Antecedents, and Repercussions.* Ithaca: Cornell UP, 1984.

Patterson, Annabel M. *Marvell and the Civic Crown.* Princeton: Princeton UP, 1978.

Pearce, Roy Harvey. *The Savages of America: A Study of the Indian and the Idea of Civilization.* Rev. ed. Baltimore: Johns Hopkins UP, 1965.

Pearl, Valerie. "Puritans and Poor Relief: The London Workhouse, 1649–1660." *Puritans and Revolutionaries: Essays in Seventeenth-Century History Presented to Christopher Hill.* Ed. Donald Pennington and Keith Thomas. Oxford, Clarendon, 1978. 206–32.

Perrot, Michelle, ed. *L'Impossible Prison: Recherches sur le Système Pénitentiarire au XIXe Siècle.* Paris: Seuil, 1980.

Phelan, John Leddy. *The Millennial Kingdom of the Franciscans in the New World: A Study of the Writings of Gerónimo de Mendieta (1525–1604).* U of California Publications in History 52. Berkeley and Los Angeles: U of California P, 1956.

Pilling, James Constantine. *Bibliography of the Algonquian Languages.* Washington, DC: Government Printing Office, 1891.

Plato, *Plato 6: The Republic.* Trans. Paul Shorey. 2 vols. The Loeb Classical Library. Cambridge: Harvard UP; London: Heinemann, 1928, 1930.

Plattes, Gabriel [attrib. to Samuel Hartlib]. *A Description of the Famous Kingdome of Macaria.* 1641. Webster, *Hartlib* 79–90.

Plockhoy, Pieter Cornelisz. *Plockhoy from Zurik-zee: The Study of a Dutch Reformer in Puritan England and Colonial America.* Ed. and introd. Leland Harder and Marvin Harder. Mennonite Historical Series 2. Newton, KS: Board of Education and Publication, 1952.

Plutarch. *The Lives of the Noble Greeks and Romans.* Trans. John Dryden and Arthur Hugh Clough. 1864. New York: Modern Library, n.d.

Pocock, J. G. A. *The Ancient Constitution and the Feudal Law: A Study of English Historical Thought in the Seventeenth Century.* 1957. New York: Norton, 1967.

————. "Contexts for the study of James Harrington." *Il Pensiero Politico* 11 (1978): 20–35.

————. "Historical Introduction." Harrington 1–152.

————. "James Harrington and the Good Old Cause: A Study of the Ideological Context of His Writings." *Journal of British Studies* 10 (1970): 30–48.

————. *The Machiavellian Moment: Florentine Political Thought and the Atlantic Republican Tradition.* Princeton: Princeton UP, 1975.

————. Politics, Language and Time: Essays on Political Thought and History. New York: Atheneum, 1971.

————. "Post-Puritan England and the Problem of the Enlightenment." Zagorin, *Culture* 91-111.

————. *Virtue, Commerce, and History: Essays on Political Thought and History, Chiefly in the Eighteenth Century.* Cambridge: Cambridge UP, 1985.

Popkin, Richard H. "Jewish Messianism and Christian Millenarianism." Zagorin, *Culture* 67–90.

Pye, Christopher. "The Sovereign, the Theater, and Kingdome of Darkenesse: Hobbes and the Spectacle of Power." *Representations* 8 (1984): 84–106.

Raab, Felix. *The English Face of Machiavelli: A Changing Interpretation, 1500–1700.* London: Routledge; Toronto: U of Toronto P, 1964.

Records of the Governor and Company of the Massachusetts Bay in New England. Vol. IV-Part II, 1661–1674. Boston, 1854.

Riley, Patrick. *Will and Political Legitimacy: A Critical Exposition of Social Contract Theory in Hobbes, Locke, Rousseau, Kant, and Hegel.* Cambridge: Harvard UP, 1982.

Ronda, James P. "'We Are Well as We Are': An Indian Critique of Seventeenth-Century Christian Missions." *William and Mary Quarterly* 3rd ser. 34 (1977): 66–82.

Rushworth, John. *Historical Collections. The Third Part; in Two Volumes.* London, 1692.

Russell-Smith, H. F. *Harrington and his Oceana: A Study of a 17th Century Utopia and Its Influence in America.* 1914. New York: Octagon, 1971.

Said, Edward W. *The World, the Text, and the Critic.* Cambridge: Harvard UP, 1983.

Salisbury, Neal. "Red Puritans: The 'Praying Indians' of Massachusetts Bay and John Eliot." *William and Mary Quarterly* 3rd ser. 31 (1974): 27–54.

Scull, G. D., ed. "English Ballads about New England." *New-England Historical and Genealogical Register* 36 (1882): 359–62.

Segal, Charles M., and David C. Stineback, eds. *Puritans, Indians, and Manifest Destiny.* New York: Putnam's, 1977.

Shanley, Mary Lyndon. "Marriage Contract and Social Contract in Seventeenth-Century English Political Thought." *The Family in Political Thought.* Ed. Jean Bethke Elshtain. Amherst: U of Massachusetts P, 1982. 80–95.

Sheehan, Bernard W. *Savagism and Civility: Indians and Englishmen in Colonial Virgina.* Cambridge: Cambridge UP, 1980.

Shklar, Judith N. "Ideology Hunting: The Case of James Harrington." *American Political Science Review* 53 (1959): 662–92.

———. "The Political Theory of Utopia: From Melancholy to Nostalgia." Manuel 101–15.

Sidney, Sir Philip, *The Countess of Pembroke's Arcadia.* Ed. Maurice Evans. Harmondsworth: Penguin, 1977.

Skinner, Quentin. "Conquest and Consent: Thomas Hobbes and the Engagement Controversy." Aylmer, *Interregnum* 79–98.

Smart, Barry. *Foucault, Marxism, and Critique.* London: Routledge, 1983.

Smith, Peter H. "Politics and Sainthood: Biography by Cotton Mather." *William and Mary Quarterly* 3rd ser. 20 (1963): 186–206.

The Souldiers Catechism. London, 1644.

The Souldiers Pocket Bible. 1643. Ed. George Livermore. Cambridge, Eng.: n.p., 1861.

Spiller, Robert E., et al., eds. "John Eliot: 1604–1690." *Literary History of the United States: Bibliography.* 4th ed. New York: Macmillan, 1974.

Sprigge, William. *A Modest Plea, For an Equal Common-wealth, Against Monarchy.* London, 1659.

Stavely, Keith W. *The Politics of Milton's Prose Style.* Yale Studies in English 185. New Haven: Yale UP, 1975.

Stearns, Raymond Phineas. "Correspondence of John Woodbridge, Jr., and Richard Baxter." *New England Quarterly* 10 (1937): 557–83.

Stein, Stephen J. "Transatlantic Extensions: Apocalyptic in Early New England." Patrides and Wittreich 266–98.

Stewart, Stanley. "Milton Revises *The Readie and Easie Way.*" *Milton Studies* 20 (1984): 205–24.

Stone, Lawrence. *The Family, Sex, and Marriage in England, 1500–1800.* New York: Harper, 1977.

Surtz, Edward. *The Praise of Pleasure: Philosophy, Education, and Communism in More's Utopia.* Cambridge: Harvard UP, 1957.

———. *The Praise of Wisdom: A Commentary on the Religious and Moral*

Problems and Backgrounds of St. Thomas More's Utopia. Chicago: Loyola UP, 1957.

Suvin, Darko. *Metamorphoses of Science Fiction: On the Poetics and History of a Literary Genre.* New Haven: Yale UP, 1979.

Syfret, R. H. "Marvell's 'Horatian Ode.'" *Review of English Studies* ns 12.46 (1961): 160–72.

Sykes, Christopher. *Crossroads to Israel, 1917–1948.* 1965. Bloomington: Indiana UP, 1973.

Tawney, R. H. *The Agrarian Problem in the Sixteenth Century.* 1912. New York: Franklin, n.d.

———. "Harrington's Interpretation of His Age." *Proceedings of the British Academy* 27 (1941): 199–223.

———. "The Rise of the Gentry, 1558–1640" *Economic History Review* 11 (1941): 1–97.

Taylor, E. G. R. *Late Tudor and Early Stuart Geography, 1583–1650.* 1934. New York: Octagon, 1968.

Thirsk, Joan. Younger Sons in the Seventeenth Century." *History* 54 (1969): 358–77.

Thomas, Keith. "The Levellers and the Franchise." Aylmer, *Interregnum* 57–78.

———. *Religion and the Decline of Magic: Studies in Popular Beliefs in Sixteenth and Seventeenth Century England.* London: Weidenfeld, 1971.

Thompson, E. P. "Time, Work-Discipline, and Industrial Capitalism." *Past and Present* 38 (1967): 56–97.

———. *Whigs and Hunters: The Origin of the Black Act.* London: Lane, 1975.

Thorowgood, Thomas. *Jewes in America.* 2nd ed. London, 1660.

Tichi, Cecelia. *New World, New Earth: Environmental Reform in American Literature from the Puritans Through Whitman.* New Haven: Yale UP, 1979.

Toland, John, ed. *The Oceana of James Harrington, Esq.; And His Other Works: With an Account of His Life Prefix'd.* Dublin, 1737.

Toliver, Harold. *Pastoral Forms and Attitudes.* Berkeley and Los Angeles: U of California P, 1971.

Toon, Peter. "The Question of Jewish Immigration." *Puritans, the Millennium and the Future of Israel: Puritan Eschatology, 1600 to 1660.* Ed. Peter Toon. Cambridge: Clark, 1970. 115–25.

Tracts Relating to the Attempts to Convert to Christianity the Indians of New England. 1647–1655. *Collections of the Massachusetts Historical Society* 3rd ser. 4 (1834): 1–287.

Trevor-Roper, H. R. *The Gentry, 1540–1640.* London: Cambridge UP, 1953.

Tuck, Richard. "Power and Authority in Seventeenth-Century England." Historical Journal 17 (1974): 43–61.

Tuveson, Ernest Lee. *Millennium and Utopia: A Study in the Background of the Idea of Progress.* 1949. New York: Harper, 1964.

―――――. *Redeemer Nation: The Idea of America's Millennial Role.* Chicago: U of Chicago P, 1968.

Vaughan, Alden T. *New England Frontier: Puritans and Indians, 1620–1675.* Boston: Little, 1965.

Vico, Giambattista. *The New Science of Giambattista Vico.* Trans. and ed. Thomas Goddard Bergin and Max Harold Fisch. Ithaca: Cornell UP, 1948.

Wallace, John M. *Destiny His Choice: The Loyalism of Andrew Marvell.* London: Cambridge UP, 1968.

―――――. "The Engagement Controversy, 1649–1652: An Annotated List of Pamphlets." *Bulletin of the New York Public Library* 68 (1964): 384–405.

Walzer, Michael. "Puritanism as a Revolutionary Ideology." *History and Theory: Studies in the Philosophy of History* 3 (1964): 59–90.

―――――. *The Revolution of the Saints: A Study in the Origins of Radical Politics.* 1965. New York: Atheneum, 1972.

Warren, Fintan B. *Vasco de Quiroga and His Pueblo-Hospitals of Santa Fe.* Washington, DC: Academy of American Franciscan History, 1963.

Webber, Everett. *Escape to Utopia: The Communal Movement in America.* New York: Hastings House, 1959.

Webber, Joan. *The Eloquent "I": Style and Self in Seventeenth-Century Prose.* Madison: U of Wisconsin P, 1968.

Weber, Max. *Economy and Society: An Outline of Interpretive Sociology.* 3 vols. Ed. Guenther Roth and Claus Wittich. New York: Bedminster, 1968.

―――――. *From Max Weber: Essays in Sociology.* Trans. H. H. Gerth and C. Wright Mills. London: Routledge, 1948.

―――――. *Max Weber: The Interpretation of Social Reality.* Ed. J. E. T. Eldridge. London: Joseph, 1971.

―――――. *The Protestant Ethic and the Spirit of Capitalism.* Trans. Talcott Parsons. New York: Scribner's, 1958.

―――――. *The Sociology of Religion.* Trans. Ephraim Fischoff. Boston: Beacon, 1963.

Webster, Charles. "The Authorship and Significance of *Macaria.*" *Past and Present* 56 (1972): 34–48. Webster, *Revolution* 369–85.

―――――. *The Great Instauration: Science, Medicine and Reform, 1626–1660.* London: Duckworth, 1975.

―――――, ed. *The Intellectual Revolution of the Seventeenth Century.* The Past and Present Series. London: Routledge, 1974.

―――――, ed. *Samuel Hartlib and the Advancement of Learning.* London: Cambridge UP, 1970.

Weis, Frederick L. "The New England Company of 1649 and Its Missionary Enterprises." *Publications of the Colonial Society of Massachusetts, Vol. 38, Transactions 1947-1951.* Boston: Colonial Society of Massachusetts, 1959. 134-219.

Wells, H. G. *A Modern Utopia.* 1905. Lincoln: U of Nebraska P, 1967.

Williams, Roger. *Key into the Language of the Indians of America. The Complete Writings of Roger Williams.* 7 vols. New York: Russell and Russell, 1963. 1: 61-284.

Wilson, A. J. N. "Andrew Marvell: 'An Horatian Ode upon Cromwel's Return from Ireland': The Thread of the Poem and Its Use of Classical Allusion." *The Critical Quarterly* 11 (1969): 325-41.

Winship, George Parker. *The Cambridge Press, 1638-1692.* Philadelphia: U of Pennsylvania P, 1945.

———, ed. *The New England Company of 1649 and John Eliot.* 1920. New York: Franklin, 1967.

Winslow, Ola Elizabeth. *John Eliot: "Apostle to the Indians."* Boston: Houghton, 1968.

Winstanley, Gerrard. *The Works of Gerrard Winstanley.* Ed. George H. Sabine. New York: Russell and Russell, 1965.

Wolfe, Don M., ed. *Leveller Manifestoes of the Puritan Revolution.* 1944. New York: Humanities, 1967.

———. *Milton in the Puritan Revolution.* 1941. New York: Humanities, 1963.

Woodhouse, A. S. P., ed. *Puritanism and Liberty, Being the Army Debates (1647-9) from the Clarke Manuscripts with Supplementary Documents.* Chicago: U of Chicago P, 1951.

Woolrych, Austin. "Historical Introduction (1659-1660)." *Complete Prose Works of John Milton.* Vol. 7. New Haven: Yale UP, 1980. 1-228. 8 vols.

Wren, Matthew [the younger]. *Considerations upon Mr. Harrington's Commonwealth of Oceana: restrained to the first Part of the Preliminaries.* London, 1657.

———. *Monarchy Asserted: Or, The State of Monarchical and Popular Government; in Vindication of the Considerations upon Mr. Harrington's Oceana.* Oxford, 1659.

Wynn, Bobby C. *Utopian Literature: Pre-1900 Imprints: A Bibliographic Guide to the Microfiche Collection.* Sanford, NC: Microfilming Corporation of America, 1981.

Yates, Frances A. *Astraea: The Imperial Theme in the Sixteenth Century.* London: Routledge, 1975.

Young, Alexander, ed. *Chronicles of the First Planters of the Colony of Massachusetts Bay, 1623-1636.* 1846. New York: Da Capo, 1970.

Young, R. F. *Comenius and the Indians of New England.* London: School of Slavonic and East European Studies in the U of London, 1929.

Youngs, J. William T., Jr. "The Indian Saints of New England." *Early American Literature* 16 (1981/1982): 241–56.

Zagorin, Perez, ed. *Culture and Politics from Puritanism to the Enlightenment.* Berkeley and Los Angeles: U of California P, 1980.

————. *A History of Political Thought in the English Revolution.* London: Routledge, 1954.

Zamiatin, Eugene. *We.* Trans. Gregory Zilboorg. New York: Dutton, 1959.

Zavala, Silvio. *Recuerdo de Vasco de Quiroga.* México: Editorial Porrúa, 1965.

Ziff, Larzer. *Puritanism in America: New Culture in a New World.* New York: Viking, 1973.

Index